H

Since the Re pture has been associated explicitly wi ...sophers and art historians have all linke... ... ...o, often in strikingly different ways. In spite of this long running interest in touch and tactility, it is vision and visuality which have tended to dominate art historical research in recent decades.

This book introduces a new impetus to the discussion of the relationship between touch and sculpture by setting up a dialogue between art historians and individuals with fresh insights who are working in disciplines beyond art history. The collection brings together a rich and diverse set of approaches, with essays tackling subjects from prehistoric figurines to the work of contemporary artists, from pre-modern ideas about the physiology of touch to tactile interaction in the museum environment, and from the phenomenology of touch in recent philosophy to the experimental findings of scientific study. It is the first volume on this subject to take such a broad approach and, as such, seeks to set the agenda for future research and collaboration in this area.

Peter Dent is lecturer in History of Art at the University of Bristol, UK.

SUBJECT/OBJECT: NEW STUDIES IN SCULPTURE

Published in association with
the Henry Moore Institute, Leeds, UK

We have become familiar with the notion that sculpture has moved into the 'expanded field', but this field has remained remarkably faithful to defining sculpture on its own terms. Sculpture can be distinct, but it is rarely autonomous. For too long studied apart, within a monographic or survey format, sculpture demands to be reintegrated with the other histories of which it is a part. In the interests of representing recent moves in this direction, this series will provide a forum for the publication and stimulation of new research examining sculpture's relationship with the world around it, with other disciplines and with other material contexts.

Other titles in the series include

Sculpture and the Vitrine
Edited by John C. Welchman

Sculpture and the Museum
Edited by Christopher R. Marshall

Sculpture and Archaeology
Edited by Paul Bonaventura and Andrew Jones

Reading the Royal Monument in Eighteenth-Century Europe
Edited by Charlotte Chastel-Rousseau

Giacometti: Critical Essays
Edited by Peter Read and Julia Kelly

Iconoclasm
Contested Objects, Contested Terms
Edited by Stacy Boldrick and Richard Clay

Sculpture and the Garden
Edited by Patrick Eyres and Fiona Russell

Sculpture and Psychoanalysis
Edited by Brandon Taylor

Figuration/Abstraction
Strategies for Public Sculpture in Europe 1945–1968
Edited by Charlotte Benton

Sculpture and Touch

Edited by Peter Dent

Routledge
Taylor & Francis Group
LONDON AND NEW YORK

First published 2014 by Ashgate Publishing

2 Park Square, Milton Park, Abingdon, Oxfordshire OX14 4RN
52 Vanderbilt Avenue, New York, NY 10017

Routledge is an imprint of the Taylor & Francis Group, an informa business

First issued in paperback 2020

British Library Cataloguing in Publication Data
A catalogue record for this book is available from the British Library.

Library of Congress Cataloging-in-Publication Data
Dent, Peter, 1975–
Sculpture and touch / by Peter Dent.
pages cm. – (Subject/object: new studies in sculpture)
Includes bibliographical references and index.
ISBN 978-1-4094-1231-1 (hardcover)
1. Sculpture and touch. I. Title.

NB1153.T68D46 2014
730.1'8–dc23

2014000527

ISBN 978-1-4094-1231-1 (hbk)
ISBN 978-0-367-66937-9 (pbk)

Contents

List of illustrations

The authors have made every effort to contact copyright holders and would be pleased to correct any errors or omissions that are brought to their attention in subsequent editions.

Pictorial essay A: Out of Sight, but not out of mind

A.1 Claude Heath, *Willendorf Venus*, 150 × 339.5 cm, alkyd resin, chalk powder, acrylic, on canvas, 1997, Walker Art Gallery, Liverpool [© Claude Heath]

A.2 Claude Heath's temporary studio at Museu Teleorman, Romania, 2010

A.3 Claude Heath, *Stone Age Flint Axe-Head*, 42 × 29.4 cm, 2010, incised paper, (residency at Museu Teleorman, Alexandria, Romania, with the Art Landscape Transformations European Commission project), Collection of Kupferstichkabinett, Museum of Prints and Drawings, Berlin, made with the Ernst Schering Foundation [© Claude Heath]

A.4 Claude Heath, *Stone Age Flint Axe-Head*, 60× 45 cm, incised paper, 2010, (residency at Museu Teleorman, Alexandria, Romania, with the Art Landscape Transformations European Commission project), Collection of Kupferstichkabinett, Museum of Prints and Drawings, Berlin, made with the Ernst Schering Foundation [© Claude Heath]

A.5 Claude Heath, *Stone Age Flint Axe-Head*, 60 × 45 cm, incised paper, 2010, (residency at Museu Teleorman, Alexandria, Romania, with the Art Landscape Transformations European Commission project), Collection of Kupferstichkabinett, Museum of Prints and Drawings, Berlin, made with the Ernst Schering Foundation [© Claude Heath]

5 A taxonomy of touch: tactile encounters in Renaissance Italy

5.1 Andrea del Verrocchio, *The Incredulity of St Thomas* (detail of Thomas' fingers about to touch Christ's wound), partially-gilded bronze, 1467–83, Or San Michele, Florence [public domain, originally published in Leo Planiscig, *Andrea del Verrocchio*, Vienna: A. Schroll, 1941]

5.2 Donatello, *Crucified Christ* (note moveable joints at the shoulders), c. 168 (h) × c. 173 (w) cm / c. 66 (h) × c. 68 (w) in., polychromed pear wood, c. 1415, Santa Croce, Florence [© Sailko (http://commons.wikimedia.org)]

5.3 Lorenzo Lotto, *Portrait of Andrea Odoni*, 104.6 × 116.6 cm / 41.2 × 45.9 in., oil on canvas, 1527, Royal Collection, London [The Royal Collection © 2010, Her Majesty Queen Elizabeth II]

5.4 Baccio Bandinelli (designer) and Agostino Veneziano (engraver), *The Academy of Baccio Bandinelli*, 27.4 × 29.8 cm / 10.8 × 11.7 in., engraving, 1531, British Museum, London [© Trustees of the British Museum]

5.5 Michelangelo Buonarroti, *Dying Slave* (detail), marble, from 1513 onwards, Musée du Louvre, Paris [© Marie-Lan Nguyen (http://commons.wikimedia.org)]

6 The neglected power of touch: what the cognitive neurosciences can tell us about the importance of touch in artistic communication

6.1 Filippo Tommaso Marinetti, *Sudan-Parigi*, mixed materials, 1922, private collection, Geneva [© DACS 2013]

6.2 Alberto Giacometti, *Disagreeable Object*, wood, 1931, The Museum of Modern Art, New York (Private Collection, promised gift to the Museum of Modern Art, in honour of Kirk Varnedoe Acc. n. PG2467.2001.0 [© 2013. Digital image, The Museum of Modern Art, New York / Scala, Florence. © The Estate of Alberto Giacometti (Fondation Giacometti, Paris and ADAGP, Paris), licensed in the UK by ACS and DACS, London 2014.]

exhibition, Hyogo Prefectural Museum of Art, Japan, 2005 [© Takao Sugiura]

8.6 Noriyuki Yamamura, *Hand*, in the *Form in Art* exhibition, Hyogo Prefectural Museum of Art, Japan, 2007 [© Noriyuki Yamamura]

9 The sculptor is a blind man: Constantin Brancusi's *Sculpture for the Blind*

9.1 Constantin Brancusi, *Sculpture for the Blind*, veined marble, c. 1920, Philadelphia Museum of Art, The Louise and Walter Arensberg Collection, 1950 [© 2013. Photo: The Philadelphia Museum of Art / Art Resource / Scala, Florence] [© ADAGP, Paris and DACS, London 2013]

9.2 Constantin Brancusi, *Hand of Mademoiselle Pogany*, 1920, Harvard Art Museums / Fogg Museum, purchase through the generosity of Mr and Mrs Max Wasserman, 1964.110 [Photo: Imaging Department © President and Fellows of Harvard College] [© ADAGP, Paris and DACS, London 2013]

10 Embracing stone, holding brushes: differentiating touch in the *Unit One* photographs

10.1 Barbara Hepworth's hands as published in *Unit One*, photograph by Paul Laib [© Bowness, Hepworth Estate]

10.2 Henry Moore's hands as published in *Unit One*, photograph by Thea Struve [Reproduced by permission of The Henry Moore Foundation]

10.3 John Bigge's hands as published in *Unit One*, photograph by Paul Laib [The de Laszlo Collection of Paul Laib Negatives, Witt Library, The Courtauld Institute of Art, London. © The de Laszlo Foundation]

10.4 Ben Nicholson's hands, photograph by Paul Laib [The de Laszlo Collection of Paul Laib Negatives, Witt Library, The Courtauld Institute of Art, London. © The de Laszlo Foundation]

10.5 Paul Nash's hands as published in *Unit One*, photograph by Francis Bruguière

10.6 Tristram Hillier's hands as published in *Unit One*, photograph by Thea Struve

10.7 Henry Moore's portrait as published in *Unit One*, photograph by Thea Struve [Reproduced by permission of The Henry Moore Foundation]

10.8 Barbara Hepworth's hands as published in *Pictorial Autobiography*, photograph by Paul Laib [© Bowness, Hepworth Estate]

Pictorial essay C: The touch of the oracle

C.1 Michael Petry, *In the Garden of Eden* (Devin Borden Hiram Butler Gallery, Houston, 2007) [© Michael Petry]

C.2 Michael Petry, *The Lovers* (*WAS: White as Snow*, DBHBG, 2004) [© Michael Petry]

C.3 Michael Petry, *Spent* (Westbrook Gallery, London, 2006) [© Michael Petry]

C.4 Michael Petry, *Tie A Knot In It*, detail (Zane Bennett Contemporary Art, Santa Fe, 2012) [© Michael Petry]

C.5 Michael Petry, *La petite mort III* (*True Love*, Muzeum Mierdzi, Legnica, Poland, 2007) [© Michael Petry]

Notes on contributors

FRANCESCA BACCI is a University Researcher at CIMeC Center for Mind and Brain Sciences at the Università di Trento and Curator of Special Projects at MART (Museum of Modern and Contemporary Art of Trento and Rovereto).

DOUG BAILEY is a professor in the Department of Anthropology at San Francisco State University.

SEBASTIANO BARASSI is Curator at the Henry Moore Foundation, Perry Green.

ANDREW BENJAMIN is Professor of Philosophy and Jewish Thought at Monash University, Melbourne and Distinguished Anniversary Professor of Philosophy and Humanities at Kingston University.

FIONA CANDLIN is a Senior Lecturer in Museum Studies in the Department of History of Art at Birkbeck College, the University of London.

JULIA CASSIM is Professor of the Kyoto Design Lab at the Kyoto Institute of Technology.

PETER DENT is a lecturer in the Department of History of Art at the University of Bristol.

ROSALYN DRISCOLL is an artist, sculptor and writer, and a member of Sensory Sites, an international art collective based in London (http://rosalyndriscoll.com/).

ALBERTO GALLACE is a University Researcher in the Department of Psychology at the Università degli Studi di Milano-Bicocca.

JAMES HALL is an art critic, historian, lecturer and broadcaster.

CLAUDE HEATH is an artist based in London (http://www.claudeheath.com/).

GERALDINE A. JOHNSON is an Associate Professor in History of Art at the University of Oxford.

HAGI KENAAN is an Associate Professor in the Department of Philosophy at Tel Aviv University.

MICHAEL PARASKOS is Director of Programmes at the Cyprus College of Art.

MICHAEL PETRY is an artist, author and Director of the Museum of Contemporary Art (MOCA), London (http://www.michaelpetry.net/).

CHARLES SPENCE is a professor in the Department of Experimental Psychology and head of the Crossmodal Research Laboratory at the University of Oxford.

Subject/Object: New Studies in Sculpture

Sculpture is formed of a narrow and specific history, concerned with processes of making and informed by the ways in which human beings use objects to attempt to make sense of the surrounding world. A sculpture sits in space, pulling or pushing all that visually surrounds it for its own ends. It is a gravity-defying object that structures the space between itself and its perceiver. It is an object that needs to be walked around, looked at and considered in relation to the space that holds it.

Subject/Object: New Studies in Sculpture emerges from an imperative to open this study by considering sculpture through other disciplines – be these thematic, monographic, art historical or the material contexts within which sculpture operates. Initiated in 2003, with Penelope Curtis as the Series Editor, the series is generated by new research originating from the Henry Moore Institute, produced in partnership with Ashgate Publishing. The Institute is a centre for the study of sculpture, based in the heart of Leeds. It is a part of The Henry Moore Foundation, set up by the sculptor Henry Moore in 1977 to encourage appreciation of the visual arts, especially sculpture. An exhibitions venue, research centre, library and sculpture archive, the Institute hosts a year-round programme of exhibitions, conferences and lectures to expand the understanding and scholarship of historical and contemporary sculpture. The starting point for all of our activities is the artwork, and our task to complicate the ways in which sculpture is understood.

Subject/Object moves through collections of critical essays on Alberto Giacometti, Henry Moore, and Auguste Rodin; through intersections and interventions into sculpture by psychoanalysis, the study of touch, film and archaeology; through the interruptions that iconoclasm, abstraction and figuration have made on dominant modes of thinking about sculpture; and through the ways sculpture has impacted on, and been impacted by, conventions of the vitrine, the monument and the museum. Each book is edited by an expert in the specific subject study area, with the contributions drawing together scholarship on the ways sculpture is understood, displayed, produced and represented. *Subject/Object* is interested in the contestation of sculpture as an autonomous discipline, seeking to produce *dissensus* rather than consensus in order to open the possibilities of perceiving, making and engaging with the object of sculpture.

Lisa Le Feuvre
Head of Sculpture Studies, Henry Moore Institute.

Acknowledgments

I would like to thank the Henry Moore Foundation and Institute for supporting this project for publication within the Subject/Object series. The original conference – Sculpture and Touch – out of which this volume grew was funded by the Research Forum at the Courtauld Institute of Art and by the Welcome Trust. The latter also funded *Sculpture and Touch,* the small associated exhibition of works by Rosalyn Driscoll, Claude Heath and Michael Petry, held at the Courtauld Institute in late 2008. A copy of the short catalogue for this exhibition is available on request from the editor of the present volume. The original conference involved more excellent contributions than could be published here, and I would particularly like to thank the authors of those not included: Toby Juliff, Carmen Windsor, Arie Hartog, Robert Hopkins, Linda Ann Nolan, Caterina Y. Pierre, Alison Wright, Shir Aloni and Anne Cranny-Francis. I have tried to cite their work in the bibliography if it has since been published elsewhere. Thanks are due to Hilly Raphael for enthusiastic help right at the beginning of this project. I have held posts in several institutions while editing this volume – the Courtauld Institute, the University of Warwick and the University of Bristol – and I am grateful for the resources that I was able to draw on in each case. Above all, I would like to thank the contributors to this volume for their patience.

Peter Dent

Introduction

Peter Dent

In the opening paragraphs of *Roads to Santiago*, a travelogue and meditation on Spanish culture and history, the Dutch writer Cees Nootebaum recounts an experience once familiar to many:

> At the entrance to the cathedral in Santiago de Compostela there is a marble column with deep impressions of fingers, an emotional, expressionistic claw created by millions of hands, including my own. But it is already a distortion to say 'including my own', for in grasping that pillar I have never felt the emotion that comes after walking for more than a year to arrive. I was not a man of the Middle Ages, I was not a believer, I arrived by car. If you disregard my hand resting on the marble, had I never been in that place, the claw would still be there, eroded in the hard stone by the fingers of all those people now dead. Yet, by laying my hand in that hollow one I was participating in a collective work of art. An idea becomes visible in matter: that is always wondrous.[1]

Nootebaum's evocative description of physical interaction with a sculptural form is far from the image that tends to spring to mind when we think of the tactile appreciation of the sculptural object: the image of a hand closing around a small-scale sculpture. That encounter surfaces repeatedly throughout this book, in the imagined interaction of the prehistoric beholder with a clay figurine (Chapter 1), in the familiar guise of the Renaissance collector portrayed with his bronze statuette (Chapter 5), and in the thought of Brancusi caressing his work with it cradled in his lap (Chapter 9).[2] This is even, in truth, the nature of the tactile encounter at the heart of the great myth of agalmatophilia, Ovid's Pygmalion, a story explored here in detail by two contributors, Hagi Kenaan and Michael Paraskos. Although representations of Pygmalion and Galatea nearly always depict her as a life-size marble statue, in the *Metamorphoses* she is first carved from ivory before becoming flesh and blood. The restrictions of this medium suggest a small articulated doll of the sort owned by young Roman women, a Barbie *avant la lettre*, but with ritual significance.[3]

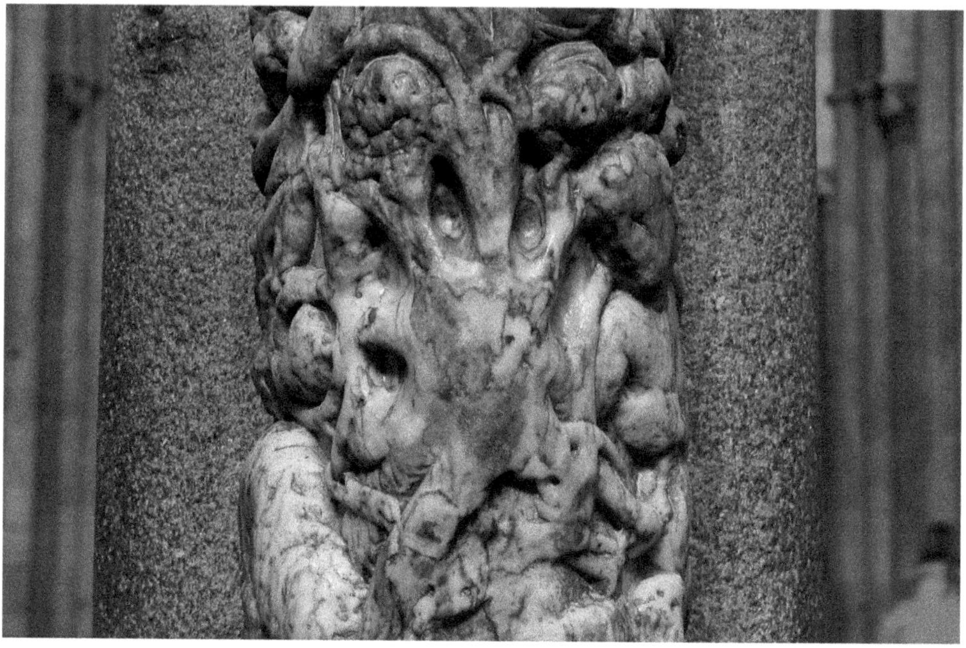

I.1 Handprint worn into the central column of the Pórtico de la Gloria, Santiago de Compostela [© Peter Dent]

In the opening chapter of this collection, Doug Bailey has interesting things to say about the psychological effects of miniaturisation on sculptural form. The idea of Pygmalion manipulating the object of his obsession in the palm of his hand introduces another, darker layer of fascination to the tale.

With this in mind, the column at Santiago may seem an unlikely point of departure, but the handprint (Figs I.1 and I.2) at Santiago is offered here by way of introduction because its idiosyncrasy throws into surprising relief the range of associations that are potentially at play in a tactile encounter with a sculptural object. The ideas woven into and around the handprint at Santiago exemplify many of the threads that run through this collection, threads that bind the separate contributions into a substantial whole.

* * *

The Pórtico de la Gloria (Figs I.3 and I.4) appeals to the senses first, and through them to the emotions and the intellect.[4] The Elders of the Apocalypse arrayed in the archivolt above Christ strike up the chords of a heavenly anthem. The column statue of King David beams out over the viewer, his face glowing with a notably early example of the so-called Gothic smile. But it is the hand

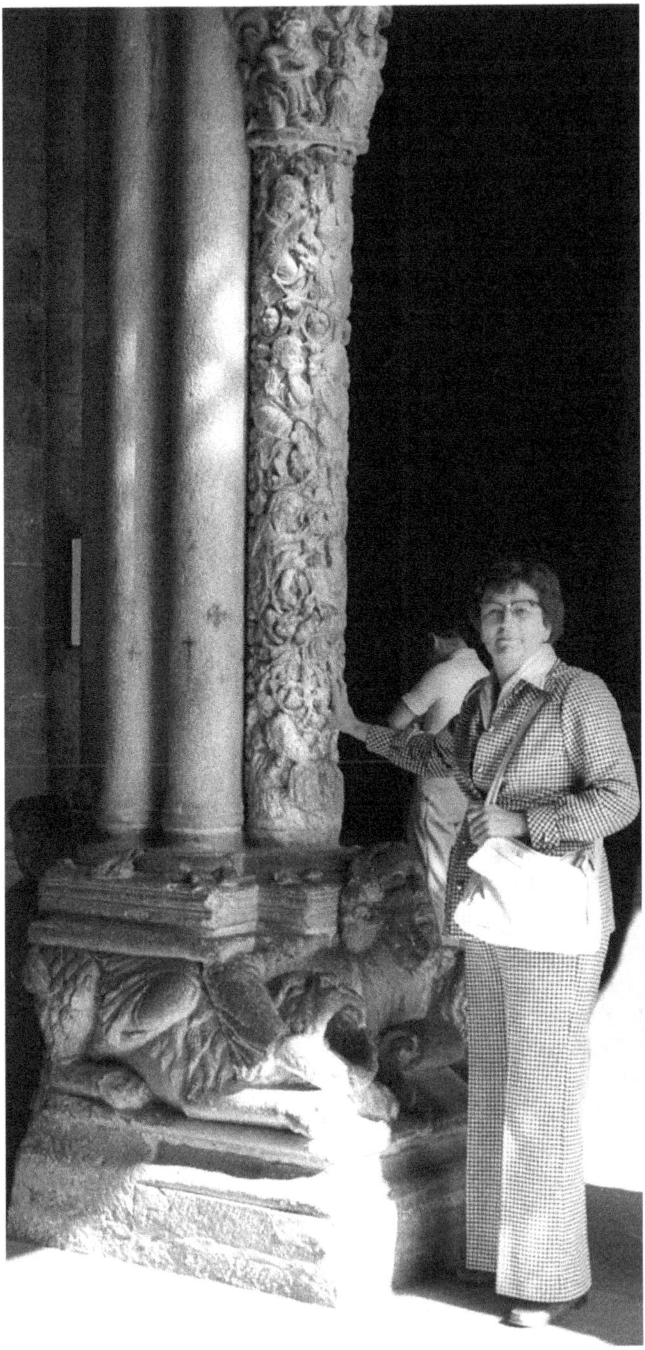

I.2 Pilgrim placing hand in handprint, Pórtico de la Gloria, Santiago de Compostela [© William J. Smither/Peregrinations]

print in the marble that gathers the individual pilgrim into a community of believers while also placing them in a personal and intimate relationship with this programmatic exposition of God's soteriological plan. The pilgrim's status is at once generalised and particularised as she steps individually forwards – one handprint, many hands – into the place of judgement, directly below the Apocalyptic Christ.[5]

In Nootebaum's account, placing his hand where other hands have been puts him viscerally 'in touch' with this community of absent others, the many pilgrims who have preceded him. The indentations in the mottled marble of the column are not immediately recognisable to the eye, but with the realisation that the five claw marks are the cumulative work of the same reverent action repeated across the centuries, the mark as hand at once becomes achingly familiar, dense with habits of social behaviour, and saturated with cultural significance. Looking at the handprint is like tracing the weight and motion of bodies worn into old flagstones, the passage of many feet that mark out paths of action and acceptable gestures for those who follow after.[6]

It must be emphasised, however, that the communicative power here lies primarily with touch, or with the thought of touching. It is less usual to think of sight operating in this fashion. The sudden revelation of the long-hidden – the unexpected flash, perhaps, of a prehistoric handprint dancing out of the pitch-dark depths of a cave into the torch's beam – can prompt the fortunate viewer to wonder who last saw such work, but the eye leaves no mark behind it.[7] In Chapter 6, Alberto Gallace and Charles Spence explore the scientific evidence for touch as a medium of artistic communication, setting out some of the complexities of thinking about touch in such a context. Across the collection as a whole, the availability of this channel of communication emerges as culturally specific, with attitudes ranging from the permissive – you may touch – to the authoritarian – you must touch, but only here, in this way, or not at all.

As a channel of communication touch has a beguiling immediacy that sometimes threatens to dull the faculties of critical reflection. Fiona Candlin in Chapter 10 identifies a certain ingenuousness running through analyses of the relationship between sculpture and touch. The under-theorisation of touch in part reflects the weight of a long tradition associating sight with intellectual acuity and touch with gross physical sensation.[8] However, the sense of immediacy in such physical contact is (literally) palpable and forms one of its essential characteristics. A number of other contributors here pursue the idea that touch renders us more aware of our bodies in a way often suppressed or hidden in visual perception. See, in particular, Kenaan's interpretation in Chapter 2 of the myth of Narcissus by way of Merleau-Ponty's embodied eye. Equally, the evidence of tactile contact is often a more effective trace of a world altered by the action of another body. Think of the simple thrill, for example, of locating a maker's fingerprints preserved in fired ceramic.[9]

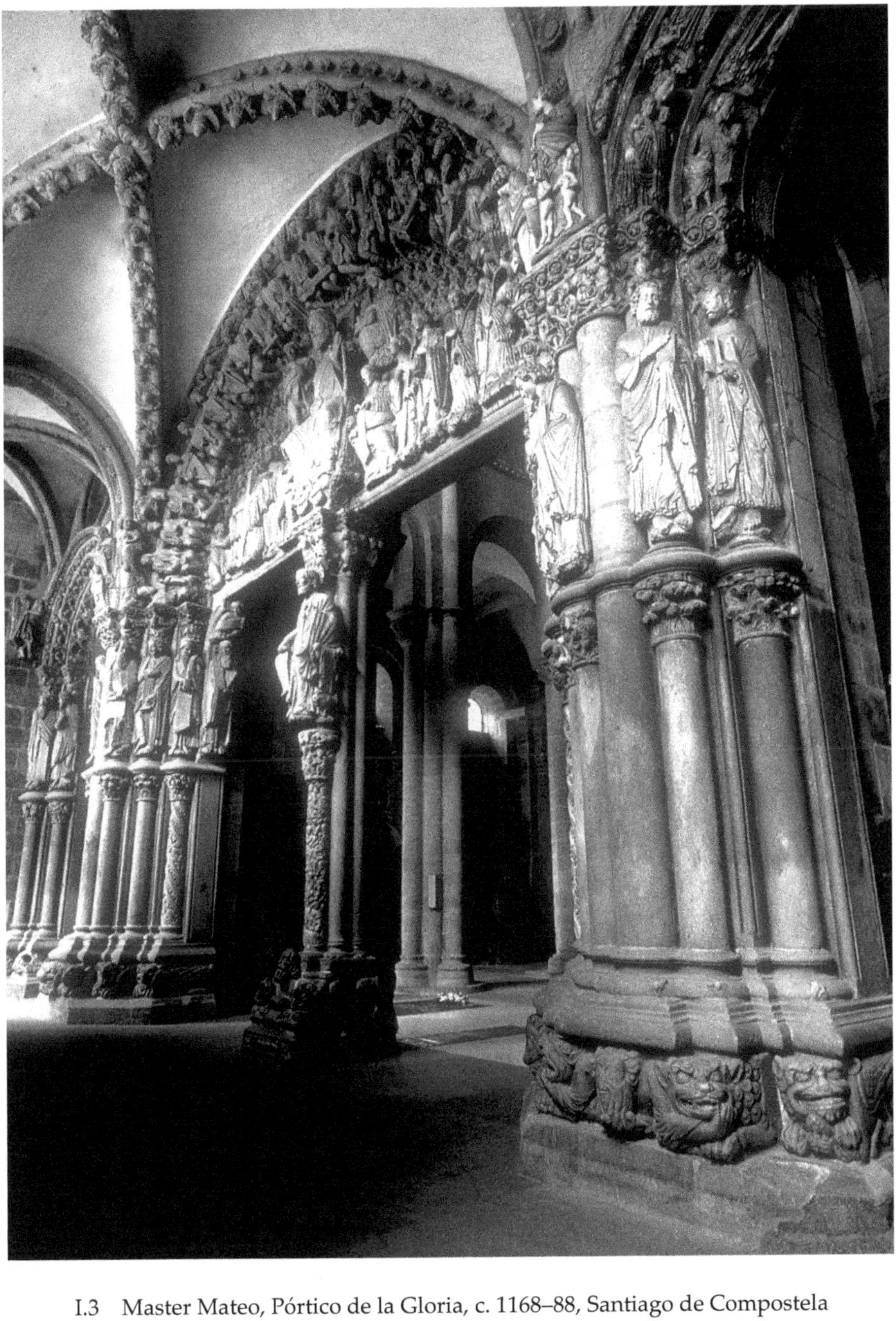

I.3 Master Mateo, Pórtico de la Gloria, c. 1168–88, Santiago de Compostela
[© William J. Smither/Peregrinations]

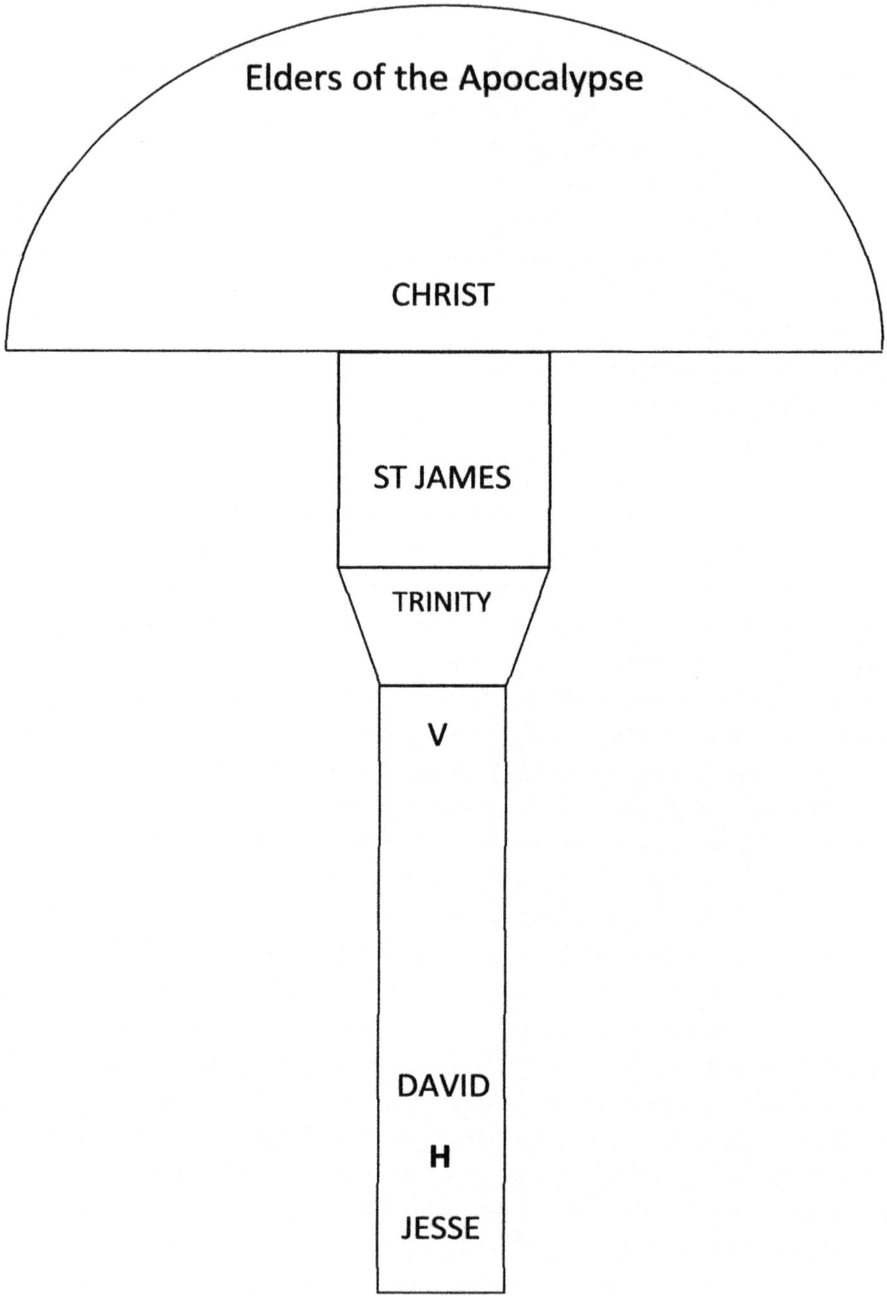

I.4 Schematic rendering of the parts of the Pórtico de la Gloria discussed in the text (V = Virgin; H = Handprint) [© Peter Dent]

But more radically, as Nootebaum seems to imply, by placing our hands where others have placed theirs, we place our bodies too, so to speak, at their disposal. We manifest for the departed a presence in this world, in the here and now, a presence with the intoxicating power to close down the great separations of space, time and cultural difference. Where this occurs through the medium of the 'monumental' art of sculpture, with all its connotations of durability and memorialisation, the juxtaposition of the fleeting fragility of individual existence with the permanence of sculptural form can be remarkably poignant.[10]

There is delusion here, of course, and Nootebaum is quick to note it. He is not a pilgrim like other pilgrims, he came by car. The point in this context is not trivial. As several contributors observe, touch and motion are intimately linked and this has implications for the perception of sculpture. Gallace and Spence, for example, report some paradoxical effects of this interrelationship observed in the scientific literature, while Andrew Benjamin in Chapter 4 follows Herder's metaphysical speculations into the never-ending exploratory movement of the hand over sculptural form as it pursues and produces its own special knowledge. In another direction, this becomes the fantasy of the moving, touching sculpture discussed by Paraskos and Kenaan in Part I.

The column at Santiago stretches this relationship to exaggeration. The body that has travelled to this threshold has come far and the extreme physical demands of that journey once served to foreground the all too human fact of embodiment itself, of which more in a moment.[11] The instant of contact is the dramatic culmination of deliberate motion, both actual and symbolic in import. This is still a threshold, however, and not quite the final destination, whether we take that to be the relics (and, indeed, sculptural images) of Saint James within the basilica itself or, in eschatological terms, reunion with the creator following the end of all things alluded to in the tympanum above.[12] In other words, contact is made but also twice deferred. Or, rather, preliminary contact is provisional; it anticipates further movement. Herder makes a telling distinction between the creative work of the hand that goes on feeling indefinitely and the poverty of the bird's-eye view (see Benjamin, Chapter 4). In this respect, it is worth remembering that sculpture is an ancient medium for marking a threshold, as though its qualities enhance the experience of the boundary state, helping both to maintain it and to move the body through it.[13] Think of Virgil's description of the doors of Apollo's temple at Cumae in the *Aeneid* or Rodin's *Gates of Hell*. Kenaan's analysis of the Narcissus myth in Chapter 2 pits painting delimited by its implicit frame against the unframed presence of sculpture within the beholder's space. In so far as the frame mediates a transition from something within the present space to something beyond (such as the painted image), one could argue that sculpture is all frame, viscerally available (touchable) to the beholder but also typically elevating that experience to another state beyond it.

Indeed, Paul Crowther has recently attempted to define the aesthetic essence of sculpture in something like these terms through the quality of transcendence.[14] Bailey's discussion of prehistoric figurines in the chapter following this Introduction argues that the common characteristics of such objects, including the fact that they can be handled, can produce significant changes in the psychological state of the beholder.

It would be well to pause a moment and think further of the beholders at Santiago, the pilgrims arriving in anticipation to be greeted by the sculptural ensemble at the western entrance. The purpose of visiting this shrine was to experience the intercessory powers of St James embodied and bestowed through his relics. Undoubtedly, as at other shrines, this attracted the disabled and diseased for whom the road to Santiago would have been particularly gruelling. Although later medieval culture was transformed by a kind of visual turn, the desire for physical contact with sanctity remained profound.[15] Several contributors argue here for the therapeutic power of touch. Indeed, for Paraskos in Chapter 3 the myth of Pygmalion and his statue encodes nothing short of a life and death argument for tactile engagement. More to the point, perhaps, is Julia Cassim's discussion in Chapter 8 of strategies adopted in exhibition practice to ensure visually impaired visitors not only physical but also cognitive access to sculptural collections. The invitation to touch the handprint on the column here offers the beholder, any beholder, a kind of cognitive access to both the contents of the basilica and some of the fundamental mysteries of Christian faith. Cassim's point is important and in this case needs unpacking a little.

When a pilgrim plants her hand into the print, she is reaching into the lower foliage of a Jesse tree, a genealogical representation of a bloodline that curls up the column from the reclining figure of Jesse at the base, past King David, and on to the Virgin seated in its canopy (Fig. I.5). In the first analysis, there is an upward trajectory here that recounts the elevation of human flesh towards a metaphysical encounter with the divine. In other words, there is hope. In a sense, in touching the column the pilgrim offers her body as confirmation of the imperfections of the fallen human condition (picture a footsore and weary traveller), while also expressly positioning that body within the path to redemption and glorification, already established in sacred history. This point is reinforced by what occurs at the top of the column's shaft. Mary appears here as the Virgin of the Annunciation. Hovering on the capital above her is the Holy Trinity. In the Incarnation, the central act of the Christian redemptive message, God descends to become flesh. This second, downward trajectory figures the mysterious moment of contact between divinity and humanity, a fundamental paradox that the believer must accept as both credible and marvellous. Indeed, it is the mystery of contact itself writ large (whether that be soul to body, spirit to matter, mind to world, or – no less mysterious in its detail – body to body).

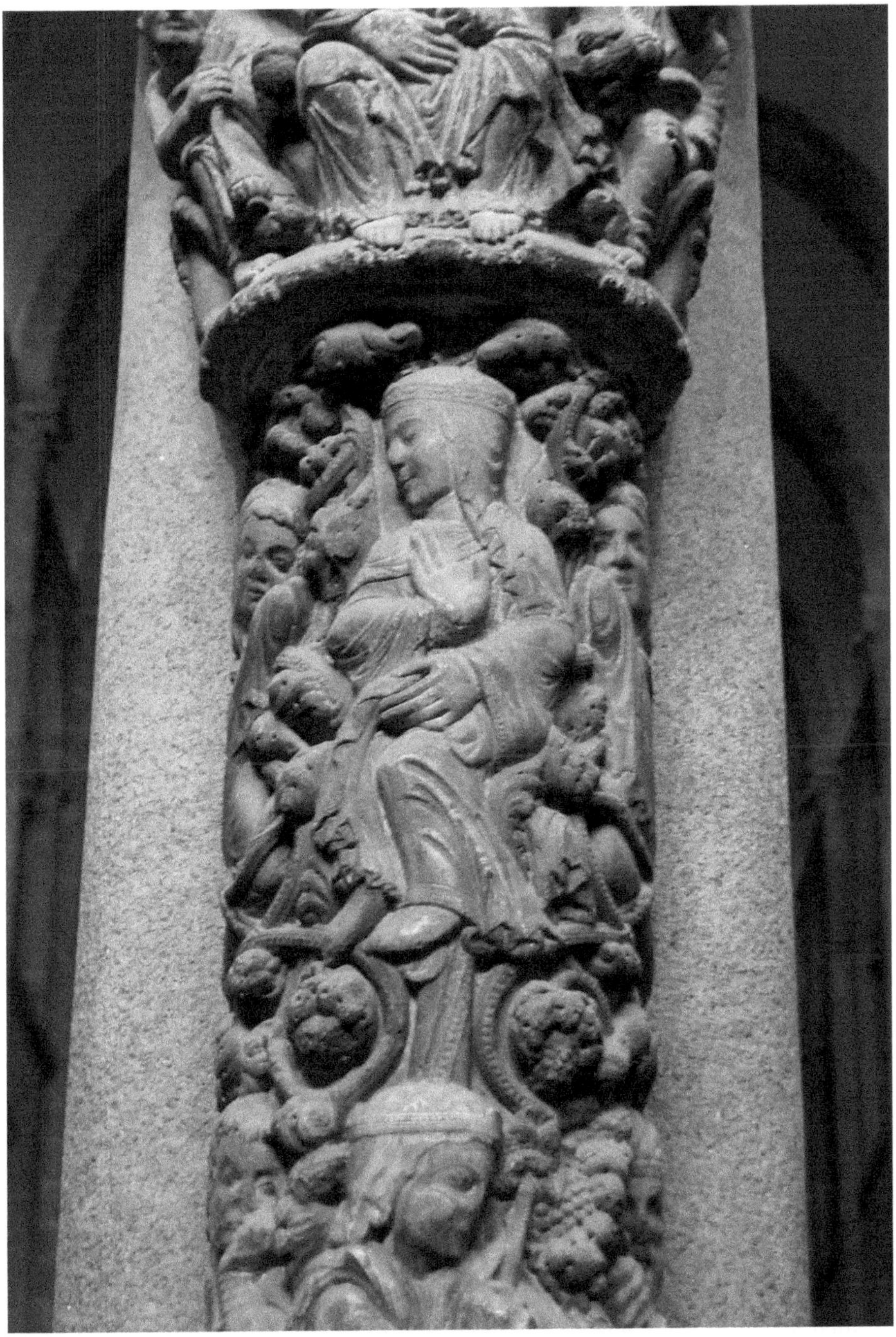

I.5 The Virgin, detail from the top of the central column of the Pórtico de la Gloria [© Peter Dent]

Placing a hand in the handprint below this special scene of contact underscores this marvel. The pilgrim offers her body a second time, this time amplifying the paradox. The Incarnation is no abstraction, the all-powerful deity represented in monumental form in the tympanum, who stands outside both space and time, is circumscribed in time and space as part of Mary's flesh, flesh as real and as particular as the viewer's own. Indeed, the point can be carried further. The column itself can be seen to embody Christ, a traditional symbolic association. It is notable that only this section of the Pórtico de la Gloria is carved in marble rather than the Galician granite used for the rest of the sculptural work.[16] The role played by different materials in the tactile appreciation of sculpture is one of the quieter themes of this collection, but it can be heard in most chapters. Perhaps the marble is a relic of the previous doorway or some other significant piece of spolia whose material marked it out for special devotional attention (one of the typologies of touch set out by Geraldine Johnson in Chapter 5), but if so the significance is long forgotten. However, if the marble of the column is taken to symbolise the manifestation of Christ in human flesh then the pilgrim here comes into contact with her incarnate saviour whose body was sacrificed on the cross for her sake.

There is no doubt that the handprint's careful staging in relation to Mary encourages the beholder to incorporate it imaginatively into any interpretation of the programme as a whole. As in the majority of Annunciations, the Virgin looks to her right, her head in profile, attentive to the transformative message. But she is seated in three-quarter view as though suspended in the act of turning. As a sign of her acceptance of God's will, she raises her arm and holds her hand, palm out, before her heart. The open palm is a gesture of receptivity to this physically transformative contact with divinity. As James Hall reveals in the final chapter of this volume, the left hand was believed to be more receptive to the lover's approach because of its proximity to the heart. Following the dominant iconography of the Annunciation, the Virgin has her right hand raised, but the significance of the gesture is broadly the same. One strand of thought running out of Aristotle placed the organ of touch in the vicinity of the heart with flesh as its medium.[17] The juxtaposition of hand over heart reveals the depth of the Virgin's transformation. This discriminates types of touch according to gender. The contact occurs between the creator, an active male, and his (ideal) creation, a passive female. Although it is common to accentuate the reciprocity of touch – as several contributors rightly do in what follows – the inflection of this reciprocity is always culturally significant. Elements of both gender and sexuality come to the fore at various points throughout this collection. The Pygmalion myth can certainly be read in such terms, but in Chapter 10 Fiona Candlin detects a complex and at times discomfiting gendering of touch occurring in twentieth-century images of sculptors, of both sexes, posing with their materials.

At Santiago the gendered touch is clearly normative for the beholder. The Virgin's open palm gesture directly addresses a pilgrim entering the church and on the vertical axis it falls into line with the worn handprint on the column below, as though one responds to the other. The pilgrim, at this point the active petitioner almost at the end of her journey, must take the Virgin as a model of submission to the vengeful and compassionate God above. In placing a hand on the handprint she is encouraged to emulate Mary's example.

There is one further element to be considered along this vertical axis containing the handprint. Between the column with its capital and the tympanum above, there is a monumental seated figure of St James. This is his basilica and the image declares it as such. In programmatic terms, James as apostle also represents the mission of the church. The work of the church in general, of his church here in Santiago, and of his relics at the altar is carried out between Christ's first appearance in the Incarnation represented on the column below and his second appearance in the Apocalypse towering over the whole ensemble. The programme offers a didactic legitimation of James' power that locates it firmly within God's plan. It interprets the anticipated contact with the relics in advance for the pilgrim. Any experience of the presence of those relics has already been framed here at the doorway. Indeed, the extent of this framing at Santiago is a useful measure of how often touch is subjected to close control as though its character is too partial, provisional, open, extended, reciprocal and contingent to be permitted unchecked. At Santiago there is a clear instruction to touch here at a single spot tied into an extensive didactic scheme. This also demonstrates how far sculpture can play a role in coding and maintaining the rules governing tactile behaviour in realms beyond the sculptural encounter itself.[18]

In tracking the interrelationship of sculpture and touch, this collection oscillates between creation and reception. The two are not always easily distinguished. Again, the Pygmalion tale is paradigmatic in this sense, but there are chapters in every part that engage with both sides of the coin. As already suggested, a combination of the creative and the receptive touch is the crux around which the sculptural programme at Santiago revolves, but the issue is more complicated than it seems on the surface because of the ambiguous status of the handprint. Nootebaum in the opening quote begins to capture some of this ambiguity when he writes of 'participating in a collective work of art. An idea becomes visible in matter: that is always wondrous.' This assumes that the print is the creation of reception itself. However, there are reasons for reconsidering at least part of this assumption. The handprint was first recorded in the late seventeenth century, but in the earliest sources there is nothing to suggest that pilgrims were responsible.[19] Instead, the print is attributed to an entirely different source. It is said to be the impression left by God's hand when, according to legend, he reoriented the basilica. If we take this at face value, it alters the interpretation advanced above, which would instead belong to a later phase of reception. The representation of Mary's passive and accepting palm at the top of the column is now correlated to the expressive force of God's active handprint. The correlation again is significant and two way. Mary and the Church are often deliberately conflated in Christian thought. If God can work the Incarnation, God can move a church. But the Incarnation itself becomes more believable because we have the physical evidence of his transformative touch before our very eyes (or rather, like Doubting Thomas, at our fingertips).

This is not the moment to work through once more the ramifications of this alternative account of the handprint for the rest of the programme. In fact it is quite possible that the seventeenth-century sources belong to the propaganda of the Counter Reformation Church, seeking, as it did elsewhere, to promote images and objects to the status of acheiropoieta – works not made by human hands – many of the most famous being contact relics of various sorts.[20] Such stories in some cases were invented where they were lacking. However, if we do accept this tradition – setting aside of course the actual account of the handprint's miraculous production – then the mark of the hand must have been artificial, initially carved on this spot to stand in for God's intervention. In other words, it would be a falsification made for visual consumption, a touch to be seen not felt.[21] There is an analogy here with one of the typologies of touch identified in Chapter 5 by Geraldine Johnson, the artist's touch. The mark, that is, of the creative hand deliberately exposed at the surface of the work as an index of its artistry, the classic case being Michelangelo's *non-finito*. Candlin's analysis in Part 3 of the *Unit One* photographs of sculptors touching their materials reveals a similar creative claim captured in a different fashion.

Whatever the origin of the handprint, at some point pilgrims to Santiago did start to touch the column. It has recently been argued that the practice may have emerged in the early twentieth century as a substitute for another tactile encounter with a column-shaped reliquary within the cathedral said to contain a relic of St James' staff.[22] This was still part of the itinerary for pilgrims in the late nineteenth century but the ritual ceased soon after, just as the first secure evidence emerges of pilgrims touching the column at the Pórtico de la Gloria. If there was a displacement, the reasons may have been tied to the reorganisation of cult activity within the church towards a more dramatic visual encounter. We might imagine such a displacement as rather like the touchable substitutes that museums now provide as a way of offering tactile access to restricted objects. The difference here of course is that the portico column already existed as a distinct work with its own predetermined meanings generated within the sculptural iconography of the whole western entrance. Whether the ritual of touching the portico column began at this point or much earlier, the activity (and its traces) introduced significant ways of encountering and understanding the programme, as suggested above. At the same time, however, other, earlier meanings were overwritten.

If there was once a carved hand of God here, this has subsequently been lost to view both in fact and in ritual memory, obliterated by the later practice. Physical contact with sculpture across many different cultures has at times been viewed in negative terms, with often less than positive results for both the object and its observer. The prohibitive fear of idolatry tends to go hand in hand with the destructive attentions of the iconoclast. The protective fear of the conservator tends to restrict the physical freedom of the beholder's experience. But touching a sculpture is not only a threat in material terms, it can also destroy the aesthetic and semantic significance of a work. In Chapter 7, Francesca Bacci explores a type of sculpture, the negative relief, whose aesthetic qualities depend upon an illusion aimed at the eye rather than the hand. Indeed, the illusion collapses under physical contact. In a slower process at Santiago, as the practice of touching the column took hold, the idea (as well as the impression) of the divine handprint was steadily but irrevocably eroded.

Nevertheless, the handprint itself has now acquired something like the status of a relic in its own right. When I visited the basilica in 2007, the column had been cordoned off with a barrier and neither pilgrim nor tourist could place a hand against the marble. There are no doubt good conservational reasons for restricting access, but the trumeau has joined the many works of sculptural art in museums now sequestered behind barriers of one type or another. One solution, mentioned above and raised by several contributors, is to provide replicas or substitutes.[23] The question is explored at length by Cassim in Chapter 8, who suggests some ways of circumventing the problem itself or of radically rethinking the strategies employed to address it. Perhaps in due course the cathedral authorities will offer some kind of alternative to satisfy the devout and the curious. In fact, at least one replica of the entire doorway already exists. The Victoria and Albert Museum possesses a full cast made by Domenico Brucciani in 1886 that faithfully captures the contours of the handprint.[24] This certainly offers a superior experience to the photographic reproduction or even the virtual sculpture rotatable in 'digital' space. However, while casts can communicate the three-dimensional extent fundamental to the experience of a sculptural object, they rarely if ever capture the kind of qualities best perceived by the hand, such as texture, temperature and fine detail (both at the surface and beneath it). A number of contributors quote the Renaissance sculptor Ghiberti who on two occasions rates the hand over the eye in the perception of surface detail (see Johnson and Hall, in particular, in Chapters 5 and 11). The identical point is made by no less a figure than Winckelmann writing of the Apollo Belvedere, whose muscles, he claimed, 'are more obvious to touch than to sight'.[25] As Barassi suggests in Chapter 9, the understated complexity of Brancusi's *Sculpture for the Blind* lies in a combination of its simple yet pregnant form with minute modulations of the surface that are perceived only at the fingertips.

Such detail is rarely captured in the cast. Indeed, casts like those at the V&A reflect a particular aesthetic attitude towards sculpture that would situate its essence in three-dimensional form, rather than in surface effect. As if in confirmation of the nature of its value, the cast at the V&A is furnished with its own 'Do not touch!' sign.

This introduction has deliberately skirted around the discourse that would define sculpture against painting as the art of touch rather than vision. That discourse begins to emerge in the Renaissance as part of the *paragone* debates that set different arts against each other (see Johnson, Chapter 5). It passes through Herder (see Benjamin, Chapter 4) and Herbert Read (see Paraskos and Candlin, Chapters 3 and 10 respectively). It continues to be the source of keen debate.[26] However, this discourse is itself framed by a broader tradition in which sculpture and touch are associated in a wider variety of ways. The metaphysical elements of contact at play in the programme at Santiago do not disappear from the desacralised account of sculpture that later emerges in aesthetic discourse. Indeed, as Benjamin indicates, Herder's take on sculptural aesthetics is in part a renegotiation of that fact. In this respect, it is worth keeping in mind that perhaps the most important image running right through the Western tradition as a general metaphor for transformative contact – particularly between material and immaterial elements – is itself sculptural: the seal matrix and its wax impression.[27]

It is the intention here and throughout this collection to suggest that the issues raised by the relationship between sculpture and touch are wider and richer than a narrower focus on aesthetic discourse alone would allow. It is well to remember that perhaps the earliest statement of medium specificity according to sensory modality takes a rather practical view of sculptural aesthetics. It occurs in one of Petrarch's dialogues on *Remedies for Fortune Fair and Foul* where Reason debates with Joy over the pleasures afforded by sculpture. When Joy declares 'Statues please me', Reason replies: 'Sculpture is nearer to nature than painting. Pictures appeal much to the eye, but sculptures can be touched, feel substantial and solid, and are of durable body.'[28] At first this looks like an argument about truth and illusion. Sculpture comes closer to true mimesis because of its greater access to the third dimension, its presence in this world. But Reason prefers to amplify the point about durability: 'This is the reason why no paintings by the ancients survive today, but countless statues.' As soon as it is vocalised, the association between sculpture and touch becomes a question of conservation! It transpires that sculptures can be touched because they can bear touching.

* * *

What follows is divided into three parts. The first, 'Origins', explores the deep history of sculptural touch in myth and the archaeological record. In Chapter 1, 'Touch and the Cheirotic Apprehension of Prehistoric Figurines', Doug Bailey adumbrates ways of thinking about touch, many of which are developed in depth elsewhere within the volume. He indicates what archaeologists stand to gain in understanding the significance of prehistoric figurines by systematically addressing the role that touch might play in their reception. He argues that the evidence linking such figurines to cult activity and religious belief is slight or non-existent. In the absence of such evidence, he casts his net wide, drawing on the analysis of elements of contemporary material culture that display similar characteristics. He identifies three features of fundamental importance to such Neolithic work. Figurines are small in scale, anthropomorphic, and three dimensional. Bailey has explored the social and psychological implications of the first two characteristics elsewhere, and summarises those findings here. Miniaturisation generates states of control and absorption; anthropomorphism foregrounds the human body as *the* contested site of identity. Bailey goes on to argue that the third characteristic – three dimensionality – in combination with the first two can make holding a figurine a deeply significant experience. As he points out, taking the long view, the history of touching sculpture is also a history of the hand itself. The implications of this should be a central part of any critical inquiry and he sketches some of the paths that an analysis attentive to such tactile interaction might need to consider.

The following two chapters, by Hagi Kenaan and Michael Paraskos, each turn to one of the foundational myths of the sculptural encounter, Pygmalion from Ovid's *Metamorphoses*. Both authors read this tale in different ways against the counter-example of Narcissus. In 'Touching Sculpture', Kenaan approaches these two protagonists as archetypes associated by earlier writers with the arts of sculpture and painting. In a discussion closely informed by Merleau-Ponty's phenomenology, he uses the comparison to explore the reductive correlation of sculpture with touch, and painting with vision. His analysis shows how touch's destructive power over Narcissus's waterborne reflection reveals the plane that becomes the site of pictorial illusion. But more than this, he emphasises the youth's physical location at the water's edge on the plane of representation itself. This throws attention back onto the embodied presence of the viewer as a condition of vision and reveals the extent to which this embodiment is easily forgotten when employing the standard pictorial metaphor of Alberti's window. He turns this insight onto the medium of sculpture in order to argue that sculpture can be distinguished from painting as an art of fantasy rather than illusion. Such an art is enlivened by its potential to act in our embodied world, encouraging an openness to reciprocity that Narcissus actively eschews.

In the second of these two chapters, 'Bringing into Being: Vivifying Sculpture through Touch', Michael Paraskos picks up on this failure of Narcissus to comprehend the reciprocity of tactility in order to engage polemically with the dematerialisation of the art work as an object from the perspective of both maker and beholder. Narcissus's rejection of the nymph Echo – a refusal to touch another – is ultimately self-destructive, a destruction of the self that is vividly conveyed every time he reaches for his own reflection in the pool. In contrast, Pygmalion remains not simply open to a physical encounter with an Other – his statue – but insistent on it. He points to Ovid's deployment of the inanimate (sculptural) body as a metaphor for negotiating the boundary between life and death throughout the poem. When Pygmalion finally coaxes life from his creation this occurs through the modality of touch, and the relationship between sculptor and sculpture becomes a double act of creation when Galatea duly gives birth to a son – a rare happy ending for an Ovidian tale. For Paraskos, this happy ending is absolutely fundamental and he employs it in a critique of conceptual art by arguing that ideas and identities acquire a necessary stability only when they can be placed beneath the hand.

The next part of the book, 'Approaches', brings together a group of chapters that address the relationship between sculpture and touch from radically different directions, the philosophical (Andrew Benjamin), the scientific (Charles Spence and Alberto Gallace) and the historical (Geraldine Johnson). The final chapter, by Francesca Bacci, combines elements of each of these different discourses. In 'To Touch: Herder and Sculpture', Benjamin picks up several threads of thought already raised in the essays of Part I, in particular the animation of matter in the act of touching and the type of knowledge that touching sculpture might deliver. While Paraskos raises contact with an animated statue in mythic terms, Benjamin scrutinises the interrelationship of form and spirit through the thought of Diderot and Herder. This link is far from casual. Herder's *Plastik* takes the myth of Pygmalion as its subtitle. Benjamin argues that what is at stake is a rethinking of matter itself. But here the issues are bound closely to the aesthetic perception of beauty as it is apprehended by the sense of touch during an incremental and endless encounter with a particular sculptural form. Indeed, it is Herder's assertion that form can only be known by the sense of touch in contrast to sight which has access merely to the illuminated surface. Illumination is important because touching can continue in its absence. However, this also raises the question of what touch touches if not the surface. Benjamin teases out some of the implications of this move for the nature of sculpture as an art form.

In 'A Taxonomy of Touch: Tactile Encounters in Renaissance Italy', Geraldine Johnson develops a careful historical analysis of the role played by touch in the reception and production of sculptural objects during the Renaissance as an antidote to the often abstract discussion of the relationship between sculpture and touch in other contexts. She offers a threefold typology of tactile appreciation covering the devotional touch, the connoisseur's touch and the artist's touch. Her analysis embeds such encounters in a set of culturally and historically specific circumstances. As she demonstrates, the sense of touch was freighted with a set of inherited values that already had a long history by the early modern period, ranging from fundamental philosophical and theological attitudes towards the nature of reality and morality, through to the status of the artist as a craftsman. She maps out the emerging aesthetic appreciation of sculpture in tactile terms along with a growing sensitivity towards the traces of the artist's shaping hand, against the medieval tradition of devotional activity. In the process, she shows not only how far these three categories overlap, but also that sculpture itself was a fluid and emerging category in this period.

Johnson's historical analysis is followed by a scientific investigation of the relationship between sculpture and touch in 'The Neglected Power of Touch: What the Cognitive Neurosciences Can Tell Us about the Importance of Touch in Artistic Communication'. The two authors, Charles Spence and Alberto Gallace are primarily concerned with how beholders encounter sculpture of various periods in contemporary contexts where the opportunities to interact with the object in tactile terms are limited or restricted by both practical considerations relating to conservation and socio-cultural norms governing such behaviour. After reviewing the potential significance of the sense of touch in various cases ranging from prehistoric figurines through to Brancusi's work (see also the chapters by Bailey and Barassi) they survey various ways in which the scientific understanding of tactility offers a series of suggestive insights into the psychological impact of certain tactile sensations, particularly in relation to pleasure and motion. They suggest these might in due course be exploited in order to develop a more nuanced awareness of the distinctive role that touch plays in sculptural encounters. As they argue, this in turn may have significant implications for the public display and reception of works of sculptural art in general.

The final chapter of this part seeks to move across the boundaries of various discourses relating to the tactile apprehension of sculpture. In 'When Touch Shatters Meaning: The Case of Sculptures Made for Sight Only', Francesca Bacci shows how the philosophical and scientific accounts of touch, particularly the question of cross-modality in relation to sight, have shaped attitudes towards sculpture as an art form. Bacci analyses this issue by focusing on works that generate and exploit conflicting sensory data supplied by different modalities, and works deliberately restricted to a uni-modal form of address. She considers, in particular, the 'hollow mask' illusion in which negative relief is interpreted as positive projection, and examines a number of cases where this type of effect is deliberately at play. This in turn serves to disturb the fundamental relationship between volume and void within sculptural aesthetics, in ways that Bacci reads out towards the work of recent artists such as Rachel Whiteread. By focusing on the interrelationship of sensory inputs – whether actual or remembered – in the act of perception, she reveals the varied extent to which our visual perception of sculptural objects is conditioned by our tactile apprehension of the world as a whole.

In the final part of the book, 'Identities', the contributors open out the parameters of the subject by interrogating the various ways in which touching sculpture entails a negotiation of identity. This extends from the artist him or herself through to the visually impaired museum goer, from the canonical Renaissance sculptor to the contemporary Japanese beholder, and from the gendered hand to the sensitivities of the otherwise much-maligned left hand. The first chapter takes us beyond the Western cultural tradition in which the discourse of sculpture and touch has been addressed most explicitly, and turns to another culture with its own historically and socially informed expectations of the sculptural encounter. In 'Beyond the Touch Tour', Julia Cassim recounts her experience of developing exhibitions in Japan for visually impaired audiences. She offers a brief history of the approaches adopted in the Anglo-American context as a point of comparison and advances an informed critique of the limitations of certain display strategies that function at times as nothing more than glorified handling sessions, or that segregate sighted from visually impaired visitors. As she argues, the real challenge for museums is not in offering physical access to their collections, but in offering cognitive access to the fullest range of audiences. Her experience in Japan also entailed working with visually impaired artists. The resulting shows, and others developed in a similar vein, not only included works that could be handled, but also objects deliberately designed to be destroyed by the act of touching, environments that required full-body immersion, and pieces that could not be touched at all. Such experimental approaches, she argues, have the potential to yield innovations well beyond the museum context.

In 'The Sculptor Is a Blind Man: Constantin Brancusi's *Sculpture for the Blind*', Sebastiano Barassi focuses on a work in several versions by Brancusi that approaches the question of tactile access and visual suppression from a different direction. Barassi situates *Sculpture for the Blind* carefully in artistic practice of the early twentieth century, arguing that the egg-shaped marble work should be seen as part of a wider-ranging interest running through several art movements in stimulating the senses. After exploring Brancusi's relationship with Duchamp and the apocryphal story of the sculpture's early display hidden within a sack with apertures through which it could be handled, Barassi carefully unpicks some of the potential associations with other similar works within Brancusi's oeuvre. He also focuses on Brancusi's tendency to group his works into meaningful sequences, in this case alongside the sculptures *Hand of Mademoiselle Pogany* and *Cup I* along with a drawing of *Mademoiselle Pogany*. These various associations lead suggestively into the realm of sleep, of dreams and of meaning hidden from the eye below the surface, meaning that may in some way be perceived by the hand. Indeed, this might connect in subtle ways with the overall form and the surface texture of the work. Nevertheless, as Barassi acknowledges, what Brancusi hoped to achieve with this work remains obscure. Indeed, the whole conception seems designed to engage with obscurity and this enigmatic quality in itself is part of the sculpture's power.

In 'Embracing Stone, Holding Brushes: Differentiating Touch in the *Unit One* Photographs', Fiona Candlin shifts attention from reception to creation and introduces the issue of gender. This chapter offers a useful corrective to some unreflective analyses that positively and unproblematically address touch, often denigrating vision in the process. In the previous chapter, Barassi describes Brancusi's habit of cradling his sculptures in his lap, a conception of the relationship between sculptor and sculpture that is analysed in some depth here. Using the photographic presentation of Unit One sculptors and painters – figures including Paul Nash, Barbara Hepworth, Henry Moore and Ben Nicholson – Candlin identifies a series of patterns in the portrayal of art and artists: painters hold the tools of their trade; sculptors hold their materials. These patterns, she argues, are rhetorical strategies designed to address the intellectual and manual skills involved in artistic activity. For the sculptors, in particular, direct contact with their materials, without the mediation of tools, implicitly places them within contemporary debates about the rigour of direct carving as a sculptural ideal. But Candlin goes on to show how the portrayal of Moore and Hepworth also engages gendered discourses around the act of creation. She scrutinises the characterisation of the active male sculptor wooing the passive female block and giving birth to sculptural offspring. As she shows, this characterisation, as old in some respects as the myth of Pygmalion, comes under various pressures in the portrayal of Hepworth, 'an anomaly, a woman carver'. At all stages, the nuances of touch set up or reinforce the governing metaphors. This more than justifies her closing shot, that 'theorists of touch may need to emulate their colleagues in visual studies to a far greater degree and to write about touch more strategically and with more specificity'.

In the final chapter, 'Lorenzo Ghiberti and Michelangelo in Search of the Feeling Hand', James Hall asks the disarmingly obvious but surprisingly revealing question, which hand? As he argues, from the historical perspective, the cultures of touch are many and varied. In the Italian Renaissance there was a careful differentiation between the touch of the left and the right hands, in terms of sensitivity, of sexual morality, of power and of status. This evaluation of the sinister side could have both negative and unexpectedly positive connotations, particularly because of its proximity to the heart. In a wide-ranging discussion of the significance of touch within Renaissance society and beyond, Hall shows how this culture of the left hand informs a number of works by Ghiberti and Michelangelo. This analysis also suggests that we might still profit from asking after which hand in cases where no hand is specified.

The juxtaposition of this chapter with Geraldine Johnson's piece earlier in the volume brings this point home clearly. Both contributors address the same historical and geographical context – even some of the same examples – but Hall reveals a different set of associations simply by shifting attention in this direction. This indicates that we lose at least as much in our ignorance of the historical and cultural dimensions of touch in relation to sculptural creation, appreciation and use, as we do when the physical act of touching sculpture is itself unavailable. While scientific study forges ahead with revelations about the sensitivity and sophistication of touch, and philosophical discourse continues to tease out the surprising and significant implications of the conceptual world of touch, the historical (and prehistorical) analysis of the social world of touch has barely begun to map the sheer wealth of possible inflections that tactility affords.

Between these parts, and as a conclusion to the book as a whole, are three pieces by artists whose work explores the relationship between sculpture and touch in strikingly different ways. The first contribution, at the end of 'Origins', comes from Claude Heath, an artist who has experimented in various ways with drawing sculptural objects that he has touched but never seen. He presents the results of a fascinating collaboration with Doug Bailey that arose during the course of this project. Heath was commissioned to produce a series of graphic works designed to capture and translate the qualities of prehistoric material as perceived by the hand. In some cases this involved using the objects themselves as drawing tools.

The second contribution, at the end of 'Approaches', comes from Rosalyn Driscoll, a sculptor whose work is deliberately created for tactile interaction. As a complement to the range of methods employed by the other contributors to Part II, she interweaves her own meditation on the significance of touch to her work with a litany of individual responses recorded by those fortunate enough to experience these pieces. Fortunate seems the right word because in many cases these experiences come across as revelatory or transcendent. If sculpture can function as threshold or frame, then the evidence of reception offered here confirms that tactile interaction with a sculptural object can open out experience in unexpected ways, something that other contributions to the volume also endorse in a variety of contexts and cases.

The third and final contribution, at the end of 'Identities', comes from Michael Petry, a contemporary installation artist. If earlier in this Introduction I suggested that the tactile appreciation of different sculptural materials was a lesser theme of the collection, it is here in the concluding part that it emerges as a fanfare. Petry opens with a poetic and evocative meditation that reads as part love song, part religious epiphany. But in the extended captions that accompany his works it becomes clear that these engage in the most physical and earthy way with the nature of sexual desire. The possibility that marble, bronze or ivory might substitute for flesh is a leitmotif of the

Western sculptural tradition. Here, however, other familiar materials with their own matrices of association, such as wood, silver, leather, pearls, string and rope, stand in not simply for bodies, but bodies engaging in sexual acts or bodily fluids such as semen and urine. The disjunction between the material at hand and the material it represents forms part of the shock and surprise of these works. This disjunction is amplified through the apparent gulf between the poetic imagery of Petry's opening text and the informative frankness of his captions. The strong element of physical desire operating in these works connects to one of the deepest strata of the relationship between sculpture and touch. In this respect, one only need recall, for example, the ancient account of a stain left on the buttocks of the Knidian Aphrodite by a love-struck devotee who then took his own life out of desperation.[29] And that of course brings us almost full circle to the *ur*-tale of sculptural touch, Pygmalion and Galatea.

Almost full circle but not quite: no sense of completion is implied or warranted. Although I have taken pains here in the Introduction to draw out some of the common concerns shared across the collection as a whole, this book is in no sense a comprehensive treatment of the subject. It would lengthen this Introduction immeasurably, not to mention the book itself, to attempt a catalogue of the many gaps and omissions that the reader will inevitably encounter. That itself is an invitation to further work. What this collection does seek to offer is an indication of the richness, legitimacy and genuine depth of this field in which a great variety of different disciplines have an interest, and through which they can enter into focused dialogue, whether that produces conflict or consensus (and both are evident here). If the sculptural ensemble of the Pórtico de la Gloria has served its purpose as the threshold for the collection, the collection itself should serve as the threshold to further engagement with this subject. There are certainly other books to be written here.

Notes

1. Cees Nootebaum, *Roads to Santiago: Detours and Riddles in the Lands and History of Spain*, trans. Ina Rilke, London: The Harvill Press, 1998, p.3.
2. A synopsis of the chapters that make up the three parts of this book can be found at the end of the Introduction.
3. Victor Stoichita, *The Pygmalion Effect: From Ovid to Hitchcock*, Chicago, IL: University of Chicago Press, 2008, pp.10–14 and George L. Hersey, *Falling in Love with Statues: Artificial Humans from Pygmalion to the Present*, Chicago, IL: University of Chicago Press, 2009, pp.32–4.
4. For up-to-date images and good details of the programme following the recent restoration, see http://www.porticodelagloria.com/el-portico-de-la-gloria.html (accessed: 26 June 2012). For a brief introduction see Ángel Sicart Giménez, 'The Pórtico de la Gloria of the Cathedral of Santiago de Compostela', in *Making Medieval Art*, Philip Lindley, ed., Donington: Tyas, 2003, pp.120–29.
5. The earliest photographic image of this practice was taken by Ksado in 1920. It shows an elderly male pilgrim. Reproduced in José Manuel García Iglesias, 'La Mano del Parteluz del Pórtico de la Gloria, Santiago de Compostela: de la leygenda a la historia', in *Boletín del Seminario de Estudios*

de Arte y Arqueología, 75, 2009, pp.31–42 (fig.6). The gendering of touch is an important factor, on which more below.

6. For a broad discussion of this wider transhistorical community of pilgrims, see Paul Genoni, 'The Pilgrim's Progress across Time: Medievalism and Modernity on the Road to Santiago', *Studies in Travel Writing*, 15 (2), 2011, pp.157–75.

7. This, of course, can only be asserted in a naïve sense. The gaze everywhere leaves its traces in the visual culture that surrounds us just as much as it shapes the social and psychological identities of both viewer and viewed. The (perceived) authenticity of the object is a crucial factor in the power of touch to collapse the distinction between past and present, see Carolyn Korsmeyer, 'Touch and the Experience of the Genuine', *British Journal of Aesthetics*, 52 (4), 2012, pp.367–77.

8. This is certainly now receiving increasing attention. See, amongst many other recent works, Constance Classen, ed., *The Book of Touch*, Oxford and New York: Berg, 2005; Mark Paterson, *The Senses of Touch: Haptics, Affects and Technologies*, Oxford and New York: Berg, 2005; Fiona Macpherson, ed., *The Senses: Classic and Contemporary Philosophical Perspectives*, Oxford: Oxford University Press, 2011; and Francesca Bacci and David Melcher, eds, *Art and the Senses*, Oxford: Oxford University Press, 2011.

9. I am thinking in particular here of the so-called Venus of Dolni Věstonice of c. 29,000–25,000 BCE with its fingerprint of a young child (Moravian Museum, Brno).

10. This sentiment informs Petrarch's identification of sculpture with the sense of touch, one of the earliest attempts of its kind (see later in this Introduction).

11. For an overview of the pilgrimage and the buildings and objects encountered on the route, see Kathleen Ashley and Marilyn Deegan, *Being a Pilgrim: Art and Ritual on the Medieval Routes to Santiago*, Farnham and Burlington, VT: Lund Humphries, 2009.

12. For an excellent discussion of all the ways in which a pilgrim might engage in mediated sensory contact with the divine in one form or another once at the basilica (including physical interaction with a life-size sculpture of James above the altar), see Kathleen M. Ashley, 'Hugging the Saint: Improvising Ritual on the Pilgrimage to Santiago de Compostela', in *Push Me, Pull You: vol. 2. Physical and Spatial Interaction in Late Medieval and Renaissance Art*, Sarah Blick and Laura D. Gelfand, eds, Leiden: Brill, 2011, pp.3–20. Ashley makes the point that some of the ritual encounters (with the statue for example) appear to have functioned as substitutes for direct access to the relics, since these appear to have been withheld from the late medieval period onwards. For images of the statue see Ashley and Deegan, *Being a Pilgrim*, chapter 9.

13. For some thoughts on this, see Øystein Hjort, '"Except on Doors": Reflections on a Curious Passage in the Letter from Hypatios of Ephesus to Julian of Atramyttion', in *Byzantine East, Latin West: Art-Historical Studies in Honor of Kurt Weitzmann*, Christopher Moss and Katherine Kiefer, eds, Princeton, NJ: Princeton University Press, 1995, pp.615–22.

14. Paul Crowther, *Phenomenology of the Visual Arts (Even the Frame)*, Stanford, CA: Stanford University Press, 2009, chapter 5 ('Sculpture and Transcendence').

15. For a critically informed discussion of the relationship between touch, vision and sculpture during the late medieval period, see Jacqueline Jung, 'The Tactile and the Visionary: Notes on the Place of Sculpture in the Medieval Religious Imagination', in *Looking Beyond: Visions, Dreams, and Insights in Medieval Art and History*, Colum Hourihane, ed., Princeton, NJ: Index of Christian Art, Princeton University, 2010, pp.203–40.

16. García Iglesias, 'La Mano', p.32.

17. For the ramifications of this in the medieval context, see Heather Webb, *The Medieval Heart*, New Haven, CT and London: Yale University Press, 2010.

18. See Ashley, 'Hugging the Saint', for the ways in which the clergy sought and seek to control the physical experiences of the pilgrim within the basilica.

19. The handprint is first mentioned in A. Jouvin, 'El viaje de España y Portugal' (1672), in J. García Mercadal, ed., *Viajes de extranjeros por España y Portuagal desde los tiempos más remotos hasta comienzos del siglo XX*, Junta de Castilla y León, 1999, vol. III, p.615. See García Iglesias, 'La Mano', pp.32–3.

20. For an acheiropoieton also involving divine action on a marble column in which the idea is linked to the Incarnation, see Herbert Kessler, *Seeing Medieval Art*, Toronto: University of Toronto Press, 2011 (2004), p.24 and fig.3.

21. The paradigm here would be Christ's footprints in the chapel of the Ascension on the Mount of Olives. It seems unlikely that anyone who came to venerate this spot actually stood

where Christ stood. See Andrea Worm, 'Steine and Fußspuren Christi auf dem Ölberg: Zu zwei ungewöhnlichen Motiven bei Darstellungen der Himmelfahrt Christi', *Zeitschrift für Kunstgeschichte*, 66 (3), 2003, pp.297–320 (I am grateful to Lucy Donkin for this reference).

22. García Iglesias, 'La Mano', pp.33–5, and Ashley, 'Hugging the Saint'.

23. For the fundamental problems posed by replicas in such experiences involving touch, see Korsmeyer, 'Touch and the Experience'.

24. See http://collections.vam.ac.uk/item/O40955/puerta-de-la-gloria-plaster-cast-the-master-matteo/ (accessed: 26 June 2012).

25. Johann Joachim Winckelmann, *History of the Art of Antiquity*, trans. H.F. Mallgrave, Los Angeles, CA: Getty Publications, 2006, X.iii.§ 18.

26. See, for example, the following by Robert Hopkins, 'Touching Pictures', *British Journal of Aesthetics* (BJA), 40 (1), 2000, pp.149–67; 'Painting, Sculpture, Sight and Touch', *BJA*, 44 (2), 2004, pp.149–66; 'Sculpture and Perspective', *BJA*, 50 (3), 2010, pp.1–17.

27. See Georges Didi-Huberman, *La resemblance par contact: archéologie, anchronisme et modernité de l'empreinte*, Paris: Ed. de Minuit, 2008.

28. Conrad H. Rawski, *Petrarch's Remedies for Fortune Fair and Foul: A Modern English Translation of De Remediis Utriusque Fortunae*, Bloomington, IN: Indiana University Press, 1991, vol.1, p.130.

29. From Pseudo-Lucian, *Erotes*. For a brief introduction, see Michael Squire, *The Art of the Body: Antiquity and Its Legacy*, London: I.B. Tauris, 2011, pp.97–100.

Bibliography

Ashley, Kathleen M., 'Hugging the Saint: Improvising Ritual on the Pilgrimage to Santiago de Compostela', in *Push Me, Pull You: vol. 2. Physical and Spatial Interaction in Late Medieval and Renaissance Art*, Sarah Blick and Laura D. Gelfand, eds, Leiden: Brill, 2011, pp.3–20.

Ashley, Kathleen and Marilyn Deegan, *Being a Pilgrim: Art and Ritual on the Medieval Routes to Santiago*, Farnham and Burlington, VT: Lund Humphries, 2009.

Bacci, Francesca and David Melcher, eds, *Art and the Senses*, Oxford: Oxford University Press, 2011.

Classen, Constance, ed., *The Book of Touch*, Oxford and New York: Berg, 2005.

Crowther, Paul, *Phenomenology of the Visual Arts (Even the Frame)*, Stanford, CA: Stanford University Press, 2009.

Didi-Huberman, Georges, *La resemblance par contact: archéologie, anchronisme et modernité de l'empreinte*, Paris: Ed. de Minuit, 2008.

García Iglesias, José Manuel, 'La Mano del Parteluz del Pórtico de la Gloria, Santiago de Compostela: de la leygenda a la historia', *Boletín del Seminario de Estudios de Arte y Arqueología*, 75, 2009, pp.31–42.

García Mercadal, J., ed., *Viajes de extranjeros por España y Portuagal desde los tiempos más remotos hasta comienzos del siglo XX*, Junta de Castilla y León, 1999.

Genoni, Paul, 'The Pilgrim's Progress across Time: Medievalism and Modernity on the Road to Santiago', *Studies in Travel Writing*, 15 (2), 2011, pp.157–75.

Hersey, George L., *Falling in Love with Statues: Artificial Humans from Pygmalion to the Present*, Chicago, IL: University of Chicago Press, 2009.

Hjort, Øystein, '"Except on Doors": Reflections on a Curious Passage in the Letter from Hypatios of Ephesus to Julian of Atramyttion', in *Byzantine East, Latin West: Art-Historical Studies in Honor of Kurt Weitzmann*, Christopher Moss and Katherine Kiefer, eds, Princeton, NJ: Princeton University Press, 1995, pp.615–22.

Hopkins, Robert, 'Touching Pictures', *British Journal of Aesthetics*, 40 (1), 2000, pp.149–67.

——, 'Painting, Sculpture, Sight and Touch', *British Journal of Aesthetics*, 44 (2), 2004, pp.149–66.
——, 'Sculpture and Perspective', *British Journal of Aesthetics*, 50 (3), 2010, pp.1–17.
Jung, Jacqueline, 'The Tactile and the Visionary: Notes on the Place of Sculpture in the Medieval Religious Imagination', in *Looking Beyond: Visions, Dreams, and Insights in Medieval Art and History*, Colum Hourihane, ed., Princeton, NJ: Index of Christian Art, Princeton University, 2010, pp.203–40.
Kessler, Herbert, *Seeing Medieval Art*, Toronto: University of Toronto Press, 2011 (2004).
Korsmeyer, Carolyn, 'Touch and the Experience of the Genuine', *British Journal of Aesthetics*, 52 (4), 2012, pp.367–77.
Macpherson, Fiona, ed., *The Senses: Classic and Contemporary Philosophical Perspectives*, Oxford: Oxford University Press, 2011.
Nootebaum, Cees, *Roads to Santiago: Detours and Riddles in the Lands and History of Spain*, trans. Ina Rilke, London: The Harvill Press, 1998.
Paterson, Mark, *The Senses of Touch: Haptics, Affects and Technologies*, Oxford and New York: Berg, 2005.
Rawski, Conrad H., *Petrarch's Remedies for Fortune Fair and Foul: A Modern English Translation of De Remediis Utriusque Fortunae*, Bloomington, IN: Indiana University Press, 1991.
Sicart Giménez, Ángel, 'The Pórtico de la Gloria of the Cathedral of Santiago de Compostela', in *Making Medieval Art*, Philip Lindley, ed., Donington: Tyas, 2003, pp.120–29.
Squire, Michael, *The Art of the Body: Antiquity and Its Legacy*, London: I.B. Tauris, 2011.
Stoichita, Victor, *The Pygmalion Effect: From Ovid to Hitchcock*, trans. Alison Anderson, Chicago, IL: University of Chicago Press, 2008.
Webb, Heather, *The Medieval Heart*, New Haven, CT and London: Yale University Press, 2010.
Winckelmann, Johann Joachim, *History of the Art of Antiquity*, trans. H.F. Mallgrave, Los Angeles, CA: Getty Publications, 2006.
Worm, Andrea, 'Steine and Fußspuren Christi auf dem Ölberg: Zu zwei ungewöhnlichen Motiven bei Darstellungen der Himmelfahrt Christi', *Zeitschrift für Kunstgeschichte*, 66 (3), 2003, pp.297–320.

Part I
Origins

1

Touch and the cheirotic apprehension of prehistoric figurines

Doug Bailey

Introduction

Standard studies of prehistoric anthropomorphic figurines have launched their analyses from an exclusively visual perspective that focuses on patterns and materials of surface decoration. I propose that a richer, more nuanced understanding of these artefacts results from a cheirotic approach, recognising that engaging an object through touch affords a particular, proximal, way of knowing that is much deeper than traditional analyses and interpretations which restrict insight to representational knowledge. A cheirotic approach examines the conditions and consequences of an object being enveloped by the hand, and thus brings the actions and consequences of touch into play. Touch as an act and a sense is intersubjective and transcendental; it engages the philosophy and psychology of the hand, hu-manualism, and the privilege of the tactile. With a cheirotic engagement, the analysis of prehistoric figurines is released from the preconceived, simplified, categories of fixed description and explanation that accompany visual-only investigation; the result is that fluid and uncertain compositions of understanding drift to the surface in a more honest, though more challenging, truth of figurines.

Prehistoric figurines

The inventory of anthropomorphic figurines from prehistoric Europe is vast with many thousands of examples, with especially numerous and varied ones recovered from sites of the Neolithic period in central and southeastern Europe (6500–3500 BC).[1] The Neolithic marks an important change in the ways that people lived their lives in prehistoric Europe. From a mode of subsistence that relied (and succeeded for tens of thousands of years) on the knowledgeable gathering and hunting and fishing of available, wild resources, there gradually emerged a dependence on the cultivation of high energy plants (such as wheat and barley) and on the breeding of animals (such as sheep, goat, pig and cattle). Accompanying this transition was the emergence of a built environment (that is, of houses and villages), as well as the adaptation of a ceramic pyrotechnology to make vessels (eventually in very large numbers) and many other objects of daily use. Figurines were one example of these new objects.

Small, and made of fired clay (animal bone and stone were also used, though much less commonly), Neolithic figurines have been recovered from domestic contexts almost exclusively (the exception is the Hamangia culture where figurines are found in burials). With the exception of the Hamangia examples (which are unique), there is no unambiguous evidence that figurines were associated with any single context, such as putative shrines or near hearths and ovens.[2] During excavation, most figurines are found in broken condition in rubbish pits or as fragments scattered across a site.[3] Interpretation is commonly crafted from reconstructions of mother goddess or fertility cults and ceremonies as popularised by the late Marija Gimbutas and widely, though uncritically, adapted by many regional specialists.[4] More recent studies have questioned the assumptions of the goddess interpretation, and have pushed research in new directions noting both the discovery of male figurines from this period as well as figures with no clearly identifiable sexual identities (that is, many are best defined as depictions of asexual, or sexually ambiguous human beings).[5]

In a recent study, I argued that the best way to think about Neolithic figurines is to look beyond particular interpretations of figurine function or meaning.[6] My proposal was to transcend suggestions made by previous scholars that figurines were goddesses or votives, or that they were toys for children, or that they were portraits of ancestors, or that they were teaching tools. I argued that these suggestions of function are nothing more than anecdotal explanations: all are based weakly on historical or ethnographic comparison; none can be (dis)proved – that is to say, we will never know what these figurines were used for, or what was the precise meaning that an individual in the Neolithic held for them. It is more honest to recognise that any individual Neolithic figurine would have had several different functions and meanings each of which would have changed during the artefact's lifetime (from creation, through use, to final discard) and each of which would have varied depending on the age, gender, experience, intention, background, needs, desires and worries and so on of the individual who made, held, used, saw, handled, broke and threw away the figurine. Critically, each of the various perceptions, uses and meanings that any single figurine might have attracted would have been equally valid and, vitally, also equally unavailable for conclusive assessment by a modern archaeologist.

My proposal was that we concentrate not on any particular (unassessible) function or meaning of any one particular figurine from a specific excavation context from a well-documented site (let alone the broad overly generalised category of 'Neolithic figurines' that wanders across regions and cultural phases). Instead, I suggested that we spend our energies considering the specific physical conditions that figurines possessed and the effects that these conditions might have had on people who daily looked at and handled these objects 8,000 years ago. I concluded that three conditions are primary: figurines are miniatures; figurines are anthropomorphic; figurines are three-dimensional. Taken together, these three conditions combine to make Neolithic figurines distinct from all other material culture from the period.[7] The condition of three-dimensionality is the stimulus for the present chapter (which in turn stimulates us to consider the significance and consequence of cheirotic apprehension), and as such will be discussed in detail further below. In advance of that discussion I need to offer a brief comment about the other two essential conditions of figurines: miniaturism and anthropomorphism.

Miniaturism and anthropomorphism

Making a small-scale version of an object or person, and then experiencing that miniature (playing with, thinking about, imagining, manipulating, holding, hiding, displaying, breaking, discarding) has unusual effects on the person experiencing the object made small. At a physical level, a person handling a miniature gains subtle empowerment and strengthening: in relation to what is represented in small-scale, one is made to feel larger in size and advanced in hierarchical position; a soothing sense of wellbeing follows. Toy manufacturers know this, as do the manufacturers and hobbyists committed to the intensely intricate model boat, car and train. It was Walt Disney, however, who exploited most publicly the potential for putting people in a scaled-down environment. Disney built Main Street in Disneyland at 5/8ths scale specifically to put people at ease, to calm them, to soothe them (this was one of his goals in creating Disneyland – to give people a place to escape from the harsh and unpleasant realities of the real world).[8] Disney's soothing of the visitors provided them with another world to visit, a world where escape and calm were powerfully implicit.

More striking than Disney's use of size-reduction on Main Street were the patterns that the University of Tennessee psychologist Alton Delong recognised among the subjects of experiments he conducted in his studies of the effects that small-scale environments have on human perception.[9] In the first of two famous studies, Delong showed that subjects who had been playing the computer game Pong on small screen televisions won more often and were happier about their gaming experience then were subjects who had played the game on larger screens; EEG records confirmed that the brain activities of small screen Pong players differed significantly from those of large screen players. In a second experiment, Delong demonstrated that the smaller the scale that people imagined that they were in, the faster their brains appeared to work. Delong asked subjects to predict the passage of time while they imagined themselves to be in miniature rooms that had been built at 1/6th, 1/12th and 1/24th scales; subject predictions of time passage were inaccurate, all were underestimates, and a clear pattern emerged in which length of each time estimate was directly related to the size of the scale reduction (the smaller the scale the shorter the time estimate). Delong concluded that when people put themselves into small-scale environments, their brain clocks slow down. For Delong's subjects, working at the small scale took them into another temporal dimension.

In these and other experiments, in small-scale arboriculture, and in work by artists intrigued by the effects that small-scale worlds have on spectators (for example, see Michael Ashkin's table-top landscapes, any bonsai tree or Anthony Gormley's *Field* series), variations of the same remarkable conclusions emerge: when people imagine themselves to be in miniature environments, they enter other worlds in which they are enlarged, soothed and able to carry out some mental tasks more efficiently and according to an altered time scale.[10]

When the object made miniature is the human body, then the consequences of miniaturism have significance at another level. Academic work on the use of dolls in therapy and psychology, police work and other areas have investigated the ways that bodies-made-small have powerful effects on people.[11] One of the most widely discussed cases is the impact that the Barbie Doll has on young girls' perceptions of their vocational potential and of their body shape.[12] Debate over the impact of Barbie on girls settles between two opposing camps: those who see her as a glorious model for young girls to gain inspiration for the limitless opportunities for professional and social development (you can do any job and achieve any position); and those who see her as a dangerous, subconscious, brainwasher of young girls and their perceptions of desirable body shape.[13] The importance of Barbie and of these debates for my suggestions about miniature bodies is not an attempt to take sides or resolve the disagreements (probably neither camp is completely correct). What is significant is that a miniature woman-shaped object (purchased and used for one reason – as a toy for a child to play with) has the potential for such strong, subconscious, effects on girls (and, strangely, on adults who wage the culture wars over those effects).

Figurines, small bodies and the Neolithic

Seen in the light of the power of miniaturism to take people into other worlds and the ways that bodies made small can affect people's perceptions of what is the correct appearance of a body (male or female), a more nuanced understanding emerges of the position that figurines may have held in the Neolithic period of central and southeastern Europe. As noted above, the Neolithic was a period of remarkable change in technology, economy and almost every other way in which people lived their lives. Accompanying the more obvious and visible changes in how people lived (for instance, how they gained their food) was a fundamental transformation in the ways that people related to one another, on individual, person-to-person, terms, as well as group-to-group. Some of this social transformation came as (probably) unintended consequences of the adaptation of the new economies and activities. For example, the collaboration and sharing (or hoarding) of trust, labour and resources that accompanied small-scale farming would have shaped social and political relationships among these small communities. Similar, also unintended effects would have resulted from the introduction of new arrangements of people in the landscape that followed the introduction of houses (and thus of households) and of the collections of particular sets of houses (and thus of village communities). In brief it was a period through which personal and group identities were finding new forms, new media and new potentials.

The powerful position that the human body occupies as the locus for social identity and which has dominated European proto-history and history emerged for the first time during the Neolithic.[14] The Neolithic emergence of the body as the primary container or canvas for personal human identity gradually replaced other, earlier ways of living and of thinking about human relationships. These ways had worked in distributing identity through less rigidly defined communities – such as hunter-gatherer-fishers – in more fluid and flexible series of calculations and negotiations. One of the clearest records of the elevation of the body to its position of pre-eminence can be seen in the (often) elaborate ways in which these communities treated the deceased. By the end of the Neolithic in southeastern Europe, for example, grand cemeteries of many hundreds of individual inhumations reveal clear patterns of unequal depositions of prestige and exotic grave goods: of Europe's earliest metals – gold and copper – and molluscs (for example shells such as *spondylus* which had local significance for projecting personal identity and, perhaps, social and political status).

While this attention to the body at time of death in the Neolithic is a well appreciated example of the emergence of the body of an individual as the key unit of identity within human society, less attention has been devoted to the powerful role that anthropomorphic figurines would have played in the same process. I have argued elsewhere that, perhaps surprisingly, it is the many thousands of figurines that made the greatest input into the elevation of the human body as the locus of personhood.[15] In brief, the presence of small human bodies – that is, figurines – variously shaped and decorated, made, used, seen and lived with, in houses and villages across the region, powered a deep and subconscious process through which the human form came to be the base currency for identity in European prehistory (and history).

The third dimension, touch and cheirotics

The understanding of Neolithic figurines that I had developed in terms of miniaturism and anthropomorphism and my arguments about the resulting elevation of the human body as the locus for identity were fine as far as they went. Regardless of the merits of those arguments, however, I realise now that my work had remained within the limitations of a visual approach, and to be honest, though I still believe in the core of the argument, I have become less convinced that I had provided any real insight into the mechanics of how the emergence and dominance of the body within European senses of identity and community had happened in the daily, lived experiences of Neolithic people. In brief, I had ignored and avoided thinking through the everyday physical practice and process of how figurines had the effects that I was suggesting that they had. I had failed to examine the third of my critical conditions of the figurines; I had neglected considering the significance and powerful consequences of knowing through touch.

Touch

When bodies made miniature are made in three dimensions, our understanding is enriched greatly if we think through the sense of touch and if we take a cheirotic approach. Coupled with their small size, figurines' physical condition of three-dimensionality generates particular interactions with people: figurines afford touching and being held in the hand.[16] Touch is a much discussed topic in the humanities and the social sciences with a broad and deep pedigree (which makes it even more striking that, beyond a very few recent attempts, especially by Lynn Meskell and Carolyn Nakamura on figurines from Çatalhöyük), the topic has not been engaged intensively by archaeologists.[17] For Aristotle, touch, touching and being touched were essential aspects for human existence (*On the Soul*, 2.II.423a–b). For Emmanuel Levinas, touch is important in its distinction from other senses: the action of one touching another propels contact beyond mere physical connection through a rich and complex engagement (which is immediate and unmediated) to a place where there are no interventions by other substances, where an 'intimate proximity' is invoked, where to submit to the action of touching or caressing is to admit that as one does not know precisely what one seeks, one must admit to the absence of predetermined knowing.[18]

For Maurice Merleau-Ponty, touch brings into play an immediacy of relationship that exceeds other attempts at interpretation or explanation where experience and knowing are reduced to simplification and generalisation.[19] In referring to this immediacy, Merleau-Ponty pushes us to reject the assumption that an object (or a body) ends at its surface (or its skin). Through touch the limit between the body and the world breaks down; the result is an intertwining, an intersection and a cross-over towards the subconscious and the metaphysical aura of touch.[20] Touch is intersubjective. Making a related point, Jacques Derrida writes that touch has a transcendental status.[21] Levinas', Merleau-Ponty's and Derrida's thoughts unbalance and unnerve me. How am I distinct from other people? Where does my being end? What is its surface and what separates that surface from the surfaces of others? If an object (or my body) does not end with its surface (or my skin), then am I distinct from other people? Indeed, does the entity 'person' have any intellectual or physical surety? By questioning the security and stability of the limits that we have assumed exist and which separate objects from people and people from people and objects from objects, we open up our understanding of our worlds in ways that are both exciting and disturbing.

The action and sense of touch, thus, can be taken to be concerned with surfaces, limits and boundaries. James Gibson tells us that the surface is where the action is, though only in the recognition, perhaps, that surfaces dissolve under the condition of touch.[22] Kevin Hetherington has argued persuasively that touch decentres the subject.[23] His work with Sarah, a blind museum visitor, reveals Sarah's tacit understanding that touch is a way of knowing that is distinct from vision (and the other senses). Touch is a way of knowing that decentres Sarah from the assumed position that she is a singular, representing subject. Hetherington and David Appelbaum ask us to think about the ways that touch is productive and performative.[24] Appelbaum argues that while the accumulation of visual knowledge is a process of consumption, the exploration by the hand is a process of making and production: touch 'concerns itself with knowledge as both performance and material accomplishment and only latterly with representation' if, indeed, it considers representation at all.[25]

Following Robert Copper and John Law, and Gabriel Josipovici, Hetherington makes the important point that the knowledge that is acquired via touch is proximal (and is distinct from distal knowledge).[26] Distal knowledge provides broad and detached understandings based on knowledge at a distance or with a concern for the big picture. Distal knowing works through representation, and focuses on an object (or person) being known in a static and completed state; it relies on preconceptions and on what is already known by illustrating boundaries and separation, distinctness and clarity, hierarchy and order.[27] Proximal knowledge is a very different animal. Proximal knowledge is context-specific, fragmentary, mundane and performative; it allows for fluidity, uncertainty, incompletion and is always partial and precarious. Proximal knowledge opens up interpretation, denying the finality that Western (social) science demands.

Standard interpretations of prehistoric figurines (and indeed explanation within archaeology more broadly witnessed) strive to produce distal knowledge, seeking clear understandings in simple terms: this figurine is a votive, that one is a toy, the other is a portrait of an ancestor. If we think about touch in the terms suggested by Levinas, Merleau-Ponty, Appelbaum and Heatherington, and if we accept the challenge of seeking proximal understandings, then the modern intellectual (and prehistoric Neolithic) engagement with figurines is an opportunity to transcend the simplicity of trying to interpret a miniature, anthropomorphic object made 8,000 years ago. To accept this challenge requires us to ask new questions about these figurines. What happens when people (past and present) take these small objects in their hands? One way to attempt an answer is to examine the process and consequences of holding and grasping an object (and a small-bodied one at that).

Cheirotics and the hand

Within an investigation of touch a cheirotic approach focuses our enquiry onto the hand: cheirotics refers to the ability of an object to be enveloped in the hand, or to the process of enveloping something in the hand; *cheir* comes from the Greek for hand or handling (for instance, a cheiropod is an animal with hands). Figurines are cheirotic objects; in their size and three dimensionality they afford being held in the hand (Figs 1.1, 1.2 and 1.3).[28] In the cheirotic sense then, when we think about figurines we would do well to think about the hand and about the particular engagement with the world that the hand allows.

For Derrida, it is the hand which makes us human as it allows for attaining, taking, comprehending, analysing and knowing. For the eighteenth-century French philosopher Françoise Maine de Biran, the hand was that thing which is properly human; Biran writes of a hu-manualism and the important role for human conscious experience that physical connections to the external world play.[29] Edmund Husserl writes about the hand and the privilege of the tactile that the hand provides for humans.[30] A psychology of the hand informs on the ways that we assess objects physically in the world. The cognitive psychologists Susan Lederman and Roberta Klatzky write about haptic apprehension and study the ways in which humans manually assess and understand the properties of objects.[31] Lederman and her colleagues suggest that in the haptic apprehension of an object, a person assesses the different properties of the object and how those properties combine to produce the whole. They contrast this process of apprehension with that of recognition or categorisation. Through touch we come to know objects in particular ways. When the hand encloses an object, it makes contact with as much of the object's surface as possible. Enclosure and envelopment are non-specialised actions which allow the taking of just enough general information about the object. They invite further investigation of a more

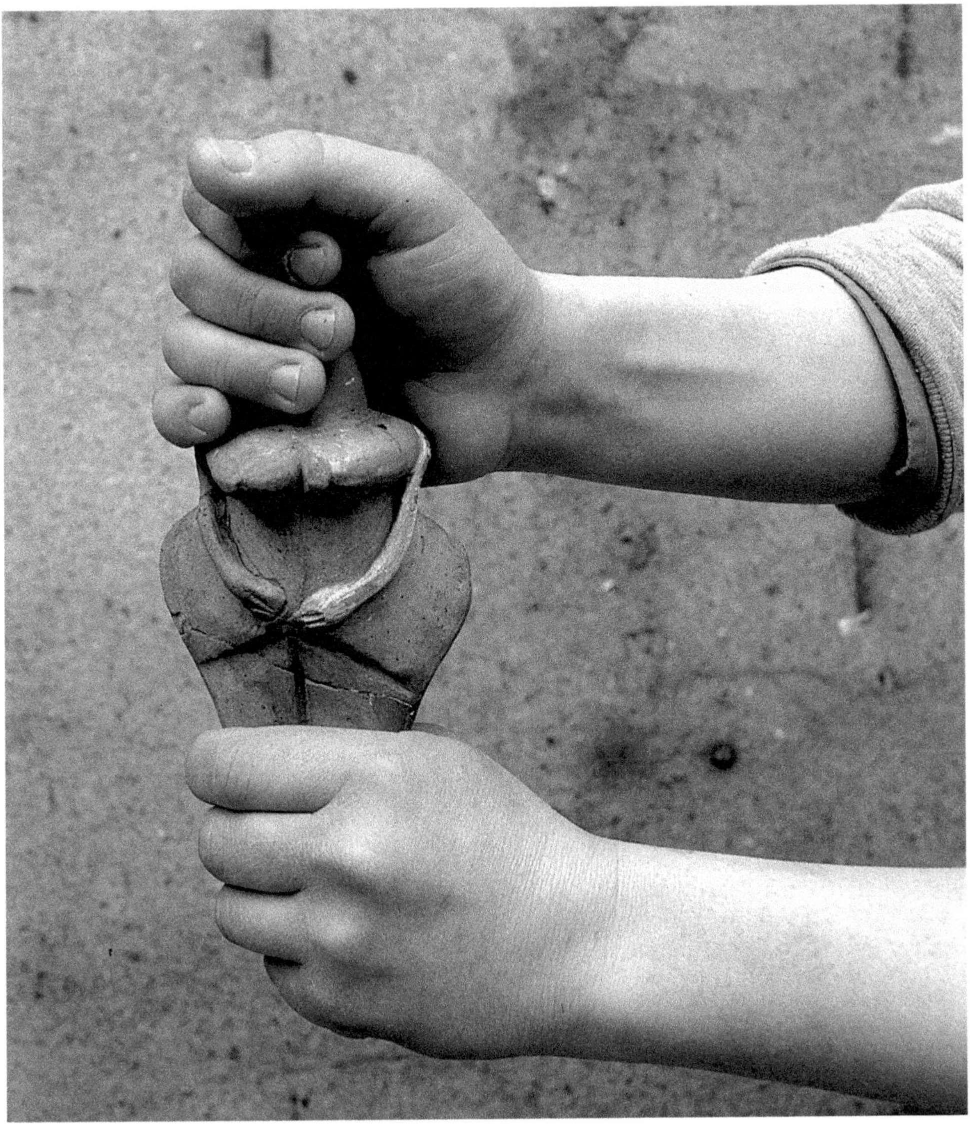

1.1 Hamangia culture figurine (5200–4500 cal BC) [© Doug Bailey]

specialised nature directed at specific parts or areas of an object, investigations which may require the use of fingers to make more precise assessments and to deepen particular apprehensions.

Have humans always had the physical abilities to engage objects in the hand as we do today? What do we know about the evolution of the hand as an anatomical and, indeed, as an intellectual capacity? There is nothing novel

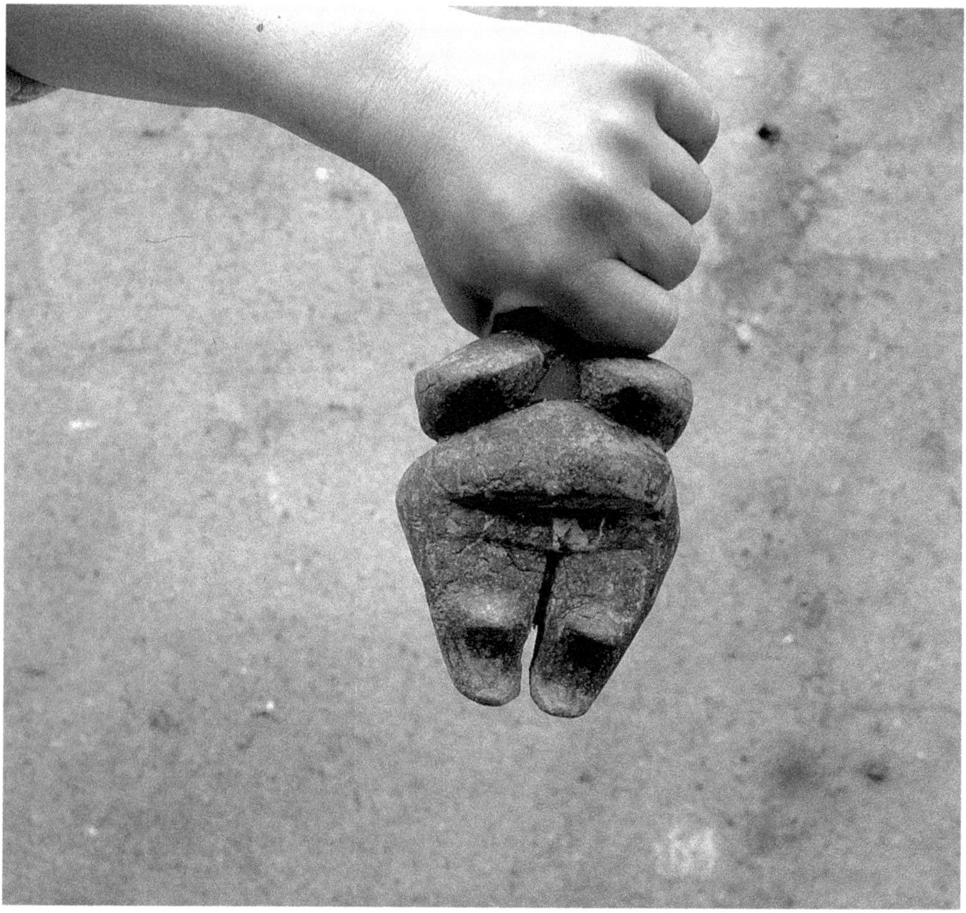

1.2 Hamangia culture figurine (5200–4500 cal BC) [© Doug Bailey]

in recognising the consequences (or could it have been a cause?) of the shift to bipedal locomotion for our ancient hominin ancestors sometime around 3.85 million years ago (or mya); hands were emancipated and could do other things, such as making and using objects like stone tools. The consequence of this development (though it could just as easily have been the cause of the shift) may well have been most important in non-functional ways, for example the importance of gesture in a symbolic sense for communication and expression. Over the longer time-scale of hominin evolution, developments in the capabilities that the human hand had for grasping and apprehending an object may well have been significant not only in functional terms (making and using tools) but also with respect to behaviour, the development of human consciousness and the human sense of what we are in relation to the world around us.

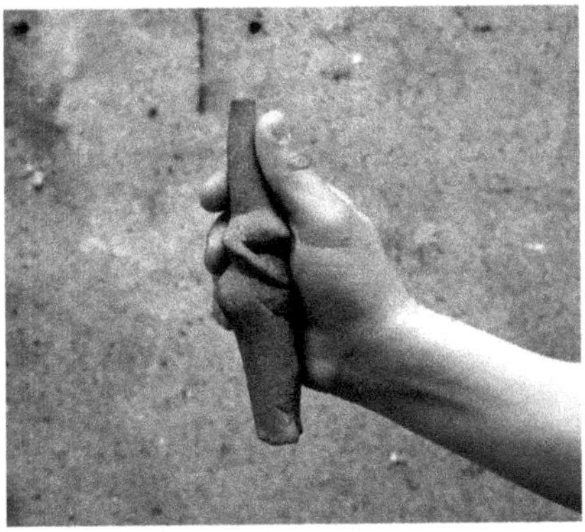
1.3 Hamangia culture figurine (5200–4500 cal BC) [© Doug Bailey]

Work by John Napier has suggested that there were two important developments in the ways that hominins used their hands to grip things (but see also the work of Mary Marzke and colleagues).[32] Napier writes of the evolution of the power grip, as used to hold a tool in the hand or wield it with striking force, as one would do with a hammer. This is an ability to be found in *Homo habilis* (the first toolmaker) and *Homo erectus* (the first hominin to move out of Africa) (from 2.4 mya and 1.9 mya respectively). Thus, Napier writes about the grip of *Homo neanderthalensis* (from as early as 200,000 years ago) as being primarily adapted for greater gripping strength and with a facility for power gripping (that is, holding objects in the palm of the hand with the thumb acting as a brace). In contrast is the precision grip which can be found with the emergence of *Homo sapiens sapiens* (anatomically modern humans – that's us) from between 200,000 and 150,000 years ago.

With the emergence of anatomically modern humans, more precise handling (and apprehension of objects) was possible through finer finger movements and oblique grips. The precision grip allowed modern humans to move an object around in their fingers. It allows you to turn the pages of this book or click the mouse to access the pdf version of this chapter. Where earlier hominins were gripping objects, modern humans (like us) were handling and manipulating them. The distinction is important, particularly in the context of the comments included above about the ways in which the handling of an object allows a person to apprehend a proximal knowledge of that object. The distinction between the handling, manipulating and manually manoeuvring of objects by modern humans on the one hand, and the earlier power gripping by *Homo habilis* and *Homo erectus* is a fundamental one. Though perhaps founded on (or at least enabled by) skeletal and musculature development, the distinction may have had most importance in terms of human cognitive abilities. If this is the case, then the consequences of the ability that modern humans have for precision handling and thus for a more nuanced, richer and deeper, haptic apprehension of objects (and of people and animals and of every other part of the world), may be more significant in terms of our intellectual abilities to think and to understand the world(s) around us than it is in terms of any new tool-based technologies or uses.

There is no question that this essential development in manual abilities accompanied technological and expressive developments both in material culture (for example the types of tools that were produced – composite tools with many parts) and in the ways in which tools could be used (for instance,

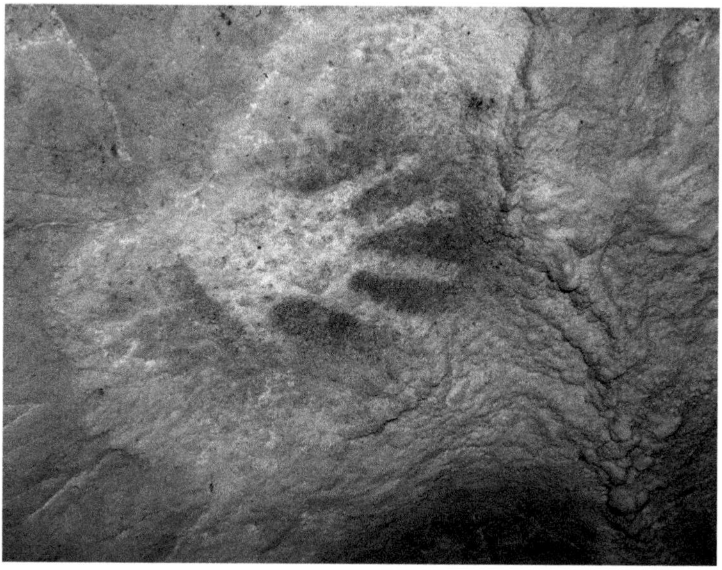

1.4 Palaeolithic handprints from the Castillo Cave, Cantabria, Northern Spain (c. 35,000 BC) [Photo courtesy and copyright of Meg Conkey]

the use of finely pointed flint objects such as burins and awls to engrave marks onto ivory and wood and to make holes in hides and softer materials). More critical, however, is the recognition that it was at this time of our evolutionary past – that is, with the appearance of anatomically modern humans – that our ancestors made the first art: representational and abstract, and including the cave paintings of western Europe and the earliest (Upper Palaeolithic) human figurines in western, central and northeastern Europe. When trying to unlock the secrets of the emergence of modern humans and their particular suite of abilities, perhaps we should focus our attention as much on the capabilities and actions of our ancestors' hands as we do on their economies – scavenging, foraging, hunting – or on their communication hardware – development of the voice box and the ability to speak a language. In addition, while so much attention has been spent dating and analysing the first art of the modern humans (the cave paintings and indeed the Upper Palaeolithic figurines), it is perhaps of at least equal importance to note that some of the most mysterious imagery on the walls of caves are the many hundreds of hand silhouettes (Fig. 1.4).

Back to the Neolithic and a cheirotics of figurines

My original proposal for a rich way to think about Neolithic figurines was to locate their emergence in the prehistoric period of Europe within the sedimentation of personal, political and social identity onto the human body. Having worked through the consequences of the hand, of holding and of the development of manipulative handling, that proposal is strengthened: a figurine's condition of three-dimensionality empowered it as an object to bring the human body into human apprehension through touch (as well, of course, as through vision). However, by thinking in terms of their cheirotic character, we can now see more clearly the strength that the Neolithic figurine had in promoting in human thinking (probably at a subconscious level) the role that the physical frame of the individual human body should play as a resting place for the human spirit.

The role that I envisage the figurines to have occupied is one in which they may well have functioned as a toy or a goddess votive. However, the critical step away from these conclusions as reductions of meaning and interpretation is to understand that touching and holding a body-made-small would have had extraordinarily powerful impacts on the ways that people in the Neolithic conceptualised their worlds. The consequences were complex and highly nuanced, and would have raised deeper, initially unanswerable questions about who and what one was and about what was an appropriate relationship of one to another.[33] These are questions of a metaphysical nature that challenge the boundaries of being, along which and beyond which people have commonly and unquestioningly lived their lives. In the sense of a proximal knowledge of self and of one's relationships to others, these figurines presented to the Neolithic people (who made, touched, handled, broke and tossed them onto a rubbish tip) an open and unending set of negotiations about the role that the human body was to have within society. We have been living with the consequences of their reactions ever since.

Notes

1. The first figurines appeared in small numbers in the Upper Palaeolithic (for example, the recent discovery of a figurine from Hohle Fels in Germany dating to 35,000 years ago; N.J. Conrad, 'A Female Figurine from the Basal Augrignacian of Hohle Fels Cave in Southwestern Germany', *Nature*, 459, 2009, pp.248–52) of western, central and Russian Europe, and though the consequences of a cheirotic approach applies equally to them as to Neolithic figurines, I restrict my discussion here to the material with which I am most familiar.

2. The widely held belief that Neolithic figurines were used and deposited in Neolithic shrines is based on false and circular reasoning: the presence of figurines is first used to define a building as a shire; and then the figurines are given a religious or ceremonial function because they are found in a shrine.

3. John Chapman and others have argued vigorously, that the deposition of figurines and figurine fragments in pits (and their scattering across sites) were ritual acts based on principles of fragmentation and enchainment. See John C. Chapman, *Fragmentation in Archaeology: People, Places and Broken Objects in the Prehistory of South Eastern Europe*, London: Routledge, 2000 and John C. Chapman and B. Gaydarska, *Parts and Whole: Fragmentation in Prehistoric Context*, Oxford: Owbow Books, 2007.

4. M. Gimbutas, *The Goddesses and Gods of Old Europe, 6500–3500 BC, Myths and Cult Images*, Berkeley, CA: University of California Press, 1982; M. Gimbutas, *The Language of the Goddess*, San Francisco, CA:

Harper Collins, 1989; M. Gimbutas, *The Civilization of the Goddess: The World of Old Europe*, San Francisco, CA: Harper Collins, 1991.

5. D.W. Bailey, 'Representing Gender: Homology or Propaganda', *Journal of European Archaeology*, 2 (2), 1994, pp.193–202; D.W. Bailey, *Prehistoric Figurines: Representation and Corporeality in the Neolithic*, London: Routledge, 2005; D.W. Bailey, 'The Figurines of Old Europe', in *The Lost World of Old Europe: The Danube Valley, 5000–3500 BC*, D.W. Anthony and J.Y. Chi, eds, Princeton, NJ: Princeton University Press, 2010, pp.113–27; D.W. Bailey, A. Cochrane and J. Zambelli, *Unearthed: A Comparative Study of Jōmon Dogū and Neolithic Figurines*, Norwich: Sainsbury Centre for the Visual Arts, 2010; D.W. Bailey, 'Figurines, Corporeality and the Origins of Gender', in *A Companion to Gender Prehistory*, D. Bolger, ed., London: Wiley, 2012, pp.244–64; P. Biehl, 'Symbolic Communication Systems: Symbols on Anthropomorphic Figurines of the Neolithic and Chalcolithic from South-eastern Europe', *Journal of European Archaeology*, 4, 1996, pp.153–76; P. Biehl, *Studien zum symbolgut des Neolithikums und der Kupferzeit in Südosteuropa* [Studies of the Symbolic Material Culture of the Neolithic and the Copper Age in Southeast Europe] (Saarbrücker Beiträge zur Altertumskunde, Bd. 64), Bonn: Dr. Rudolt Habelt Verlag, 2003; P. Biehl, 'Figurines in Action: Methods and Theories in Figurine Research', in *Festschrift Peter Ucko: A Future for Archaeology – the Past as the Present*, R. Layton, S. Shennan and P. Stone, eds, London: UCL Press, 2006, pp.199–215; M. Conkey and R. Tringham, 'Archaeology and the Goddess: Exploring the Contours of Feminist Archaeology', in *Feminism in the Academy*, D.C. Stanton and A.J. Stewart, eds, Ann Arbor, MI: The University of Michigan Press, 1995, pp.199–247; R. Hardie, 'Gender Tensions in Figurines in SE Europe', in *Cult in Context: Reconsidering Ritual in Archaeology*, D.A. Barrowclough and C. Malone, eds, Oxford: Oxbow Books, 2007, pp.82–9; L.M. Meskell, 'Goddesses, Gimbutas, and "New Age" Archaeology', *Antiquity*, 69, 1995, pp.74–86; L.M. Meskell, 'Oh My Goddess: Ecofeminism, Sexuality and Archaeology', *Archaeological Dialogues*, 5 (2), 1998, pp.126–42; L.M. Meskell, 'Divine Things', in *Rethinking Materiality: The Engagement of Mind with the Material World*, E. DeMarrais, C. Gosden and C. Renfrew, eds, Cambridge: McDonald Institute for Archaeological Research, 2004, pp.249–59; L.M. Meskell, 'Refiguring the Corpus at Çatalhöyük', in *Image and Imagination: A Global Prehistory of Figurative Representation*, C. Renfrew and I. Morley, eds, Cambridge: McDonald Institute Monographs, 2007, pp.137–49; L.M. Meskell, C. Nakamura, R. King and S. Farid, 'Figured Lifeworlds and Depositional Practices at Çatalhöyük', *Cambridge Archaeological Journal*, 18, 2008, pp.139–61.

6. Bailey, *Prehistoric Figurines*.

7. Of related interest are other miniature objects such as small-scale house and furniture models and animal figurines, though both of these types of artefacts appear much less frequently than do anthropomorphic figurines.

8. E. Doss, 'Making Imaginations Age in the 1950s: Disneyland's Fantasy Art and Architecture', in *Designing Disney's Theme Parks: The Architecture of Reassurance*, K.A. Marling, ed., New York: Flammarion, 1977, pp.179–89; R. Schickel, *The Disney Version: The Life, Times, Art and Commerce of Walt Disney*, New York: Ivan R. Dee, 1993.

9. A.J. Delong, 'Phenomenological Space-Time: Towards an Experimental Relativity', *Science* (7 August), 1981, pp.681–2; A.J. Delong, 'Spatial Scale, Temporal Experience and Information Processing: An Empirical Examination of Experimental Reality', *Man-Environment Systems*, 13, 1983, pp.77–86.

10. Bailey, *Prehistoric Figurines*.

11. I.A. James, L. Mackenize and E. Mukaetova-Ladinska, 'Doll Use in Care Homes for People with Dementia', *International Journal of Geriatric Psychiatry*, 21 (11), 2006, pp.1093–8; M. Morgan, *How to Interview Sex Abuse Victims: Including the Use of Anatomical Dolls*, London: Sage, 1995.

12. M.G. Lord, *Forever Barbie: The Unauthorized Biography of a Real Doll*, New York: William Morrow and Company, 1994.

13. K.D. Brownell, M.A. Napolitano, 'Distorting Reality for Children: Body Size Proportions of Barbie and Ken Dolls', *International Journal of Eating Disorders*, 18 (3), 2006, pp.295–8.

14. D.W. Bailey, 'The Corporeal Politics of Being in the Neolithic', in *Past Bodies: Centred Research in Archaeology*, J. Robb and D. Borić, eds, Oxford: Oxbow Books, 2008, pp.9–18.

15. D.W. Bailey, 'Figurines, Corporeality and the Origins of Gender', in *A Companion to Gender Prehistory*, D. Bolger, ed., London: Wiley, 2012, pp.244–64.

16. I refer to J.J. Gibson's sense of affordance J.J. Gibson, *The Ecological Approach to Visual Perception*, Boston, MA: Houghton Mifflin, 1979.

17. C. Nakamura and L. Meskell, 'Articulate Bodies: Forms and Figures at Çatalhöyük', *Journal of Archaeological Method and Theory*, 16, 2009, pp.205–30.

18. E. Levinas, *Time and the Other*, Pittsburgh, PA: Duquesne University Press, 1990; E. Levinas, *Totality and Infinity: An Essay on Exteriority*, Pittsburgh, PA: Duquesne University Press, 1969, p.257; E. Levinas, *Existence and Existents*, trans. A. Lingis, The Hague: Nijhoff, 1978.

19. M. Merleau-Ponty, *The Visible and the Invisible, Followed by Working Notes*, trans. Alphonso Lingis, Evanston, IL: Northwestern University Press, 1968.

20. Merleau-Ponty, *The Visible*, p.138.

21. J. Derrida, *On Touching: Jean-Luc Nancy*, Palo Alto, CA: Stanford University Press, 2005, pp.146–7.

22. Gibson, *Ecological Approach*, p.23.

23. K. Hetherington, 'Spatial Textures: Making Place through Touch', *Environment and Planning A*, 35 (11), 2003, pp.1933–44.

24. D. Appelbaum, *The Stop*, Albany, NY: State University of New York, 1995.

25. Appelbaum, *The Stop*.

26. R. Cooper and J. Law, 'Organisation: Distal and Proximal Views', in *The Sociology of Organizations*, S. Bacharach, ed., Greenwich, CT: JAI, 1994, pp.123–45 and G. Josipovici, *Touch: An Essay*, New Haven, CT: Yale University Press, 1996.

27. Heatherington, 'Spatial Textures', p.239.

28. There are of course Neolithic figurines which cannot be completely held in the hand, figurines which are larger. However, the vast majority of figurines from the Neolithic of central and southeastern Europe afford being held in the hand.

29. F-P. de Biran, *Oeuvres Philosophiques de Maine de Biran, Paris: Librairie de Ladrange, 1841;* A. Kühtmann, *Maine de Biran: Ein Beitrag zur Geschichte der Metaphysik under der Psychologie des Willens*, Bremen: Max Nössler, 1901; A. Lang, *Maine de Biran und die Neuere Philosophie*, Cologne, 1901; M. Couailhac, *Maine de Biran*, Paris: Félix Alcan, 1905.

30. E. Husserl, *Ideas Pertaining to a Pure Phenomenology and to a Phenomenological Philosophy: Second Book: Studies in the Phenomenology of Constitution*, London: Springer, 1990.

31. S.J. Lederman and R.L. Klatzky, 'Hand Movements: A Window into Haptic Object Recognition', *Cognitive Psychology*, 19, 1987, pp.342–68; S.J. Lederman and R. Klatzky, 'Haptic Explanation and Object Representation', in *Vision and Action: The Control Grasping*, M.A. Goodale, ed., Norwood, NJ: Ablex, 1990, pp.98–110.

32. J.R. Napier, 'The Evolution of the Hand', *Scientific American*, 207, 1962, pp.56–62; J.R. Napier and R. Tuttle, *Hands*, Princeton, NJ: Princeton University Press, 1993; M.W. Marzke, K.L. Wullstein and S.F. Viegas, 'Evolution of the Power ("Squeeze") Grip and Its Morphological Correlates in Hominids', *American Journal of Physical Anthropology*, 89 (3), 1992, pp.283–98; M.W. Marzke, 'Precision Grips, Hand Morphology, and Tools', *American Journal of Physical Anthropology*, 102 (1), 1997, pp.91–110.

33. In a recent article, I have made the case that prehistoric European figurines were one of the key mechanisms in the development of modern, Western conceptions of gender and of the sedimentation of gendered identity in the body; Bailey, 'Figurines, Corporeality, and the Origins of Gender'.

Bibliography

Appelbaum, D., *The Stop*, Albany, NY: State University of New York, 1995.

Bailey, D.W., 'Representing Gender: Homology or Propaganda', *Journal of European Archaeology*, 2 (2), 1994, pp.193–202.

——, *Prehistoric Figurines: Representation and Corporeality in the Neolithic*, London: Routledge, 2005.

——, 'The Anti-rhetorical Power of Representational Absence: Faceless Figurines in the Balkan Neolithic', in *Material Beginnings: A Global Prehistory of Figurative Representation*, C. Renfrew and I. Morley, eds, Cambridge: McDonald Institute, 2007, pp.117–26.

——, 'The Corporeal Politics of Being in the Neolithic', in *Past Bodies: Centred Research in Archaeology*, J. Robb and D. Borić, eds, Oxford: Oxbow Books, 2008, pp.9–18.

——, 'The Figurines of Old Europe', in *The Lost World of Old Europe: The Danube Valley, 5000–3500 BC*, D.W. Anthony and J.Y. Chi, eds, Princeton, NJ: Princeton University Press, 2010, pp.113–27.

——, 'Figurines, Corporeality and the Origins of Gender', in *A Companion to Gender Prehistory*, D. Bolger, ed., London: Wiley, 2012, pp.244–64.

Bailey, D.W., A. Cochrane and J. Zambelli, *Unearthed: A Comparative Study of Jōmon Dogū and Neolithic Figurines*, Norwich: Sainsbury Centre for the Visual Arts, 2010.

Biehl, P., 'Symbolic Communication Systems: Symbols on Anthropomorphic Figurines of the Neolithic and Chalcolithic from South-eastern Europe', *Journal of European Archaeology*, 4, 1996, pp.153–76.

——, *Studien zum symbolgut des Neolithikums und der Kupferzeit in Südosteuropa* [Studies of the Symbolic Material Culture of the Neolithic and the Copper Age in Southeast Europe] (Saarbrücker Beiträge zur Altertumskunde, Bd. 64), Bonn: Dr. Rudolt Habelt Verlag, 2003.

——, 'Figurines in Action: Methods and Theories in Figurine Research', in *Festschrift Peter Ucko: A Future for Archaeology – the Past as the Present*, R. Layton, S. Shennan and P. Stone, eds, London: UCL Press, 2006, pp.199–215.

Brownell, K.D. and M.A. Napolitano, 'Distorting Reality for Children: Body Size Proportions of Barbie and Ken Dolls', *International Journal of Eating Disorders*, 18 (3), 2006, pp.295–8.

Chapman, John C., *Fragmentation in Archaeology: People, Places and Broken Objects in the Prehistory of South Eastern Europe*, London: Routledge, 2000.

Chapman, John C., and B. Gaydarska, *Parts and Whole: Fragmentation in Prehistoric Context*, Oxford: Owbow Books, 2007.

Conkey, M. and R. Tringham, 'Archaeology and the Goddess: Exploring the Contours of Feminist Archaeology', in *Feminism in the Academy*, D.C. Stanton and A.J. Stewart, eds, Ann Arbor, MI: The University of Michigan Press, 1995, pp.199–247.

Conrad, N.J., 'A Female Figurine from the Basal Augrignacian of Hohle Fels Cave in Southwestern Germany', *Nature*, 459, 2009, pp.248–52.

Cooper, R. and J. Law, 'Organisation: Distal and Proximal Views', in *The Sociology of Organizations*, S. Bacharach, ed., Greenwich, CT: JAI, 1994, pp.123–45.

Couailhac, M., *Maine de Biran*, Paris: Félix Alcan, 1905.

de Biran, F-P., *Oeuvres philosophiques de Maine de Biran*, Paris: Librairie de Ladrange, 1841.

Delong, A.J., 'Phenomenological Space-Time: Towards an Experimental Relativity', *Science* (7 August), 1981, pp.681–2.

——, 'Spatial Scale, Temporal Experience and Information Processing: An Empirical Examination of Experimental Reality', *Man-Environment Systems*, 13, 1983, pp.77–86.

Derrida, J., *On Touching: Jean-Luc Nancy*, Palo Alto, CA: Stanford University Press, 2005, pp.146–7.

Doss, E., 'Making Imaginations Age in the 1950s: Disneyland's Fantasy Art and Architecture', in *Designing Disney's Theme Parks: The Architecture of Reassurance*, K.A. Marling, ed., New York: Flammarion, 1977, pp.179–89.

Gibson, J.J., *The Ecological Approach to Visual Perception*, Boston, MA: Houghton Mifflin, 1979.

Gimbutas, M., *The Goddesses and Gods of Old Europe, 6500–3500 BC, Myths and Cult Images*, Berkeley, CA: University of California Press, 1982.
——, *The Language of the Goddess*, San Francisco, CA: Harper Collins, 1989.
——, *The Civilization of the Goddess: The World of Old Europe*, San Francisco, CA: Harper Collins, 1991.
Hardie, R., 'Gender Tensions in Figurines in SE Europe', in *Cult in Context: Reconsidering Ritual in Archaeology*, D.A. Barrowclough and C. Malone, eds, Oxford: Oxbow Books, 2007, pp.82–9.
Hetherington, K., 'Spatial Textures: Making Place through Touch', *Environment and Planning A*, 35 (11), 2003, pp.1933–44.
Husserl, E., *Ideas Pertaining to a Pure Phenomenology and to a Phenomenological Philosophy: Second Book: Studies in the Phenomenology of Constitution*, London: Springer, 1990.
James, I.A., L. Mackenize and E. Mukaetova-Ladinska, 'Doll Use in Care Homes for People with Dementia', *International Journal of Geriatric Psychiatry*, 21 (11), 2006, pp.1093–8.
Josipovici, G., *Touch: An Essay*, New Haven, CT: Yale University Press, 1996.
Kühtmann, A., *Maine de Biran: Ein Beitrag zur Geschichte der Metaphysik under der Psychologie des Willens*, Bremen: Max Nössler, 1901.
Lang, A., *Maine de Biran und die Neuere Philosophie*, Cologne, 1901.
Lederman, S.J. and R.L. Klatzky, 'Hand Movements: A Window into Haptic Object Recognition', *Cognitive Psychology*, 19, 1987, pp.342–68.
——, 'Haptic Explanation and Object Representation', in *Vision and Action: The Control Grasping*, M.A. Goodale, ed., Norwood, NJ: Ablex, 1990, pp.98–110.
Levinas, E., *Totality and Infinity: An Essay on Exteriority*, Pittsburgh, PA: Duquesne University Press, 1969.
——, *Existence and Existents*, trans. A. Lingis, The Hague: Nijhoff, 1978.
——, *Time and the Other*, Pittsburgh, PA: Duquesne University Press, 1990.
Lord, M.G., *Forever Barbie: The Unauthorized Biography of a Real Doll*, New York: William Morrow and Company, 1994.
Marzke, M.W., 'Precision Grips, Hand Morphology, and Tools', *American Journal of Physical Anthropology*, 102 (1), 1997, pp.91–110.
Marzke, M.W., K.L. Wullstein and S.F. Viegas, 'Evolution of the Power ("Squeeze") Grip and Its Morphological Correlates in Hominids', *American Journal of Physical Anthropology*, 89 (3), 1992, pp.283–98.
Merleau-Ponty, M., *The Visible and the Invisible, Followed by Working Notes*, trans. Alphonso Lingis, Evanston, IL: Northwestern University Press, 1968.
Meskell, L.M., 'Goddesses, Gimbutas, and "New Age" Archaeology', *Antiquity*, 69, 1995, pp.74–86.
——, 'Oh My Goddess: Ecofeminism, Sexuality and Archaeology', *Archaeological Dialogues*, 5 (2), 1998, pp.126–42.
——, 'Divine Things', in *Rethinking Materiality: The Engagement of Mind with the Material World*, E. DeMarrais, C. Gosden and C. Renfrew, eds, Cambridge: McDonald Institute for Archaeological Research, 2004, pp.249–59.
——, 'Refiguring the Corpus at Çatalhöyük', in *Image and Imagination: A Global Prehistory of Figurative Representation*, C. Renfrew and I. Morley, eds, Cambridge: McDonald Institute Monographs, 2007, pp.137–49.
Meskell, L.M., C. Nakamura, R. King and S. Farid, 'Figured Lifeworlds and Depositional Practices at Çatalhöyük', *Cambridge Archaeological Journal*, 18, 2008, pp.139–61.

Morgan, M., *How to Interview Sex Abuse Victims: Including the Use of Anatomical Dolls*, London: Sage, 1995.
Nakamura, C. and L. Meskell, 'Articulate Bodies: Forms and Figures at Çatalhöyük', *Journal of Archaeological Method and Theory*, 16, 2009, pp.205–30.
Napier, J.R., 'The Evolution of the Hand', *Scientific American*, 207, 1962, pp.56–62.
Napier, J.R. and R. Tuttle, *Hands*, Princeton, NJ: Princeton University Press, 1993.
Schickel, R., *The Disney Version: The Life, Times, Art and Commerce of Walt Disney*, New York: Ivan R. Dee, 1993.

2

Touching sculpture

Hagi Kenaan

Sculpture, vision, touch

The desire to touch is typically part of our encounter with sculptures. But, what is the significance of this common experience? Can it provide a key to any deeper understanding of sculpture's essence? While responses to these questions clearly vary, it is interesting to notice that there is, nevertheless, a certain similarity in the manner in which accounts of sculpture appropriate the primary experience from which the problem of touch arises in the first place. Embracing or rejecting the idea that sculpture speaks to touch in a unique manner, accounts of sculpture typically do so by integrating the ordinary experience of 'wanting to touch the sculptures we see' into a general conceptual framework in which that primary experience can only echo as a mere symptom of an allegedly more basic aspect of sculpture.

Furthermore, even when the intimate relationship between sculpture and touch does become an explicit theme, it is not so much the actual character of their intimacy (or, again, of our experience) that invites reflection. What typically seems to matter in these cases, rather, are the implications that such a connection carries for a more generic understanding of the place of sculpture among the plastic arts and specifically vis-à-vis painting – an echo of a *paragone*. Hence, for example, as Herbert Read explains his influential understanding of sculpture as 'an art of palpation', he writes:

> An art owes its particularity to the emphasis or preference given to any one organ of sensation. If sculpture has any such particularity it is to be distinguished from painting as the plastic art that gives preference to tactile sensations as against visual sensations, and it is precisely when this preference is clearly stated that sculpture attains its highest and its unique aesthetic values.[1]

For Read, the coupling of sculpture and touch is grounded in an essential division of the senses which corresponds to an analogous division of the arts: the clear-cut distinction made between touch and sight finds its correlation in the distinction between sculpture and painting. Read's intuition about the essential connection between touch and sculpture thus serves as grounds for establishing the identity of sculpture vis-à-vis painting, but the specificity of this connection is left unexamined and will, in fact, ineluctably remain unexamined as long as one thinks of sculpture (and painting) in terms of a clear-cut distinction between touch and sight. Using this distinction as a background for thinking about sculpture not only blurs the manner in which perception depends on a constant intertwining of the senses, but it more importantly veils the unique rootedness of sculpture in the visual. Sculpture's intimacy with touch is not opposed to, but rather 'fills in' or 'adumbrates' – to use a term from Husserl – an essentially visual mode of presence. In other words, sculpture does not address our tactile sensibilities independently of vision; on the contrary, its tactility manifests itself precisely within the confines of what the eye reveals to us. Hence, instead of debating whether sculpture is closer to touch or to vision, the question that needs to be asked should be one that invites us to explore an intersection, a double proximity, a tactility whose resonance is visual and a visuality whose inner pulse is the desire to touch.

In viewing sculpture, the eye can never forget – it is obliged to bear witness to – its condition of embodiment. Sculpture can meet the eye only in the form of an intertwining – a 'chiasmus' as Merleau-Ponty calls it – of vision and the body. Indeed, in the literature on sculpture, from Rosalind Krauss's *Passages in Modern Sculpture* to Alex Potts's *The Sculptural Imagination*, Merleau-Ponty's phenomenology of the body has established itself as an important point of reference, a starting point perhaps, for a radical reevaluation of the conditions of vision relevant for understanding the visuality of sculpture.[2] Merleau-Ponty's positing of the lived body as the gravitational centre of the field of vision, his elaboration of the intrinsic corporeality of the visual, is clearly pertinent to the direction in which I wish to be heading. At the same time, however, beyond a general consideration of the embodied vision elicited by sculpture, the question on which I wish to focus is a more specific one, dealing with the manner in which touching becomes operative in the visuality of sculpture. In other words, in opening itself to our sense of touch, what kind of spectatorship – what kind of optics – does sculpture call for?

Narcissus's touch

In addressing this question, I shall ultimately return to Merleau-Ponty, but will do so by introducing a more specific, even if rudimentary, concept of experience that he began to develop in his later writings. This is his notion of 'narcissism' – which is, in many respects, a philosophical attempt of releasing Narcissus from the grip of its problematic Freudian connotations. However, since the mythical figure of Narcissus remains, in itself, unspoken of by Merleau-Ponty, I shall first offer a reading that underlines the lessons which, I believe, can be drawn by thinking with Narcissus.

Although their stories intersect in interesting ways, Narcissus is no Pygmalion. Unlike the mythical king who succeeds in bringing the coupling of sculpture and touch into fruition, Narcissus's relation to touch is less obvious and less happy. He is no sculptor, but, as he lies motionless, 'smitten by the beautiful form' of the one he takes to be his beloved, he is, interestingly, described by Ovid as 'a statue carved from Parian marble'.[3] What is the significance of the connection Ovid draws between Narcissus and a sculpture? And, what is the role of touch in Narcissus's story of self-love and illusion?

Touch is not part of Narcissus's repertoire. In his short life, he touches nobody and is touched by no one. Yet, this absence of touch is dramatically present in the Narcissus story. It appears as a recurring theme whose centrality may suggest a reading of Ovid's Narcissus as a moral tale about the avoidance of touch and ultimately the failure to touch. The Ovidian version of Narcissus consists of two main parts: first, the story of Narcissus's relation with the nymph Echo and, then, the relationship with his own reflected image. While the first part of the story is marked by the claim of the vocal and the second part is dedicated to the question of visual representation, touch is a theme that runs through both of these parts. The tale begins with Narcissus's avoidance or rejection of the touch of others. 'Many youths and many maidens sought his love; but, in that slender form was pride so cold that no youth, no maiden *touched* his heart.'[4] In response to the loving gestures of the nymph Echo, Narcissus retorts: 'hands off! Embrace me not! May I die before I give you power over me.'[5] Narcissus cannot bear the thought of being touched. Is he afraid? Disgusted? Why does he associate the experience of being touched with a state of subjection to the other's power? Can he only experience the other's touch as an exertion of force, a form of violence? Is Narcissus's tragically narrow understanding of touch tied, perhaps, to the fact that he himself was born into the world as an outcome of the violent rape suffered by his mother, Liriope?

As Narcissus encounters his own reflected image, however, his aversion against being touched gives way to a new intense desire to touch – to be the one who touches – what he sees. Narcissus is captivated by the sight of beauty – the beauty of what appears to be another person. This turning point in which Narcissus 'looks in speechless wonder at himself' is, as suggested, also the point in which Ovid compares him to 'a statue carved from Parian marble.' Thus,

> Unwittingly he desires himself ... equally he kindles love and burns with love. How often did he offer vain kisses on the elusive pool?

How often did he plunge his arms into the water seeking to clasp
the neck he sees there, but did not clasp himself in them![6]

Narcissus wants to touch his beloved but is unable to do so. He has indeed changed in his new desire to touch; but does this mean he has also acquired a new, or broader, perception of what touch may be like? Ovid seems to suggest that Narcissus is still captivated by his original understanding of touch as an act of seizing. His continuous attempts in touching are thus self-defeating. And, as Narcissus describes his predicament, the painful impossibility of touch becomes an explicit issue for him:

'… I am charmed and I see; but, what I see and what charms me I cannot find' – so serious is the lover's delusion – 'and to make me grieve the more, no mighty ocean separates us, no long road, no mountain ranges, no city walls with close-shut gates; by a thin barrier of water we are kept apart. He himself is eager to be embraced. For, often as I stretch my lips towards the lucent wave, so often with upturned face he strives to lift his lips to mine. You would think he could be touched – so small a thing it is that separates our loving hearts.'[7]

The 'small thing' that, according to Narcissus, separates him from his lover, barring him from embracing the object of his desire is the mirroring surface – 'a thin barrier of water' – which is, in fact, the enabling condition of visual illusion.

Narcissus and the ground of vision

Indeed, for the tradition of reflecting on the visual arts, Narcissus has been a consistent trope for the essence of visual representation, a principle of mirroring. Looking back to the Second Sophistic, for example, Jas Elsner shows how the figure of Narcissus becomes a regulating theme in ancient conceptions of naturalism. Narcissus exemplifies a form of absorption in the visual, a self-forgetting, that is a necessary condition for the possibility of visual illusion. According to Elsner,

Narcissus's remarkable inability to see that he himself is the object reflected on the pool of water seems a striking example of that fact that, for the deceptions of naturalism to work, one must blind oneself to one's own collusion with them. In blinding himself in this way … Narcissus shows himself to be a perfect viewer of art in the mode of naturalism.[8]

There is a complicated and interesting story to be told of the different figurations of Narcissus in theories of the visual arts. One of the important chapters in such a story has to do with the appearance of Narcissus in the founding text of Renaissance art theory, Alberti's *On Painting*, in which Narcissus is crowned as 'the inventor of painting'.[9]

In book 2 of *On Painting*, as he reflects on the essence and origins of his subject matter, Alberti writes:

> I say among my friends that Narcissus who was changed into a flower, according to the poets, was the inventor of painting. Since painting is already the flower of every art, the story of Narcissus is most to the point. What else can you call painting but a similar embracing with art of what is presented on the surface of the water in the fountain?[10]

Alberti's celebration of Narcissus as the inventor of painting is not at all self-evident. And as shown by Stephen Bann, and in a different way by Karsten Harries, for example, the negative connotations of the Narcissus myth make Alberti's choice not only surprising but also, in many ways, subversive.[11] Yet, what exactly are the visual implications of Alberti's turn to Narcissus? Or, to connect more directly to our original question, what kind of optics – what kind of gaze – is evoked by the figure of Narcissus? For Alberti, 'Narcissus ... was the inventor of painting' since painting is an 'embracing with art of what is presented on the surface of the water in the fountain'. While in itself, the water's surface is of no concern to Alberti, a similar kind of surface does occupy the centre of his perspective construction. This is the transparent surface of a window pane which functions, in Alberti, as a regulating model for understanding the picture surface. The window-surface is not only a framed transparency that allows the rays reflected from objects to reach our eye, but is also in itself a medium of representation. Intersecting with the visual pyramid, it presents a full mapping of the visual field, creating a screen of appearances whose virtual double is the picture surface. Lacking any real depth, the picture surface – just like the window – opens up as if it were an actual visual field. Yet, in order to represent things 'as they appear', the painter must come to terms with the unique presence of that infinitely thin surface which makes his appearances possible and yet which, in itself, needs to be concealed so as to allow the eye to enter the painting's virtual visual space. In other words, the painter needs to learn how to 'embrace' the substratum of appearances.

This is precisely where the figure of Narcissus becomes relevant. Narcissus is affected by and falls in love with his own image, reflected in the water. Indeed, Narcissus embodies a principle of reflection; but, the common understanding of Narcissus and narcissism in terms of the question of mirroring may conceal a crucial dimension of the story. Something hides between the Narcissus who looks and the Narcissus who is looked at: the surface of the water. This is an infinitely thin plane that nevertheless contains within itself both the possibility of reflection and that of transparency. This surface on which the visual drama initially transpires is something that hardly ever calls attention to itself. Narcissus, however, is the one whose attentiveness uncovers this domain of the in-between. Thus, Narcissus not only surrenders to a visual illusion, not only falls in love with an object that turns out to be an image, but in doing this he also ends up making the dramatic discovery of a concealed region hidden between the object and its reflection. With Narcissus a new kind of human look is born – a liberated gaze that, in its deep sorrow, can see beyond the object-form of that which appears. 'His tears ruffled the water, and dimly the image came back from the troubled pool.'[12] What Narcissus sees for the first time is the inner layer of the field of visual appearances – a discovery that indeed inaugurates the possibility of painting.

Narcissus's gaze embraces the presence of a surface that underlies the possibility of representation, a surface which typically remains hidden by the actuality of appearances. Yet, what Narcissus discovers is not just a prototypical version of the Albertian window. In fact, it is important to recognise that the medium of representation which Narcissus uncovers is constituted in a manner that sets it apart from the Albertian window. Reading Narcissus beyond Alberti, we may notice that the visual surface that concerns him is not located in front of him, but is a horizontal visual plane on which his eyes and his body intersect. When gazing, he 'stretches on the shaded grass'. When staring at his image, Narcissus – and this is, in my view, important to remember – is *humi positus* 'prone to the ground'.[13] Narcissus's relation to the ground has been well intuited by the pictorial tradition from the fresco of Narcissus at the house of Marcus Lucretius Fronto in Pompeii (Fig. 2.1) to the famous Caravaggio painting (Fig. 2.2), in which the surface which reflects Narcissus's image is one to which Narcissus has to bend. He is located on, supported by, the same plane that opens up as a visual domain. The visuality that is opened up by the ground – and from the ground up – is of a kind that maintains an atypical relation to the viewer's gaze. While intersecting with the gaze, the pool's surface is that which never fully faces – is never in front of – the viewer. The narcissistic gaze is thus never frontal. The viewer is never parallel to and separate from the image's surface, but always already implanted in it. Whereas the framing of an image in a picture hanging on a wall in front of us is dependent on the picture's distance and separation from the viewer, the ground's surface enables the visual to appear only because the viewer is connected directly and bodily to it.

Narcissus's oblique gaze thus uncovers a primary dimension of the visual, one that is so easily forgotten in a standardised space whose fundamental axes are the vertical and the horizontal. In such a space, 'narcissistic' visuality typically remains buried by the common kind of vision that appropriates the visual head on. This is what happens, for example, in Alberti's construction in which the unique possibility of the diagonal gaze is completely erased by the established isomorphism between the eye's relation to the floor (x1x2) and its relation to a vertical screen of appearances (for example a window in which the floor appears, y1y2) (Fig. 2.3).

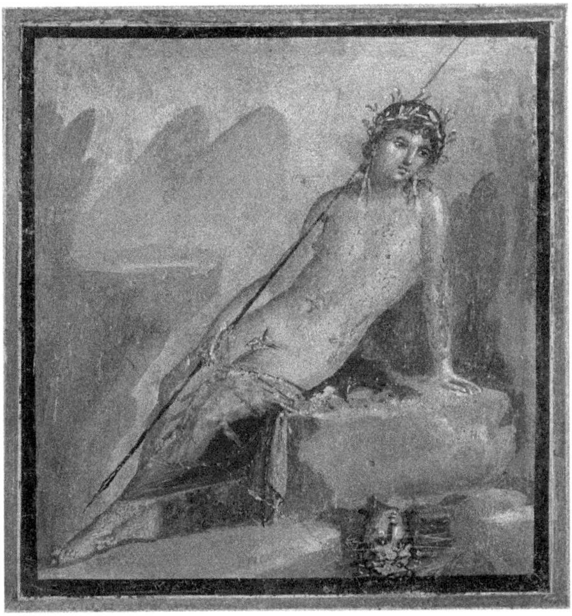

2.1 *Narcissus*, fresco, third quarter of the third century AD, House of Marcus Lucretius Fronto, Pompeii [© Mimmo Jodice/Corbis]

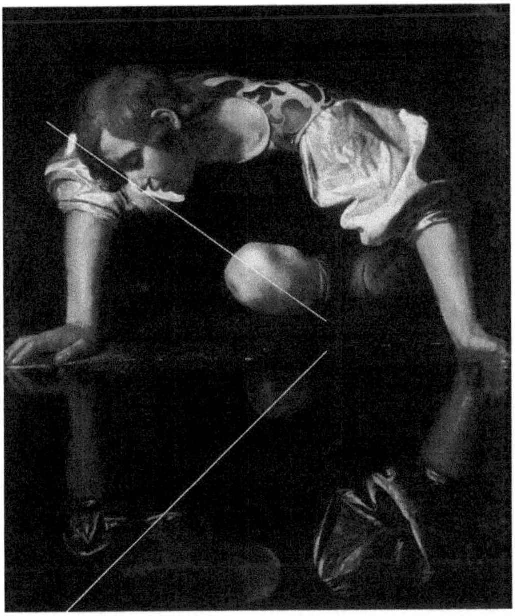

2.2 Caravaggio, *Narcissus*, oil on canvas, 1597–1599, Galleria Nazionale d'Arte Antica, Rome (with author's additions) [© Araldo de Luca/Corbis]

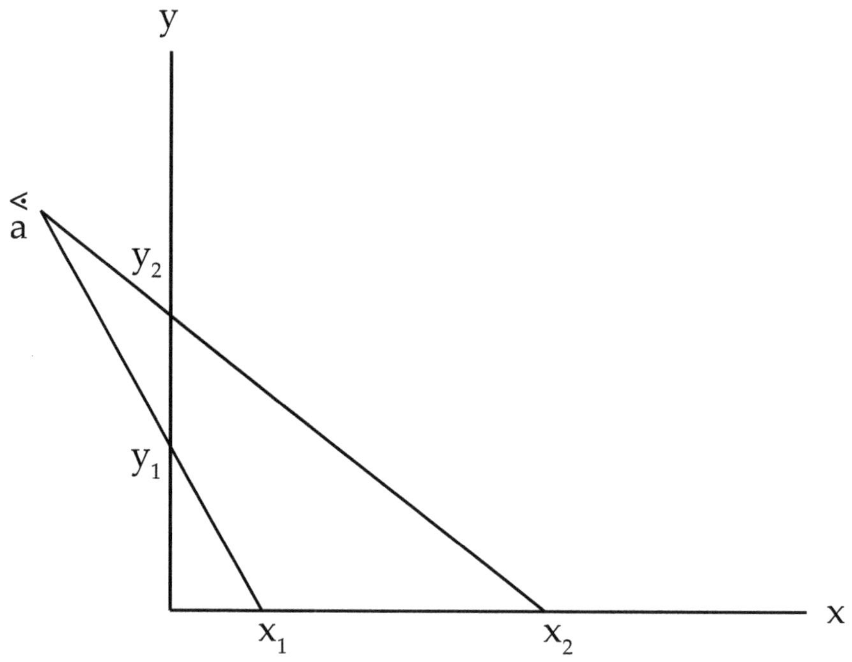

2.3 Alberti's window: the frontal and the oblique [© Hagi Kenaan]

Hence, I think that Narcissus allows us to recall a dimension of the visual which is constantly there to be seen and, yet, cannot be framed or captured in any direct or frontal manner. Narcissus, as I understand him, is a figure for a visuality that depends on our relation to the ground on which we stand, a relation which allows the gaze to remember the weight of our body, the rhythm of our pace and – tying things back to our discussion – the desire to touch. This is precisely where the experience of sculpture becomes relevant again.

Illusion and/or fantasy

How is Narcissus's gaze relevant for understanding the visuality of sculpture? Being three-dimensional, sculptures are always part of a place and, as such, they also belong to a human space in which the body is the underlying condition of vision. In other words, since they share with their viewers the same three-dimensional space, sculptures are always located on the potential maps of our bodily movement and here, as suggested, Merleau-Ponty's thinking has been particularly influential for art theory in its ability to articulate the manner in which embodiment is a fundamental condition of vision and visuality.

For Merleau-Ponty, embodiment is the condition of a being 'caught in the fabric of the world'. The embodied self is riveted to the materiality of the world. 'Its cohesion is that of a thing ... things are an annex or prolongation of itself. They are incrusted into its flesh, they are part of its full definition; the world is made of the same stuff as the body.'[14] This means, however, that human vision is never 'a view upon an outside, a merely physical–optical relation to the world'. For Merleau-Ponty, seeing is not an event that can occur inside an independent or virtual mind; it is not a relation between an ideal viewer and an image, but a real condition of our moving about in this world. The visual field is not a rear screen of a *camera obscura*, but a life-world that opens up through the 'intersection', as he calls it, between the eye and the body's possible routes of action. 'This extraordinary overlapping', he writes 'forbids us to conceive of vision as an operation of thought that would set up before the mind a picture or a representation of the world ... immersed in the visible by his body, itself visible, the seer does not appropriate what he sees. He merely approaches it by looking.'[15] And indeed, approaching by looking and looking by approaching is central to the ways we experience sculpture.

When we face a sculpture our body is always an issue. Not only is the unfolding of the sculpture's different facets dependent on our body's movement, but the solidity and size, the measurements – colossal or miniature – of sculptures can become meaningful – from an archaic *kouros* to a Donatello, a Giacometti, David Smith, Richard Serra or Anish Kapoor – only in relation to the actuality of the viewer's body. Paintings, too, relate to our bodies. And, not only when they are carried or shipped, but, as they face us, from the walls on which they hang. Standing in front of *Las Meninas* is different, in this respect, from facing a relatively small Zurbaran, just as the viewing of Veronese's panoramic *Wedding at Cana* is so different from looking at his small *Rape of Europa*. However, while the relationship with our body may indeed be significant in approaching the framed painting *qua* object, we need to ask whether our body is also significant in relation to our experience of the pictorial world opened up 'in' the picture. Facing a picture, it seems that the measurements of that which belongs to the pictorial world do not speak directly to the body, but become meaningful only in the context and through the mediation of the matrix of internal relations within that world.[16] Regarding touch, the case is, in many ways, analogous: unlike the case of sculpture in which the viewer's body and the sculpted figure share a world, the painted world is one that may accommodate the eye, but grants no access to the viewer's body. While we view sculptures by entering their space – a hall, a garden or city square – our bodies can never actually inhabit a pictorial space. Moreover, the separation of the viewer's body from the course of the eye is – at least traditionally – a necessary condition for viewing the painting. That is to say, the visuality of a painting can open up to a viewer, for example as three dimensional, only on the condition that the eye forgets the claims of the body. The body of an exemplary viewer is thus one that neither moves nor touches. It assumes a given perspective, takes the form of a fixed point of view. Another way to put this is to say that in facing a painting, a viewer must internalise the rule of the painting's frame. The frame, in this respect, is not just a contingent fact about paintings, but is, rather, the condition of a painting's visuality. It makes illusion possible by separating off and thus singling out the pictorial world. The frame is what allows our eyes to look through and enter the depth of the painted world. But, it also marks a threshold which our body can never cross. Our experience with sculpture is very different in this respect: since we are always already within a sculpture's frame of reference, a sculpture is that which, in principle, cannot be framed.

We arrive at the question of touching. Whereas touching is continuous with our being with sculpture, a painted figure is not something we can ever touch. We may, of course, touch a painting *qua* an object, that is, let our fingers trace a certain area of the canvas or allow our hand to feel the coldness or dampness of a fresco; but, we can never touch the bed we see in Van Gogh's painting of his bedroom or the crows flying over his corn field. And, again, not only does our hand remain an outsider in relation to the painted world, but the very gesture of touching a painting is one that threatens to ruin the cohesiveness – the illusion – of that world. To attend to a painting via the touching hand is a known recipe for making the illusion disappear. In painting, touch kills illusion. And, in this sense, I suggest that sculpture, unlike painting, is ultimately not about illusion.

But if not an illusion, is there another modality of the imagination to which a sculpture speaks? Indeed, sculpture plays with the imagination in a different way than painting does. I think that what is at stake here is the order of 'fantasy' which differs from illusion in a few important ways. First, illusion is a state of captivation. Facing a painting, we are captivated by a fictional world. Our eyes transport us into that world which structures our present. Looking at a painting, we are, temporally speaking, *in* the present, a virtual present. Fantasy, on the other hand, is always future oriented. It is a play with that which is about to happen, with what might happen.

Both illusion and fantasy, painting and sculpture, walk the line between the real and the unreal. But they do so in different ways. For painting, the question is how to open up a surface onto depth. Will the two dimensional surface open up as a three dimensional world, a place for voluminous objects and figures to present themselves and for the viewer to explore? Coloured by the effect of fantasy, sculpture's question takes a different form: will the statue come to life? Will it move or respond in any ways to my touch? Whereas illusionistic painting plays with the possibility of simulating depth or objecthood on a flat surface, sculpture plays with the possibility of finding life in formed matter. In other words, while paintings invite us to enter their world, sculptures are experienced through the possibility that they will enter and become active in our world.

Paintings, too, may elicit in us a desire to touch. But touching them often seems different from touching sculpture due to the kind of 'concerns' the hand has. Touching a painting, the hand that touches typically wants to know how the virtual space seen by the eye is made possible. In touching sculpture, however, our hand is less interested in its conditions of possibility, but rather in its conditions of actuality – its potential livelihood. As such, the question of the hand touching a statue is an open one, yearning for the unexpected, projecting itself, like Pygmalion, onto the openness of a future.

Sculpture and narcissism

To tie things back to the figure of Narcissus, let us consider the conception of narcissism that Merleau-Ponty, in his later writings, attempts to develop. Embodiment has been a central theme in Merleau-Ponty's philosophy at least since his *Phenomenology of Perception* (1944). In the last years of his life, however, Merleau-Ponty tried to radicalise these earlier philosophical articulations of the significance of the body by searching for a new philosophical language that would allow him to finally break away from deeply-rooted philosophical oppositions that, he felt, continued to haunt his writing despite itself. Embracing the body as the foundation of subjectivity appeared to be insufficient as long as its grounding field of thought remained polarised by the subject–object, inner–outer or the mind–body opposition. In this context, the term 'narcissism' is introduced as part of a new philosophical vocabulary revolving around the notion of 'flesh' (*chair*) which expands – and in a certain sense, sublates – the notion of the body (*corps*) so as to reshape the whole topography of thinking beyond traditional oppositions. Merleau-Ponty writes:

> The flesh is a mirror phenomenon and the mirror is an extension of my relation with my body ... to touch oneself, to see oneself, is to obtain a specular extract of oneself, i.e., fission of appearance and Being – a fission that already takes place in the touch ... and which, with the mirror (Narcissus) is only a more profound adhesion to self.[17]

For Merleau-Ponty, embodiment is more primary than either body or mind. And the fact that the embodied self 'is caught in the fabric of the world' is, in itself, indicative of a metaphysical condition that is more primary than either self or world. Or, in other words, the fact of embodiment depends (conceptually and ontologically) on an underlying grid, a grounding relation from which the distinction between world and self can develop. Hence, whereas the terms 'reversibility' and 'mirroring' serve Merleau-Ponty in attending to the relational structure of this primordial stratum of being, 'narcissism' is used by him to refer to the same phenomenon from the perspective of selfhood:

> The enigma is that my body simultaneously sees and is seen. That which looks at things can also look at itself and recognize in what it sees, the 'other side' of its power of looking. It sees itself seeing. It touches itself touching. … it is not a self through transparence, like thought which only thinks its object by assimilating it, by constituting it, by transforming it into thought. It is a self through confusion, narcissism, through inherence of the one who sees in that which he sees and through inherence of the sensing in the sensed – a self, therefore, that is caught up in things, that has a front and a back, a past and a future ….[18]

The narcissistic structure of selfhood is an indissoluble tie, one which the reflective self will constantly try to untie by thinking of itself and its relation to the world. For Merleau-Ponty, vision and touch are key examples for unpacking the workings of – and the complexities created by – a mirroring which is always already operative in the most basic forms of our encounter with the world. One of the important aspects of such a mirroring is its intertwining of activity and passivity:

> Since the seer is caught up in what he sees, it is still himself he sees: there is a fundamental narcissism of all vision. And thus for the same reason, the vision he exercises, he also undergoes from the things, such that, as many painters have said, I feel myself looked at by the things, my activity is equally passivity – which is the second and more profound sense of the narcissism.[19]

For Merleau-Ponty, the 'profound sense of narcissism' – that 'my activity is equally my passivity' – shows itself in vision and touch, but ultimately refers beyond them to a deeper, more general, reversibility – a chiasmatic inception from which self and world emerge: the unfolding of being is a 'mirror phenomenon'. For our purposes, however, we may remain with touch and vision and specifically, here, with touch which exemplifies the idea of activity as passivity in a more intuitive way than vision.

When we ordinarily speak of touching, we typically envision an intentional action to which we tend to ascribe certain ends, a directionality and teleology of sorts (we touch 'in order to …'). Understanding touching in this manner easily hides, however, a passive dimension that, at first sight, might not be seen. In touching, we open up to the world through the intersection of two different, at times conflicting, forms of intentionality: one is directed at objects or a given content while the other reveals itself in sensation or in the form of an affect. The specificity of this latter form of experience typically conceals itself when we frame the occurrence of a touching as a kind of act. Hence, to put this simply, you cannot touch without being touched by that which you touch. The experience of touching always involves the experience of being touched. Touching is a twofold phenomenon of which reversibility is always a part. And this, of course, holds true also when it comes to touching sculpture.

Touching a statue, one is necessarily also touched by that statue. When, in a museum, we secretly act against the signs of prohibition and allow our fingers to touch a Sphinx or an Aphrodite, our sensation is structured in a two directional form: our human hand feels Aphrodite's marble body as its correlative object of touch, but, in the very gesture of touching the goddess, our hand also becomes, itself, the bearer of her touch. In a corollary manner, we may thus say that the desire to touch a statue cannot be separated from a desire to be touched by it. And, more generally, as we desire to touch someone or something, the possibility of being touched by them is intrinsic to that desire, even if our awareness of the passivity of touch is not complete.

In this context, Ovid's Narcissus should be read, I suggest, as exemplifying a form of resistance or closure in the face of the reversibility of touch. Putting this anachronistically, Narcissus refuses to accept the condition of selfhood that Merleau-Ponty terms 'narcissism'. Narcissus is captivated by a form of vision that fails to make room for touching. And this failure to open vision to a dimension of touch is due to his understanding of touch as a one-dimensional form of action. As suggested, since touching, for him, is an act of force, the field of options is predetermined in a binary way: it is either 'Hands off! Embrace me not!' or an active seeking on his part 'to clasp the neck he sees'. Narcissus cannot recognise the other side of touching – a passivity that constantly resonates in the activity of touching. He does recognise that in touching one is always also being touched and that in being touched one can also be active. But, it is not only a theoretical issue that Narcissus fails to grasp. What Narcissus is primarily blind to is the deep need, his own need, to be touched. Indeed, Narcissus's narcissism – closer to Freud than to Merleau-Ponty – is a condition of captivation in a visuality that is allegedly self-sufficient. In our context, this means a vision, an optics, that closes itself off from the claims of the touching body and thus from the alterity of the other person which the reversibility of touch brings in. Deaf to the reciprocity of touch – and more generally, to the fact that his 'flesh is a mirror phenomenon', that he is 'a self through confusion, narcissism' – Narcissus continues to keep guard against any sign of a touch that may invade his subjectivity. Unable to integrate touch into vision, Narcissus is thus held captive by a virtual picture which, as a picture, he can never inhabit. The tragic aspect of Narcissus's story is not only that his desire to be touched remained unacknowledged and thus unfulfilled, but that while never fully given as a fact of the matter, the possibility of being touched was nevertheless always already there for Narcissus, open and waiting for him.

Hence, in gesturing toward a conclusion, what I have tried to suggest is that the figure of Narcissus provides a fruitful lens for articulating the intimacy between sculpture and touch. Moreover, I have tried to show that the experience of sculpture opens for us a particularly interesting angle on the manner in which the drama of narcissism plays itself out. In touching a sculpture, we are touching, running against the limits, of fantasy: is the sculpture secretly alive? Will it unexpectedly respond to my touch, to my desire to be touched? Will it touch me back? Between hope and incredulity, we thus encounter sculpture under the sign of a more fundamental question: am I alone in the world or do I have the capacity – perhaps the sheer luck – to be touched? In this respect, the desire to touch sculptures is an important reminder.

Notes

1. Herbert Read, *The Art of Sculpture*, London: Faber & Faber, 1956, p.70.
2. First of all, post-war minimalist sculpture.
3. Ovid, *Met.* 3.419: 'ut e Pario formatum marmore'. All translations from Ovid are from, Ovid, *Metamorphoses*, ed. and trans. F.J. Miller, Cambridge, MA: The Loeb Classical Library, Harvard University Press, 1984.
4. 'multi illum iuvenes, multae cupiere puellae. Sed fuit in tenera tam dura superba forma, nulli illum iuvenes, nullae tetigere puellae.' Ovid, *Met.* 3.353. My emphasis.
5. '"manus conplexibus aufer! Ante" ait "emoriar, quam sit tibi copia nostri."' Ovid, *Met.* 3.390–91.
6. 'se cupit inprudens ... pariterque accendit et ardet. Inrita fallacy quotiens dedit oscula fonti, in mediis quotiens visum captantia collum brachia mersit aquis nec se deprendit in illis!' Ovid, *Met.* 3.425–9.
7. '"... et placet et video; sed quod videoque placetque, non tamen inventio" – tantus tenet error amantem – "quoque magis doleam, nec nos mare separate ingens nec via nec montes nec clausismoenia portis; exigua prohibemur aqua! Cupit ipse teneri: nam quotiens liquidis porreximus oscula lymphis, hic totiens ad me resupino nititur ore. Posse putes tangi: minimum est, quod amantibus obstat."' Ovid, *Met.* 3.446–53.
8. Jas Elsner, *Roman Eyes: Visuality and Subjectivity in Art and Text*, Princeton, NJ: Princeton University Press, 2007, p.49.
9. Part two on 'The Self' of Stephen Bann's, *The True Vine: On Visual Representation and the Western Tradition*, Cambridge: Cambridge University Press, 1989 does precisely that and offers an analysis of Narcissus's role in Alberti as part of an exceptionally rich and insightful account of the figurations of Narcissus in art theory from Philosostratus to contemporary art.
10. Leon Battista Alberti, *On Painting*, trans. J.R. Spencer, New York and London: Yale University Press, 1966, p.64.
11. 'Is Alberti saying', Harries asks, that 'the art of the painter originates in the same pride that caused Narcissus to perish, only that the painter escapes his precursor's fate by substituting the creation of an art-work for the futile attempt actually to embrace himself?' Karsten Harries, *The Broken Frame*, Washington, DC: The Catholic University of America Press, 1989, p.15. In 'Alberti and Perspective Construction', *Infinity and Perspective*, Cambridge, MA: MIT Press, 2001, pp.64–9, Harries argues that Alberti's Narcissus is a figure that should be read against the background of a complex set of tensions that are central to Alberti's writing and, specifically, in connection with 'Alberti's proto-Nietzschean praise of painting' whose presentation of the artist as a second creator, ultimately 'threatens to usurp the place of God'.
12. 'Et lacrimis turbavit aquas, obscuraque moto reddita forma lacu est.' Ovid, *Met.* 3.475–6.
13. Ovid, *Met.* 3.420.
14. Maurice Merleau-Ponty, 'Eye and Mind', *The Primacy of Perception*, trans. W. Cobb, Evanston, IL: Northwestern University Press, 1964, p.163.
15. Merleau-Ponty, 'Eye and Mind', p.162.
16. There are, of course, borderline and exceptional cases and perhaps the story is completely different in non-figurative painting. The size of a Barnett Newman, for example, is clearly related to – and affects – the body. Can we say that, in this sense, it has sculptural qualities?
17. Maurice Merleau-Ponty, *The Visible and the Invisible*, trans. A. Lingis, Evanston, IL: Northwestern University Press, 1960, p.256.

18. Merleau-Ponty, 'Eye and Mind', pp.162–3.
19. Merleau-Ponty, *The Visible and the Invisible*, p.139.

Bibliography

Alberti, Leon Battista, *On Painting*, trans. J.R. Spencer, New York and London: Yale University Press, 1966.

Bann, Stephen, *The True Vine: On Visual Representation and the Western Tradition*, Cambridge: Cambridge University Press, 1989.

Elsner, Jas, *Roman Eyes: Visuality and Subjectivity in Art and Text*, Princeton, NJ: Princeton University Press, 2007.

Harries, Karsten, *The Broken Frame*, Washington, DC: The Catholic University of America Press, 1989.

——, *Infinity and Perspective*, Cambridge, MA: MIT Press, 2001.

Merleau-Ponty, Maurice, *The Visible and the Invisible*, trans. A. Lingis, Evanston, IL: Northwestern University Press, 1960.

——, *The Primacy of Perception*, trans. W. Cobb, Evanston, IL: Northwestern University Press, 1964.

Ovid, *Metamorphoses*, ed. and trans. F.J. Miller, Cambridge, MA: The Loeb Classical Library, Harvard University Press, 1984.

Read, Herbert, *The Art of Sculpture*, London: Faber & Faber, 1956.

3

Bringing into being: vivifying sculpture through touch

Michael Paraskos

Anyone who knows the Greek myth of Pygmalion and Galatea, particularly as told by the Roman writer Ovid in *Metamorphoses*, will be aware of how much touching goes on in it. Indeed, it is not an exaggeration to say that Ovid's version of the story is full of groping hands. This can be contrasted to the lack of touch that takes place in another of Ovid's tales, 'Echo and Narcissus'. In fact, 'Echo and Narcissus' is the story of a boy repulsed by even the idea of being touched.

Both tales are well-enough known not to need retelling in detail, and while it would be easy to treat them as no more than pretty fairy tales, a case can be made that Ovid is using them to offer up a lesson in the importance of human touch, and the jeopardy that awaits those who reject the tactile senses. Significantly, however, in that lesson there seems to be an emphasis placed on sculpture as a manifestation of touch, or more accurately the tactile human senses. What I would like to do here is first discuss the relationship of touch to both the stories of 'Pygmalion and Galatea' and 'Echo and Narcissus'; then look at more general studies into the importance of the tactile senses in human life; and finally concentrate on the specific issue of sculpture as a tactile form, using both Ovid and the English art theorist Herbert Read as my guide. Indeed, Read is the key to understanding the perspective from which I am considering both Ovid's tales and the essential nature of sculpture.

There can be little doubt that in the West we live in a culture in which touch is deeply problematic. Even in art, which was once the epitome of physicality, the rush towards non-physical forms of visual image making, whether virtual, or digital, or photographic, in the last half century or more, has made those who have maintained a physical connection with their art practice appear quixotic. Some art theories have exacerbated this trend by positing that art is not a physical thing (an art work) but the signifier of an art idea (an art object). Consequently the idea that an artist has to make his or her art work in a direct physical way has been cast aside by many. Arguably this has its roots in the long history in Western society of elevating non-physical cerebral work above physical manual labour, or we could say of thinkers above doers. This can be taken back to the Platonic origins of our current understanding of aesthetics, in which the senses of sight and hearing were prioritised over touch and taste because they were distanced from the originating stimulus, thereby allowing contemplative detachment to be maintained. But we can also see that a social class distinction is maintained through this prioritisation, between thinkers who did not touch, and doers who did.[1] Other writers too have commented on the priority traditional aesthetics has given to non-tactile senses, particularly to sight. Most notably F. David Martin, has written extensively on this phenomenon, and labelled it the 'eminence of the eye'.[2] Although the eminence of the eye can be explained in intellectual terms, there is also something like a fear of touching that has an impact on how we relate to art in the West. Constance Classen has noted that unregulated tactility is threatening to contemporary Western society in general,[3] and coming from an Eastern Orthodox Christian tradition myself, I do sometimes wonder if Western visitors are engrossed by the tactility of the worship in Eastern churches, or slightly repulsed at the sight of us kissing religious icons. Certainly it is rarely understood. I also recall taking a group of MA Sculpture Studies students from Leeds University out on a walking tour of the public sculpture of Leeds one year, and trying to encourage them to touch the sculptures we visited. It was difficult, even with the sensuous curves of a Henry Moore, and impossible with the realist sculpture of Roger Burnett. Indeed, the Burnett, which was not hyper-realist, seemed to elicit fear when I suggested touching one of the figures. That fear is, I believe, deeply engrained, and well illustrated not by a sculpture, but a painting of a sculpture by Edward Coley Burne-Jones, entitled *The Hand Refrains*, which forms part of a series of illustrations of the Pygmalion and Galatea story.[4] In this image Burne-Jones shows a highly chaste Pygmalion seemingly too frightened to touch his own carving. This stands in stark contrast to Ovid's description of Pygmalion's highly physical relationship to the sculpture before it becomes human, which verges on the sexual:

> Often he ran his hands over the work, feeling to see whether it was flesh or ivory, and would not yet admit that ivory was all it was. He kissed the statue, and imagined that it kissed him back, spoke to it and embraced it, and thought he felt his fingers sink into the limbs he touched, so that he was afraid lest a bruise appear where he had pressed the flesh.[5]

While it might be tempting to write off Burne-Jones's depiction as Victorian prudery it is worth keeping in mind Classen's comment that tactility is: 'as threatening to contemporary Western society as it was to the Victorians'.[6]

This passage from 'Pygmalion and Galatea' can be contrasted sharply with 'Echo and Narcissus'. In Ovid's retelling of the tale, Narcissus fell in love with his own reflection, but each time he attempted to touch that reflection it disappeared. 'How often did he vainly kiss the treacherous pool', Ovid tells us. 'How often plunge his arms deep in the waters, as he tried to clasp the neck he saw! But he could not lay hold upon himself.' I would ask you to keep that phrase in mind for later: *he could not lay hold upon himself.* The important thing in this story at this point, however, is not that Narcissus is a fool for falling in love with his own reflection, but that he has, in fact, been cursed by the gods, and for the specific reason that he refused to accept the physical touch of other people. Narcissus was, according to Ovid, so beautiful that, 'Many a lad and many girls fell in love with him, but his soft young body housed a pride so unyielding that none of those boys or girls dared touch him'. The consequences of Narcissus's failure to accept his own tactile senses is seen when the nymph Echo falls in love with him. One day she tried to embrace Narcissus only to be rebuffed with the words, 'Away with these embraces! I would die before I would have you touch me!' It is this, Ovid says, that leads Nemesis to curse Narcissus. Even the fact he is cursed by Nemesis, a goddess whose attributes were more like a personification of 'just deserts', than the powers of a human-like god, is important here. 'Echo and Narcissus' is really a story that suggests Narcissus brings his situation on himself. His lack of physical engagement is his own fault and it results in a personal unhappiness, psychological unhealthiness and ultimately death. Conversely 'Pygmalion and Galatea' is a story in which happiness, mental well-being and even life itself depend upon a tactile engagement with the world. This is a lesson Pygmalion has to learn as his initial response to physical, and specifically sexual, touch is very similar to that of Narcissus. Pygmalion begins as someone who is revolted by the daughters of Propoetus who had been punished for insulting Aphrodite by being turned into the first prostitutes. By deciding to reject physical love Pygmalion appears to be on the same path as Narcissus, but he is saved from this by the physicality of sculpted art.

In all of this Ovid was playing with the popular understanding of sculpture in the Roman world in which he lived. Sculpture was conceptualised at the time as something both dead and alive. In her studies into Archaic and Classical attitudes to sculpture Deborah Steiner has argued that although sculptures were often thought of as living things, and treated accordingly, there was also a very definite conceptual link in the ancient world between the immobility of the dead and the immobility of statuary. According to Steiner the word *empedos*, the inability to move, was applied in Greek poetry and drama equally to sculptures and the dead, and stone representations of dead people on funeral monuments were not intended to represent those figures as they had been when alive, but as they were once they were dead. In other words, once a person died they became like stone, or like funeral monuments, and there are many examples from the ancient world of descriptions of the dead in Hades being statue-like and immobile.[7] This meant the souls of the dead were not deceased in the sense of ceasing to exist, but had become immobile like sculpture, and in that immobility they had lost one of the key defining characteristics of living humanity. Thus in 'Echo and Narcissus' Ovid described the still living Narcissus as if he was already dead, like a statue: 'Spellbound by his own self, he remained there motionless, with fixed gaze, like a statue carved from Parian marble.' With this Ovid was indicating that even if Narcissus's body was not dead at this point in the tale, his humanity was dead as he was unwilling or unable to respond to the tactile embrace of Echo.

Pygmalion responds very differently, however, and it is through his touch that the sculpture comes to life. The reason for this is simply that the deadliness of sculpture is, like the deadliness of Narcissus, rooted in its indifference to other beings. Sculpture, far from being a physical intervention in the reality of our world, can be said to always remain obstinately in its own reality, in a bubble of space that is indifferent to our existence, and even our touch. We can touch it, but it never really touches us. It is only by his persistent touching (and some divine intervention) that Pygmalion is able to break through this inhuman and deathly indifference, and vivify the sculpture into his living reality. As Douglas Bauer has stated: 'That the ivory statue melted to life under the loving touch of Pygmalion [is] surely the most significant feature of his story and the one on which his entire allegory hinges.'[8] More recently Victor Stoichita has made the same point, arguing that Pygmalion undertakes two related acts – the first to turn the inanimate raw material into mimetic art, and the second to turn the mimetic art into flesh. This second act is 'made through feeling, touching, caressing', and ultimately through kissing. In other words, through sexual touch.[9]

If we set 'Pygmalion and Galatea' alongside 'Echo and Narcissus' it becomes even more clear that the internal logic of *Metamorphoses* rejects the idea that looking alone can enliven. On the contrary, looking alone deadens, progressively devitalising the human spirit until there is no longer anything human remaining. That is the fate of both Echo and Narcissus and it stands in stark contrast to the fates of Pygmalion and Galatea, whose story is almost unique in the text for ending happily. The measure of that happiness is perhaps divined most strongly from the end of Ovid's retelling of their story when the link between Ovid as the author of *Metamorphoses* and Ovid as the author of some of the most bawdy love poems ever written becomes clear:

> When Pygmalion returned home, he made straight for the statue of the girl he loved, leaned over the couch, and kissed her. She seemed warm: he laid his lips on hers again, and touched her breast with his hands: at his touch the ivory lost its hardness, and grew soft: his fingers made an imprint on the yielding surface, just as wax of Hymettos melts in the sun and, worked by men's fingers, is fashioned into many different shapes, and made fit for use by being used. The lover stood, amazed, afraid of being mistaken, his joy tempered with doubt, and again and again stroked the object of his prayers. It was indeed a human body! The veins throbbed as he pressed them with his thumb.

Of course this might appear to have less to do with the importance of touch in human happiness than the importance of love, or even sex. But it really is a question of tactility, and in this Bauer's view that the over-riding theme in the whole of *Metamorphoses* is the contrast between forces of love and death is pivotal. In 'Pygmalion and Galatea' we have the only story in which there is a happy resolution of this theme, and it is a resolution that is achieved through touch, both before the sculpture comes to life (in the touch of the artist) and afterwards (in the touch of the lovers). Both Pygmalion and Galatea gain life, not only in the sense that they both become living beings, but in the happy-ever-after resolution of their tale which results in fertility and the birth of a son, called Paphos. There is nothing else quite like it in *Metamorphoses,* and in a complex series of tables and diagrams Bauer attempted to show how the tale is not just a happy interlude in an otherwise beautiful but unremittingly tragic series of stories; rather it was the resolution of the plethora of related tragedies that form *Metamorphoses*. What *Metamorphoses* can be seen as is a series of failed attempts to elude death-like states, by which is meant 'states of being' that are not like being human. This would include being turned into a plant – Narcissus, Daphne and others – or being turned into an animal – Philomela, Procne and others. In other words, *Metamorphoses* has the twin themes of about being human and failing to be human, the former cognate with life and the latter with death. This is apparent right from the start of the text when Ovid retells the story of the Greek equivalent of Noah and the Cataclysm. In this the two survivors of the flood, Deucalion and Pyrrha, do not repopulate the world through their children, as in the Bible's version of the story, but by casting stones behind them, each of which turns into a human being as it lands. As told in the first book of *Metamorphoses,* this story makes one immediately aware that all human beings begin as dead (that is, as stone). As Bauer shows, this leitmotif recurs in each of the subsequent chapters of *Metamorphoses,* both directly and indirectly. Medusa, in Book IV of *Metamorphoses,* turns anyone who looks at her into stone, whilst Narcissus possesses a physique and character that resembles stone.[10] What this suggests is that Ovid is using *Metamorphoses* to imply that the process begun by Deucalion and Pyrrha of bringing stones to life by making them human is incomplete, or at the very least that the humans created by Deucalion and Pyrrha are forever on the verge of reverting to their origins, to a non-human death state, like stony statues.

The only exception to that is in the story of 'Pygmalion and Galatea'. By connecting this story specifically with that of 'Echo and Narcissus', therefore, we see that the means for escaping from one's stony origin is not by human sight, which failed to save Echo and Narcissus, but through licit human touch – through tactility. And in saying this I think we need to take issue with another writer who has commented at length on Ovid's stories, David Freedberg. Curiously Freedberg tends to diminish the importance of touch in 'Pygmalion and Galatea', despite citing in his writing numerous other examples of people touching sculptures throughout history, including people having sexual relations with sculptures.[11] In the case of 'Pygmalion and Galatea', however, Freedberg tends to place Pygmalion's relationship to his sculpture purely into an ocular framework. Pygmalion's sculpture ceases to be art, and becomes alive, Freedberg says, because 'it has been enlivened by looking'.[12] This seems particularly problematic within 'Pygmalion and Galatea' when there is simply so much touching going on. It is true we are told that after he had completed the statue, 'Pygmalion gazed in wonder', but the result of that gaze is that Pygmalion developed a passionate physical love for what was, after all, an object and not, strictly speaking, an image.

Alongside all this we can also set the writings of the anthropologist Ashley Montagu who argued specifically for the importance of touch as a vivifying force, not in art, but in life. In his 1971 book *Touching: The Significance of the Skin,* Montagu argued that the lack of touch diminished not only the physical but the psychological health and well-being of a number of animals, including humans. In this Montagu drew partly on psychoanalytical writings, including Anna Freud's claim that early experiences of touch, such as stroking, cuddling and tactile soothing help 'to build up a healthy body image and body ego, increases its cathexis with narcissistic libido, and simultaneously promotes the development of object love by cementing the bond between child and mother'.[13] But he also made wide ranging use of anthropology, zoology, biology and sociology to argue that for humans and other mammals the physical touch of others is required for them to become well-rounded creatures, and even to survive in the early years of life. In animals, individual creatures that are touched in a gentle way (the phrase Montagu uses is 'gentled') are physically healthier than those neglected, with stronger bone and body growth. They also show signs of greater emotional stability, and in humans, Montagu claimed, the findings are similar.[14] This begins to answer one of the criticisms that might be levelled at my reading of *Metamorphoses,* that even if human touch is a force for good, the touch hankered after in many of its stories is often violent and abusive. Montagu's emphasis on 'gentling' as the form of touch might address that concern. Yet in this context the most important aspect of Montagu's study is the way touch is linked to the development of self-identity. Citing Alexander Lowen's 1967 book *The Betrayal of the Body,* Montagu states that 'Lowen shows that the feeling of identity arises from a feeling of contact with the body'. According to Montagu the failure of this in humans leads to 'disassociation', a failure to correlate the image a person has about him or herself to the way that person feels about him or herself. 'Loss of touch with the body results in loss of touch with reality', Montagu claims.[15]

Although Montagu did not address sculpture or art directly in his study, something close to his ideas is hinted at in Jean-Jacques Rousseau's dramatic retelling of the Pygmalion and Galatea tale written in 1762. In Rousseau's version of the story, when Galatea comes to life, she touches herself repeatedly, almost as if to bring herself into being. 'This is me', she says, touching her own body. And then, 'This is not me', as she touches a block of marble. Each time she does this she is seen to create a sense of self-identity through touch.

Similar ideas in relation to art were also lighted on by Herbert Read, again in connection with the stories of Ovid. In his 1954 Mellon Lectures, reproduced as the book *The Art of Sculpture*, Read noted that the death of Narcissus came about due to his inability to endow his own reflection with corporeality. In other words, Narcissus could not touch his reflection. What this represented, Read thought, was the 'deep-seated longing that man has to project an icon, a material counterpart of his mental image of himself'.[16] Like Wilhelm Worringer before him,[17] Read was using Ovid's story to posit a function for art whereby it provided an escape from the mentally disturbing and fluid actuality of existence. Art did this by giving the human mind a fabricated reality that is relatively firm and stable. What Read emphasised, however, was the importance of the physicality of art in this process, so that it was no use simply *thinking* of a firm and stable reality, it is necessary to create physical objects to embody that firm and stable reality. Only in that way does the created reality gain some degree of permanence by being touched. This is not a difficult concept to understand if one thinks of the dreams we have when we sleep. For a few moments after waking the reality of a dream remains very vivid and can be recalled quite easily. Very soon, however, it seems to evaporate and we often do not remember it at all, let alone in detail. Art is, in a sense, a way of giving a 'dream', some degree of physical permanence.

In the case of sculpture, therefore, the creation of a human-shaped object is the product of the mind wanting to create a stable image of the self, and the physicality of that object is necessary to prevent that self-image from evaporating like a dream. As Read states, 'Only by conceiving an *image* of the body can we situate the *idea* of ourselves in the external world.' Once that self-image comes into existence, however, it attains some degree of independence from the self, so that we can, like Rousseau's Galatea, say it is both 'me' and 'not me'. It is the dialectical relationship between the 'me' and 'not me' that Read put forward as the basis for consciousness itself.

As I have said, in Read's view Narcissus was doomed because he could not touch his own reflection, whereas Ovid's Pygmalion touches Galatea repeatedly. In Read's schema, this tactility is of the utmost importance as it is the touch of physical objects that gives them reality, not simply their sight. As Read stated:

> To arrive at a satisfactory image of ourselves, we must … touch our bodies and must take account of all our internal bodily sensations, particularly those of muscular tensions of movement and lassitude, and of gravity and weight. We assemble and compare all these different impressions and sensations, and from that total evidence we construct the body image.[18]

What is being indicated here is that without an embodied and tactile sense of self, and equally an embodied and tactile sense of non-self, we risk ceasing to be conscious, as though we can revert back to the unconscious stones that Deucalion and Pyrrha cast over their shoulders, becoming like images made from Parian marble, or even like the dead themselves. Physical objects fix reality, but tactile interaction with them establishes a sense of self and non-self, and out of that dialectic consciousness emerges. Ovid's entire *Metamorphoses* suggests that to cease to engage in this process is to risk reverting to a non-conscious, stone-like and moribund state.

I would just like to end with the question of whether this reading of Ovid has important implications for the place of art in society today, and significantly the way we teach art practice to students, display it in our museums, and even select what is celebrated as worthwhile art in our society. As our society appears to be adopting a culture that seems to be becoming ever more virtual should we not ask ourselves whether or not the legitimate role of art in society is to counteract this move? By counteract I do not necessarily mean be opposed to virtual reality and virtual lives, but simply act as a counterbalance to this increasing virtuality in order to maintain a healthy equilibrium. From this we might want to suggest that if society is determined to become ever more virtual then art should become ever more physical in order to provide a psychological balance to maintain the well-being of human consciousness. I am not alone in asking this question, as the recent writings of Matthew Crawford demonstrate,[19] but it is still a minority who seem to be addressing the risks we run in diverting our attention from the tactility and physicality of engaging with the material world in favour of an immaterial and ultimately unreal world that cannot satisfy our longings. This is, I would suggest, the very real lesson of Ovid's *Metamorphoses*, and with that lesson comes a very serious warning of the possible consequences if we do not.

Notes

1. See Arnold Berleant, 'The Sensuous and the Sensual in Aesthetics', *The Journal of Aesthetics and Art Criticism*, 23 (2), Winter 1964, pp.186ff.
2. F. David Martin, 'The Autonomy of Sculpture', *The Journal of Aesthetics and Art Criticism*, 34 (3), Spring 1976, pp.273–86, *passim*.
3. Constance Classen, *The Book of Touch*, Oxford: Berg, 2005, p.259 and *passim*.
4. Now in Birmingham City Art Gallery.
5. All quotations from Ovid are taken from Ovid, *Metamorphoses*, Book III, trans. Mary Innes, London: Penguin Books, 1955.
6. Classen, *Book of Touch*, p.262.
7. Deborah Steiner, *Images in Mind*, Princeton, NJ: Princeton University Press, 2001, p.145f.
8. Douglas F. Bauer, 'The Function of Pygmalion in the Metamorphoses of Ovid', *Transactions and Proceedings of the American Philological Association*, 93, 1962, p.16.

9. Victor Stoichita, *The Pygmalion Effect*, trans. Alison Anderson, Chicago, IL: University of Chicago Press, 2008, p.14.
10. Bauer, 'Function of Pygmalion', p.2f.
11. David Freedberg, *The Power of Images*, Chicago, IL: University of Chicago Press, 1991, p.326f.
12. Freedberg, *Power of Images*, p.344.
13. Quoted in Ashley Montagu, *Touching: The Human Significance of the Skin*, New York: Columbia University Press, 1971, p.163.
14. Montagu, *Touching*, p.85f., and *passim*.
15. Montagu, *Touching*, pp.205–6.
16. Herbert Read, *The Art of Sculpture*, New York: Bollingen Foundation, 1956, p.29.
17. Wilhelm Worringer, *Form in Gothic*, trans. Herbert Read, London: Putnams, 1927, *passim*.
18. Read, *Art of Sculpture*, p.29.
19. Matthew Crawford, *The Case for Working with Your Hands*, London: Penguin Books, 2009.

Bibliography

Bauer, Douglas F., 'The Function of Pygmalion in the Metamorphoses of Ovid', *Transactions and Proceedings of the American Philological Association*, 93, 1962, pp.1–21.

Berleant, Arnold, 'The Sensuous and the Sensual in Aesthetics', *The Journal of Aesthetics and Art Criticism*, 23 (2), 1964, pp.185–92.

Classen, Constance, *The Book of Touch*, Oxford: Berg, 2005.

Crawford, Matthew, *The Case for Working with Your Hands*, London: Penguin Books, 2009.

Freedberg, David, *The Power of Images*, Chicago, IL: University of Chicago Press, 1991.

Martin, F. David, 'The Autonomy of Sculpture', *The Journal of Aesthetics and Art Criticism*, 34 (3), 1976, pp.273–86.

Montagu, Ashley, *Touching: The Human Significance of the Skin*, New York: Columbia University Press, 1971.

Ovid, *Metamorphoses*, trans. Mary Innes, London: Penguin Books, 1955.

Read, Herbert, *The Art of Sculpture*, New York: Bollingen Foundation, 1956.

Steiner, Deborah, *Images in Mind*, Princeton, NJ: Princeton University Press, 2001.

Stoichita, Victor, *The Pygmalion Effect*, trans. Alison Anderson, Chicago, IL: University of Chicago Press, 2008.

Worringer, Wilhelm, *Form in Gothic*, trans. Herbert Read, London: Putnams, 1927.

Pictorial essay A: Out of sight, but not out of mind

Claude Heath

In 2008 I gave a presentation at the *Sculpture and Touch* conference at the Courtauld Institute in London and described a drawing I had made of the four-inch-high prehistoric figurine known as the *Venus of Willendorf.*

This drawing was made wearing a blindfold and recording what my touching left hand was sensing, translating sensations into marks on the paper with my right hand. The drawing of the Venus had followed the sculpture's contours, turning it through 180 degrees in stages, animating the figurine (Fig. A.1 shows a painting based upon this drawing). After the presentation, archaeologist Doug Bailey introduced himself and, following some discussion, we agreed that it would be exciting to revisit this blindfold technique and to examine the possibility that touch could reorganise our perceptions of newly excavated artefacts from his dig in Romania, sight unseen.

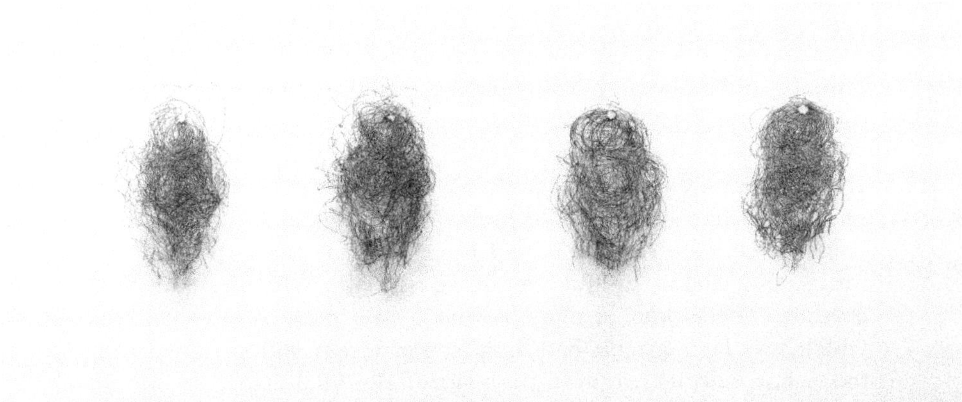

A.1 Claude Heath, *Willendorf Venus*, 150 × 339.5 cm, alkyd resin, chalk powder, acrylic, on canvas, 1997, Walker Art Gallery, Liverpool [© Claude Heath]

The first object I was presented with was hidden inside a cardboard box. It weighed heavily in the hand, a chunk of rock with a very sharp edge, bound to a wooden shaft by a frayed cord of some kind. It was clearly a flint axe-head with a modern handle, or perhaps a completely modern flint axe-head, or so I guessed. The resident team of archaeologists who were working at the museum in Alexandria, Romania, were acting under strict instructions not to tell me anything about the objects that had been chosen for me to draw. So, to avoid accidentally seeing the selected items, we set up a covered desk area that was screened off by hanging cloths where the objects could be safely stored and where I could work in the intense heat of the day without seeing them or the drawings (Fig. A.2). As time progressed, it became evident to me that it was better to work without a blindfold, while my hands busied themselves inside the tented working area, out of sight, sometimes taking drawings out to look at them or to put them away.

Being confronted with a flint axe-head raised what seemed like a common-sense question in the circumstances: what instruments should I use to draw an instrument that has its own definite physical capacities? The answer that came to mind was to use the axe-head to draw itself, so that I could touch and hold it while drawing it at the same time. I used the flint edge to incise and tear drawn marks on the paper sheets (being careful not to damage the object in any way), and so it was possible to feel the marks left behind on the paper, which had become a tactile drawing. Then, rocking the gently curving edge of the axe-head repeatedly across the sheet in a slow grinding action with the handle as the fulcrum, I left, to my surprise, a trail of tiny indentations and tears that reshaped the paper into broad furrows (Fig. A.3). These lacerations revealed the tiniest details about the individual planes, the smaller and larger pieces chipped off the flint block, that constitute its cutting edge. The paper held even the slightest traces of this action. In due course, drawings made with scalpels to cut the paper, guided by touch, evolved from this scraping of flints into the paper surface (Figs. A.4 and A.5). Drawings of different objects were also made by pressing and embossing heavy paper, until the shapes began to feel like the objects themselves. Ink drawings were created too, describing the patterns in flint surfaces that seemed to hold clues as to the meaning of these pieces, although this was probably an illusory impression of encoding.

The selection was a mix of prehistoric things as well as related modern ones. There were flint tools and their residual parts, dry clay forms, one rough and friable, another moulded smooth, with the marks of fingers present. There was also a well-used and very sturdy wooden stool, which was later established as a Roma design still current in the region today but with its origin in prehistory. The final object was unmistakable to the touch: a bust of Nicolae Ceauşescu, his name clearly spelt out in coarsely-cut relief lettering at the base. The beaked nose and chin, the thick cloak over his shoulders, like wings, his hand clasping a scroll:

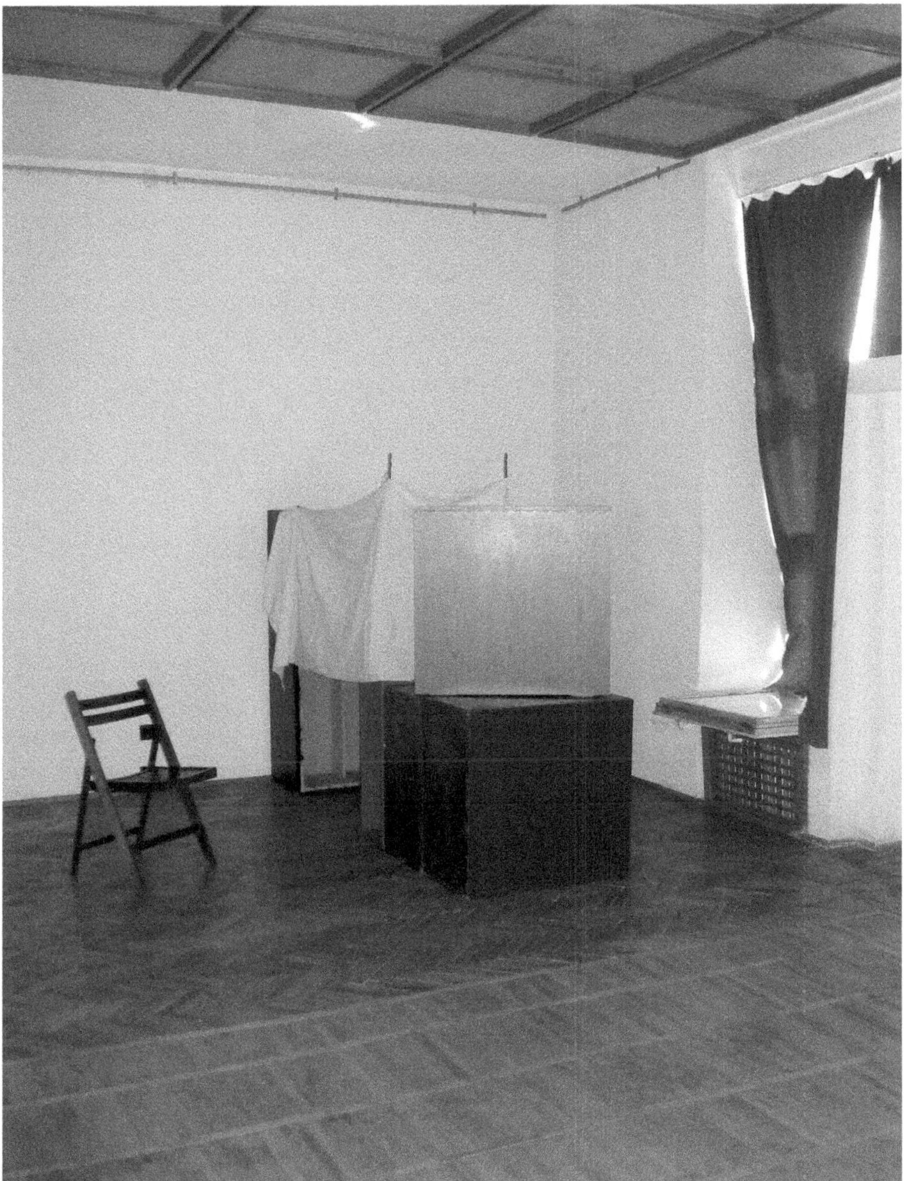

A.2 Claude Heath's temporary studio at Museu Teleorman, Romania, 2010

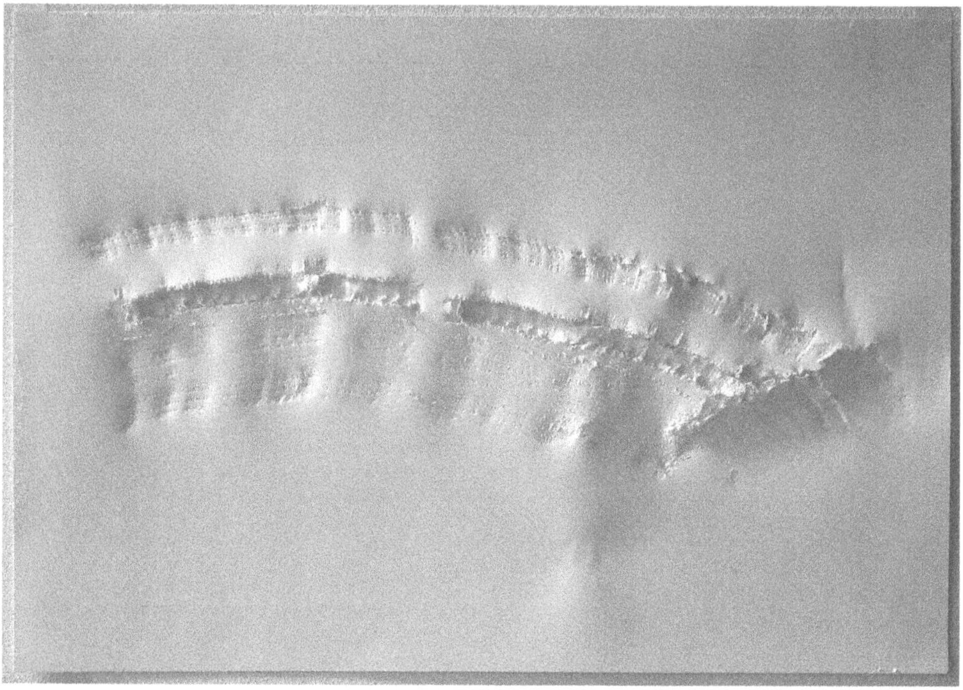

A.3 Claude Heath, *Stone Age Flint Axe-Head*, 42 × 29.4 cm, 2010, incised paper, (residency at Museu Teleorman, Alexandria, Romania, with the Art Landscape Transformations European Commission project), Collection of Kupferstichkabinett, Museum of Prints and Drawings, Berlin, made with the Ernst Schering Foundation [© Claude Heath]

all of this convinced me, as it appeared to the sense of touch, that the maker of this portrait had intended it as a satiric representation of the politician. The evidence suggested that Ceauşescu was being remade as a metaphorical bird of prey with potentially lethal powers. Before leaving Romania, when I did finally see this sculpture, these layers of interpretation immediately evaporated, and it was clear that this was a dry, white, standardised bust of the Romanian leader in the realist style, an image of the state-ratified kind that now lies covered in weeds in various parts of the world.

Soon after I handled the *Flint Axe-Head* in Romania, Focillon's suggestive description of a Stone-Age knife came to mind: 'The implement itself is no less remarkable than the use to which it is put. It is both a value and a result in itself.'[1]

Notes

1. Henri Focillon, *The Life of Forms in Art*, George Kubler, trans., New York: Zone Books, 1989, p.165.

A.4 Claude Heath, *Stone Age Flint Axe-Head*, 60 × 45 cm, incised paper, 2010, (residency at Museu Teleorman, Alexandria, Romania, with the Art Landscape Transformations European Commission project), Collection of Kupferstichkabinett, Museum of Prints and Drawings, Berlin, made with the Ernst Schering Foundation [© Claude Heath]

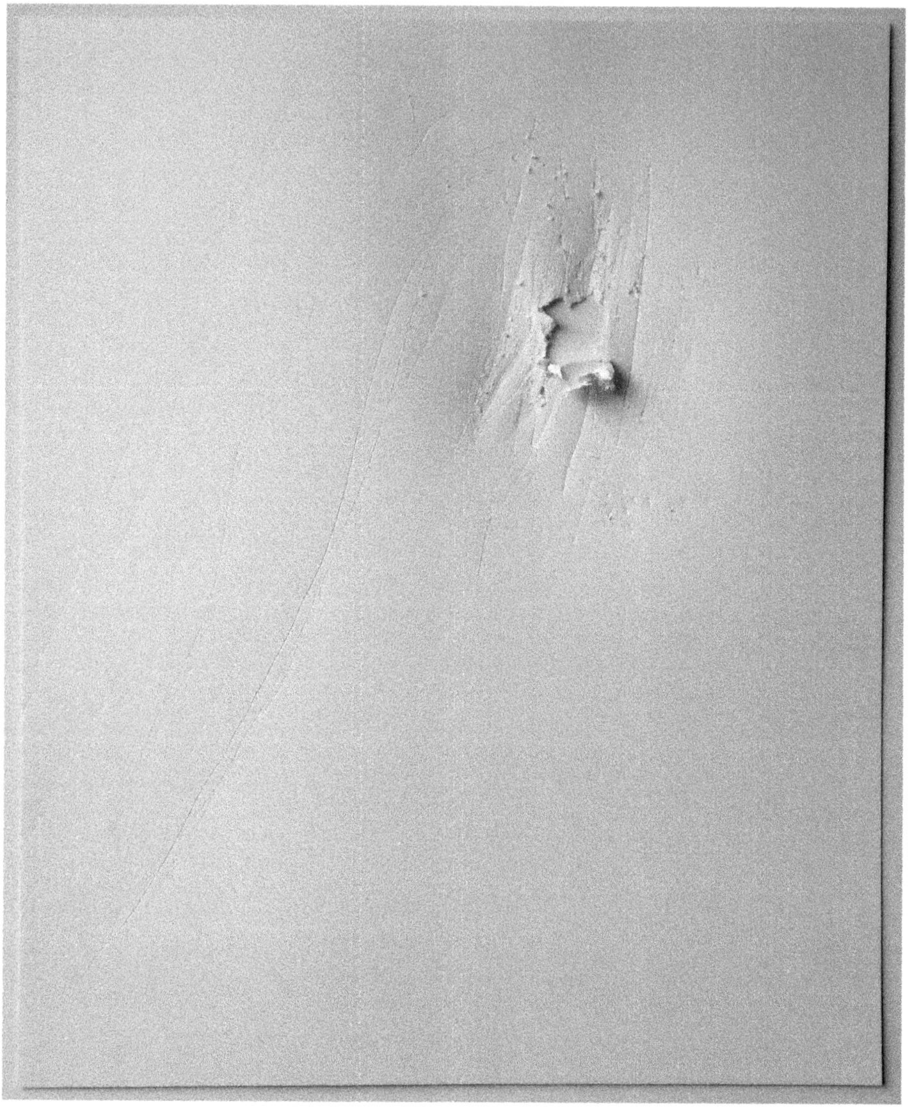

A.5 Claude Heath, *Stone Age Flint Axe-Head*, 60 × 45 cm, incised paper, 2010, (residency at Museu Teleorman, Alexandria, Romania, with the Art Landscape Transformations European Commission project), Collection of Kupferstichkabinett, Museum of Prints and Drawings, Berlin, made with the Ernst Schering Foundation [© Claude Heath]

Part II
Approaches

4

To touch: Herder and sculpture

Andrew Benjamin

A hand touches a face. Beginning with the nose – either at the tip or to one side – it matters little, what counts is that the hand is moving. The hand slides. A movement, which could be as much an inquiry, thus yielding the question – whose face is this? – as it is a caress and thus an encounter with skin demanding pleasure. The moving hand has an inherently ambiguous status. Moving from nose to cheek returning prior to tracing with finger tips extended the way the cheek will suddenly, though smoothly, become an ear. Perhaps the finger moves on discovering a change of texture, moving backwards and forwards at the point at which texture changes prior to allowing itself the discovery of what at first is a warm then moist opening which in opening up, perhaps beneath the finger, becomes the mouth. Diderot describes the same when writing of '*l'existence successive*' of the hand. The hand cannot stop touching precisely because there is no point at which the touching should stop. Not only does this provide access to the way for the one born blind, there emerges what for Diderot is the '*notion de direction*'. Equally, it is also clear that the direction in question is not from beginning to end. Rather direction is movement itself. Movement is inherently directional. Even the backward and forward movement that satisfies when the nose itches remains movement. Is it only for the blind – and this may indeed be Diderot's implicit conjecture – that the 'skin' (*la peau*) is beautiful? Beauty now involves neither image nor representation. The capacity to register beauty's presence, for Diderot, may lie in the moving finger and thus in touching.[1] As Diderot notes in relation to the one born blind, 'Il juge de la beauté par le toucher'.[2] The skin in question therefore is not the exquisite pink skin elegantly captured by Chardin in his painting of the schoolmistress if that skin were thought to be no more than a surface, rather it is the skin under my fingers – my blind fingers – when they touch. This does, of course, open up the possibility of another approach to Chardin's painting. One already there in Diderot's own writings on Chardin and in which there is a fundamental transformation in how the 'surface' is understood. The surface will have been animated site, infused with 'spirit'. For Diderot, as the line above suggests, beauty is felt. In being felt it is no longer a question of the subject's response to an object's presentation but of a reworking of the nature as well as the contents of the subject/object relation.

The question of the finger is not foreign to Herder's concerns. Herder suggests were something to appear 'doubtful' or contradictory' to the 'art student' then the student should make use of, 'the fingers of his inner sense (*den Finger seines innern Sinnes*) in order to discover that which he could not otherwise identify: the shape of the *sprit* within the form (*Gestalt des Geistes in dieser Form*)'.[3] As a prelude to a direct concern with Herder it is vital to note two important moments that occur in this passage. The first is the one away from a literalisation of both the finger and touch. Hence the reference made, in the passage, to the 'fingers of his inner sense'. The second is the position of a relationship between 'form' (*Form*) understood as material presence and 'spirit' (*Geist*). The latter could be understood as much as a gesture to a form of idealism as it is to the presence of immateriality. The latter – the immaterial (named in this context as *Geist*) – emerges once there is a sustained attempt to effect a separation between materialism and empiricism. In other words, the conjecture, as has already been noted, is that once the material and the empirical have been separated then implicit within the work and as part of the object's material presence is an active quality that is inherently immaterial.

There is an important echo of such a possibility in Diderot. What is interesting is that Diderot, almost despite his commitment to differing forms of philosophical materialism, leaves open the space for what emerges as the ineliminability of the immaterial once there is a commitment to a form of materialism. To be precise, the immaterial occurs in the space provided by the severance of the equation of the material and the empirical. This is clear, not only in Diderot's treatment of painting within the *Essais sur la peinture*, it is also there in his work on specific painters. In regards to the latter, in writing about Chardin, he notes:

> Chardin is between nature and art; he consigns the other imitations to the third rank. With him, you are never reminded of the palette. There is a harmony there beyond which nothing is felt to be wanting; it winds its way imperceptibly through his composition, fully present within every part of the whole canvas; it is, as the theologians say of the spirit, discernable everywhere and hidden at every point.[4]

What is significant in this formulation is the recognition, and this despite the language in which it tries to find expression, of a quality that is always in excess of that which is there to be described and yet which is at work within what would have been described. The reference to 'spirit' (*l'esprit*) is not to an externality and thus not to that which in being external would have had a determining effect on both the quality as well as the identity of the object's internality. 'Spirit' is a quality of the object. What is of significance here is the impossibility of any complete separation of 'spirit' and the object's material presence. Its presence is 'sensible' yet 'secret'. In other words, it is an immaterial force as part of matter, occasioning as a consequence a rethinking of matter as an already present site of activity. The move to Diderot, one in which Herder can be located, is the repositioning of the 'soul' from the subject to the object. It should go without saying that this repositioning has to be understood as an emphatic reconsideration of the aesthetic. A reconsideration in which the significant element is the emergence of the 'object' as an entity defined in relation to modes of animation. With both Diderot, and as will be suggested Herder, there is the move from the 'form' of the object – that is, the object's generalisable conditions of intuitabiliy – as the basis of aesthetics to the object itself.[5] However, it is the object within an emergent materialism and thus not the object of mere sensation.

Herder

Written in the wake of Diderot's *Lettre,* Herder's *Plastik* (1778) is one of the first attempts to present a philosophical account of sculpture. More as a prelude than an introduction – that will occur in a moment – Herder's enterprise, perhaps its capacity for disruption, can be noted in the way a relation to Greece is established. In a discussion of Anacreon's *Bathyllus,* a poetic enterprise concerned with the move from poetry to painting, Herder writes that 'the Greeks never conceived beauty other than in *determinate form (in bestimmter Form)*'.[6] The reference to the already determined nature of 'form' does not mean that there is the complete absence of any vestige of idealism in Herder. On one level it would seem as though the retention of terms such as 'spirit' and 'soul' (and perhaps even 'beauty') defined Herder's project as straightforwardly idealist. However, once it is recognised that 'soul' and 'spirit' retain their philosophical hold as that which animates and thus gives life to material presence, where the soul's presence is defined in terms of internality rather than externality, then this opens up the possibility that both 'soul' and 'spirit' allow for their own radical reinterpretation. What is important is the philosophical space they identify. Thus it will be essential, following from what has already been noted in relation to Diderot, to return to what the concession of animate matter allows in terms of what it provides for another possibility within the history of aesthetics.

The retention of a version of idealism, a version that can be recast in terms of the relationship between the material and the immaterial, indicates that, in this instance, the problematic of vision that defines the way beauty is formulated in the Platonic Dialogues is, for Herder, no longer apposite as the basis for developing an understanding of painting and sculpture in the

Hellenic period. The other element that is at play within such a setting is not just form, but the sense proper to form, namely touch. The disruptive claim concerning the quality of the already 'determinate form' means that there cannot be for Herder a question of beauty as an end in itself. Nor more exactly is it possible to abstract beauty from the specific determination marking its presence – that is, the determinate presence of sculpture as opposed to poetry, or painting. It is as though Plato's insistence that what needs to be pursued is 'absolute beauty', since it is that which accounts for the way a given particular is beautiful, has itself become impossible.[7] The Platonic move is always to argue that while there are determinate beautiful things they attain that state due to the operation of the Beautiful. It functions as the cause. This self-referential universal would then become the object of philosophical study *par excellence*.[8] For Herder, 'beauty' is a quality of the object. Moreover, it is a quality that does not depend upon Beauty's externality.

Herder's *Plastik* opens with a reference to Diderot. With Herder, in a sense following Diderot, the hand takes on a more complex configuration. (It will always need to be noted, albeit parenthetically, that there cannot be a history of either the hand or touch as though what is at work is the same in every instance.[9]) Nonetheless, what has to be remembered is that the hand is timed. The claim here is that the overall project of Herder's text is announced in one of its opening moves. The opening is staged in relation to Diderot and specifically Diderot's preoccupation with the effect of cataract operations on the blind. The central question therefore is: With sight what do the once blind see? In relation to a question of this nature Herder begins thus:

> What do these strange experiences teach us? Something that we ourselves could experience daily if we were to acknowledge that *sight* (*Gesicht*) *reveals merely shapes*, but *touch* (*Gefühl*) alone reveals bodies: that *everything that has form is known only through the sense of touch* (*nur durchs tastende Gefühl*) and that *sight reveals only visible surfaces* (*nur Fläche*) – moreover, not the surfaces of bodies but solely *surfaces exposed to light*.[10]

This positioning of the surface, as linked to the eye, sanctions an important development within philosophical writings on art (and within that positioning note the way in which what is 'touched' is other than the literal 'surface').[11] While both Kant and Hegel will allow for different treatments of painting as opposed to sculpture, neither link the particularity of each to the operation of a different sense. In part this is the originality of Herder's initial approach. And yet it is subtler since it is only in terms of touch, and thus the centrality of the hand, that form and the relations between forms in painting can be understood. There has been a move therefore from the literal hand to giving the hand, and with it touch, the major role in any account of the operation of art's work. However, while in terms of experience this is of great significance, of equal importance is the way there is a transformation of the object.

The object that is touched is different, it will have to be argued, in terms of its ontological status from the one that is merely seen. Hence the need to see touching.

Touch must remain for Herder that which guarantees seeing. Precisely because seeing is bound up with surfaces, it is for Herder linked to the dream since the latter is the surface with neither depth nor internal connection: 'Sight gives us *dreams*, touch gives us *truth*'.[12] Hence, Herder writes,

> Pity the lover who gazes upon his beloved from a distance as if she were an image on a surface and for whom this suffices! Pity the sculptor of an Apollo or a Hercules who has never embraced the body of an Apollo, who has never touched, even in a dream, the breast or the back of a Hercules. Truly from *nothing*, there can arise only *nothing*: the ray of light, touching nothing, can never become the warm, creative hand.[13]

For Herder it is in relation to his treatment of sculpture that it becomes possible to return to the more general treatment of the philosophy of art. Sculpture is both an exceptional case and yet precisely in being exceptional it provides the measure in which it becomes possible to generalise. In terms of the strategy adopted by Herder in *Plastik* it is the 'infinite sublime' – an engagement staged in relation to Job and Burke amongst others and yet reducible neither to the simply theological nor the merely physiological – that plays a central role. The 'colossal' provides both the '*origin*' (*Ursprungs*) and the '*essence*' (*Wessen*) of sculpture.[14] Sculpture is presented not just in relation to its inherent spatiality but also in regards to its having an active quality; matter as dynamic. Being is acting out and what is acted out is the work's matter. Matter therefore is an activity. As such the work of matter (a state of affairs that incorporates work as matter) has to be rethought as always already dynamic. Hence Herder's remarkable claim that sculpture, 'speaks to us as an *act*' (*als Tat, zu uns spricht*).[15] Solidity had acquired a potential and consequently materiality now insists within a form of potentiality. It matters. It will be vital to return to this point. What it indicates, to reiterate the point already noted, is a transformation of the object occurring within the move towards the centrality of touch. As such, what is needed is another account of matter's presence. An account that links potentiality and materiality such that what is at work is both the presence of an immaterial force though equally a dynamic conception of matter.[16] The co-presence of the two demands a shift on the level of nomenclature. The static connotations of 'matter' need to cede their place to a term which attributes to the work of art a workful quality; as such matter becomes *mattering*.[17]

Rather than the flat surface on which light is projected, sculpture captures and reflects light, holds it and passes it on. Captures it, for a face is bathed in light; moves it, as there is the casting of shadows. Light falls on a cheek – in part – in the movement across the face, a movement, which while marking the movement of the eye is one in which the eye is touching. The eye is becoming the hand. It is not just that the object brings a form of the infinite into play; defining sculpture in terms of an act locates the infinite as much in the object's mode of presentation as it does in the condition of a response. Art, taking sculpture as a type of paradigm, can as a condition of its being – the being of art – never be finished. The infinite sublime is not just the truth of sculpture. In enacting the unending it acts out the being of the art object: being as mattering. The detail here is essential since for Herder sublimity brings the 'true image of the gods and heroes' into play.[18] There is a need therefore to work through these formulations rather than take them as designating an already determined and structured field of inquiry. Hence, the reworking of Herder.

Herder starts his treatment of the infinite sublime by identifying sculpture as that which does not have a single point of orientation, rather it 'explores everything in the dark' (*im Dunkel*).[19] Countering an aesthetics of light, an epistemology of illumination and an ontology of delimited singularity – one bearing, as has already been indicated, an important connection to the object of Cartesian 'clear and distinct perception' – there is the productive condition of the dark; of touching *im Dunkel*. What is staged here does, of course, need to be understood as a form of blindness working beyond the hold of the literal. While the part of the argumentation that emerges at this point in the book's development returns to the general, if not more traditional, conceptions of the sublime, namely as that which is already in excess, Herder introduces an important difference. Rather than excess engendering, of necessity, a transcendental realm, in this context it is linked to another conception of the unending or infinite. Rather than the infinite as the non-representational as though all that was involved is a limit in relation to the comprehension of the object – this would of course be the position for Kant – for Herder what the infinite sets in play is a fundamentally different state of affairs. For Herder the limit is given by the being of the object. The move from subject to object has been completed. The passage, in which this other infinite emerges, even though Herder does of course not present it in terms that underscore the centrality of the object, in lieu of the subject, is the following:

> the hand never touches the *entire* object. It cannot grasp a form *all at once*, with the exception of the sphere, which is the form of stasis and contains perfection in itself. The hand can rest on the sphere and the sphere in the hand. But with articulated forms, the work of the hand is never complete (*nie zu Ende*): it goes on feeling as it were indefinitely (*immer unendlich*).[20]

The counter to any sense of closure is not an opening in which the claim that it would always be possible to search out additional elements could then be made. Such a response would be no more than a gloss on a hermeneutic project stemming from a preoccupation with meaning. A preoccupation that leaves the object untouched. It would not pertain to the object and would not be defined in terms of the relation that a transformation of the object's status would have demanded. Rather, difficult as it may be, there is the need to hold to '*obscurity*' (*Dunkel*), and thus to the '*night*' (*Nacht*).[21] Neither term diminishes the object; indeed they get close to its truth. Neither term obfuscates. They identify the condition of meaning. The night is the time of the always more; the time resisting an end, the time of a darkness in which the hand works endlessly. That on which the hand works cannot be mastered, the infinite stands in the way, stands almost as a between, such that the continuity of movement, the operation of the blind hand uncovers more but preserves the site as one of continual uncovering. It is a continuity made possible by the 'soul', though only on the condition that the presence of the soul is defined in terms of an operative, thus workful, sense of internality.

Herder's retention of the 'soul' locates his work, as has already been indicated, within the history of idealism. However, it is that history that has to be reconsidered. This location does not involve clear distinctions. Idealism is at its most productive when it can be understood as asserting firstly the irreducibility of material presence to empirical presence and secondly the co-presence of the immaterial and the material as constitutive of an object. Hence there will be an important distinction between the ideal found, for example in Plato and Goethe for whom that which is external to particulars ('forms' and '*Ur-phenomena*') have a causal relation to the identity of particulars on the one hand, and the forms of idealism at work in both Hegel and Herder on the other.[22] While it occurs in different ways, in both instances the 'ideal' is integral to the work itself.[23] In the case of Herder, to reiterate the general points noted above, the irreducibility of matter to the empirical involves in the first instance the introduction of an immaterial presence as that which informs matter and secondly the interplay between the material and the immaterial accounts for the way in which the infinite is at work within Herder's conception of the art object. Within such a setting idealism acquires a different character. It becomes an account of the interplay between mediacy and immateriality. Eschewed by such a setting is what may be described as the counter-positioning of the immediate and the empirical (which is itself a position that is inextricably bound up with what has already been identified as the literalisation of the eye and the hand.) In order to take this reworking of idealism a stage further there needs to be a return to both 'spirit' and the 'soul'.

The inevitable concession concerning 'spirit' noted in Diderot reappears in Herder. Herder describes the presence of the soul in ways that escape any quick identification of the soul with a form of transcendence where transcendence assumes both externality and causality. The soul is defined in terms of life and the animate. Herder's formulation is both deliberate and careful and takes the particularity of sculpture as its point of departure. Herder's claim is that, what 'sculpture should create ... are forms in which the living soul pervades the entire body (*einen edlen Körper durchhaucht*).[24] As such art has the 'task of representing the *embodied soul*' (*Seele im Körper darzustellen*).[25] It is in relation to this setting of work that it becomes possible to situate beauty; for Herder, 'Beauty ... is always only the shining through of *form*, the *sensible expression of perfection* ... (*Schönheit ist also nur immer Durchschein Form, sinnlicher Ausdruck der Vollkommenheit ...*)'.[26] To begin to work through this complex of relations it is essential to note that what is central is Herder's insistence that the work of art is the work of matter – hence the work of art is its 'act'. Accepting the link between work and 'act' is to assume that the work of art *is* – 'is' in the strong sense of exists, thus what is involved is a claim about the ontology of art work – in its being at work. Work therefore has an inherently actative dimension. To account for matter as work necessitates recourse to matter as dynamic. The work of matter is the ground of meaning. Attributions of meaning are therefore always the after effect of the work of matter. Indeed, whether it is recognised or not, work is the precondition for the attribution of meaning. The impossibility of an identification of meaning and finality cannot be explained in terms of relativity on the level of meaning. The contrary is the case. Meaning's lack of finality has its conditions of existence in a conception of the object defined by the 'unending'. This is Herder's point concerning the relationship between touch and the object: a relation in which there had been a transformation of its constitutive elements. As such, questions of interpretation have to be redefined in terms of the nature of the connection between the finitude of the interpretative decision and the work as itself defined by the potential infinite of matter, where matter is understood as always already the site of its own animation. (Matter as *mattering*.)

Herder's account of this set up has recourse to both 'spirit' and the 'soul'. However, the presence of the soul is not to be accounted for in terms of the latter's presence within the object that then allows for the possibility that the soul could have an existence and thus a possible history that is external to its having been objectified. This is the difference between Hegel and Schelling on the one hand and Herder on the other. And yet there are moments of equivocation. As part of a complex argument sculpture is taken as inherently allegorical because it involves the presentation of '*one thing through another*' (*Eins durchs Andere*).[27] Indeed, Herder goes on to suggest that sculpture as an instance of what he refers to as '*daß bildende Kunst*' (which are the visual arts in general) is in a state of what he describes as 'permanent allegory' precisely because sculptures 'image the soul through the body' (*sie bildet Seele durch Körper*).[28] This needs to be interpreted, however, in light of the passage already noted in which it was argued that the 'fingers' of 'inner sense' discovered the 'shape of the *spirit* within the form' (*Gestalt des Geistes in dieser Form*).[29] Both 'soul' and 'spirit' open up a concern with 'beauty'. There is an important set of interconnections. Soul pervades matter. It animates matter. Beauty becomes form's shining. Beauty is not the form. It is its mode of being present; presenting as shining. Beauty is bound up with the inherently actative nature of matter. Beauty becomes a quality of the object; a quality that shines. Shining has a genuine accord with matter's animation and the soul's pervasive presence.

While it is always possible to uncover those moments within *Plastik* within which more conventional understandings of the role of both 'spirit' and 'soul' can be discerned, hence the reference above to Herder's equivocation, it is nonetheless still possible to insist on the centrality of the work of matter within Herder's own position. Insisting on that work involves a return to touch. Touch, while bringing the opposition between sensation and cognition into play, does so on the basis that the conventional determinations of that opposition no longer play a determining role within the subject/object relation that characterises every philosophical concern with the work of art. Another philosophical project is announced. Once touch can be incorporated in ways that reposition both the nature of the subject and the object, as well as the content of their relation, a transformation in which references to the 'soul' move from the subject to the object, there is an accompanying transformation of the nature of the object.[30] The object becomes that which in resisting its reduction to the literal acquires a quality that announces the reduction's impossibility. Touch, therefore, in introducing a temporal dimension that is not circumscribed by immediacy, in yielding a conception of the object in which its *mattering* is central, stages different dimensions of the structure of thought that are essential to the development of a materialist philosophy of art.

Notes

1. While it cannot be argued for in this context, the essential difference between Kant on the one hand and Herder and Diderot on the other is the latter's concern with the nature of the object and not with the subject's response to the presentation of an object. In regards to the specific claim concerning immediacy this can be understood in terms of the absence of the concept – where the concept's presence would be understood as that which mediated (determined) in advance claims about the object's beauty. To this end see the argumentation of §9 of the *Critique of the Power of Judgment*. Also the claim made in §6 that 'the person making the judgment feels himself to be completely free (*frei*) with regard to the satisfaction he devotes to the object'. The state of being 'free' is another instance of a structure of immediacy. References to Kant are to: *Critique of the Aesthetic Power of Judgment*, trans. Paul Guyer and Eric Matthews, Cambridge: Cambridge University Press, 2000 and I. Kant, 'Kritik der Urtheilskaft', in *Kants Werke, Akademie Textausgabe*, Berlin: Walter de Gruyter, 1968. For an expanded discussion of many of the points raised in this chapter, especially those in the first section, see the forthcoming volume, Andrew Benjamin, *Art's Philosophical Practice*.
2. Denis Diderot, *Lettre sur les aveugles* (1749), in Diderot, *Oeuvres philosophiques*, ed. Paul Vernière, Paris: Garnier, 1992, p.90.
3. Herder, Johann Gottfried, *Sculpture: Some Observations on Shape and Form from Pygmalion's Creative Dream*, ed. and trans. Jason Gaiger, Chicago, IL and London: University of Chicago Press, 2002, p.90; Johann Gottfried Herder, *Plastik: einige Wahrnehmungen über Form und Gestalt aus Pygmalions bildendem Traume*, in Johann Gottfried Herder, *Werke*, ed. Günter Arnold et al., vol. 3, *Schriften zu Philosophie, Literatur, Kunst und Altertum 1774–1787*, ed. Jürgen Brummack and Martin Bollacher, Frankfurt am Main: Deutscher Klassiker Verlag, 1994, p.311.
4. 'Chardin est entre la nature et l'art: il relègue les autres imitations au troisième rang. Il n'y a rien en lui qui sente la palette. C'est une harmonie au delà de laquelle on ne songe pas à désirer: elle serpente imperceptiblement dans sa composition, tout sous chaque partie de l'étendue de sa toile; c'est, comme les théologiens dissent de l'esprit, sensible dans le tout et secret en chaque point.' Denis Diderot, *Oeuvres esthétiques*, Paris: Classiques Garniers, 1994, p.495.

5. Hence there is the need to distinguish this position outlined here from the one presented by Kant in §15 of the *Critique of the Aesthetic Power of Judgment*. In that Section it is clear that a concern with the object is a philosophical impossibility for a judgement of taste. Judgments that evince such concerns – judgments in which 'charm' and 'emotion' play a role (cf. §13) – are judgments that allow for the object and are correspondingly not 'pure judgments of taste'. Impossibility, in this context, has to be understood within terms set by the relationship between the subject and the form of the object. Kant's position is presented in the following formulation of the aesthetic judgment: '... an aesthetic judgment is of a unique kind and affords absolutely no cognition (*kein Erkenntnis*) (not even a confused one) of the object, which happens only in a logical judgment; while the former by contrast, relates, the representation by which an object is given solely to the subject, and does not bring our attention to any property of the object, but only the purposive form in the determination of the powers of representation that are occupied with it.' (pp.113/228).

6. Herder, *Sculpture*, p.80; Herder, *Plastik*, p.300.

7. Plato, *Phaedo*, 100D.

8. In this regards see my 'A Missed Encounter: Plato's Socrates and Geach's Euthyphro', *Grazer Philosophische Studien*, 29, 1987, pp.145–70.

9. For two instances of the many ways in which the history of touch and the history of the hand can be deployed see: Sander Gilman, 'Touch, Sexuality and Disease', in *Medicine and the Five Senses*, W.F. Bynun and Roy Porter, eds, Cambridge: Cambridge University Press, 1993, pp.198–225, and the collection *Manus Loquens: Medium der Geste – Geste der Medien*, Matthias Bickenbach, Annina Klappert and Hedwig Pompe, eds, Cologne: Dumont Buchverlag, 2003. Moreover, the history of both touch and the hand cannot escape having to consider the injunction within the history of Christianity, that is, Christ's words to Mary Magdalene, *noli me tangere* (John 20:17). The Latin invokes the touch in a far more emphatic way than the original Greek. It is the Latin that had the determining effect on the history of art. Diderot and Herder can be seen therefore as attempts to 'desacralise' the art work through their insistence on a transformation of touch.

10. Herder, *Sculpture*, p.35; Herder, *Plastik*, p.247.

11. I have taken up the question of the surface's problematisation as it occurs in Walter Benjamin's early writings on art in my 'Framing Pictures, Transcending Marks: Walter Benjamin's "Paintings, or Signs and Marks"', in *Walter Benjamin and the Architecture of Modernity*, Andrew Benjamin and Charles Rice, eds, Melbourne: Re:press Books, 2009, pp.129–42.

12. Herder, *Sculpture*, p.38; Herder, *Plastik*, p.250.

13. Herder, *Sculpture*, p.42; Herder, *Plastik*, p.255.

14. Herder, *Sculpture*, p.93; Herder, *Plastik*, p.313.

15. Herder, *Sculpture*, p.80; Herder, *Plastik*, p.300.

16. I have, in collaboration with Howard Caygill, as part of a more general research project on the concept of force, edited an issue of *Parallax*, whose papers offer the beginnings of a sustained repositioning and thus reworking of force. See *Parallax*, 15 (51), 2009. In addition see our 'Introduction' to this issue: 'Of Force', pp.1–4. While it does not form part of the above project it is clear that recent work by Christophe Menke is also involved in a rethinking of the concept of force and thus by extension of what has been described here as the immaterial. See his 'Force: Towards an Aesthetic Concept of Life', *MLN*, 125 (3), April 2010 (German Issue), pp.552–70. Fundamental to Menke's position is the following contention: 'The aesthetic force is an endless generation and dissolution of expressions, an endless transformation of expression into different expression. The operation of the aesthetic force thus consists at any moment in transcending what it has itself engendered. The aesthetic force creates new expression by withdrawing from its previous expression' (p.567).

17. A further explication of what is meant by *mattering* is an ongoing project. See my 'Colouring Philosophy: Appel, Lyotard and Art's Work', *Critical Horizons: A Journal of Philosophy and Social Theory*, 11 (2), 2010, pp.379–95. Here as part of a general engagement with the question of colour I argue that: 'the ontology of art work – i.e. the being proper to art – is defined in terms of activity. The work of art works. It is a dynamic process that always has its own complex economies. The second is that meaning is always, and only, an after effect of the way matters works. As such, the working of matter is the precondition for the possibility of meaning. This aspect of a work can be understood as its *mattering*. Mattering as the work of matter is, within a materialist aesthetics, the *conditio sine qua non* for attributions of meaning. Moreover, to insist on mattering is both to maintain the centrality of matter thought as a locus of activity rather than a merely static event, while at the same time holding to the necessity of the particularity of a given work. The mattering of one work is always distinct from that of another.'

18. Herder, *Sculpture*, p.93; Herder, *Plastik*, p.314.

19. Herder, *Sculpture*, p.93; Herder, *Plastik*, p.314.

20. Herder, *Sculpture*, p.94; Herder, *Plastik*, p.316. The translation in this instance has been slightly modified.

21. Herder, *Sculpture*, p.94; Herder, *Plastik*, p.316.

22. Walter Benjamin's treatment of this aspect of Goethe's conception of the artwork, precisely because of the externality of the 'Ur-phenomena', leads Benjamin to conclude that such a conception makes art uncriticisable. And yet the move to criticism necessitates allowing the work a quality that cannot be equated with either description or commentary. The work of art will always be more. The limit of Goethe, for Benjamin, is clear. In his formulation for Goethe, art 'itself does not create the archetypes they rest prior to all created work, in that sphere of art where is not creation but nature' (p.180). See in this regard Benjamin's 'The Concept of Criticism in German Romanticism', in Walter Benjamin, *Selected Writings*, vol. 1, ed. Marcus Bullock and Michael W. Jennings, Cambridge MA: Harvard University Press, 1996, pp.180–82 in particular.

23. The relationship between Hegel and Herder is an extremely fruitful area of inquiry. What matters is how the question of 'soul' is to be understood. In this regard see Linda Walsh, 'The "Hard Form" of Sculpture: Marble, Matter and Spirit in European Sculpture from the Enlightenment through Romanticism', *Modern Intellectual History*, 5 (3), 2008, pp.455–86. For the discussion of the relationship between Hegel and Herder, pp.479–80. For an important statement of how that relation might be understood see Kristin Gjesdal, 'Hegel and Herder on Art History and Reason', *Philosophy and Literature*, 30, 2006, pp.17–32. Central to Gjsdal's characterisation of the difference is the way that their differing philosophy's of history – the absence of teleology in Herder – means that works would have a different sense of expression (expression in relation to what has been called in the argument of this paper the 'immaterial') and thus there would be a historically determined hierarchy within artworks.

    The difference between Herder and Hegel is, in other words, not only that Herder does not turn Greek art into the ideal of art as such, but also that he takes no art-form to be the privileged or paradigmatic expression within the boundaries of Greek culture. There are no normative hierarchies among the periods, nor among the aesthetic forms of expression within a given, historical paradigm. No type of art manifests the essence of art as such, and to perceive tragedy as less perfect an art-form than sculpture (yet as more attuned to modern spirit) would simply not be an option for Herder (p.26).

24. Herder, *Sculpture*, p.45; Herder, *Plastik*, p.259. The translation in this instance has been slightly modified.

25. Herder, *Sculpture*, p.45; Herder, *Plastik*, p.259.

26. Herder, *Sculpture*, p.78; Herder, *Plastik*, p.297.

27. Herder, *Sculpture*, p.96; Herder, *Plastik*, p.318.

28. Herder, *Sculpture*, p.96; Herder, *Plastik*, p.319. The translation in this instance has been slightly modified.

29. Herder, *Sculpture*, p.90; Herder, *Plastik*, p.311.

30. Rachel Zuckert, 'Sculpture and Touch: Herder's Aesthetics of Sculpture', *The Journal of Aesthetics and Art Criticism*, 67 (3), Summer 2009, pp.285–99: 'Imaginative proprioceptive identification allows us, Herder suggests, to understand the expressiveness of the sculpture, the way in which the comportment of the sculpture can express fitness, health, strength, well-being, emotional states, or tendencies to action, that is, the way in which this (represented) body is "ensouled," "alive," active' (p.285).

    Zuckert goes on to argue that this position can be understood in terms of a new conception of embodiment. The contention here is that it is the transformation of the conception of seeing that allows for the already present sense of embodied subjectivity.

Bibliography

Benjamin, Andrew, 'A Missed Encounter: Plato's Socrates and Geach's Euthyphro', *Grazer Philosophische Studien*, 29, 1987, pp.145–70.

——, 'Framing Pictures, Transcending Marks: Walter Benjamin's "Paintings, or Signs and Marks"', in *Walter Benjamin and the Architecture of Modernity*, Andrew Benjamin and Charles Rice, eds, Melbourne: Re:press Books, 2009, pp.129–42.

——, 'Colouring Philosophy: Appel, Lyotard and Art's Work', *Critical Horizons: A Journal of Philosophy and Social Theory*, 11 (2), 2010, pp.379–95.
Benjamin, Andrew and Howard Caygill, 'Introduction', *Parallax*, 15 (51), 2009, pp.1–4.
Benjamin, Walter, *Selected Writings*, vol. 1, ed. Marcus Bullock and Michael W. Jennings, Cambridge MA: Harvard University Press, 1996.
Bickenbach, Matthias, Annina Klappert and Hedwig Pompe, eds, *Manus Loquens. Medium der Geste – Geste der Medien*, Cologne: Dumont Buchverlag, 2003.
Diderot, Denis, *Oeuvres philosophiques*, ed. Paul Vernière, Paris: Garnier, 1992.
——, *Oeuvres esthétiques*, ed. Paul Vernière, Paris: Classiques Garniers, 1994.
Gilman, Sander, 'Touch, Sexuality and Disease', in *Medicine and the Five Senses*, W.F. Bynun and Roy Porter, eds, Cambridge: Cambridge University Press, 1993, pp.198–225.
Gjesdal, Kristin, 'Hegel and Herder on Art History and Reason', *Philosophy and Literature*, 30, 2006, pp.17–32.
Herder, Johann Gottfried, *Plastik: einige Wahrnehmungen über Form und Gestalt aus Pygmalions bildendem Traume*, in Johann Gottfried Herder, *Werke*, ed. Günter Arnold et al., vol. 3, *Schriften zu Philosophie, Literatur, Kunst und Altertum 1774–1787*, ed. Jürgen Brummack and Martin Bollacher, Frankfurt am Main: Deutscher Klassiker Verlag, 1994, pp.243–326.
——, *Sculpture: Some Observations on Shape and Form from Pygmalion's Creative Dream*, ed. and trans. Jason Gaiger, Chicago, IL and London: University of Chicago Press, 2002.
Kant, Immanuel, 'Kritik der Urtheilskaft', in *Kants Werke, Akademie Textausgabe*, Berlin: Walter de Gruyter, 1968.
——, *Critique of the Aesthetic Power of Judgment*, trans. Paul Guyer and Eric Matthews, Cambridge: Cambridge University Press, 2000.
Menke, Christophe, 'Force: Towards an Aesthetic Concept of Life', *MLN*, 125 (3), 2010 (German Issue), pp.552–70.
Walsh, Linda, 'The "Hard Form" of Sculpture: Marble, Matter and Spirit in European Sculpture from the Enlightenment through Romanticism', *Modern Intellectual History*, 5 (3), 2008, pp.455–86.
Zuckert, Rachel, 'Sculpture and Touch: Herder's Aesthetics of Sculpture', *The Journal of Aesthetics and Art Criticism*, 67 (3), 2009, pp.285–99.

5

A taxonomy of touch: tactile encounters in Renaissance Italy

Geraldine A. Johnson

Until recently, very few art historians had considered the sense of touch in the production and reception of art in Renaissance Italy – or, indeed, in most other periods and places – a legacy, at least in part, of the role photographs have played in the development of Art History as a discipline, with their inevitable tendency to de-materialise even the most tactile sculpted object.[1] Tactility as an abstract concept, however, has an impressive pedigree in art historical studies, beginning with the work of Adolf von Hildebrand, Bernard Berenson, Alois Riegl and Heinrich Wölfflin in the late nineteenth and early twentieth century.[2] More recently, philosophers and intellectual historians such as Maurice Merleau-Ponty, Michel Foucault, Luce Irigaray and Martin Jay have likewise considered tactility, especially in contrast to vision.[3] In the past decade, interest in the senses in general and touch in particular has exploded, especially in fields such as anthropology, sociology and literary studies, a phenomenon sometimes referred to as 'the material turn'.[4] Art historians have also begun to reconsider tactility not merely as an abstract concept, but as a phenomenon involving real objects made and encountered in specific historical and physical circumstances, as is evident in some of the chapters found in the present volume and in a few other recent publications. Nevertheless, it is striking that, with a few exceptions, most scholars of Early Modern art in particular have only rarely touched on the question of touch.[5]

The sense of touch, however, was actually of great interest in fifteenth-, sixteenth- and seventeenth-century Italy. Early Modern notions about touch grew out of a tradition that can be traced back to ancient Greece, where both Plato and Aristotle ranked touch below sight in terms of its relative dignity. Such attitudes continued to be espoused in the Renaissance by figures such Leonardo da Vinci and Leon Battista Alberti.[6] Indeed, Alberti not only codified the supremely ocularcentric practice of linear perspective in his influential *Della pittura*, but even used a winged eye as his personal device when designing his self-portrait for a bronze plaquette (Washington, DC, National Gallery of Art).

Some Renaissance writers and artists, however, resisted such visual paradigms. In fact, the humanist Mario Equicola went as far as proclaiming touch to be the most dignified of all the senses.[7] And while artists such as Leonardo continued to prioritise vision, others demonstrated a fascination with touch, including the fifteenth-century painter and sculptor Andrea del Verrocchio, Leonardo's teacher. This is suggested by Verrocchio's two-figure bronze group for the Florentine guild church of Or San Michele depicting the Gospel story of the Incredulity of St Thomas in which the apostle refused to believe in the Resurrection until he had literally touched Christ's wounds with his hands (Fig. 5.1). In the Gospel, Thomas states that, until 'I shall … put my finger into the print of the nails, and thrust my hand into his side, I will not believe' (John 20:25). It was precisely sculpture's ability to give tactile proof to doubtful beholders that became a key theme of many pro-sculpture arguments presented by Early Modern writers.

Other artists, both painters and sculptors, likewise explored the complex implications of the sense of touch in images concerned with tactile themes as, for example, in Michelangelo Merisi da Caravaggio's famous painted version of the *Incredulity of St Thomas* (Potsdam, Sanssouci) or in images illustrating Christ's command to Mary Magdalen *not* to touch him – *Noli me tangere* – by artists ranging from Fra Angelico (Florence, San Marco) in the fifteenth century to Agnolo Bronzino (Paris, Musée du Louvre) in the sixteenth.[8] Bronzino was, in fact, interested in tactility not only as a pictorial theme, but also as part of the wider debate on the *paragone*, the theoretical discussion on the relative merits of sculpture versus painting in which the sense of touch played a crucial role.[9]

In their writings, Bronzino and other advocates of painting used sculpture's tactile qualities as evidence of its lower status, while those who favoured sculpture saw tactility as a highly positive attribute. For example, the sixteenth-century sculptor Niccolò Tribolo made touch a central part of his argument in favour of sculpture:

> if a blind man … only having the sense of touch … encountered a marble or wood or clay figure, he would declare that it was the figure of a man, … woman, … [or] child; and contrarily, if it had been a painting … he would have discovered nothing at all, … [because] sculpture is the real thing, and painting is a lie.[10]

The humanist Benedetto Varchi likewise claimed that vision

> often deceives … [while] the most reliable sense is touch … .[W]hen we see something and we are doubtful about it, … we use touch to verify it. Everyone thus knows that touching a statue confirms everything the eye sees … therefore sculptors say that their art is truthful and painting is [not].[11]

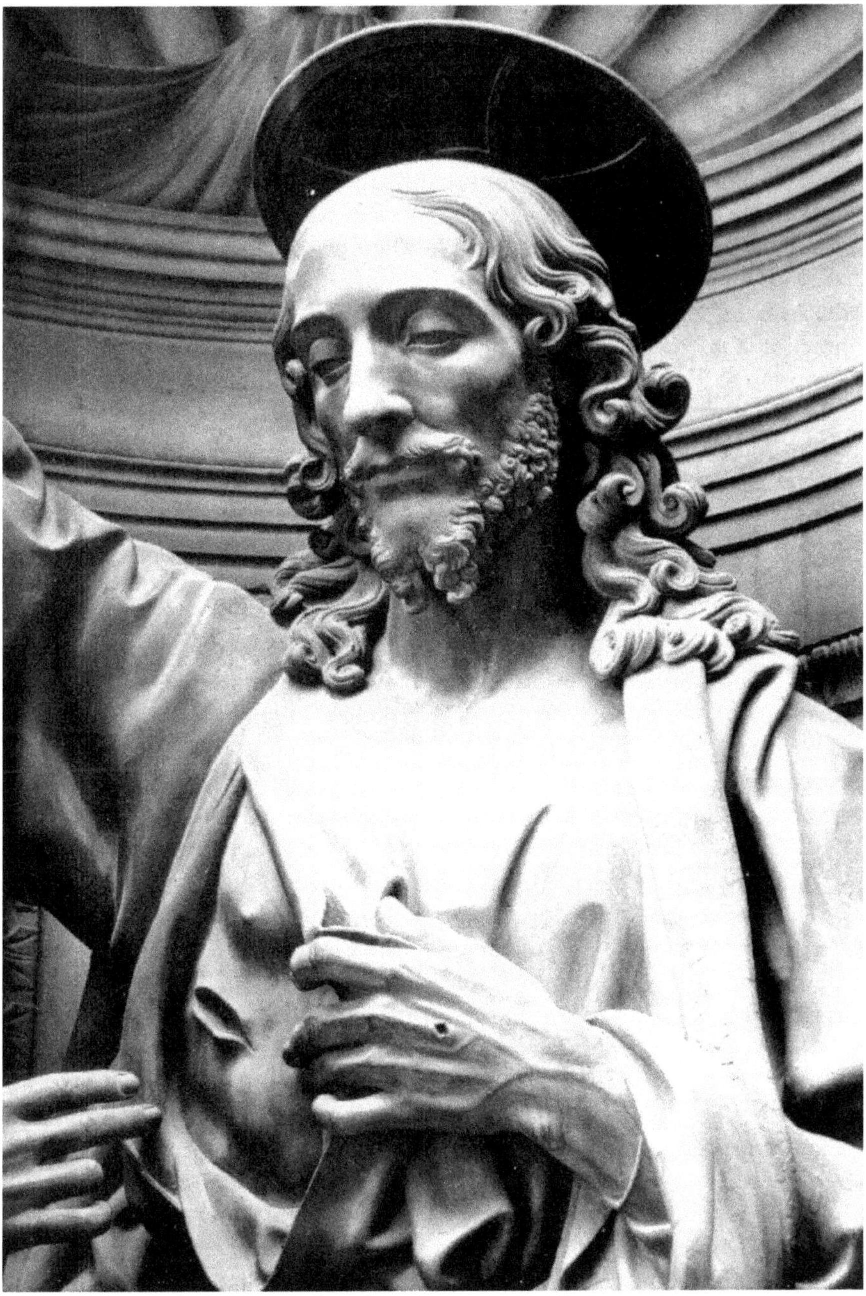

5.1 Andrea del Verrocchio, *The Incredulity of St Thomas* (detail of Thomas' fingers about to touch Christ's wound), partially-gilded bronze, 1467–83, Or San Michele, Florence [public domain, originally published in Leo Planiscig, *Andrea del Verrocchio*, Vienna: A. Schroll, 1941]

In contrast, sculpture's tactile qualities were presented very negatively by writers intent on proving painting's superiority. For instance, in the sixteenth century, the director of Florence's Academy of Design, Vincenzio Borghini, stated that touch was 'the coarsest sense' of all and ridiculed Tribolo's example of the blind man.[12] Galileo Galilei did so as well when he claimed in 1612 that only the 'simple-minded … [would] think that sculpture can deceive the sense of touch … .Who would believe that a man, when touching a statue, would think that it is a living human being?'[13] Clearly, the sense of touch was a point of contention in the *paragone* debate. But rather than focusing on such abstract discussions, it is perhaps equally interesting to consider instead tactility in practice, that is, how it was physically manifested in the production and reception of Renaissance art. What follows, therefore, is a kind of taxonomy of touch as it was actually experienced by Italian artists, patrons and beholders in the Early Modern period.

The most common type of touch deployed by rich and poor, male and female, lay and cleric alike was probably the devotional touch, which was evident in everything from how small statues, reliefs and even religious paintings were literally handled in the domestic sphere, to the much more public rituals involving sculpted objects that were performed in churches and convents. In the 'public' category, one should also include pilgrims touching and kissing saintly statues or the carved and cast containers made for holy relics. In paintings like Gentile da Fabriano's *Pilgrims Visiting the Shrine of St Nicholas of Bari* (Washington, DC, National Gallery of Art), the talismanic properties of touch are implied in the eager, outstretched hands of the sick and crippled pilgrims who reach up to touch a carved saint's tomb, while the Late Medieval bronze statue of St Peter in the Vatican attributed to Arnolfo di Cambio is still the object of tactile veneration by present-day pilgrims.

The devotional touch in this period and, indeed, earlier, ran along a continuum from touching the actual body or relics of a saint, to touching a tomb or reliquary housing such remains, to, finally, touching a statue serving as a substitute for a holy figure. Sculpture could thus provide a means of both mediating and controlling tactile engagements with real as well as simulated sacred bodies. But Late Medieval and Early Modern beholders did not have to go on pilgrimages in order to engage the devotional touch. For instance, we know that some of the dozens (if not hundreds) of life-size wooden figures of the Crucified Christ found in churches throughout Italy and beyond were physically handled during rituals associated with Holy Week. As with the pilgrim's touch, the distinction between reality and simulation, between living (or dead) bodies and their sculpted representations could be elided by such three-dimensional figures, which could include wigs made of real human hair and loin-clothes fashioned from real pieces of cloth.

A number of these sculptures were even taken down manually from their supporting crosses on Good Friday and symbolically 'buried' in temporary altar-tombs elsewhere in their churches. A few – including an example carved by Donatello in the early fifteenth century for the Florentine church of Santa Croce – had movable arms to facilitate the very tactile reenactment of Christ's deposition and burial performed by a priest and his acolytes (Fig. 5.2). Lay worshippers may also have been allowed to venerate such sculpted figures physically during rituals involving kneeling before, touching and even kissing them on Good Friday. The physical handling and veneration of these sculptures suggests that many painted and sculpted depictions of the Deposition and Lamentation, such as examples by Rosso Fiorentino (Volterra, Pinacoteca) or Ercole de' Roberti (Liverpool, Walker Art Gallery), should perhaps be understood not only as imagined representations of long-ago Biblical events, but also ever-present reminders of very real contemporary rituals of touch and devotion.

It was not just statues of the dead, adult Christ that were subject to tactile handling by devotees. Statues of the living Infant Christ, often made of wood or plaster, were also literally manipulated, especially when displayed in Christmas-time crêches – a custom already evoked in the early fourteenth-century fresco in the upper church of San Francesco in Assisi of the so-called Miracle at Greccio, which shows this type of sculpture coming to life in the hands of St Francis. Documents describe nuns cradling statues of the Christ Child as well, with these objects also occasionally appearing to come to life – sometimes even to the point of seeming to suckle at the nuns' breasts.[14]

Desiderio da Settignano's mid-fifteenth-century marble Christ Child made for the top of a tabernacle in the church of San Lorenzo in Florence was likewise subject to the devotional touch.[15] In 1497, for instance, the figure seems to have served as the model for a statue that was carried by hand by four young boys during a highly emotional procession through the streets of Florence. Two decades later, Desiderio's original marble figure, while on display at Christmas time on a ground-level altar, was tenderly embraced by the future Medici pope Leo X, who was so emotionally overwhelmed that he didn't know whether to laugh or cry, which suggests just how powerful tactile encounters with sculpted objects could be for even the most educated and elite of beholders. It is again worth keeping such encounters in mind when looking at contemporary paintings of the Madonna and Child, since some examples may well reflect the very real interactions contemporary beholders had with sculpted effigies of the Infant Jesus.

Such encounters were not limited to public contexts such as churches, nor to elite beholders such as popes. In fact, images of the Madonna and Child were probably the single most common type of artwork found in Renaissance homes at all levels of society. Less well-off beholders would have limited their tactile encounters to handling mass-produced prints of the Madonna and Child, while more well-to-do beholders could have afforded painted or even sculpted versions, with the latter especially allowing for various types of

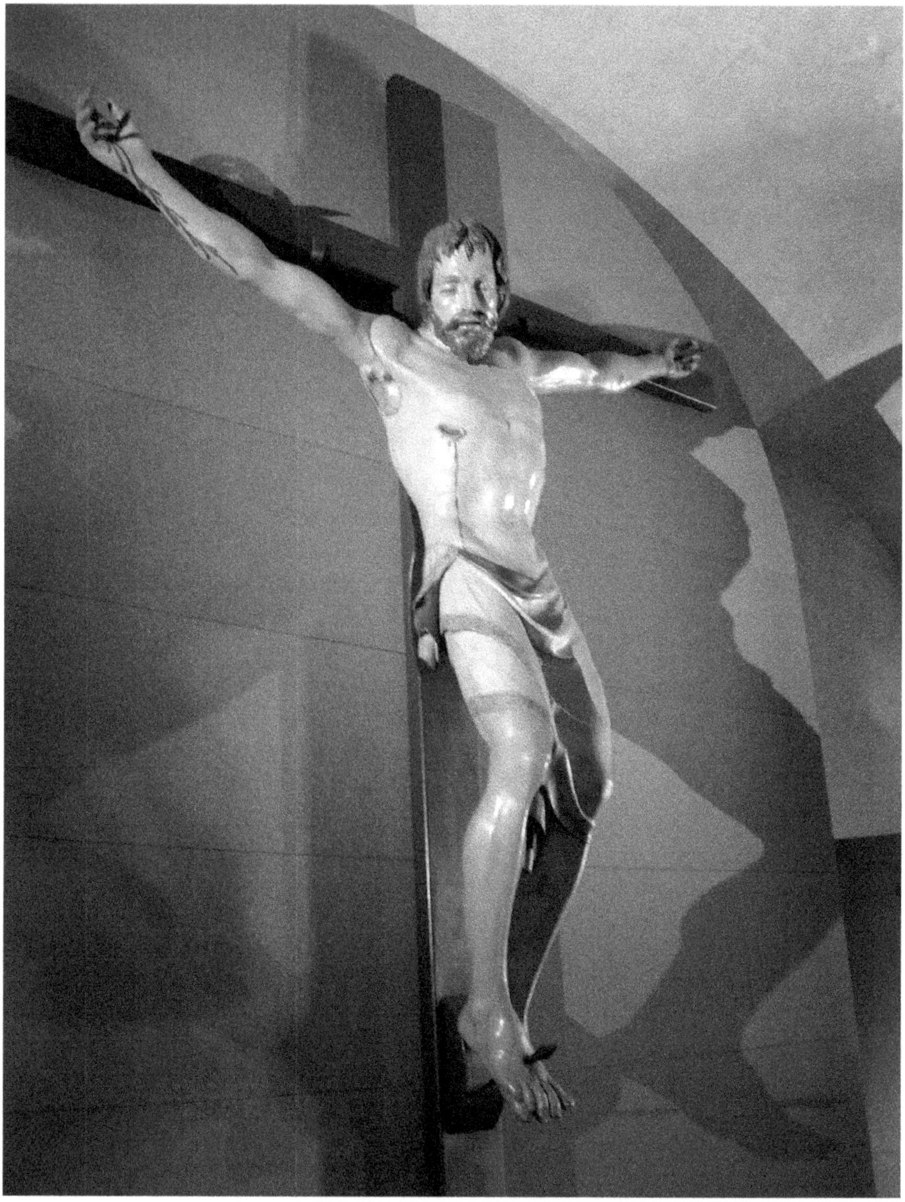

5.2 Donatello, *Crucified Christ* (note moveable joints at the shoulders), c. 168 (h) × c. 173 (w) cm / c. 66 (h) × c. 68 (w) in., polychromed pear wood, c. 1415, Santa Croce, Florence [© Sailko (http://commons.wikimedia.org)]

physical interaction. In some sculpted examples, such as a half-length Marian relief based on a popular design by Lorenzo Ghiberti that is now in the Ashmolean Museum in Oxford, hooks at the wrist and neck suggest that clothing or jewellery may have once been put on and taken off such objects. Thanks to the three-dimensional qualities of sculpture as a medium, such tactile interactions in the domestic sphere would have been made both possible and legitimate.[16]

The question of licit versus illicit devotional touching merits further consideration. In the early fifteenth century, Giovanni di Pagolo Morelli vividly described his fevered embracing, kissing and touching of a Crucifixion image while overwhelmed with grief at the death of his beloved son, which suggests just how highly tactile licit devotional practices involving art objects could be in this period.[17] In contrast, highly-charged prints produced in the seventeenth century by Marcantonio Bellavia of Mary Magdalen sensually caressing a disturbingly life-like sculpture of the Crucified Christ (New York Public Library) hint at the dangers illicit touching could have in a devotional context – especially in light of Christ's explicit command to the Magdalen *not* to touch him.[18]

The question of licit and illicit touching, especially as inflected by gender and desire, is also relevant to a second type of touch, namely, that of the collector and connoisseur, whose possessive hand forms a secular counterpart to the touch of the religious devotee, especially from the later fifteenth century onwards.[19] For instance, in Lorenzo Lotto's 1527 portrait of the Venetian collector Andrea Odoni (London, Royal Collection), the sitter dramatically proffers an *all'antica* female statuette to an implied external beholder (Fig. 5.3). Further tactile encounters are imbedded within the composition, first and foremost in the gold crucifix in Odoni's other hand, which he presses close to his heart. The book, coins and gems scattered on the green felt tablecloth beside him and the sculptures within hand's reach also hint at previous and potential tactile encounters. Even the shadowy figure of Susanna stepping into her bath just above Odoni's bent elbow, a bronze statuette that may well have been used as an inkstand, has a kind of implicit tactile functionality.

The humanist collector's study or *studiolo* would have been full of such insistently tactile objects, from exquisitely-finished bronze statuettes designed by artists such as Pier-Jacopo Alari Bonacolsi (better known as Antico) or Giambologna to sculpted objects that straddle the object-art divide, like elaborate door knockers or hand-bells, as well as natural curiosities like branches of coral and even paintings, prints and books, all of which could be subject to the touch of the connoisseur. Such objects would have been stored and presented in a variety of ways. For instance, in Vittore Carpaccio's early sixteenth-century fictional depiction of St Augustine in his study (Venice, Scuola di San Giorgio degli Schiavone), figurative statuettes are displayed on a raised ledge, while a bronze hand-bell, books and other objects associated with scholarly pursuits are kept literally within hand's reach on the desk.

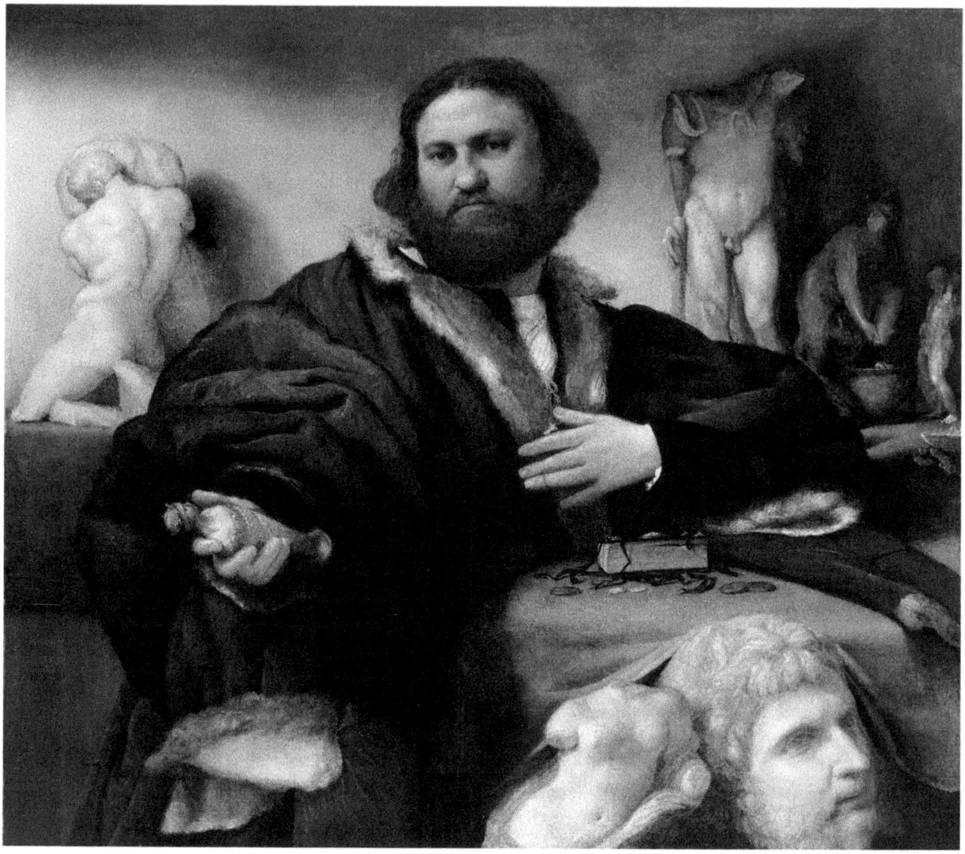

5.3 Lorenzo Lotto, *Portrait of Andrea Odoni*, 104.6 × 116.6 cm / 41.2 × 45.9 in., oil on canvas, 1527, Royal Collection, London [The Royal Collection © 2010, Her Majesty Queen Elizabeth II]

We know that sculptures and other items stored in such studies were handled by their owners, as when Lorenzo de' Medici lovingly presented a visiting cardinal with some of the highlights of his father Piero's collection, which he had inherited.[20]

However, tactile encounters with sculptures in particular could also be viewed in much more negative terms. For example, the art theorist Paolo Pino ridiculed sculpture's tempting tactility by citing the story of an ancient Athenian youth who had sexually assaulted a statue of Venus.[21] Such responses confirm a general sense of anxiety about the potential dangers of mis-handling sculpted objects, especially by allowing them to become objects of sexual desire. This is particularly evident in depictions of female statuettes literally being man-handled. For instance, in Titian's c. 1567 portrait of the collector and art dealer Jacopo Strada (Vienna, Kunsthistorisches Museum), the sitter grasps a female statuette without, it seems, daring to engage her visually. Clearly, the sense of male possessive, sexual entitlement to the female body that is characteristic of Early Modern culture in general is evident in such images, but so too is a sense of the potential sensory dangers (as well as pleasures) involved in actively engaging sculpted works of art.

In a fascinating text, the sculptor and art theorist Lorenzo Ghiberti vividly described his own manual encounters with various life-sized statues. When writing in the abstract about sculpture, Ghiberti stresses the importance of vision, optics and lighting effects in how they are displayed and interpreted. When he begins discussing actual statues he has personally encountered, however, Ghiberti often invokes the sense of touch. For instance, Ghiberti describes his encounter with a classical female statue by stating that looking at it with one's eyes was not enough, since its beauty could only be properly appreciated by 'the hand touching it'. Elsewhere, Ghiberti records his encounter with an ancient statue of an Hermaphrodite, a work that had 'the greatest refinement, [but] which the face [*il viso*, that is, looking with one's eyes] would not have seen, had not the touch [of] the hand sought it out'.[22] Touch, even more than light or vision, was thus crucial for assessing and admiring sculpture according to Ghiberti.

Ghiberti has been invoked here in the context of the collector and connoisseur's touch, but he was also, of course, a practising sculptor, which suggests yet another type of touch, that of the artist. The sculptor's touch was, in fact, a key issue in discussions about the relative status of painters versus sculptors. Although sculptors were often depicted handling sculpted objects, artists with social and intellectual aspirations used a variety of strategies to try to downplay the very manual labour involved in actually producing sculpture in order to confirm their status as gentlemen-artists rather than as mere artisans. For instance, in a print illustrating a fortune-telling book published in 1527, Sigismondo Fanti's *Triompho di Fortuna* (Cambridge, MA, Harvard University, Houghton Library), the great Michelangelo himself is shown carving his marble figure of Dawn in an *all'antica* setting in which he appears in the guise of a loin-cloth-wearing classical sculptor. However, despite the scene's learned allusions, the woodcut also unavoidably highlights the intense physical labour involved in marble carving, with the sculptor's vigorously-raised arm raining hammer blows down onto the marble figure emerging beneath him.[23]

In another print, the sixteenth-century sculptor Baccio Bandinelli very self-consciously sought to present himself not as an *all'antica* sculptor, but rather as a contemporary gentleman and artist-scholar who would soon be knighted by Emperor Charles V (London, British Museum)[24] (Fig. 5.4). In this image, designed by Bandinelli himself, the sculptor seems, at first glance, to have succeeded in banishing any trace of hard physical labour

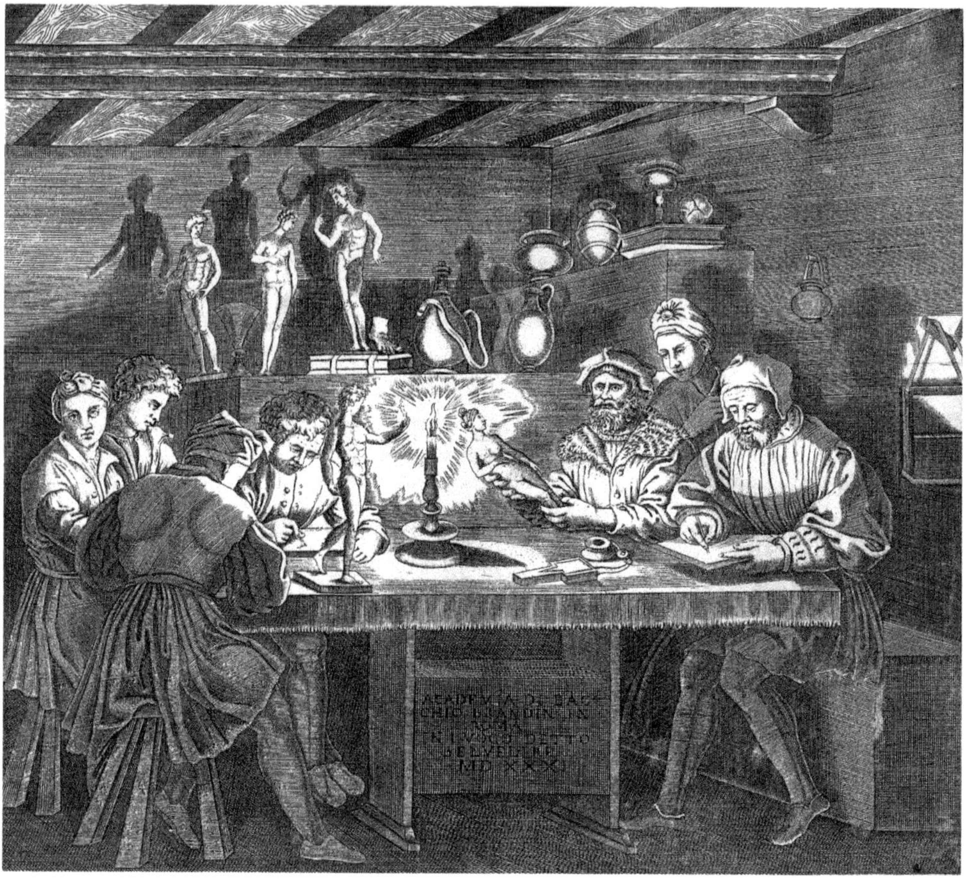

5.4 Baccio Bandinelli (designer) and Agostino Veneziano (engraver), *The Academy of Baccio Bandinelli*, 27.4 × 29.8 cm / 10.8 × 11.7 in., engraving, 1531, British Museum, London [© Trustees of the British Museum]

from his sculpture academy. Instead, he is seated near the centre of the composition, surrounded by well-dressed apprentices making drawings after antique-inspired statuettes. However, in an unintentionally telling detail, we see that Bandinelli, despite his social and academic pretensions, simply can't keep his hands off of sculpture – the inevitable tactile allure of the art he practices is instead demonstrated by the firm grip with which he holds a nude female statuette.

The significance of the sculptor's touch is also suggested by physical evidence. For instance, Michelangelo became famous (or rather, infamous) for leaving many of his sculpted works unfinished. Although his *non-finito* was often due to changing circumstances and overly ambitious deadlines, in some works, Michelangelo may have left his marble surfaces unfinished in order to attest to the presence and potency of his hand. While the perfectly smooth contours of bronze statuettes by sculptors such as Antico or Giambologna seem to have been designed to erase any vestiges of the maker's hand, thereby enticing the inquisitive and acquisitive hands of the collector-connoisseur, Michelangelo's rough surfaces suggest instead a desire to preserve the tactile traces of the sculptor's touch.

Michelangelo's interest in touch is also evident in his poetry. For instance, in some of his sonnets, the sculptor's God-like hand is seen as a powerful, life-giving force capable of animating carved figures.[25] Michelangelo similarly thematised the hand itself in many of his statues. The auto-erotic, probing hand of the so-called *Dying Slave* (Paris, Musée du Louvre), for instance, recalls the hand of the sculptor-as-lover described in some of his poems (Fig. 5.5). Likewise, Michelangelo's *Moses*, who insistently fingers his flowing beard without even deigning to look down at it, once again alludes to sculpture's inherent tactility. The prominence of hands in many of Michelangelo's works thus suggests that, at some level, this member may have functioned for the sculptor as a visual synecdoche, that is, as a part symbolically representing the sculptor – or perhaps the art of sculpture – as a whole.

The three types of touch highlighted in this chapter – that of the devotee, the collector and the artist – are each, in turn, further inflected by their makers' and beholders' gender, their public and private roles, their social and economic circumstances, and whether they were lay or clerical. Sculptural tactility in this period could also be a real, physical phenomenon, as well as a theoretical construct, a poetical metaphor or an implied desire. Perhaps most intriguing, by considering the sense of touch in Renaissance Italy, we can begin to rethink the very category of sculpture itself. While tactility in theory and practice was used to define the 'high' art of sculpture practised by artists like Michelangelo, tactility was also an inevitable feature of the production and reception of everything from bronze statuettes and plaquettes to much more obviously 'functional' objects in the domestic sphere, and from three-dimensional sculpted objects to supposedly two-dimensional 'flat' art such as paintings and prints. Thus, while elite theoretical debates like the *paragone* clearly sought to use touch to define and distinguish painting from sculpture, in practice, the tactile production and handling of a wide range of sculpted and other hand-crafted images and objects that often do not conform to traditional art historical definitions of sculpture suggests that perhaps sculpture itself as a category was still in flux in the Renaissance, at least when considered in terms of the sense of touch.

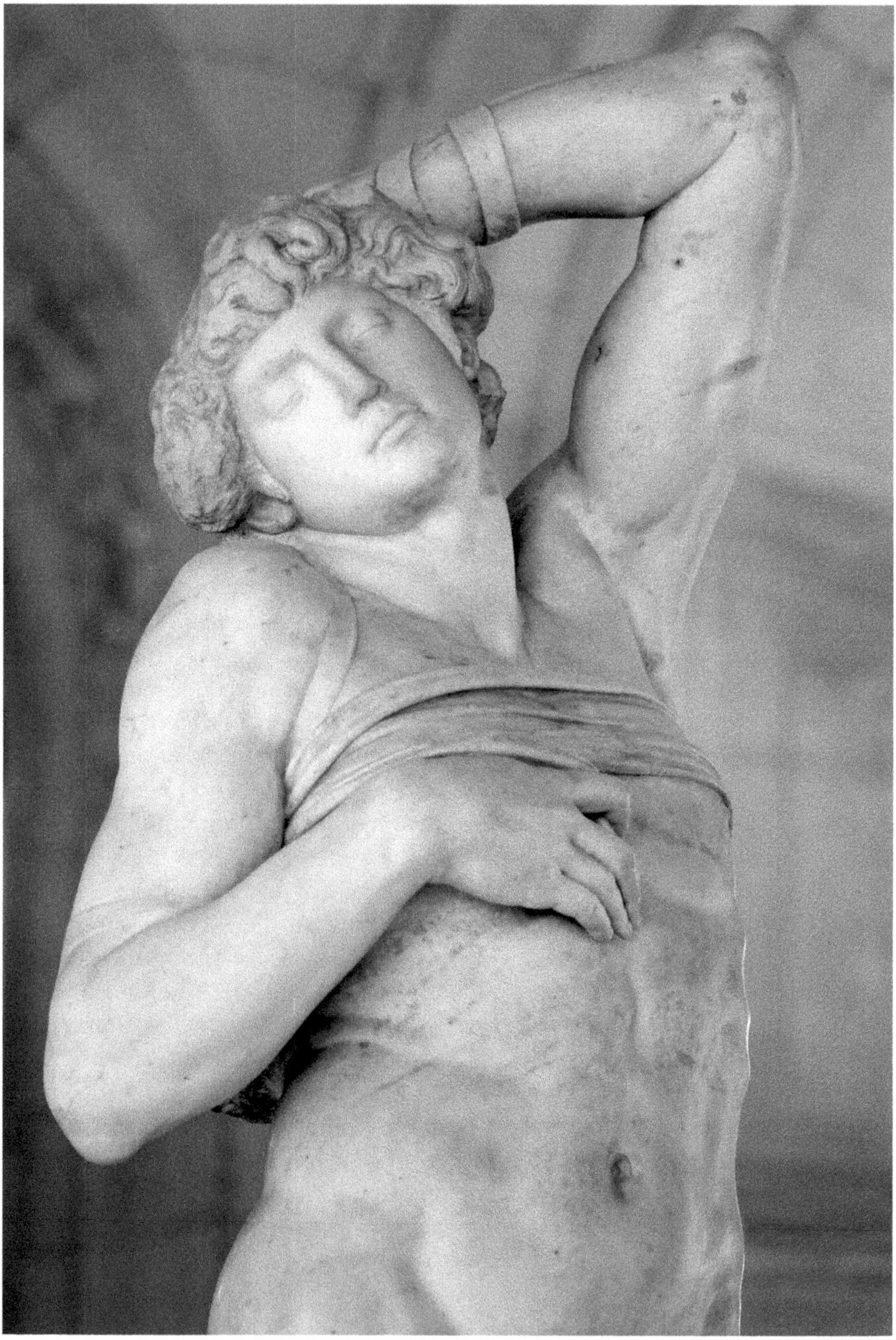

5.5 Michelangelo Buonarroti, *Dying Slave* (detail), marble, from 1513 onwards, Musée du Louvre, Paris [© Marie-Lan Nguyen (http://commons.wikimedia.org)]

Notes

1. For an expanded discussion of many of the points raised in this chapter, see Geraldine A. Johnson, 'The Art of Touch in Early Modern Italy', in *Art and the Senses*, F. Bacci and D. Melcher, eds, Oxford: Oxford University Press, 2011, pp.59–84. See also Geraldine A. Johnson, 'Touch, Tactility and the Reception of Sculpture in Early Modern Italy', in *A Companion to Art Theory*, P. Smith and C. Wilde, eds, Oxford: Blackwell Publishers, 2002, pp.61–74. On the role played by photographs, especially of Italian Renaissance sculpture, in the history of art history, see Geraldine A. Johnson, 'Using the Photographic Archive: On the Life (and Death) of Images', in *Photo Archives and the Photographic Memory of Art History*, C. Caraffa, ed., Berlin and Munich: Deutscher Kunstverlag, 2011, pp.145–56, and Geraldine A. Johnson, '*(Un)richtige Aufnahme*: Renaissance Sculpture and the Visual Historiography of Art History', *Art History*, 36, 2013, pp.12–51.

2. Adolf von Hildebrand, *Das Problem der Form in der bildenden Kunst*, Strasbourg: J.H.E. Heitz, 1893; Bernard Berenson, *The Central Italian Painters of the Renaissance*, New York: G.P. Putnam's Sons, 1897; Alois Riegl, *Die spätrömische Kunst-Industrie, nach den Funden in Österreich-Ungarn*, Vienna: K.K. Hof- und Staatsdruckerei, 1901, vol. 1; and Heinrich Wölfflin, *Kunstgeschichtliche Grundbegriffe: Das Problem der Stilentwicklung in der neueren Kunst*, Munich: F. Bruckmann, 1915.

3. Maurice Merleau-Ponty, *Phenomenology of Perception*, trans. C. Smith, London: Routledge and Kegan Paul, 1962; Michel Foucault, *The Birth of the Clinic: An Archaeology of Medical Perception*, trans. A.M. Sheridan Smith, New York: Pantheon Books, 1973; Luce Irigaray, *Ce sexe qui n'en est pas un*, Paris: Éditions de Minuit, 1977; and Martin Jay, *Downcast Eyes: The Denigration of Vision in Twentieth-Century French Thought*, Berkeley, CA: University of California Press, 1993.

4. For example, see: Laura U. Marks, *Touch: Sensuous Theory and Multisensory Media*, Minneapolis, MN: University of Minnesota Press, 2002; Susan Stewart, *Poetry and the Fate of the Senses*, Chicago, IL: University of Chicago Press, 2002; David Howes, *Sensual Relations: Engaging the Senses in Culture and Social Theory*, Ann Arbor, MI: University of Michigan Press, 2003; Constance Classen, ed., *The Book of Touch*, Oxford: Berg, 2005; Mark M. Smith, *Sensory History*, Oxford: Berg, 2007; Tony Bennett and Patrick Joyce, eds, *Material Powers: Cultural Studies, History and the Material Turn*, London and New York: Routledge, 2010; and Dan Hicks and Mary C. Beaudry, eds, *The Oxford Handbook of Material Cultural Studies*, Oxford and New York: Oxford University Press, 2010.

5. On art and the senses in Early Modern culture in general, see especially François Quiviger, *The Sensory World of Italian Renaissance Art*, London: Reaktion Books, 2010, and Alice E. Sanger and Siv Tove Kulbrandstad Walker, eds, *Sense and the Senses in Early Modern Art and Cultural Practice*, Aldershot: Ashgate, 2012.

6. David Summers, *The Judgment of Sense: Renaissance Naturalism and the Rise of Aesthetics*, Cambridge: Cambridge University Press, 1987, pp.32 ff.

7. Stephen J. Campbell, *The Cabinet of Eros: Renaissance Mythological Painting and the Studiolo of Isabella d'Este*, New Haven, CT: Yale University Press, 2004, p.110.

8. On the *Noli me tangere* theme, see the recent essay by Lisa M. Rafanelli, 'Thematizing Vision in the Renaissance: The *Noli Me Tangere* as a Metaphor for Art Making', in *Sense and the Senses in Early Modern Art and Cultural Practice*, A.E. Sanger and S.T. Kulbrandstad Walker, eds, Aldershot: Ashgate, 2012, pp.149–68.

9. On the *paragone* debate, see among others: Leatrice Mendelsohn, *Paragoni: Benedetto Varchi's Due Lezzioni and Cinquecento Art Theory*, Ann Arbor, MI: UMI Research Press, 1982; Ben Thomas, 'The *Paragone* Debate and Sixteenth-century Italian Art', D.Phil., University of Oxford, 1996, 2 vols; and Simonetta La Barbera Bellia, *Il paragone delle arti nella teoria artistica del Cinquecento*, Bhageria: Cafaro, 1997.

10. Paola Barocchi, ed., *Scritti d'arte del cinquecento: Pittura e scultura*, Milan and Naples: Riccardo Ricciardi editore, 1971, vol. 3, p.518.

11. Barocchi, *Scritti d'arte*, pp.533–4.

12. Barocchi, *Scritti d'arte*, p.637.

13. Erwin Panofsky, *Galileo as a Critic of the Arts*, The Hague: Matinus Nijhoff, 1954, p.35.

14. On this phenomenon, see especially Christiane Klapisch-Zuber, 'Holy Dolls: Play and Piety in Florence in the Quattrocento', in *Women, Family, and Ritual in Renaissance Italy*, trans. L.G. Cochrane, Chicago, IL: University of Chicago Press, 1985, pp.310–29.

15. On this statue, see Andrew Butterfield and Caroline Elam, 'Desiderio da Settignano's Tabernacle of the Sacrament', *Mitteilungen des Kunsthistorischen Institutes in Florenz*, 43, 1999, pp.333–57.

16. On half-length Marian reliefs, see Geraldine A. Johnson, 'Beautiful Brides and Model Mothers: The Devotional and Talismanic Functions of Early Modern Marian Reliefs', in *The Material Culture of Sex, Procreation, and Marriage in Premodern Europe*, A.L. McClanan and K.R. Encarnación, eds, New York: Palgrave, 2002, pp.135–61.

17. On Giovanni's veneration of the *Crucifixion* and the related visions he experienced, see Giovanni di Pagolo Morelli, *Ricordi*, ed. V. Branca, Florence: Felice Le Monnier, 1956, pp.476–516.

18. The prints are illustrated in Debora Kuller Shuger, *The Renaissance Bible: Scholarship, Sacrifice, and Subjectivity*, Berkeley, CA: University of California Press, 1994, figs 3a and 3b.

19. For an extended discussion of the collector's touch, see Geraldine A. Johnson, 'In the Hand of the Beholder: Isabella d'Este and the Sensory Allure of Sculpture', in *Sense and the Senses in Early Modern Art and Culture Practice*, A. Sanger and S.T. Kulbrandstad Walker, eds, Farnham: Ashgate, 2012, pp.183–97.

20. Luke Syson, 'The Medici Study', in *At Home in Renaissance Italy*, M. Ajmar-Wollheim and F. Dennis, eds, London: V&A, 2006, p.288.

21. Barocchi, *Scritti d'arte*, p.550.

22. Lorenzo Ghiberti, *I commentari*, ed. O. Morisani, Naples: Riccardo Ricciardi editore, 1947, pp.54–5.

23. The woodcut is discussed in Geraldine A. Johnson, 'Michelangelo, Canon Formation and Fortune Telling in Fanti's *Triompho di Fortuna*', in *Coming About: A Festschrift for John Shearman*, L. Jones and L. Matthew, eds, Cambridge, MA: Harvard University Art Museums, 2002, pp.199–205.

24. On this print, see Ben Thomas, 'The Academy of Baccio Bandinelli', *Print Quarterly*, 22, 2005, pp.3–14. I would like to thank Dr Thomas for kindly sending me a copy of this article.

25. James M. Saslow, *The Poetry of Michelangelo: An Annotated Translation*, New Haven, CT: Yale University Press, 1991, *passim*.

Bibliography

Barocchi, Paola, ed., *Scritti d'arte del cinquecento: Pittura e scultura*, Milan and Naples: Riccardo Ricciardi editore, 1971, vol. 3.

Bennett, Tony and Patrick Joyce, eds, *Material Powers: Cultural Studies, History and the Material Turn*, London and New York: Routledge, 2010.

Berenson, Bernard, *The Central Italian Painters of the Renaissance*, New York: G.P. Putnam's Sons, 1897.

Butterfield, Andrew and Caroline Elam, 'Desiderio da Settignano's Tabernacle of the Sacrament', *Mitteilungen des Kunsthistorischen Institutes in Florenz*, 43, 1999, pp.333–57.

Campbell, Stephen J., *The Cabinet of Eros: Renaissance Mythological Painting and the Studiolo of Isabella d'Este*, New Haven, CT: Yale University Press, 2004.

Classen, Constance, ed., *The Book of Touch*, Oxford: Berg, 2005.

Foucault, Michel, *The Birth of the Clinic: An Archaeology of Medical Perception*, trans. A.M. Sheridan Smith, New York: Pantheon Books, 1973.

Ghiberti, Lorenzo, *I commentari*, ed. O. Morisani, Naples: Riccardo Ricciardi editore, 1947.

Hicks, Dan and Mary C. Beaudry, eds, *The Oxford Handbook of Material Cultural Studies*, Oxford and New York: Oxford University Press, 2010.

Hildebrand, Adolf von, *Das Problem der Form in der bildenden Kunst*, Strasbourg: J.H.E. Heitz, 1893.

Howes, David, *Sensual Relations: Engaging the Senses in Culture and Social Theory*, Ann Arbor, MI: University of Michigan Press, 2003.

Irigaray, Luce, *Ce sexe qui n'en est pas un*, Paris: Éditions de Minuit, 1977.

Jay, Martin, *Downcast Eyes: The Denigration of Vision in Twentieth-Century French Thought*, Berkeley, CA: University of California Press, 1993.

Johnson, Geraldine A., 'Beautiful Brides and Model Mothers: The Devotional and Talismanic Functions of Early Modern Marian Reliefs', in *The Material Culture of Sex, Procreation, and Marriage in Premodern Europe*, A.L. McClanan and K.R. Encarnación, eds, New York: Palgrave, 2002, pp.135–61.

——, 'Michelangelo, Canon Formation and Fortune Telling in Fanti's Triompho di Fortuna', in *Coming About: A Festschrift for John Shearman*, L. Jones and L. Matthew, eds, Cambridge, MA: Harvard University Art Museums, 2002, pp.199–205.

——, 'Touch, Tactility and the Reception of Sculpture in Early Modern Italy', in *A Companion to Art Theory*, P. Smith and C. Wilde, eds, Oxford: Blackwell Publishers, 2002, pp.61–74.

——, 'The Art of Touch in Early Modern Italy', in *Art and the Senses*, F. Bacci and D. Melcher, eds, Oxford: Oxford University Press, 2011, pp.59–84.

——, 'Using the Photographic Archive: On the Life (and Death) of Images', in *Photo Archives and the Photographic Memory of Art History*, C. Caraffa, ed., Berlin and Munich: Deutscher Kunstverlag, 2011, pp.145–56.

——, 'In the Hand of the Beholder: Isabella d'Este and the Sensory Allure of Sculpture', in *Sense and the Senses in Early Modern Art and Culture Practice*, A. Sanger and S.T. Kulbrandstad Walker, eds, Farnham: Ashgate, 2012, pp.183–97.

——, '*(Un)richtige Aufnahme*: Renaissance Sculpture and the Visual Historiography of Art History', *Art History*, 36, 2013, pp.12–51.

Klapisch-Zuber, Christiane, 'Holy Dolls: Play and Piety in Florence in the Quattrocento', in *Women, Family, and Ritual in Renaissance Italy*, trans. L.G. Cochrane, Chicago, IL: University of Chicago Press, 1985, pp.310–29.

La Barbera Bellia, Simonetta, *Il paragone delle arti nella teoria artistica del Cinquecento*, Bhageria: Cafaro, 1997.

Marks, Laura U., *Touch: Sensuous Theory and Multisensory Media*, Minneapolis, MN: University of Minnesota Press, 2002.

Mendelsohn, Leatrice, *Paragoni: Benedetto Varchi's Due Lezzioni and Cinquecento Art Theory*, Ann Arbor, MI: UMI Research Press, 1982.

Merleau-Ponty, Maurice, *Phenomenology of Perception*, trans. C. Smith, London: Routledge and Kegan Paul, 1962.

Morelli, Giovanni di Pagolo, *Ricordi*, ed. V. Branca, Florence: Felice Le Monnier, 1956.

Panofsky, Erwin, *Galileo as a Critic of the Arts*, The Hague: Matinus Nijhoff, 1954.

Quiviger, François, *The Sensory World of Italian Renaissance Art*, London: Reaktion Books, 2010.

Rafanelli, Lisa M., 'Thematizing Vision in the Renaissance: The *Noli Me Tangere* as a Metaphor for Art Making', in *Sense and the Senses in Early Modern Art and Cultural Practice*, A.E. Sanger and S.T. Kulbrandstad Walker, eds, Aldershot: Ashgate, 2012, pp.149–68.

Riegl, Alois, *Die spätrömische Kunst-Industrie, nach den Funden in Österreich-Ungarn*, Vienna: K.K. Hof- und Staatsdruckerei, 1901.

Sanger, Alice E. and Siv Tove Kulbrandstad Walker, eds, *Sense and the Senses in Early Modern Art and Cultural Practice*, Aldershot: Ashgate, 2012.

Saslow, James M., *The Poetry of Michelangelo: An Annotated Translation*, New Haven, CT: Yale University Press, 1991.

Shuger, Debora Kuller, *The Renaissance Bible: Scholarship, Sacrifice, and Subjectivity*, Berkeley, CA: University of California Press, 1994.

Smith, Mark M., *Sensory History*, Oxford: Berg, 2007.

Stewart, Susan, *Poetry and the Fate of the Senses*, Chicago, IL: University of Chicago Press, 2002.

Summers, David, *The Judgment of Sense: Renaissance Naturalism and the Rise of Aesthetics*, Cambridge: Cambridge University Press, 1987.
Syson, Luke, 'The Medici Study', in *At Home in Renaissance Italy*, M. Ajmar-Wollheim and F. Dennis, eds, London: V&A, 2006, p.288.
Thomas, Ben, 'The Paragone Debate and Sixteenth-century Italian Art', D.Phil., University of Oxford, 1996, 2 vols.
——, 'The Academy of Baccio Bandinelli', *Print Quarterly*, 22, 2005, pp.3–14.
Wölfflin, Heinrich, *Kunstgeschichtliche Grundbegriffe: Das Problem der Stilentwicklung in der neueren Kunst*, Munich: F. Bruckmann, 1915.

The neglected power of touch: what the cognitive neurosciences can tell us about the importance of touch in artistic communication

Alberto Gallace and Charles Spence

> Touch reaches in man the maximum of discriminative accuracy. While in respect of all the other senses we fall below many species of animals, in respect of touch we far excel all other species in exactness of discrimination. That is why man is the most intelligent of all animals. This is confirmed by the fact that it is to differences in the organ of touch and to nothing else that the differences between man and man in respect of natural endowment are due; men whose flesh is hard are ill-endowed by nature, men whose flesh is soft, well-endowed.
>
> Aristotle, *On the Soul*, Book 2, part 9 (421a 20–25)

Introduction

It has been argued that among all of the senses, touch is the one that embodies the strongest emotional content.[1] The importance of the sense of touch has been recognised by many cultures in the ancient world (for example, see the above quote from Aristotle). In the past, touch has often been described as the natural barrier between that which is human and that which is divine. The Latin expression 'noli me tangere', do not touch me, the statement used by the resurrected Jesus before reaching a higher spiritual world, was a concept that was often reiterated in the medieval period. This expression was used to strengthen the idea that touch is 'the' human sense. Certainly, this could not come without a set of more-or-less obvious consequences. Since that time, touch has been indivisibly linked to sin, vice, sexuality, perversion, and even impurity as opposed to the holiness and purity of vision.

The Catholic Church has always recognised the risk of the voluptuous emotions that can result from tactile contact, and the facility with which even the most innocent of contacts may take on a libidinous character (see the

Moechialogia).[2] In fact, at certain points in human history, women were not even allowed to touch the altar cloth or receive the communion with their bare hands (see *Concil. Autissiodor.* AD 578, Can. 37 and 36, respectively).[3] In other words, over the years, religious and social restrictions have primarily been directed at the sense of touch rather than to the senses of vision or audition. Such restrictions regarding the possibility of people touching certain objects can also be found in contemporary society.[4]

As the quote with which we started this article shows, Aristotle defined touch as the sense that characterises and distinguishes humans from other animals. As the most human of our senses, touch is somehow perceived as an 'emotional' sense. Anger, fear, love, affection, sexual desire, all of these emotions are often easier to express, and to be understood, via the sense of touch.[5] On the basis of such considerations, it should not come as any surprise to find that artists (with their uncanny ability to anticipate and oftentimes 'understand' the properties of nature before scientists) have for many years been exploiting the sense of touch for both communicative and hedonic purposes.[6]

If one considers a stock definition of art culled for this purpose from Wikipedia as the 'product of deliberately arranging elements in a way to affect the senses or emotions', touch can certainly be considered among the more 'artistic' of the senses. As Rosalyn Driscoll notes, 'nothing arouses you like touch'. It is therefore in some respects surprising to see that, at various points in history, touch has been 'excluded' from the field of art (not only when actually restricted but also when artistic production has concentrated on two-dimensional images).[7] Ironically, even those pieces of art that were deliberately created in order to be touched have often, at a later date, been placed out-of-bounds to the human hand.[8] In fact, it is common practice for art galleries and museums to buy works of art that were created with the desire that they should be touched only to prohibit people (in particular, the public) from touching them in order to preserve them.

In this chapter, after briefly outlining a few of the key moments in the history of the use of touch in art, we discuss the importance of adding tactile contact for the artistic appreciation of a given object, be it a piece of art or merely a household object. That is, we try to answer the question of what exactly is lost when touch is prevented (or, in other words, what is special or unique about the sense of touch). In order to do this, we briefly summarise some of the key studies that have investigated the cognitive and neuroscientific aspects of tactile information processing in humans and which are especially relevant to this topic. This body of evidence unequivocally suggests that tactile contact has extremely important consequences for both our cognition and emotion. We conclude by arguing that preventing people from touching sculptures (or at least the replicas of works of art) and objects that have specifically been made to be touched severely hampers those educational benefits that constituted a critical element in the early development of museums and, to a lesser extent, art galleries. That is, showing sculpture without allowing people to touch it, might be usefully compared with asking customers to sit in a restaurant without permitting them to taste their food.

Tactile art

> Artists and designers love physical objects, especially if they have had a hand in making them. When people experience an art object tactilely, actually hold it in their hand, they understand something of what the artist was thinking when they created it.[9]

It is difficult to track back to the very origins of tactile art (or at least the desire to stimulate the sense of touch for the purpose of artistic expression), especially since, in this case, the work of anthropologists has typically been dominated (with very few exceptions, but see Doug Bailey's chapter earlier in this collection) by the visual attributes and qualities of their finds.[10] However, a few initial points can still be made on the basis of some of the earliest surviving works of art. Consider, for example, the 'Venus of Willendorf' (Naturhistorisches Museum, Vienna), a small statue representing a female figure with large breasts and hips estimated to have been created somewhere between 24,000–22,000 BC. This work seems to have been made to be touched. Its size (11.1 cm tall), and even its shape, mean that it would fit perfectly in the palm of one's hand. Even more relevant to this claim is the fact that the statue's feet do not allow it to stand-up by itself. In other words, it seems likely that the Venus had to be held in the hands of our ancestors in order to be properly appreciated. What is more, this object is made of limestone, a very heavy material. It seems possible that this tactile quality (that is, the weight) of the material used, might have been exploited explicitly by the piece's creator in order to express the status of the object (or even to communicate the concept of status itself).[11] Therefore, although the meaning of this sculpture (and of other similar statues from the Palaeolithic period) is still the object of much debate (with possible interpretations ranging from representations of security and success, a fertility icon, pornographic imagery, a direct representation of a woman/goddess or even a self-portrait), its strong relationship with the sense of touch certainly appears significant.[12] The existence of such objects might suggest, then, that the sense of touch played an important role in artistic expression and appreciation (and, more generally, in the life) of some of the earliest human cultures.[13]

Since the Renaissance, at least, the medium of sculpture has been explicitly linked to the sense of touch.[14] Certain artists have highlighted the importance of touch in their work. Brancusi, for example, suggested that 'Sculpture must be lovely to touch, friendly to live with, not only well made'.[15] Actually, anecdotal reports suggest that the artist loved to have his egg-shaped sculpture the *Beginning of the World* lying on a cushion or on his couch or, even better, on his lap, where he would touch it with his eyes closed).[16] It should also be noted here that Brancusi himself created a seminal piece of sculpture entitled *Sculpture for the Blind* (see Barassi's detailed discussion in Chapter 9 of this volume). This piece of art, when originally exhibited in New York in 1917, was apparently enclosed in a bag with two holes for the museum-goer's hands to pass through. The egg-like shape of this piece (a form common to several of Brancusi's works), was thought to represent the profundity of interiors and the mystery of creation.[17] The sense of touch thus seems to be connected in Brancusi's work with primitive and profound emotional content.

The use of touch constituted a particularly important aspect of the twentieth-century art movement known as 'Futurism'. Filippo Tommaso Marinetti defined 'Tattilismo' (or the 'Art of Touch') as a central aspect of his newly-created movement, a 'multisensorial' evolution of Futurism.[18] Marinetti even went so far as to suggest that humans might be able to 'penetrate' the very essence of matter without the aid of any scientific knowledge by means of 'Tattilismo'. People were, for example, invited to follow coloured tracks across 'tactile boards' made by the futurist artists. Sensations and rhythms were elicited by means of the progression of different materials (such as sponge, sandpaper, wool, brush, foil paper and velvet).

In one of Marinetti's boards, entitled *Sudan-Parigi* (*Sudan-Paris*) (see Fig. 6.1), Sudan was represented by materials and textures (such as sandpaper and metal brushes) giving rise to rough tactile sensations if touched. The sea was represented by materials associated with 'metallic' sensations (such as foil), and the city of Paris by softer materials including velvet, silk and feathers. Note that most of the meanings communicated by these objects and their surfaces cannot be fully apprehended by vision alone without reference to the tactile sensations elicited by touching such materials themselves.

Touch (and tactile stimulation) was a key aspect of the Futurist movement. A 'tactile theatre' was even created, in which the audience was presented with tactile stimulation (by means of a conveyor belt) that was harmonised with visual, auditory and/or olfactory stimuli.[19] In roughly the same period when Marinetti was presenting his 'Manifesto' of Tattilismo (and was taking people on 'hand journeys'[20]), a new educational current developed in Italy, one that made tactile experience an important component of the learning and creative process. In Montessori schools, young children were asked to follow the edges of three dimensional letters with the tips of their fingers in order to improve their reading and writing abilities.[21] Recently, it has been demonstrated that students educated in Montessori schools (that can now be found all over the globe) are significantly better at reading and mathematics, executive functions, social abilities and creativity under test conditions than children who have not been educated with these methods.[22] In other words,

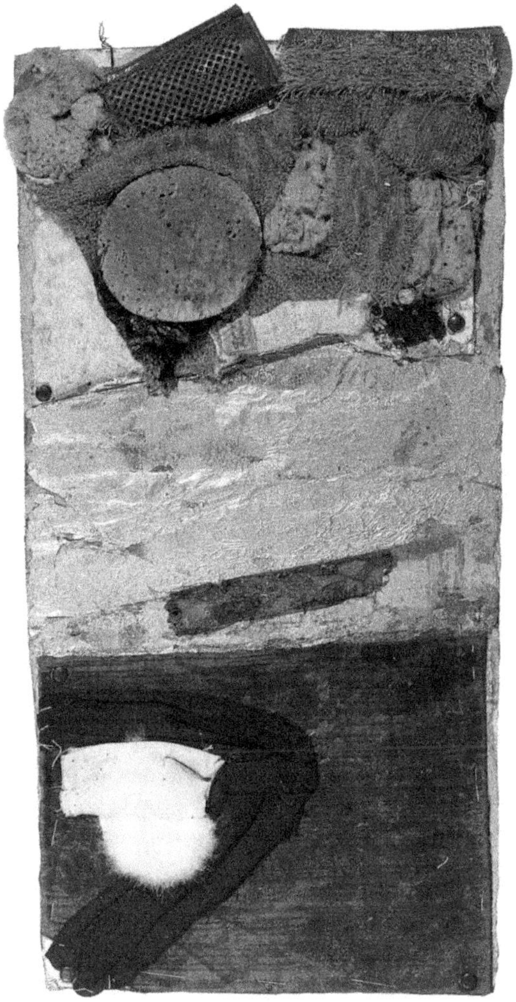

6.1 Filippo Tommaso Marinetti, *Sudan-Parigi*, mixed materials, 1922, private collection, Geneva [© DACS 2013]

the introduction of touch and, more generally, of a plethora of different sensory experiences in an educational context seems to enhance human learning and creativity.[23]

Surrealism also seems to have responded to the rising popularity of the sense of touch in education and artistic expression. This is witnessed by the increasing presence in the production of this artistic and cultural movement of the representation (in sculpture, just as in painting) of the human hand or of the glove as its simulacrum (mediating a concept related to the true expression of the conscious and unconscious self via automatic movements).[24]

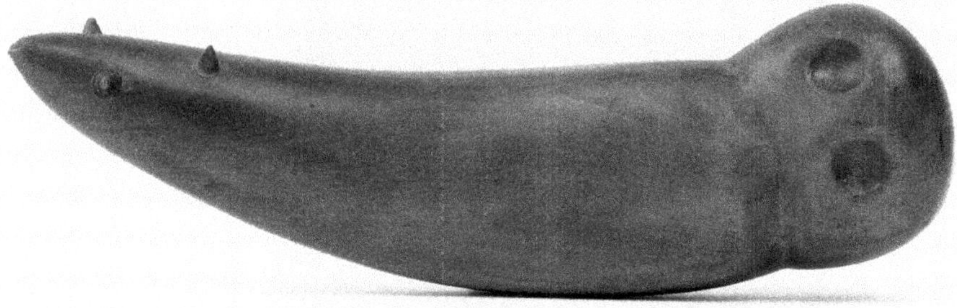

6.2 Alberto Giacometti, *Disagreeable Object*, wood, 1931, The Museum of Modern Art, New York (Private Collection, promised gift to the Museum of Modern Art, in honour of Kirk Varnedoe Acc. n. PG2467.2001.0) [© 2013. Digital image, The Museum of Modern Art, New York / Scala, Florence. © The Estate of Alberto Giacometti (Fondation Giacometti, Paris and ADAGP, Paris), licensed in the UK by ACS and DACS, London 2014.]

In 1930, in roughly the same period during which the Italian Futurist movement flourished, a more 'extremist' section of the French avant-garde begun to produce artistic works designed to appeal first and foremost to the sense of touch. One classic example of this trend is the *Disagreeable Object* (1931), a phallic-form sculpture (see Fig. 6.2) meant by its creator, Alberto Giacometti, to be touched. In this sculpture, just as in many other works by the same artist, there is always an allusion to the hand as the 'vital organ of sensual perception'.[25] Once again, touch was used here to stress the concept of sensuality and, more generally, to highlight the importance of bodily sensations to our aesthetic experiences (see also Michael Petry's *Party Number 1*).[26]

More recently, touch (or haptics as it is sometimes now called in order to stress the active, rather than passive, nature of most meaningful tactile stimulation) seems once again to have captured the interest of a new generation of artists. For example, in the Brazilian artist Ernesto Neto's work, smell and touch are just as important as sight.[27] Indeed, he uses materials that engage many of the senses. In certain of his productions, Neto creates semi-transparent rooms and soft cubes that recall skin-like membranes

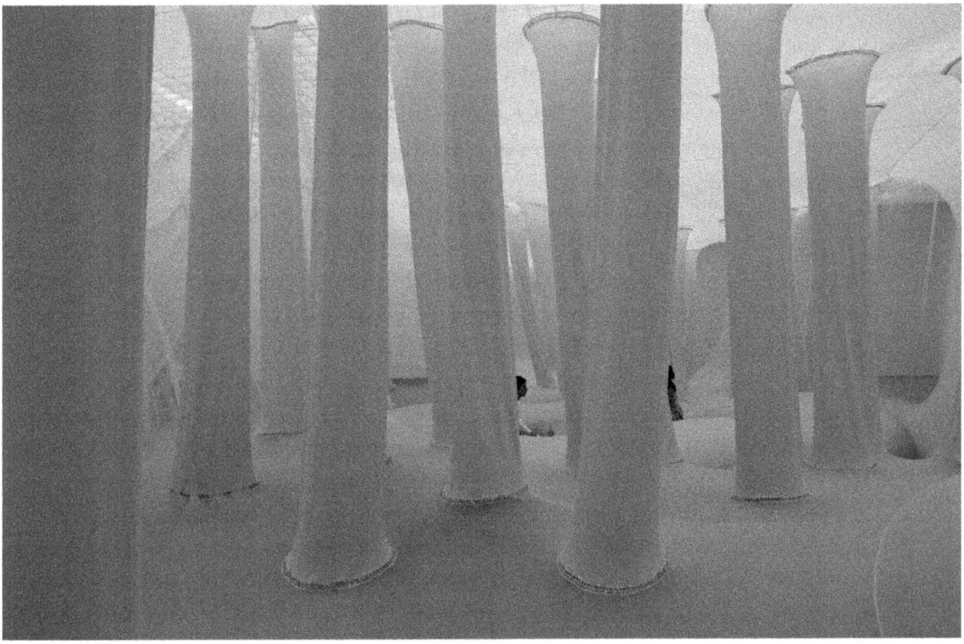

6.3 Ernesto Neto, *Cellula Nave*, mixed materials, Museum Booijmans van Beuningen, Rotterdam [© Niels (http://commons.wikimedia.org)]

(see, for example, his installation *Nude Plasmic*). These environments remind the visitor of the body's interior, something that is definitely 'organic'. The viewer enters these rooms and literally gets in touch with the work by pushing and pulling the materials while walking through and exploring the space. The fabric almost feels like a soft skin that necessitates a 'physical' relationship with the audience. In Neto's work, active 'interactions', where tactile sensations assume a leading role, are designed to provide a more intimate relationship between the artwork and the viewer (see Fig. 6.3).

The German artist Lilli Muller also requests her audience to interact with, and touch, her artworks.[28] These depict anamorphous shapes, part-human, part-plant, reminiscent of abstracted limbs and body-parts, and intestinal and sexual organs. By interacting with her sculptures and installations, often composed of huge foam balls, it is hoped that the audience begins to 'see' the unnoticeable, something that can only become apparent via touching or handling. Thus, the work of Lilli Muller, like that of Ernesto Neto, can be seen as highlighting the importance of the sense of touch as a source of deep emotional knowledge (by direct contact with the piece of art).

Another artist who has made touch her artistic signature is Rosalyn Driscoll.[29] The importance of touch for this artist is explicit: 'The language of the body is touch. I make sculptures that people can touch or that evoke the sense of touch. Aesthetic touch generates different connections, awareness and insights than looking. As someone said, "When you look it's an object, but when you touch it's a journey".' In Driscoll's works, which typically consist of diverse arrays of textured materials, such as stone, metal, rope and handmade paper, the viewer can trace the contours of her sculpture, feel its materials, and participate in its forms in ways similar to the artist's process of making objects. She suggests that works where the sense of touch is central bring more dimensions of one's being to the encounter and in the process create access to more sources of meaning.[30] Indeed, it is important to highlight here that touch is thought to encompass cutaneous contact, kinaesthesia and proprioception, and therefore, in some sense, the whole body.[31]

Finally, another contemporary artist who considers touch to constitute an important component of her artistic work is Miho Suganami.[32] In one of her projects, entitled *Have You Touched Your Hands*, members of the public made moulds of their hands. Miho then made castings of everyone's hands with plaster. These plaster hands were then mounted on a wall, and the audience invited to touch them. In a different session, the owners of the hands had to try to recognise their own hands from amongst the others, whilst blindfolded. The aim here was to make participants rediscover their own body and to demonstrate that sight is not necessarily always the most important of our senses.

The work of the contemporary artists cited in this section clearly suggests that the sense of touch is assuming a growing importance in artistic production.[33] There are a number of reasons why this trend is likely to continue. These factors include: a) a desire to breach the limits imposed by a society that may be making many people suffer from what Field has defined as 'touch hunger';[34] b) a belief that the sense of touch (and, more generally, multisensory stimulation) can lead to a more profound and emotional contact with art than that provided by unimodal visual stimulation; and c) the importance of making art accessible to the visually-impaired museum visitor.

It is somehow reassuring to see that despite all of the prohibitions that different cultures in different ages have more or less explicitly imposed on touching (of which the 'do not touch' signs in museums, art galleries, shops and so on are only the most recent),[35] artists belonging to different cultures have been able to exploit touch for their own artistic ends (even in Suganami's case making a piece of art consisting of a warm brick on which was etched the message 'Do not touch'). By contrast, it is rather unfortunate that even pieces of art that have been explicitly made to be touched are placed off-limits when acquired by museums and art institutions.[36] In summary, the examples reported in this section demonstrate that the sense of touch (perhaps because of its close links with bodily sensations) is often selected whenever very deep, primitive, emotional and sensual ideas are to be communicated. With this in mind, one may be justified in wondering what is lost when tactile content is prevented.

What is lost in terms of aesthetic appreciation when touch is prevented?

As my fingertips trace line and curve, they discover the thought and emotion which the artist has portrayed. I can feel in the faces of gods and heroes, hate, courage and love, just as I can detect them in living faces I am permitted to touch ... I sometimes wonder if the hand is not more sensitive to the beauties of sculpture than the eye. I should think the wonderful rhythmical flow of lines and curves could be more subtly felt than seen ... I know that I can feel the heart-throbs of the ancient Greeks in the marble gods and goddesses.[37]

A large body of research demonstrates that tactile contact can have a positive effect on our emotional and cognitive processes and on our general well-being. Part of this evidence comes from the literature on interpersonal touch (that is, human-to-human touch), and will not be discussed here (in part, because it is unclear how similar interpersonal touch is to inanimate, or object, touch).[38] But how important is human-to-object tactile contact, that is, inanimate touch? Are these aspects of our perception qualitatively significant or can everything of worth simply be appreciated by the eyes only (that is, by viewing the object)?

Both field and laboratory studies have suggested that touch plays an important role in shaping and affecting our experiences, that is, our aesthetic experiences, of many objects.[39] For instance, allowing people to touch objects (for example the objects placed on a touch table in a science museum or art gallery) increases the attention of the museum visitor and their subsequent ability to recall the experience.[40] This result accords well with a set of laboratory-based results showing that people can remember a given object or situation better if the information is presented from more than one sensory modality.[41] One gets a hint of the amount of information that is missed when people are not allowed to experience an object by touch from MacGregor regarding his haptic sensory analysis of a set of Scottish carved stone balls (CSBs):

The first thing that you notice when your hands close around a CSB is their coolness to the touch. As the lateral motion of the fingers explores the form of the object, the texture rapidly becomes apparent ... The initial enclosure of the hands rapidly established the sub-spherical shape of these objects and the exact form of them was rapidly determined by following their contours. In the case of the balls with a limited number of knobs, the number is readily and quickly established. When a larger number of knobs are present it becomes harder to establish the exact number by touch alone.[42]

The idea that vision alone is insufficient for the appreciation of certain qualities of sculpture seems to be expressed even more explicitly by Ghiberti, writing in the mid-fifteenth century: 'I have seen by diffused light ... a statue of Hermaphrodite ... that has been made with admirable skill ... In this [statue] there was the greatest refinement, which the eye would not have discovered, had not the hand sought it out.'[43]

Interestingly, a recent series of psychological experiments has shown that touching an inanimate object can even influence impression formation and decision-making outcomes regarding unrelated people and situations.[44] On the basis of such results, one can easily conclude that a given object can be experienced by people as being more important or serious than others, simply by changing its haptically-perceived temperature or weight (or, even more surprisingly, on the basis of changes regarding the perceived weight of the clipboard where participants have to write their rating!).

It turns out that there are receptors in the human non-glabrous skin that appear to code for pleasant touch,[45] and which respond vigorously to the slow stroking of the skin.[46] Even more importantly, it has been shown that certain areas of the brain, such as the orbitofrontal cortex (OFC), respond to 'pleasant touch' (as compared to neutral touch), such as the feel of velvet on the skin.[47]

Neuroimaging studies have shown that the OFC is involved in the representation of the reward value and of the subjective pleasantness of sensory stimuli.[48] It is worth noting here that neurophysiological studies on animals have shown that the OFC receives robust input from sensory cortices and associative information from the amygdale (a brain structure involved in the processing of emotional stimuli), and it sends both motor and limbic outputs to the striatum and nucleus accumbens.[49] That is, this structure appears to constitute the ideal candidate in terms of evaluating the affective value of sensory experiences and initiating a possible reaction to them.[50] Moreover, in humans, disruption of cortical activity in orbitofrontal, insular and other limbic regions has been shown to correlate with 'anhedonia' (a condition often associated with depression).[51]

Finally, activity in the OFC (as well as in the anterior cingulate cortex, insular cortex, amygdala, nucleus accumbens and related striatum, ventral pallidum and brainstem sites) appears to code for the occurrence of pleasure in humans and animals (see Fig. 6.4, for a representation of the position of the OFC in the human brain).[52] Therefore, it seems likely that this structure may play an important role in mediating our emotional responses to tactile stimuli. One important question here is: to what extent does tactile information contribute to the activation of the OFC when a multisensory stimulus is presented? And is the activation of the OFC elicited by visual stimuli alone sufficient to activate those neural networks responsible for our aesthetic evaluations? Finally, one might also wonder whether the activation of the OFC generated by stimuli that are designed to be touched is reduced when the same stimuli can only be seen. We believe that answering these questions will certainly help to determine, also from a neural point of view, what is really lost when people are not allowed to touch a given piece of art.

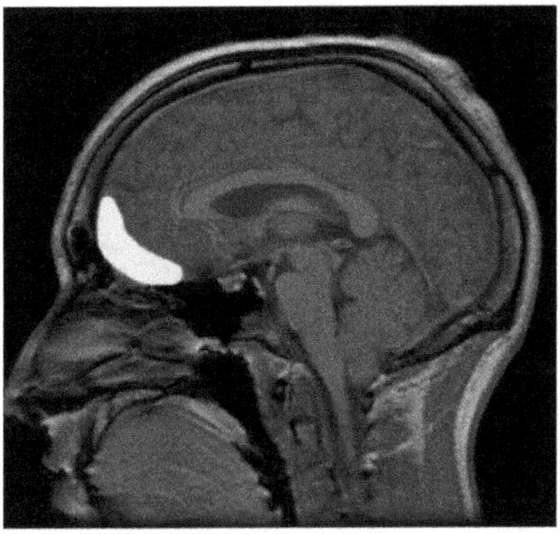

6.4 A representation of the position of the orbitofrontal cortex in the human brain [© Paul Wicks (http://commons.wikimedia.org)]

What is special in touch? The role of movement or 'when the viewer (user) becomes the artist'

> The tactual properties of our surroundings do not chatter at us like their colors; they remain mute until we make them speak. By our muscular activities we produce such properties as roughness and smoothness, and hardness and softness. We are truly the creators of these qualities.[53]

With these words, Katz gestures at the close relationship between the sense of touch and the ability to move our bodies in space. Note also that certain properties of the stimuli that we explore by touch (such as their weight and shape) are mainly determined by the effort exerted by our muscles on a given object.[54] The fact that, when touch is involved, we are necessarily actively engaged in the exploration of a given object makes the relationship between artist and perceiver all the more subtle. That is, as Katz would seem to suggest in the quote above, our decision regarding how to explore a given piece of art makes us similar to the creator of that art itself. Moreover, the infinite modes of haptic exploration associated with a given shape entail that any two people who explore the same object by touch will never have exactly the same experience of it. This peculiarity of touch is captured in the well-known ancient Indian tale in which a group of blind men (or blindfolded men) touch an elephant to learn what it is like. Each one of them handles a different part, such as the leg or the trunk. They then compare their opinions on what they felt, and understand that they are in complete disagreement (see Fig. 6.5). In other words, where tactile experiences are concerned the piece of art is not only unique in terms of its creation, but also in terms of the way in which it is explored.

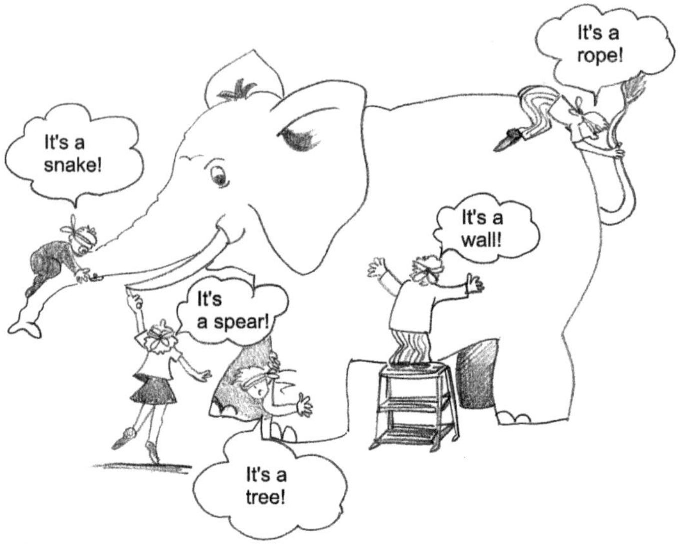

6.5 A representation of 'the blind men and the elephant' tale (see the main text for details) [© Elena Ceriotti]

The close link between touch and movement is something that has been one of the more widely-studied (although still least understood) aspects of human information processing in scientific research circles. For example, in the 1960s, researchers started to seriously consider this link while investigating the possibility of providing distal visual information via tactile interfaces to blind individuals. In particular, from the very beginnings of research on this topic, it has been shown that blind participants who have tried to use the tactile-visual sensory substitution (TVSS) system were only able to recognise the visual objects that had been 'translated' into tactile images when they were free to move the camera used to provide the visual input to the system.[55] The conclusion would appear to be that the perception of complex tactile stimuli always requires movement (or scanning) in order to be effective.

Interestingly, the relationship between touch and movement also works in the opposite direction. In particular, studies of 'sensory suppression' have demonstrated that whenever we move our bodies in space our sensitivity to detect the presence of tactile stimuli decreases.[56] That is, once again, there appears to be a fundamental relationship between our perception of touch and our movement. This relationship is also highlighted by the study of the neural aspects of tactile information processing. In fact, the tactile and motor areas of the brain are especially heavily interconnected (here one cannot help but point out the strict point-to-point anatomical correspondence between the sensory and motor maps on the precentral and postcentral gyrus of the brain).[57]

These observations strengthen the claim that in touch perceiving is not something passive, something that is mainly determined by the qualities of the object that we experience, but is a much more active process that cannot be fully separated from our active (or haptic) exploration of it. This is the reason why tactile contact reduces the boundaries between the artist and the perceiver. Given this distinctive aspect of touch, one might wonder to what extent our society is really willing to give up tactile contact in museums or art galleries. That is, for how long will we still limit this intimate and unique relationship between artist, viewer (or perhaps that should be user) and art?

Conclusions

Touch has always been important to artistic expression, even if for centuries those interpreting works of art have chosen instead to focus on their visual attributes. Interestingly, sculptors and artists have perhaps correctly intuited the phenomenal power of touch to communicate emotions and to affect our aesthetic judgments. However, it is only now that these intuitions can be complemented by the guidelines emerging from laboratory research. For example, cognitive neuroscience research has shown that our judgments of importance, weight, attractiveness and so on can all be affected by the object that we happen to be holding in our hands.[58] Indeed, the available neuroscience research now supports the claim that 'a weighty issue' is more than just a metaphorical expression!

Neuroscience research also shows that certain tactile stimuli (such as the feel of velvet on the skin) are effective in modulating the activation of certain areas of the brain involved in the perception of pleasure. Finally, the important link between touch and active movement, something that contributes to making the relationship between a person and a piece of art more intimate (and also reduces the physical distance between the observer and the observed object), has been highlighted in a number of studies. Given the above considerations, we believe that it is unfortunate that we do not let people touch artistic works more, despite the obvious political, curatorial and conservational issues around touch and sculpture.[59]

Certainly, one cannot avoid the fact that touching slowly destroys the object that is touched, and that art galleries obviously need to exercise their duty of care to preserve the works of art for future generations. One solution to this problem that has been raised elsewhere is to provide accurate replicas (accurate both in terms of their material properties and, ideally, size) of those artworks that are better experienced also by touch. Here, research in the cognitive neurosciences might help to provide the guidelines for the construction of these replicas.[60] For example, one might select characteristics that elicit similar patterns of neural activity as those provoked by the real objects when touched. We believe that a synergy of efforts between cognitive neuroscientists and art curators might offer important opportunities for the development of more complete and educational ways of experiencing art in museums and art galleries.

Notes

1. For reviews see T. Field, *Touch*, Cambridge, MA: MIT Press, 2001 and A. Gallace, and C. Spence, 'The Science of Interpersonal Touch: An Overview', *Neuroscience and Neurobehavioral Reviews*, 34, 2010, pp.246–59.
2. H. Ellis, *Studies in the Psychology of Sex*, New York: Random House, 1936.
3. O.J. Reichel, *A Complete Manual of Canon Law*, London: John Hodges, 1896.
4. See, for example, F. Candlin, 'Blindness, Art and Exclusion in Museums and Galleries', *Journal of Art and Design Education*, 22, 2003, pp.100–110; F. Candlin, 'Don't Touch! Hand Off! Art, Blindness and the Conservation of Expertise', *Body and Society*, 10, 2004, pp.71–90; F. Candlin, 'Touch and the Limits of the Rational Museum', *The Senses and Society*, 3, 2008, pp.277–92.
5. See M.J. Hertenstein, J.M. Verkamp, A.M. Kerestes and R.M., Holmes, 'The Communicative Functions of Touch in Humans, Nonhuman Primates, and Rats: A Review and Synthesis of the Empirical Research', *Genetic, Social, and General Psychology Monographs*, 132 (1), 2006, pp.5–94.
6. For example, R. Driscoll, *Aesthetic Touch/Haptic Art: Proceedings of the Eurohaptics 2006 Conference*, Paris, 2006; F.T. Marinetti, *Il manifesto del tattilismo* [The Futurist Manifesto], Milano: Comoaedia, 1921.
7. See J. Hall, *The World as Sculpture*, London: Random House, 1999.
8. See Candlin, 'Blindness', Candlin, 'Don't Touch!' and F. Bacci, 'Sculpture and Touch?', in *Art and the Senses*, F. Bacci and D. Mecher, eds, Oxford: Oxford University Press, 2011, pp.133–48.
9. R. Munoz, 'Foreword', in *Touch Graphics: The Power of Tactile Design*, R. Street and F. Lewis, eds, Gloucester, MA: Rockport, 2001, p.9.
10. See also G.A. Johnson, 'Touch, Tactility, and the Reception of Sculpture in Early Modern Italy', in *A Companion to Art Theory*, P. Smith and C. Wilde, eds, Oxford: Blackwell, 2002, pp.61–74.
11. J.M. Ackerman, C.C. Nocera and J.A. Bargh, 'Incidental Haptic Sensations Influence Social Judgments and Decisions', *Science*, 328, pp.1712–15.
12. L. McDermott, 'Self-representation in Upper Paleolithic Female Figurines', *Current Anthropology*, 37, 1996, pp.227–76; V.S. Ramachandran and W. Hirstein, 'The Science of Art: A Neurological Theory of Aesthetic Experience', *Journal of Consciousness Studies*, 6, 1999, pp.15–51.
13. Probably much more so than it does now; see T.R. Williams, 'Cultural Structuring of Tactile Experience in a Borneo Society', *American Anthropologist*, 68, 1966, pp.27–39, for an anthropological study of a tribe in Borneo showing the importance of touch in everyday life for people belonging to this 'primitive' culture.
14. See, for example, B. Berenson, *The Venetian Painters of the Renaissance: With an Index to Their Works*, New York: G. Putnam's Sons, 1894; R. Etlin, 'Aesthetics and the Spatial Sense of Self', *The Journal of Aesthetics and Art Criticism*, 56 (1), 1998, pp.1–19; Johnson, 'Touch and Tactility'; M. Merleau-Ponty, *Phenomenologie de la Perception* [The Phenomenology of Perception], Paris: Gallimard, 1945; though see also Hall, *World as Sculpture*.
15. See A.C. Tacha, 'Brancusi: Legend, Reality and Impact', *Art Journal*, 22, 1963, pp.240–41.
16. Tacha, 'Brancusi'.
17. Tacha, 'Brancusi'.
18. Marinetti, *Tattilismo*.
19. Marinetti, *Tattilismo*.
20. See Bacci, 'Sculpture and Touch?'.

21. See M. Montessori, *Il Metodo della Pedagogia Scientifica applicato all'educazione infantile nelle Case dei Bambini*, Lapi: Città di Castello, 1909 (first published in English as *The Montessori Method*, 1912); M. Montessori, *Come educare il potenziale umano* [How to Educate the Human Potential], Milano: Garzanti, 1943; M. Montessori, *Educazione per un mondo nuovo* [Education for a New World], Milan: Garzanti, 1991; A.S. Lillard and N.M. Else-Quest, 'An Evaluation of Montessori Education', *Science*, 313, 2006, pp.1893–4.

22. Lillard and Else-Quest, 'Montessori'.

23. See also J. Minogue and M.G. Jones, 'Haptics in Education: Exploring an Untapped Sensory Modality', *Review of Educational Research*, 76, 2006, pp.317–48.

24. See K.H. Powell, 'Hands on Surrealism', *Art History*, 20, 1997, pp.516–33.

25. A. Jolles, 'The Tactile Turn: Envisioning a Postcolonial Aesthetic in France', *Yale French Studies*, 109, 2006 (*Surrealism and Its Others*), pp.17–38).

26. Bacci, 'Sculpture and touch?'.

27. D. Ebony, 'Ernesto Neto at Bonakdar Jancou', *Art in America*, 87, 1999, p.11.

28. http://lillimuller.com/ (accessed: 1 May 2010).

29. http://www.rosalyndriscoll.com/ (accessed: 1 May 2010).

30. Driscoll, *Aesthetic Touch*.

31. R.L. Klatzky and S.J. Lederman, 'Touch', in *Experimental Psychology*, A.F. Healy and R.W. Proctor, eds, vol. 4 in *Handbook of Psychology*, I.B. Weiner, ed., New York: Wiley, 2002, pp.147–76.

32. http://www.suganami.freeserve.co.uk/ (accessed: 1 May 2010).

33. See also M. Diaconu, 'The Rebellion of the "Lower" Senses: A Phenomenological Aesthetics of Touch, Smell, and Taste', in *Essays in Celebration of the Founding of the Organization of Phenomenological Organizations*, H. Chan-Fai, I. Chvatik, I. Copoeru, L. Embree, J. Iribarne and H.R. Sepp, eds, 2003 [online] available at www.o-p-o.net (accessed: 3 March 2014); M. Diaconu, 'Reflections on an Aesthetics of Touch, Smell and Taste', *Contemporary Aesthetics*, 4, 2006 [online] available at www.contempaesthetics.org (accessed: 3 March 2014).

34. Field, *Touch*.

35. Candlin 'Blindness', and Candlin 'Don't Touch!'.

36. Candlin 'Blindness', Candlin, 'Don't Touch!' and Candlin, 'Touch and the Limits'.

37. H. Keller, *The Story of My Life*, London: George G. Harrap, 1923, pp.126–7.

38. See Gallace and Spence, 'Interpersonal Touch' for a review of this topic.

39. C. Jansson-Boyd and N. Marlow, 'Not Only in the Eye of the Beholder: Tactile Information Can Affect Aesthetic Evaluation', *Psychology of Aesthetics, Creativity, and the Arts*, 1, 2007, pp.170–73.

40. C. Spence and A. Gallace, 'Making Sense of Touch', in *Touch in Museums: Policy and Practice in Object Handling*, H. Chatterjee, ed., Oxford: Berg, 2008, pp.21–40.

41. See A. Gallace and C. Spence, 'The Cognitive and Neural Correlates of Tactile Memory', *Psychological Bulletin*, 135, 2009, pp.380–406, for a review.

42. G. MacGregor, 'Making Sense of the Past in the Present: A Sensory Analysis of Carved Stone Balls', *World Archaeology*, 31, 1999, pp.258–71, p.265 in particular.

43. L. Ghiberti, *I Commentari* [The Commentaries], ed. O. Morisani, Naples: Riccardo Ricciardi Editore, 1947, pp.54–5.

44. Ackerman, Nocera and Bargh, 'Haptic Sensations'.

45. F. McGlone, A.B. Vallbo, L. Loken and J. Wessberg, 'Discriminative Touch and Emotional Touch', *Canadian Journal of Experimental Psychology*, 61, 2007, pp.173–83.

46. For example, P. Bessou, P.R. Burgess, E.R. Perl and C.B. Taylor, 'Dynamic Properties of Mechanoreceptors with Unmyelinated (C) Fibers', *Journal of Neurophysiology*, 34, 1971, pp.116–31.

47. S. Francis, E.T. Rolls, R. Bowtell, F. McGlone, J. O'Doherty, A. Browning, S. Clare and E. Smith, 'The Representation of Pleasant Touch in the Brain and Its Relationship with Taste and Olfactory Areas', *Neuroreport*, 25, 1999, pp.453–9.

48. For example, E.T. Rolls, 'The Orbitofrontal Cortex and Reward', *Cerebral Cortex*, 10, 2000, pp.284–94.
49. G. Schoenbaum, M.R. Roesch and T.A. Stalnaker, 'Orbitofrontal Cortex, Decision-making and Drug Addiction', *Trends in Neurosciences*, 29, 2006, pp.116–24.
50. A. Dickinson and B. Balleine, 'Hedonics: The Cognitive-Motivational Interface', in *Pleasures of the Brain*, M.L. Kringelbach and K.C. Berridge, eds, Oxford: Oxford University Press, 2009, pp.74–84.
51. P.A. Keedwell, C. Andrew, S.C. Williams, M.J. Brammer and M.L. Phillips, 'The Neural Correlates of Anhedonia in Major Depressive Disorder', *Biological Psychiatry*, 58, 2005, pp.843–53.
52. See K.C. Berridge and M.L. Kringelbach, 'Affective Neuroscience of Pleasure: Reward in Humans and Animals', *Psychopharmacology*, 99, 2008, pp.457–80, for a review.
53. D. Katz, *The World of Touch*, Hillsdale, NJ: Erlbaum Associates, 1989, p.240.
54. S.J. Lederman and R.L Klatzky, 'Multisensory Texture Perception', in *The Handbook of Multisensory Processes*, G.A. Calvert, C. Spence and B.E. Stein, eds, Cambridge, MA: MIT Press, 2004, pp.107–22.
55. See, for example, P. Bach-y-Rita, *Brain Mechanisms in Sensory Substitution*, New York: Academic Press, 1972; P. Bach-y-Rita, C.C. Collins, F. Saunders, B. White and L. Scadden, 'Vision Substitution by Tactile Image Projection', *Nature*, 221, 1969, pp.963–4.
56. See Gallace and Spence, 'Interpersonal Touch' and G. Juravle, H. Deubel, H.Z. Tan and C. Spence, 'Changes in Tactile Sensitivity over the Timecourse of a Goal-directed Movement', *Behavioural Brain Research*, 208, 2010, pp.391–401.
57. D.J. Felleman and D.C. Van Essen, 'Distributed Hierarchical Processing in Primate Cerebral Cortex', *Cerebral Cortex*, 1, 1991, pp.1–47; W. Penfield and E. Boldrey, 'Somatic Motor and Sensory Representation in the Cerebral Cortex of Man as Studied by Electrical Stimulation', *Brain*, 60, 1937, pp.389–443.
58. For example, L.E. Williams and J.A. Bargh, 'Experiencing Physical Warmth Promotes Interpersonal Warmth', *Science*, 322, 2008, pp.606–7.
59. See also Bacci, 'Sculpture and Touch?'.
60. Spence and Gallace, 'Making Sense' and M. Karlsson and A.V. Velasco, 'Designing for the Tactile Sense: Investigating the Relation between Surface Properties, Perceptions and Preferences', *CoDesign*, 3 (Supplement 1), 2007, pp.123–33.

Bibliography

Ackerman, J.M., C.C. Nocera and J.A. Bargh, 'Incidental Haptic Sensations Influence Social Judgments and Decisions', *Science*, 328, 2010, pp.1712–15.

Bacci, Francesca, 'Sculpture and Touch', in *Art and the Senses*, Francesca Bacci and David Melcher, eds, Oxford: Oxford University Press, 2011, pp.133–48.

Bach-y-Rita, P., *Brain Mechanisms in Sensory Substitution*, New York: Academic Press, 1972.

Bach-y-Rita, P., C.C. Collins, F. Saunders, B. White and L. Scadden, 'Vision Substitution by Tactile Image Projection', *Nature*, 221, 1969, pp.963–4.

Berenson, B., *The Venetian Painters of the Renaissance: With an Index to Their Works*, New York: G. Putnam's Sons, 1894.

Berridge, K.C. and M.L. Kringelbach, 'Affective Neuroscience of Pleasure: Reward in Humans and Animals', *Psychopharmacology*, 99, 2008, pp.457–80.

Bessou, P., P.R. Burgess, E.R. Perl and C.B. Taylor, 'Dynamic Properties of Mechanoreceptors with Unmyelinated (C) Fibers', *Journal of Neurophysiology*, 34, 1971, pp.116–31.

Candlin, Fiona, 'Blindness, Art and Exclusion in Museums and Galleries', *Journal of Art and Design Education*, 22, 2003, pp.100–110.

——, 'Don't Touch! Hands Off! Art, Blindness and the Conservation of Expertise', *Body and Society*, 10, 2004, pp.71–90.

——, 'Touch and the Limits of the Rational Museum', *The Senses and Society*, 3, 2008, pp.277–92.
Diaconu, M., 'The Rebellion of the "Lower" Senses: A Phenomenological Aesthetics of Touch, Smell, and Taste', in *Essays in Celebration of the Founding of the Organization of Phenomenological Organizations*, H. Chan-Fai, I. Chvatik, I. Copoeru, L. Embree, J. Iribarne and H.R. Sepp, eds, 2003 [online] available at www.o-p-o.net (accessed: 3 March 2014).
——, 'Reflections on an Aesthetics of Touch, Smell and Taste', *Contemporary Aesthetics*, 4, 2006 [online] available at www.contempaesthetics.org (accessed: 3 March 2014).
Dickinson, A. and B. Balleine, 'Hedonics: The Cognitive-Motivational Interface', in *Pleasures of the Brain*, M.L. Kringelbach and K.C. Berridge, eds, Oxford: Oxford University Press, 2009, pp.74–84.
Driscoll, Rosalyn, *Aesthetic Touch/Haptic Art: Proceedings of the Eurohaptics 2006 Conference*, Paris, 2006.
Ebony, D., 'Ernesto Neto at Bonakdar Jancou', *Art in America*, 87, 1999, p.11.
Ellis, H., *Studies in the Psychology of Sex*, New York: Random House, 1936.
Etlin, R., 'Aesthetics and the Spatial Sense of Self', *The Journal of Aesthetics and Art Criticism*, 56 (1), 1998, pp.1–19.
Felleman, D.J. and D.C. Van Essen, 'Distributed Hierarchical Processing in Primate Cerebral Cortex', *Cerebral Cortex*, 1, 1991, pp.1–47.
Field, T., *Touch*, Cambridge, MA: MIT Press, 2001.
Francis, S., E.T. Rolls, R. Bowtell, F. McGlone, J. O'Doherty, A. Browning, S. Clare and E. Smith, 'The Representation of Pleasant Touch in the Brain and Its Relationship with Taste and Olfactory Areas', *Neuroreport*, 25, 1999, pp.453–9.
Gallace, Alberto and Charles Spence, 'The Cognitive and Neural Correlates of Tactile Memory', *Psychological Bulletin*, 135, 2009, pp.380–406.
——, 'The Science of Interpersonal Touch: An Overview', *Neuroscience and Neurobehavioral Reviews*, 34, 2010, pp.246–59.
Ghiberti, Lorenzo, *I commentari*, O. Morisani, ed., Naples: Riccardo Ricciardi Editore, 1947.
Hall, James, *The World as Sculpture*, London: Random House, 1999.
Hertenstein, M.J., J.M. Verkamp, A.M. Kerestes and R.M. Holmes, 'The Communicative Functions of Touch in Humans, Nonhuman Primates, and Rats: A Review and Synthesis of the Empirical Research', *Genetic, Social, and General Psychology Monographs*, 132 (1), 2006, pp.5–94.
Jansson-Boyd, C. and N. Marlow, 'Not Only in the Eye of the Beholder: Tactile Information Can Affect Aesthetic Evaluation', *Psychology of Aesthetics, Creativity, and the Arts*, 1, 2007, pp.170–73.
Johnson, Geraldine A., 'Touch, Tactility, and the Reception of Sculpture in Early Modern Italy', in *A Companion to Art Theory*, P. Smith and C. Wilde, eds, Oxford: Blackwell, 2002, pp.61–74.
Jolles, A., 'The Tactile Turn: Envisioning a Postcolonial Aesthetic in France', *Yale French Studies*, 109, 2006 (*Surrealism and Its Others*), pp.17–38.
Juravle, G., H. Deubel, H.Z. Tan and C. Spence, 'Changes in Tactile Sensitivity over the Timecourse of a Goal-directed Movement', *Behavioural Brain Research*, 208, 2010, pp.391–401.
Karlsson, M. and A.V. Velasco, 'Designing for the Tactile Sense: Investigating the Relation between Surface Properties, Perceptions and Preferences', *CoDesign*, 3 (Supplement 1), 2007, pp.123–33.
Katz, D., *The World of Touch*, Hillsdale, NJ: Erlbaum Associates, 1989.
Keedwell, P.A., C. Andrew, S.C. Williams, M.J. Brammer and M.L. Phillips, 'The Neural Correlates of Anhedonia in Major Depressive Disorder', *Biological Psychiatry*, 58, 2005, pp.843–53.

Keller, H., *The Story of My Life*, London: George G. Harrap, 1923.
Klatzky, R.L. and S.J. Lederman, 'Touch', in *Experimental Psychology*, A.F. Healy and R.W. Proctor eds, vol. 4 in *Handbook of Psychology*, I.B. Weiner, ed., New York: Wiley, 2002, pp.147–76.
Lederman, S.J. and R.L. Klatzky, 'Multisensory Texture Perception', in *The Handbook of Multisensory Processes*, G.A. Calvert, C. Spence and B.E. Stein, eds, Cambridge, MA: MIT Press, 2004, pp.107–22.
Lillard, A.S. and N.M. Else-Quest, 'An Evaluation of Montessori Education', *Science*, 313, 2006, pp.1893–4.
MacGregor, G., 'Making Sense of the Past in the Present: A Sensory Analysis of Carved Stone Balls', *World Archaeology*, 31, 1999, pp.258–71.
Marinetti, F.T., *Il manifesto del tattilismo*, Milano: Comoaedia, 1921.
McDermott, L., 'Self-representation in Upper Paleolithic Female Figurines', *Current Anthropology*, 37, 1996, pp.227–76.
McGlone, F., A.B. Vallbo, L. Loken and J. Wessberg, 'Discriminative Touch and Emotional Touch', *Canadian Journal of Experimental Psychology*, 61, 2007, pp.173–83.
Merleau-Ponty, M., *Phenomenologie de la perception*, Paris: Gallimard, 1945.
Minogue, J. and M.G. Jones, 'Haptics in Education: Exploring an Untapped Sensory Modality', *Review of Educational Research*, 76, 2006, pp.317–48.
Montessori, M., *Il Metodo della Pedagogia Scientifica applicato all'educazione infantile nelle Case dei Bambini*, Lapi: Città di Castello, 1909.
——, *Come educare il potenziale umano*, Milano: Garzanti, 1943.
——, *Educazione per un mondo nuovo*, Milan: Garzanti, 1991.
Munoz, R., 'Foreword', in *Touch Graphics: The Power of Tactile Design*, R. Street and F. Lewis, eds, Gloucester, MA: Rockport, 2001, p.9.
Penfield, W. and E. Boldrey, 'Somatic Motor and Sensory Representation in the Cerebral Cortex of Man as Studied by Electrical Stimulation', *Brain*, 60, 1937, pp.389–443.
Powell, K.H., 'Hands-on Surrealism', *Art History*, 20, 1997, pp.516–33.
Ramachandran, V.S. and W. Hirstein, 'The Science of Art: A Neurological Theory of Aesthetic Experience', *Journal of Consciousness Studies*, 6, 1999, pp.15–51.
Reichel, O.J., *A Complete Manual of Canon Law*, London: John Hodges, 1896.
Rolls, E.T., 'The Orbitofrontal Cortex and Reward', *Cerebral Cortex*, 10, 2000, pp.284–94.
Schoenbaum, G., M.R. Roesch and T.A. Stalnaker, 'Orbitofrontal Cortex, Decision-making and Drug Addiction', *Trends in Neurosciences*, 29, 2006, pp.116–24.
Spence, C. and A. Gallace, 'Making Sense of Touch', in *Touch in Museums: Policy and Practice in Object Handling*, H. Chatterjee, ed., Oxford: Berg, 2008, pp.21–40.
Tacha, A.C., 'Brancusi: Legend, Reality and Impact', *Art Journal*, 22, 1963, pp.240–41.
Williams, L.E. and J.A. Bargh, 'Experiencing Physical Warmth Promotes Interpersonal Warmth', *Science*, 322, 2008, pp.606–7.
Williams, T.R., 'Cultural Structuring of Tactile Experience in a Borneo Society', *American Anthropologist*, 68, 1966, pp.27–39.

7

When touch shatters meaning: the case of sculptures made for sight only

Francesca Bacci

The relationship between touch and sculpture is rich and complex. In the act of sculpting, the gesture that imposes the shaping will onto the formless matter performs an action but also receives feedback through the sense of touch. The reaction of the matter to the gesture yields a great amount of information. If this tactile and sensory-motor information is received by an experienced sculptor (that is, by an individual with an extensive knowledge of past interaction with clay, plaster or stone), then it will sensibly modify and regulate every further action that the artist will undertake upon the medium. It is this accumulation of hand experiences with the material that, ultimately, influences greatly the artist's style.

This seldom considered phenomenon appears evident to practising sculptors who work in traditional media such as wood, clay or marble, as American sculptor Malvina Hoffman (1887–1966) exemplarily reported. In 1939, she authored an instruction manual for young artists, titled *Sculpture Inside and Out*. One of the tenets of her method was an insistence on extensive practice as a necessary route to students achieving mastery over the medium, to 'train their hands to obey their minds'.[1] This was encouraged not so that the students would become able to subjugate the matter to their own will, but in order to allow the expression of one's own style to flow freely, unobstructed by the incompetence of the hands. However, such style – and here comes the most surprising point – is largely determined by the medium of sculpture itself. She wrote:

> It would be well for students to understand why they should carve directly in stone while they are studying the first principles of sculpture. … The resistance of the stone controls their minds; the appearance of forms as they emerge in the stone gives the carver a new demonstration of why the stone demands a solid form. Details and personal attributes are automatically subordinated to

> the basic needs of the material. Training that is limited to modelling in clay, for casting into bronze, is liable to lead the student into dangerous channels. He will probably become intrigued in the details of drapery, expression of the face, gestures of action, etc. The plastic consistency of clay is a temptation to model unessentials. … The discipline which stone and marble impose upon the artist, however, is unquestionably the best teacher that a student could have. Stone is a taskmaster that is unprejudiced, that presents the same obstacles to every student, old or young, archaic or modern, that commands undivided attention and tenacity of purpose, strong steady hands, and infinite patience.[2]

In other words, Hoffman reported that tactile acquisition of information during the carving of stone is responsible for the artist's stylistic choices. What expert hands have learnt to discern are 'the needs of the material' and 'the resistance of stone'. It is this tactile learning that shapes the formal thinking of the sculptor. According to Hoffman, style would develop as a consequence of tactile interaction with the raw matter, and not, as more commonly held, as a visually-guided choice.

Correspondingly, some scientists came to believe that the sense of sight learns to identify objects upon matching their visual features to sensory information coming from touch. As Aristotle had already noticed in the fourth century BC, '… this sense in man is highly discriminating; in the other senses he is behind many kinds of animal, but in touch he is much more discriminating than the other animals'.[3] It was Bishop George Berkeley, in 1709, who theorised the superiority of touch over sight in his *Essay Towards a New Theory of Vision*, where he maintained that touch teaches vision and, empirically, that space is not understood visually but haptically.[4] In 1866, the German scientist Hermann von Helmholtz described visual perceptions as unconscious inferences from sensory data and knowledge derived from the past.[5] More recently, following von Helmholtz's lead, vision scientist Richard Gregory wrote that 'knowledge is necessary for vision because retinal images are inherently ambiguous (for example for size, shape and distance of objects), and because many properties that are vital for behaviour cannot be signalled by the eyes, such as hardness and weight, hot or cold, edible or poisonous'. Moreover, 'perceptions are hypotheses, predicting unsensed characteristics of objects, and predicting in time, to compensate neural signalling delay'.[6]

Perception, especially vision, is not a passive window on the world, but it requires intelligent problem-solving based on knowledge. Instructive in this regard is the experience of Gregory with a patient, Mr Bradford, who acquired sight via corneal grafts after a lifetime of blindness. To his surprise, the man was immediately able to read the time on a wall-clock, despite having never seen one before – but having touched the clock's hands for a lifetime. Technically, the patient showed cross-modal transfer from touch to vision, so he was able to solve the problem of the meaning of what he was seeing for the first time. 'Vision was generally thought to be separate from the other senses' wrote Gregory, 'and is still mainly studied in isolation; yet Bradford showed that exploratory touch – as well no doubt as taste, sound and other sensory experiences – gives richness and meaning to retinal images. For optical images are but ghosts, materialised into objects by perceptual experience of the non-visual properties of things.'[7] These modern discoveries seem to partially confirm a very old hypothesis. What Aristotle had called *sensus communis* was the part of the psyche responsible for binding the inputs of the individual sense organs into a coherent and intelligible representation. According to the philosopher and theologian Thomas Aquinas, the fundamental basis for the *sensus communis* is to be found in the sense of touch, as he wrote in his commentary to Aristotle's *De anima* (3. lect. 3. 602): '[Touch] is the first and in a way the root and foundation of all senses. ... This power is attributed to the sense of touch not as a proper sense, but because it is the foundation of all senses and the closest to the fontal root of all senses, which is common sense.'[8]

At the same time, other scientists have focused on the ways in which sight can influence tactile perception.[9] As early as 1832, Sir David Brewster considered the question of sensory dominance in his book *Natural Magic.* He described

> how optically left-right reversing an indented object (an engraved watch seal) results in the concavities (or depressions) of the seal appearing visually as protuberances (or elevations) instead. According to Brewster, the seal will actually '*feel*' as if it is elevated as well when explored haptically, thus showing the dominance of vision over the conflicting tactile/haptic sensations.[10]

In an influential study, Ernst and Banks varied the reliability of visual and haptic information and found that judgments optimally combined the data from the two senses, weighing more the sense which displays a more accurate input.[11] But what happens when the information coming from the two different sensory modalities is not only different, but contradictory? What if the visually-constructed idea of the object that forms in our awareness is subverted, if not destroyed, upon touching that object? Despite the interconnectedness of the senses of touch and sight, and the powerful embodied feel of visual input, there are artworks that are best apprehended uni-modally, and the simultaneous information coming from two different senses may threaten their aesthetic effect.

In sculpture, the most striking case may be that of negative-relief, that is a bas-relief that is concave rather than convex, developing in depth rather than projecting out. We are mostly accustomed to seeing this type of relief when looking at plaster moulds bearing the imprint of a three-dimensional shape. With proper lighting, these negative-reliefs can create a powerful visual illusion that makes them appear as if they were projecting out. This phenomenon, called the 'hollow mask illusion', was described in great detail by Gregory in an elegant experiment using a mask of Charlie Chaplin. Viewing the mask from the hollow side with both eyes, it appears convex. If the mask is rotated, or the observer moves, it appears to rotate in the opposite

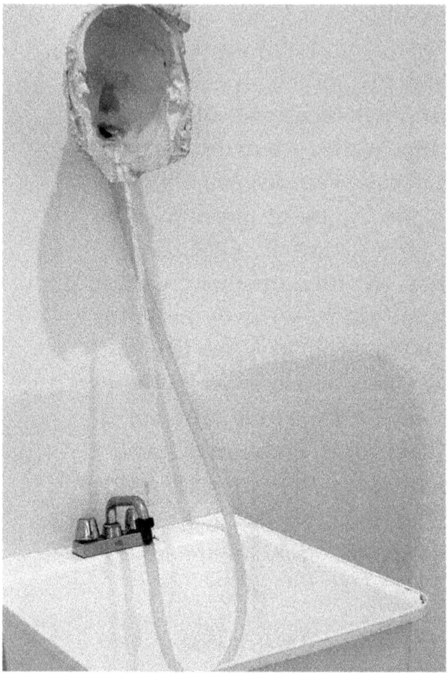

7.1 Bruce Nauman, *Fountain*, mixed materials, 2007, Venice Biennale. Courtesy Amie Lawless

to normal direction, at twice the speed. Gregory observed that our experience of faces being convex prevails over the sensory data suggesting that what we are observing may be hollow – or in his words 'top-down knowledge of faces is pitted against bottom-up signalled information'.[12] Touching the face will interfere with the illusion, making it confusing for the brain to integrate the information from the two modalities. An installation which exploited this effect for artistic purposes is Bruce Nauman's *Fountain*, presented at the Venice Biennale in 2007 (Fig. 7.1), in an exhibition aptly titled *Think With the Senses, Feel With the Mind: Art in the Present Tense*. The artist assembled a sink and a bucket with a cast of a face hanging above, connecting them with clear plastic tubing so that the water would spurt out of the figure's mouth. This detail reinforced the impression that the face must be positive, as indeed all real faces are, while cleverly referencing one of the most famous works by Nauman, *Self-Portrait as Fountain* (1966).

The effect of the sensation of convexity in a concave form had been noticed long before in the artistic *milieu*, as a photograph published in Malvina Hoffman's 1939 book demonstrates (in the caption, one can read: 'note the effect of top lighting on concave forms, giving illusion of positive relief lighted from below').[13] Specifically, in modern times the interest in inverting the relationship between hollow and full in sculpture can be traced back to the experiments of the Constructivist artist Naum Gabo (1890–1977). He developed a method called 'stereometric construction', which consisted in conveying the idea of volume through the use of a combination of planes and hollow spaces rather than portraying the volume through the use of masses. A series of heads and figures dating 1915–1920 are exemplary of the application of this system (see, for example, Gabo's *Head No. 2*, 1916, made in cor-ten steel and presently in the Tate's Collection). In these sculptures the face appears as if drawn in three dimensions, with the contour lines made by the edge of solid planes connecting at the core of the form. The volume of the figure is no longer made visible through a solid mass, of the sort typically employed in sculpture, but it is replaced by wedges of empty space filled only by air. Clearly a tactile approach to these sculptures would yield very confusing information regarding the identity of the subject, which is effectively drawn in space.

One complex instance of exploitation of the artistic potential of negative forms is the work of Rachel Whiteread. The British artist produces massive casts of the space which is not occupied by objects, such as the underside of chairs or of an entire staircase, which she calls 'negative spaces'. What is significant to the artist's message is that these normally unacknowledged spaces become solid, thus making their presence visible. In an essay on Whiteread's work, David Batchelor suggests that these casts elicit a 'strange familiarity':

> once more we have to learn to see cavities as protrusions ... and protrusions as cavities. In this way, moving around the work and inspecting the details, we gradually build up a picture of something very familiar – a living room. Something so familiar we would never normally spend much time or attention looking at it.

He then proceeds to compare the process of the creation of these sculptures to photography:

> as with photography, casting's relationship with its original is indexical rather than autographic. Each represents by leaving a trace of one material upon another .... The process is closer to transfer than to translation. And in each certain properties are transferred while others are omitted. Whiteread's sculptures are in this sense monochrome monotone negatives – utterly faithful to and yet at the same time utterly unlike the subjects from which they are derived.[14]

Touching such works can turn them into new objects to apprehend, rather than the recognisable solidified spaces that they are intended to be. It is already quite compelling, for the public, to reconstruct via inversion the visual identity of an object from its cast, where convexities are concavities and vice versa. Adding touch to the equation may potentially disrupt the apprehension of the piece – and yet, conceptually, touch is very present in these works, albeit in a sublimated form. We, the onlookers, come to physically occupy a space which is usually full of something else – of static objects, of lack of air – a space that has been freed for us by the inversion that the artist has performed, and that our touch could not usually penetrate.

It is worth noticing that on occasion, artists can attribute symbolic meanings to the presence or absence of matter. The figure of the angel cast on the bronze doors of the Cathedral of Concordia Sagittaria, Venice (Fig. 7.2) utilises the formal device of negative-relief to convey the spiritual nature of the character, which does not have a material body. In contrast, the adjacent figure of Christ, resurrected in flesh and in spirit, is represented in bas-relief to underline that it is his body too, and not just his soul, that is ascending to heaven. The artist has thus created a personal iconography where the alternating appearance of void and volume comes to symbolise the two natures of Jesus (spiritual and earthly/bodily).

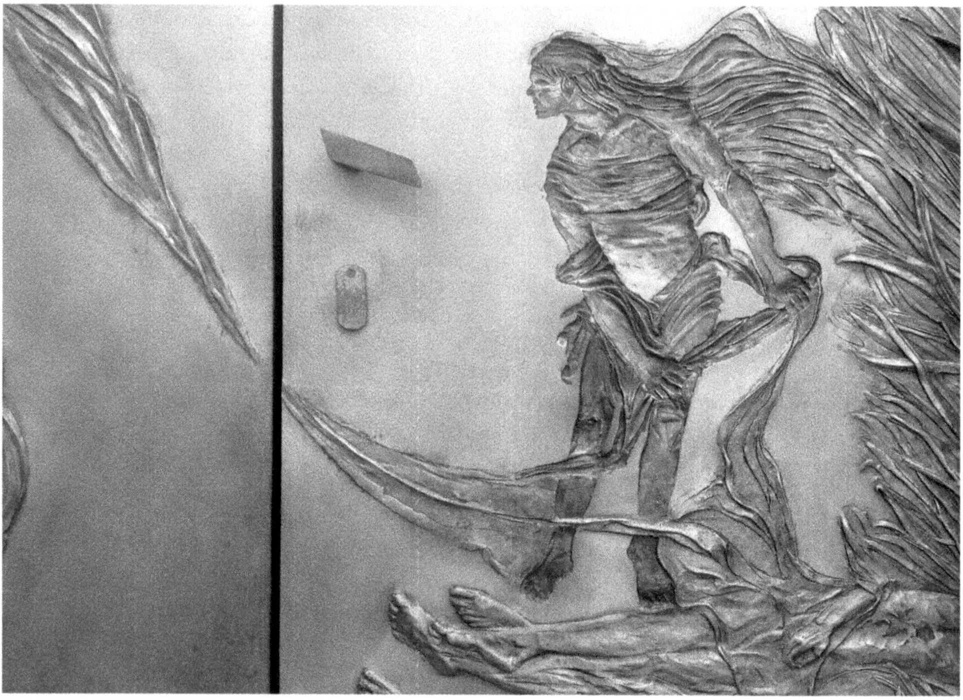

7.2 Fiorenzo Bacci, *Angel*, bronze, Cathedral, Concordia Sagittaria, Venice [© Francesca Bacci]

One perceptually interesting case is that of ambiguous wire figures. When viewed from a distance greater than one meter, Alberto Giacometti's sculpture *Study for the Palace at 4 a.m.* (1932) reveals an analogous type of spatial ambiguity. The relationship between the figures and the fragmentary nature of the architecture, where actions occur simultaneously in time and space, are embodied in the visual instability of the palace, which mirrors the dream-like quality of this Surrealist object. As noticed by Ruth Markus, 'the *Palace* meets Dalí's criteria of the Surrealistic object, that is, it contains mutually contradictory objects and situations existing side by side, located in a non-consecutive space, in a stream of time that flows impossibly back and forth'.[15] This ambiguity is not only intentional, but indeed necessary to the artwork's expressive power and could be lost by the simple touch of the hand.

Around 1928, Picasso dedicated numerous drawings, *maquettes* and sculptures to the exploration of this type of spatial ambiguity.[16] In his *carnets* there are a number of preparatory ink drawings through which he elaborated the three-dimensional *maquettes* for a monument to Apollinaire. From these graphic renderings there is no way of telling which of the physical wires, each represented by an ink line, will be in front of which. This ambiguity is preserved almost intact in the three-dimensional work, which needs to be inspected from different angles in order to be mentally rendered in 3-D. For it is obvious that these ambiguities are readily resolved through sensory-motor interaction of the observer with the work – through considering the sculpture from different viewpoints one can combine the different visual information in the correct spatial layout. But, although this information can be gathered visually, it nonetheless refers to the solidity of the object, to its material being, in its tactile physical presence; in other words to those *qualia* that characterise the object, which have been learnt through the sense of touch.

Giacometti's and Picasso's artworks just discussed are reminiscent of a famous ambiguous figure, extensively studied by vision scientists, called the Necker cube. It is a line drawing of a cube in isometric perspective, with the parallel edges of the cube drawn as parallel lines in the picture. When two lines cross, the picture does not show which is in front and which is behind. This makes the picture ambiguous, as it can be interpreted in two different ways. This cube has also been produced in three dimensions, and it appears to retain a great deal of perceptual ambiguity even as a form in the round.[17]

Apart from the concerns of conservators relating to potential damage caused by the improper handling of historical art objects,[18] there are also numerous cases in which we are constrained within the modality of vision because the hands' touch can immediately threaten the existence of a sculpture, by changing its physical characteristics. One example of such cases, which tend to occur more frequently among contemporary artworks due to the wide variety of new materials available, is Jeppe Hein's sculptural installation titled *Between Fire and Water* (2006; Figs 7.3 and 7.4). This young Danish artist enjoys surprising the public's expectations and undermining common assumptions. In this work the observer is confronted with two water jets which spring from opposite directions forming an arch. Where they meet, a burning flame originates. The assumption that the combination of the opposing elements of water and fire cannot occur in nature makes the observer want to touch the installation, to investigate further how this could be possible – perhaps there is something in the water that may feel different; solving the puzzle requires the joint effort of different senses. Yet actually touching the work would cause a disruption of the water jets and could expose the observer to the risk of getting burnt, should the flammable substance present in the water wet the hands and catch fire.

One last but widespread case of the constrained use of visuality in the sensory approach to three-dimensional artworks is that of photographs of sculpture. In some instances, the photograph of a sculpture can serve as an indicator of the precise lighting and angle that the artist wishes to impose as the ideal viewing condition for the piece. In *Das Problem der Form in der bildenden Kunst* (1893), Adolf von Hildebrand theorised that sculpture should strive to present the viewer with a clear image, thus not obliging a person to walk around a piece to figure out what it may represent. He therefore thought that each sculpture presented an ideal viewing point, and that this ideal was best embodied by relief sculpture rather than sculpture in the round.

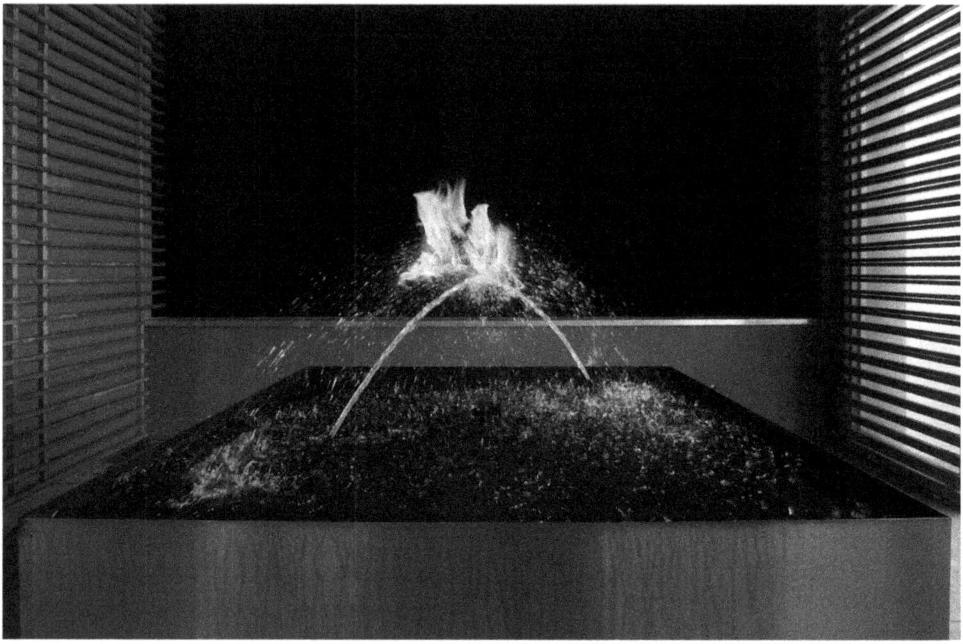

7.3 Jeppe Hein, *Between Fire and Water*, 90 × 200 × 200 cm, stainless steel, pump, nozzles, sensor, butane, computer control mechanism, 2006 [Courtesy Johann König, Berlin and 303 Gallery, New York / Photo credits: Agostino Osio]

In accordance with this standpoint, the sculptor Medardo Rosso (1858–1928) carefully staged his works so that they may be viewed to their best advantage, and went as far as requiring the beholder to look at the sculpture only from the prescribed angle and distance. Bringing Hildebrand's idea to full fruition, Rosso created sculpture which he intended should be seen exclusively from a unique vantage point – the same as that from which the artist received his 'first impression' of the subject – so that the observer could share his emotion. This viewing modality is the visual equivalent of observing a flat object, and does not encompass much tactile information. To restrict haptic access to his sculptures even further, Rosso often displayed them in vitrines, which also have the effect of framing the image as if it were bi-dimensional. This would explain why it has been claimed that the work of the Italian artist (who photographed his own sculptures and disseminated these images)[19] was created for the camera, through which it reaches its highest expressive potential. Rosso went as far as demanding that the observer should consider his sculpture as if it were a painting. 'My work must be looked at as a painting, from the optical distance, where it recomposes itself with the collaboration of your retina'.[20]

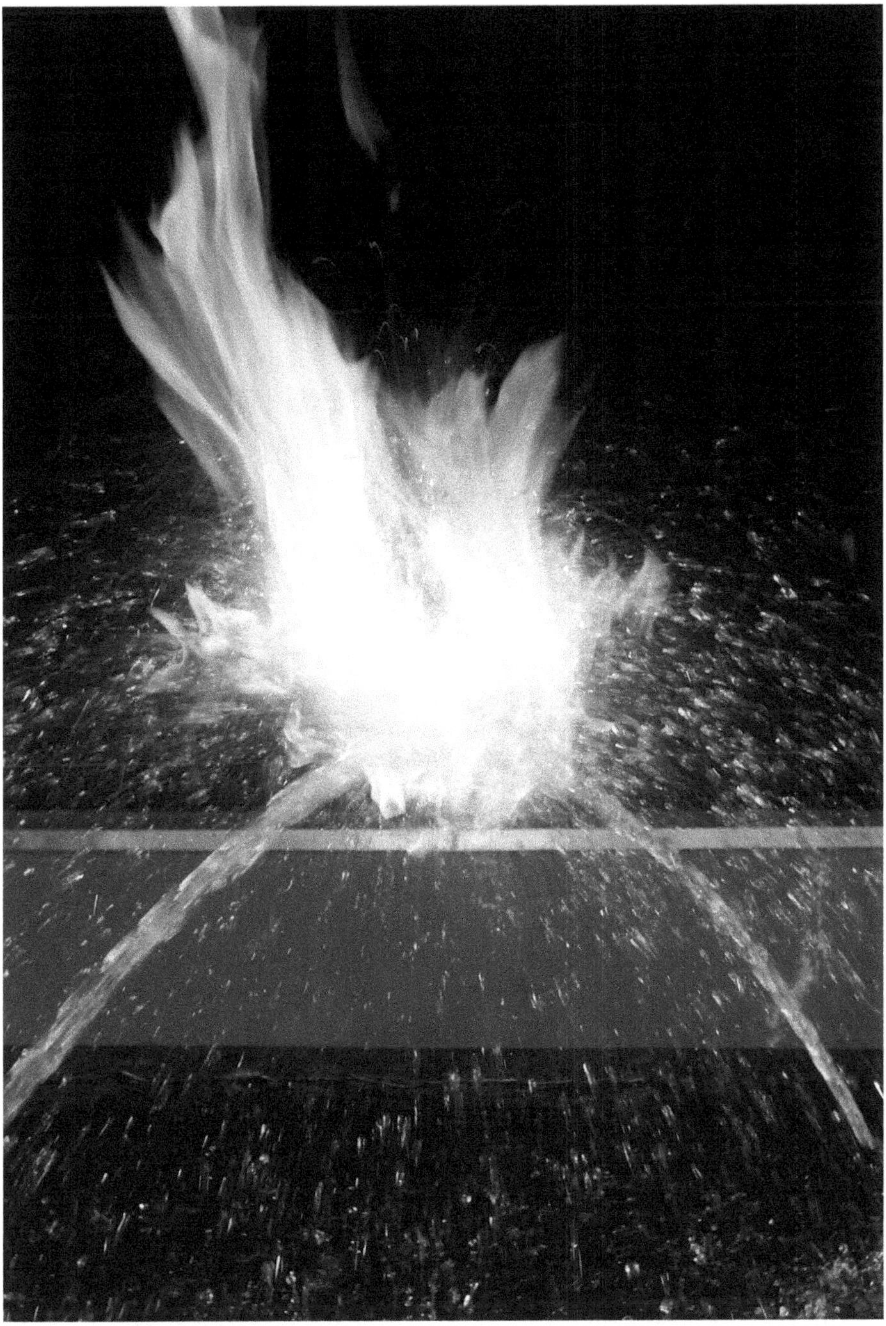

7.4 Jeppe Hein, *Between Fire and Water*, detail, 90 × 200 × 200 cm, stainless steel, pump, nozzles, sensor, butane, computer control mechanism, 2006 [Courtesy Johann König, Berlin and 303 Gallery, New York / Photo credits: Agostino Osio]

> A work of sculpture is not made to be touched, but to be seen at such or such a distance, according to the effect intended by the artist. Our hand does not permit us to bring to our consciousness the values, the tones, the colours – in a word, the life of the thing. For seizing the inner significance of a work of art, we should rely entirely on the visual impression.[21]

By ensuring the impossibility of physical touch, the photographic rendering of a sculpture can enforce the artist's need to control all of the variables that three-dimensional environments entail, hence the sculpture's final effect. Rosso also enjoyed the ambiguity conveyed by the photographs over the material nature of his work. Notoriously, he was flattered when Degas mistakenly thought that a photograph of *Impression d'omnibus* (1884–1885) represented a drawing. This was consistent with his theoretical belief that 'what is important in art is to make one forget matter'.[22]

In contemporary works, often a photograph is all that remains to testify to the existence of a sculptural installation, so that the visual route is the only available link to retrieve the memory of the piece, even when this is eminently tactile in nature. Such is the case, for example, with Ana Mendieta's *Siluetas*, which powerfully acknowledges that our entire body is capable of touching. In fact, the most interesting characteristic of this sense is its reciprocity, the unique sensation that whenever we touch we are also touched – everything touches everything. This concept is expressed almost literally in the *Siluetas*, in which the artwork is nothing more than an imprint, a witness to the act of reciprocal touching, where one can feel the friction between two extraneous bodies through the channel of the eyes. The traces of the contact between the artist's naked body and the earth are further 'touched' by the natural elements, through which they undergo a slow but inevitable consumption. This process, other than commenting on the fleeting nature of our bodily existence and on the inexorable passing of time, has the effect of humanising nature, attributing to it a sensory and sentient capacity. Paradoxically, although perceived exclusively through the eyes in the form of photographs, and thus being 'untouchable', Mendieta's sculptural interventions appeal directly to our tactile sensibility, in order to fully express the complex feelings of physical bond with the homeland, of nostalgia, absence, ageing and decay, of familiarity and division that are the main themes of her work. Appropriately, the sculptor Rosalyn Driscoll wrote that 'touch functions on a continuum between objective and subjective, not only providing knowledge about the object, but also about ourselves. The sense of touch generates meanings that emerge from the body as well as the mind.'[23]

Touching is a natural instinct, while the practice of uni-modal apprehension of art through sight only is not. One would expect that touching would be the default approach to three-dimensional artworks, unless otherwise indicated. Yet today, in museums worldwide, sculpture is institutionally protected from touch. This intriguing and relatively recent fact is mainly caused by a refusal to accept the transience of art – its physical destruction being equivalent to the loss of an economic good. By capitalising on the impossibility of laying our hands on the exhibited artworks, some contemporary sculptors choose to overcome this limit by producing works that thrive on perceptual ambiguity, as we have seen, challenging us to employ all of our sensory arsenal in ever new ways.

Notes

1. Malvina Hoffman, *Sculpture Inside and Out*, New York: W.W. Norton, 1939, p.82.
2. Hoffman, *Sculpture*, pp.157–8.
3. Aristotle, *On the Soul; Parva Naturalia; On Breath*, W.S. Hett, trans., rev. ed., Cambridge, MA and London: Harvard University Press, 1957, p.121.
4. George Berkeley, *An Essay Towards a New Theory of Vision*, Dublin: printed by Aaron Rhames, for Jeremy Pepyat, 1709. Full text available online at http://www.gutenberg.org/files/4722/4722-h/4722-h.htm#sect136 (accessed: 3 March 2014).
5. Hermann von Helmholtz, 'Concerning the Perceptions in General', in *Treatise on Physiological Optics*, vol. 3, 3rd edn, 1866 (trans. J.P.C. Southall 1925 *Opt. Soc. Am.* Section 26, reprinted New York: Dover, 1962).
6. Richard L. Gregory, 'Knowledge in Perception and Illusion', *Philosophical Transactions of the Royal Society of London*, B, 352, 1997, pp.1121–8 [online] available at http://www.richardgregory.org/papers/brainy_mind/brainy-mind.htm (accessed: 3 March 2014).
7. Richard L. Gregory, 'The Blind Leading the Sighted: An Eye-opening Experience of the Wonders of Perception', *Nature*, 430 (836), 19 August 2004, p.1.
8. Thomas Aquinas, *A Commentary on Aristotle's 'De anima'*, trans. Robert Pasnau, New Haven, CT: Yale University Press, 1999.
9. See, for example, I. Rock and J. Victor, 'Vision and Touch: An Experimentally Created Conflict between the Two Senses', *Science*, 143 (3606), 1964, pp.594–6.
10. Charles Spence, 'The Multisensory Perception of Touch', in *Art and the Senses*, F. Bacci and D. Melcher, eds, Oxford: Oxford University Press, 2011, p.86. Please refer to this essay for an overview of the debate on sensory dominance in science.
11. M.O. Ernst and Martin S. Banks, 'Humans Integrate Visual and Haptic Information in a Statistically Optimal Fashion', *Nature*, 415, 24 January 2002, pp.429–33.
12. Gregory, 'Knowledge in perception'.
13. Hoffman, *Sculpture*, p.160.
14. D. Batchelor, 'A Strange Familiarity', in *Rachel Whiteread: Plaster Sculptures*, London: Karsten Schubert, 1993, pp.6–9.
15. Ruth Markus, 'Giacometti's "The Palace at 4 a.m." (1932–33) as a Stage Design', *Scenography International*, 8, 2004 [online] available at http://www2.tau.ac.il/InternetFiles/Segel/Art/UserFiles/file/scenography%20-%20Giacometti%20Palace.pdf (accessed: 3 March 2014). Quoted from Salvador Dalí (1931–32), 'The Object as Revealed in Surrealist Experiment', in *Theories of Modern Art*, H.B. Chipp, ed., Berkeley, CA: University of California Press, 1968, pp.417–27.
16. See, for example, the drawings in a sketch album in the Marina Picasso Collection, dated 27 July – 17 December 1928, Dinard-Paris, specifically page 20, dated 3 august 1928. A reproduction is published in C. Lichtenstern, *Picasso, monument à Apollinaire: Project pour une humanisation de l'espace*, Paris: Adam Biro, 1990, p.48.
17. M. Bertamini, L. Masala, G. Meyer and N. Bruno, 'Vision, Haptics, and Attention: New Data from a Multisensory Necker Cube', *Perception*, 39 (2), 2010, pp.195–207 and N. Bruno, A. Jacomuzzi, M. Bertamini and G. Meyer, 'A Visual-Haptic Necker Cube Reveals Temporal Constraints on

Intersensory Merging during Perceptual Exploration', *Neuropsychologia*, 45 (3), 1 February 2007, pp.469–75.

18. On this topic see Fiona Candlin, 'Touch and the Limits of the Rational Museum', *Senses and Society*, 3 (3), 2008, pp.277–92; Fiona Candlin, 'Museums, Modernity and the Class Politics of Touching Objects', in *Touch in Museums: Policy and Practice in Object Handling*, Helen Chatterjee, ed., London: Berg, 2008, pp.9–20; Fiona Candlin, 'The Dubious Inheritance of Touch: Art History and Museum Access', *Journal of Visual Culture*, 5 (2), 2006, pp.137–54.

19. For more information on Rosso's use of photography, see F. Bacci, 'Impressions in Light: Photographs of Sculptures by Medardo Rosso (1858–1928)', New Brunswick, NJ: Rutgers University, 2005 (unpublished dissertation) and F. Bacci, 'Sculpting the Immaterial, Modelling the Light: Presenting Medardo Rosso's Photographic Oeuvre', *Sculpture Journal*, 15 (2), 2006, pp.223–38.

20. My translation from the French by L. Vauxcelles, 'Medardo Rosso', preface to Rosso retrospective in *Salon d'Automne, Catalogue des ouvrages de peinture, sculpture, dessin, gravure, architecture et art décoratif*, Paris: Grand Palais des Champs-Elysées, 1929, p.331.

21. M. Rosso, 'Impressionism in Sculpture, an Explanation', *The Daily Mail*, London, 17 October 1907. Republished in L. Caramel, ed., *Mostra di Medardo Rosso (1858–1928)*, Milan: Società per le Belle Arti ed Esposizione Permanente, 1979, pp.68ff.

22. 'Ce qui importe pour moi en art, c'est de faire oublier la matière', in E. Claris, *De l'Impressionisme en sculpture – Auguste Rodin et Medardo Rosso*, Paris: Éditions de 'La Nouvelle Revue', 1902, p.51.

23. Rosalyn Driscoll, 'By the Light of the Body', 2009 (unpublished manuscript).

Bibliography

Aquinas, Thomas, *A Commentary on Aristotle's 'De anima'*, trans. Robert Pasnau, New Haven, CT: Yale University Press, 1999.

Aristotle, *On the Soul; Parva Naturalia; On Breath*, W.S. Hett, trans., rev. ed., Cambridge, MA and London: Harvard University Press, 1957.

Bacci, Francesca, 'Impressions in Light: Photographs of Sculptures by Medardo Rosso (1858–1928)', New Brunswick, NJ: Rutgers University, 2005 (unpublished dissertation).

——, 'Sculpting the Immaterial, Modelling the Light: Presenting Medardo Rosso's Photographic Oeuvre', *Sculpture Journal*, 15 (2), 2006, pp.223–38.

Batchelor, D., 'A Strange Familiarity', in *Rachel Whiteread: Plaster Sculptures*, London: Karsten Schubert, 1993, pp.6–9.

Berkeley, George, *An Essay Towards a New Theory of Vision*, Dublin: printed by Aaron Rhames, for Jeremy Pepyat, 1709. Full text available online at http://www.gutenberg.org/files/4722/4722-h/4722-h.htm#sect136 (accessed: 3 March 2014).

Bertamini, M., L. Masala, G. Meyer and N. Bruno, 'Vision, Haptics, and Attention: New Data from a Multisensory Necker Cube', *Perception*, 39 (2), 2010, pp.195–207.

Bruno, N., A. Jacomuzzi, M. Bertamini and G. Meyer, 'A Visual-Haptic Necker Cube Reveals Temporal Constraints on Intersensory Merging during Perceptual Exploration', *Neuropsychologia*, 45 (3), 1 February 2007, pp.469–75.

Candlin, Fiona, 'The Dubious Inheritance of Touch: Art History and Museum Access', *Journal of Visual Culture*, 5 (2), 2006, pp.137–54.

——, 'Museums, Modernity and the Class Politics of Touching Objects', in *Touch in Museums: Policy and Practice in Object Handling*, Helen Chatterjee, ed., London: Berg, 2008, pp.9–20.

——, 'Touch and the Limits of the Rational Museum', *Senses and Society*, 3 (3), 2008, pp.277–92.

Caramel, L., ed., *Mostra di Medardo Rosso (1858–1928)*, Milan: Società per le Belle Arti ed Esposizione Permanente, 1979.
Chipp, H.B., ed., *Theories of Modern Art*, Berkeley, CA: University of California Press, 1968.
Claris, E., *De l'Impressionisme en sculpture – Auguste Rodin et Medardo Rosso*, Paris: Éditions de 'La Nouvelle Revue', 1902.
Driscoll, Rosalyn, 'By the Light of the Body', 2009 (unpublished manuscript).
Ernst, M.O. and Martin S. Banks, 'Humans Integrate Visual and Haptic Information in a Statistically Optimal Fashion', *Nature*, 415, 24 January 2002, pp.429–33.
Gregory, Richard L., 'Knowledge in Perception and Illusion', *Philosophical Transactions of the Royal Society of London*, B, 352, 1997, pp.1121–8 [online] available at http://www.richardgregory.org/papers/brainy_mind/brainy-mind.htm (accessed: 3 March 2014).
——, 'The Blind Leading the Sighted: An Eye-opening Experience of the Wonders of Perception', *Nature*, 430 (836), 19 August 2004, p.1.
Helmholtz, Hermann von, 'Concerning the Perceptions in General', in *Treatise on Physiological Optics*, vol. 3, 3rd edn, 1866 (translated by J.P.C. Southall 1925 *Opt. Soc. Am.* Section 26, reprinted New York: Dover, 1962).
Hoffman, Malvina, *Sculpture Inside and Out*, New York: W.W. Norton, 1939.
Lichtenstern, C., *Picasso, monument à Apollinaire. Project pour une humanisation de l'espace*, Paris: Adam Biro, 1990.
Markus, Ruth, 'Giacometti's "The Palace at 4 a.m." (1932–33) as a Stage Design', *Scenography International*, 8, 2004 [online] available at http://www2.tau.ac.il/Internet Files/Segel/Art/UserFiles/file/scenography%20-%20Giacometti%20Palace.pdf (accessed: 3 March 2014).
Rock, I. and J. Victor, 'Vision and Touch: An Experimentally Created Conflict between the Two Senses', *Science*, 143 (3606), 1964, pp.594–6.
Spence, Charles, 'The Multisensory Perception of Touch', in *Art and the Senses*, F. Bacci and D. Melcher, eds, Oxford: Oxford University Press, 2011, pp.85–106.
Vauxcelles, L., 'Medardo Rosso', preface to Rosso retrospective in *Salon d'Automne, Catalogue des ouvrages de peinture, sculpture, dessin, gravure, architecture et art décoratif*, Paris: Grand Palais des Champs-Elysées, 1929.

Pictorial essay B: Playing with fire

Rosalyn Driscoll

Every winter morning I play with fire. I build a fire in the woodstove that heats our house. To ensure the flames take hold I adjust all the conditions: remaining embers, size of the logs, spacing and draft. I am playing with an element – fire – that can be dangerous but here is contained and beneficial.

There are faster, easier ways to generate heat, but building fires feeds my work as an artist. Like making a fire, making an artwork requires observation and use of elements and forces, both physical and psychological; they take physical form as materials, gravity, light, structure, colour and relationships; they take psychological form as memories, emotions, passions, views and imagination.

When you integrate the sense of touch into making and experiencing art, you add fire to the artistic arsenal – again, both physical and psychological. Touch is an elemental, embodied way of knowing. It is also intimate, provocative and affective. To include touch in art is to play with fire; it invites interaction with elements and forces that are powerful yet contained by the work of art.

I have made and exhibited tactile sculptures for the last 20 years. By observing and recording people's responses to touching my work – especially when they touch without sight, using a blindfold – I am developing an understanding of aesthetic touch. Some of their comments, in italics, illustrate my thoughts. The parts of touch I address here are its fiery aspects – its sensory physicality and its unconscious, emotional dimensions.

Touch is a multivalent network of nerves running from the surface of the skin deep into the interior of the body. This network spans many functions: contact with the surroundings; movements of muscle and bone; the feeling of presence; balance; pressure; temperature; the sensations of emotions like the shiver of fear or the knot of anger; as well as pain and pleasure. The word 'touch' is shorthand for all these *somatic* senses. As such, touch monitors the conditions of the body-mind; it provides information about the body's activities and how the body is affected by things, as well as information about the things themselves. Touch connects the outer and inner dimensions of our being by its very structure and function, creating dynamic loops of sensing, knowing, acting and being.

Because touch is essential to the body, it remains fundamental to human survival and well-being from earliest childhood until the day we die. Touch is inextricably fused with pleasure, pain, sexuality, visceral feelings and emotional states.

By integrating the sense of touch into the experience of art, we tap into these deeply felt, often unconscious responses. Bodily history, habits, drives and passions come into play. After touching my sculpture, a Japanese gentleman said:

This experience is very fundamental, basic, primitive, more direct than intellectual experiences and therefore stronger.

Touch remains coloured by early experiences as children when touch was the primary way of interacting with the world, and assurance and comfort were afforded by tactile exchanges with the mother. Touching – even of sculpture – is infused with memories of the polymorphous pleasures of childhood.

There was such a sense of freedom: no barriers, no age, no survival, just bliss. Permission! Being a kid! Atavistic. A return to childhood.

Sculptures are often unfamiliar objects made of sensuous, appealing materials; touching allows us to know them the way we came to know things as children. An artist combines the playful, open investigation of the child with the discerning discrimination of the adult; touching is a way for people to tap into that blend of freedom and awareness, to re-connect with their childhood hapticity and dynamism, and to resonate with the artist's creativity.

I felt a strong stirring in my soul for some sense I'd long hidden.

The ease and frequency of touching and being touched that occurs in childhood diminishes as we mature. Conscious, sensuous touch can eventually become limited to sexual encounters. Touching sculpture may call up sexual associations, even if the artwork is not figurative.

I never considered touching in another atmosphere than the intimate.

Touch, sex and pleasure can become linked in a trio that excludes other kinds of tactile exchange or sensuous pleasure, reducing sensitivity and openness to tactility.

Sight is safe, touch is erotic.

This state of affairs makes touching sculpture potentially charged, intensifying the encounter. Touching sculpture can be enriching, as it provides a way to cultivate non-sexual touch within the safety of the aesthetic experience.

Apart from the erotic or pleasurable aspects of sexual relations, their *mutuality* conveys the reciprocal nature of touch. We are touched as well as touching. When we touch, we are intimately engaged, even with a work of art.

It's all about relationship. When I touch, I enter into a relationship with what I'm touching. I can't remain with my superficial ideas of what something is. I'm invited to go deeper.

Mutuality and reciprocity underlie touch, raising the stakes; we cannot remain aloof, apart, detached or at a distance, as we can with sight.

When I was touching the sculptures, they were the whole world. I was inside the experience.

Such close engagement can incite pleasure but also discomfort. Touch brings us into contact with things that can hurt us; risk and vulnerability underlie the experience of touching sculpture.

Does it have any sharp places? Will it bite?

It took trust. I had to trust there wouldn't be anything sharp.

We are also psychologically vulnerable when we touch; the sensations of touch can trigger the sensations of emotions. In touching sculpture we open ourselves to the possibility of disturbing feelings as well as pleasurable ones. I learned that both fear and exhilaration can result from people encountering edges, holes, sudden transitions, unexpected materials, or open spaces.

Such a dynamic experience, very deep with curiosity and anxiety.

The encounter with art provides an opportunity to notice and feel emotions in an aesthetic context where we refrain from acting on our feelings, and are free to explore them in depth.

There are so many emotions attached to the closeness and innocence of touch.

Touching sculpture grounds emotions in sensations, giving the feelings an immediacy and reality that renders them more accessible: a steel passage feels cold, making me fearful; a wooden area feels warm so I relax; a leather hammock is reassuring; a tight fit causes panic; a keen edge worries me.

And gravity! My stomach and guts got involved. When I touched the cloth that was wrapping something vertical, I felt nausea. I love the way things wiggle when suspended. I like having to squat down.

It brought me back down to earth, back into my individual psyche,
using my own senses to form my reality in my surroundings.

Feeling is believing.

Movement is central to the haptic experience. Touching a sculpture, I translate its forms and spaces into motion, activating the artwork. My motions translate the sculpture into bodily experience for a more deeply felt understanding.

Information taken in through the fingers was tactile and spatial, but
it was a sense of space I have never experienced before because it was
not made finite and given limits by visual measurement.

Because movement produces sensations in the body, it can draw attention to the inner dimensions of being.

I could feel sensations deep inside my body as I touched. And while exploring with
my hands, memories of early spaces, of rooms, came into my mind. The air, the
space that my hand had to travel from touch to touch became very palpable.

When we touch a sculpture, we invite movement and touch – which are normally unconscious – into conscious awareness and even into the realm of aesthetics and meaning. In so doing we create connections between conscious and unconscious aspects of our being, integrating higher and lower functions.

It broke the lock, the hold that sight has on me. It got me off the highway
that goes between eye and brain that you don't even know you're on.
Wait a minute, you say, there's this whole other road to travel.

Touching requires a level of commitment that does not exist with sight; we must reach out, make a connection, explore the unknown, and open ourselves to discovery.

At first I was afraid – how could I know*? Then, on first touch, joy, a different kind of knowing.*

You can't just look at something and walk away.

Touching deeply defines one's sense of self, shaping the body maps generated in the brain. I learn *who* and *how* I am through my motions and interactions with the world. When I touch a sculpture – a complex, articulate object – I learn even more. Touching sculpture provides contact with unusual materials, unfamiliar sensations, new movement patterns, and opportunities for empathy and emotional exploration.

Worked aluminium surface felt softer than paper. Copper felt softer
than wood, more impressionable. Astonishing that such a hard
surface could feel so soft; it seemed softer than my skin.

Embodying different movement patterns creates meanings we feel and know in the body. Such movement directions as simple as left and right, high and low, narrow and wide, generate different qualities and meanings.

My hand was forced to go flat on the surface by the narrowness of the space,
a way of feeling I hadn't done before, very different than fingertips.

We are able to embody and even identify with the qualities of the sculpture, whether pleasurable, useful, disturbing or challenging.

When I got to a place that went deeper, it felt like an infinite cavity, and that felt risky.

In any perceptual act, we arrive at understanding through a process that is dynamic, fluid and constantly in motion. In the words of perceptual psychologist Rudolf Arnheim, we experience:

> … the challenge, the productive confusion, the promising leads, the partial solutions, the disturbing contradictions, the flash appearance of a stable solution whose adequacy is self-evident, the structural changes brought about by the pressure of changing total situations, the resemblance discovered among different patterns ….[1]

This description of the dynamic quality of perception holds true for any of the senses, but especially for haptic perception, which does not name, categorise and fix objects in the way that sight does.

If you look at a piece of art it's an object, but if you touch it, it's a journey.

Tactile perception is so much slower and more accessible to awareness than sight that we can actually track the processes of perception.

I not only tried to map it, but also to figure out the space it occupied.
The more I touched it, the more it took shape in my head. At first I would leave
one side and it wouldn't be there anymore, but as I kept touching, the other
side would begin to exist when I left it – the permanence of the object.

People touching my sculpture report such challenges, productive confusion, promising leads, partial solutions, contradictions, resolutions and changing conditions. Haptic perception *consists* of this dynamic evolution.

The lid looks like stone, so when I touched it and discovered it was
leather, I felt as if I'd been shocked. I was so surprised I pulled my hands
away. And then I discovered the shadow actually was stone!

Knowing a sculpture through touch provides an embodied experience of the changing, mobile nature of reality itself – of both the world and myself. I move and change as I explore a sculpture, and my impressions of the artwork change. There is no summative moment of completion.

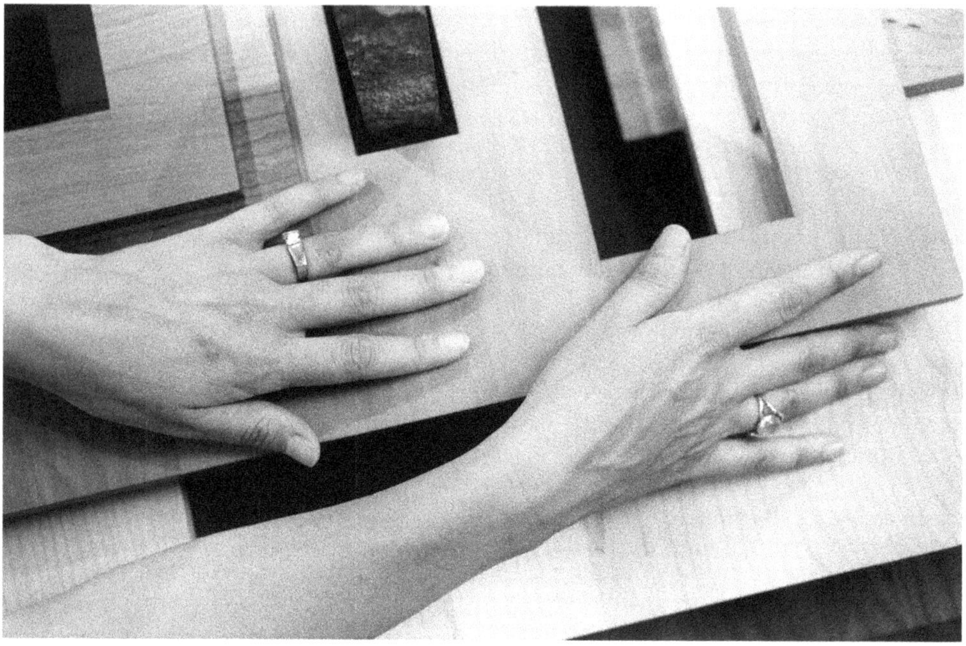

B.1 Rosalyn Driscoll, *A Natural History*, 178 × 132 × 112 cm / 70 × 52 × 44 in., wood, stone, steel, 1998 [© Rosalyn Driscoll]

I wanted to know the sculpture's dimensions. At first I expected it to be small, but when I reached across it, my arm kept going on and on and it seemed huge. Then I walked around it and it seemed smaller.

Knowing through touch imbues sculpture with motion and transformation that become integral to the experience, to the object, and to one's self. This perception of mutability reflects the underlying truth of reality as impermanent, ever-changing processes rather than immutable, fixed forms – like fire itself.

Notes

1. Rudolf Arnheim, *Visual Thinking*, Berkeley and Los Angeles, CA: University of California Press, 1969, pp.76–7.

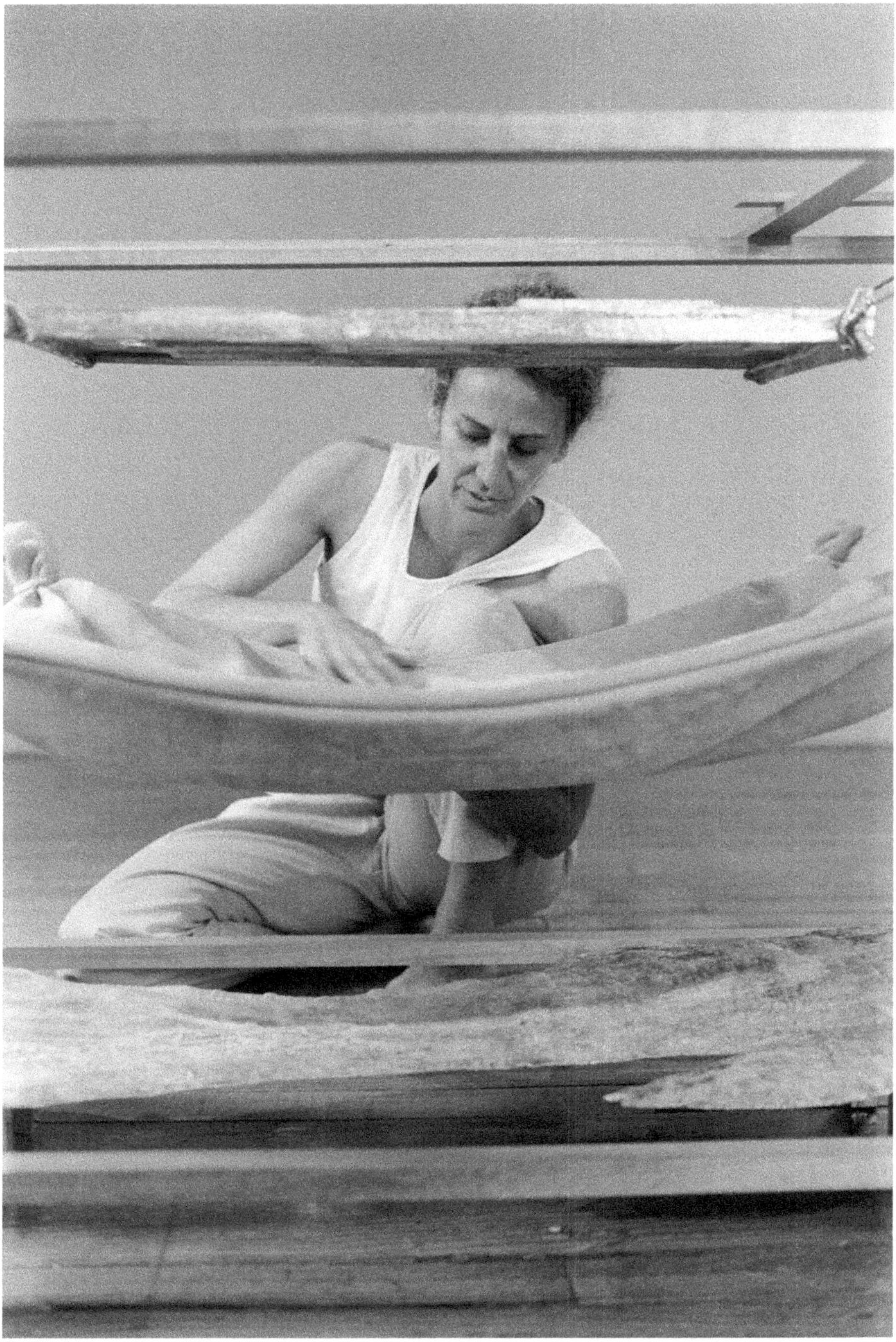

B.2 Rosalyn Driscoll, *Anatomy*, 137 × 86 × 147 cm / 54 × 34 × 58 in., wood, copper, leather, 1998 [© Rosalyn Driscoll]

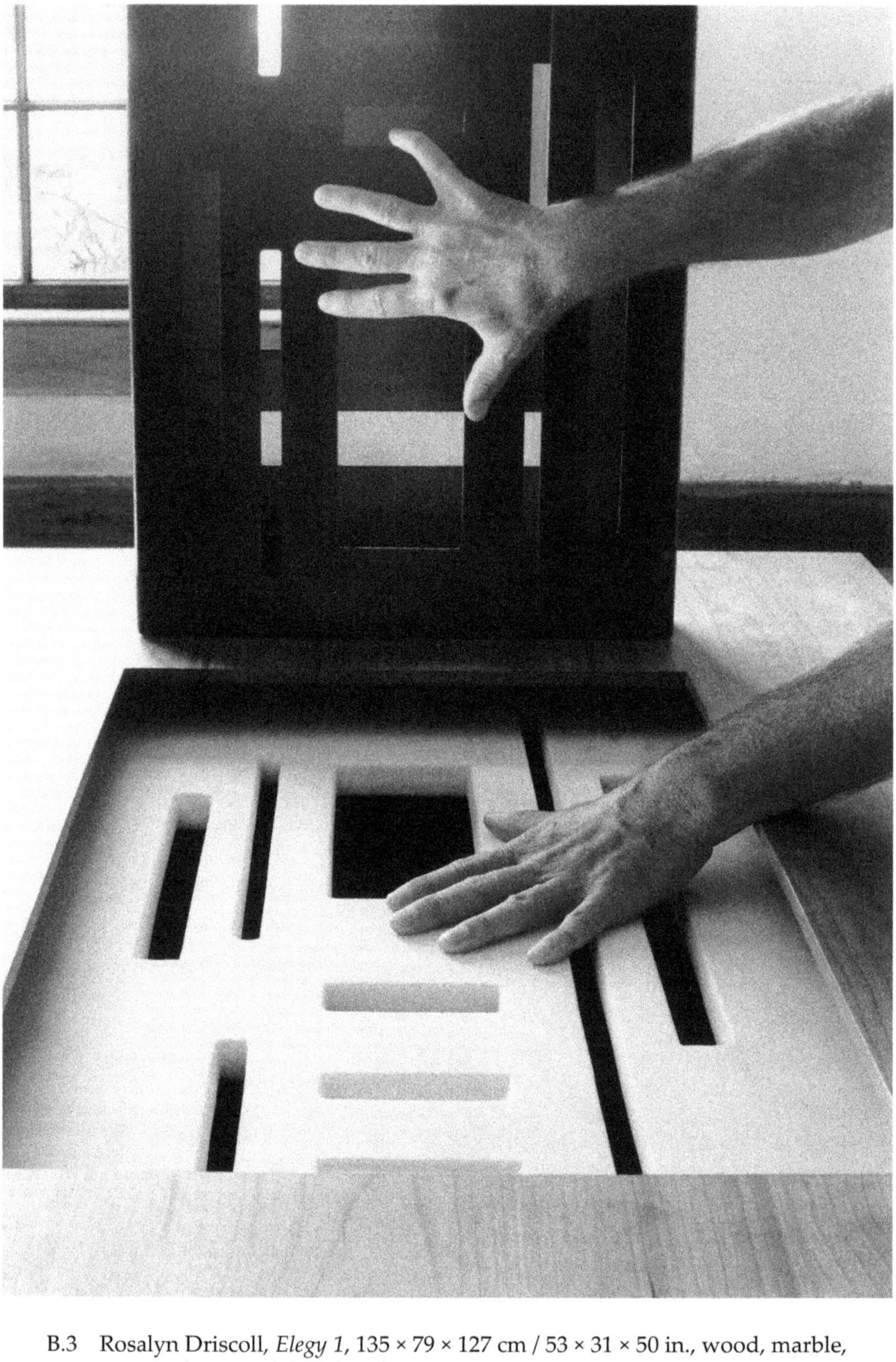

B.3 Rosalyn Driscoll, *Elegy 1*, 135 × 79 × 127 cm / 53 × 31 × 50 in., wood, marble, schist, steel, handmade paper, 1995 [© Rosalyn Driscoll]

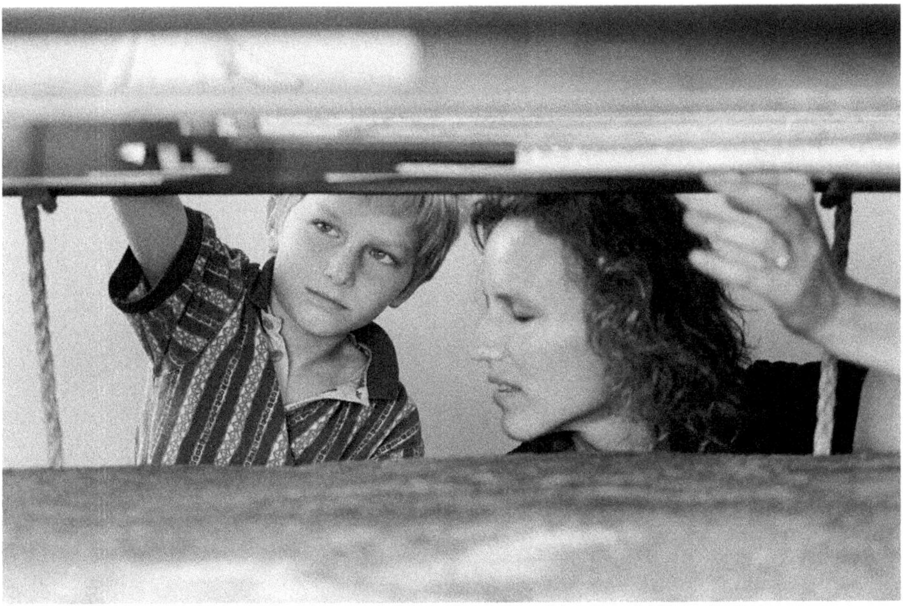

B.4 Rosalyn Driscoll, *Elegy 5*, 132 × 81 × 132 cm / 52 × 32 × 52 in., steel, stone, leather, rope, gauze, 1996 [© Rosalyn Driscoll]

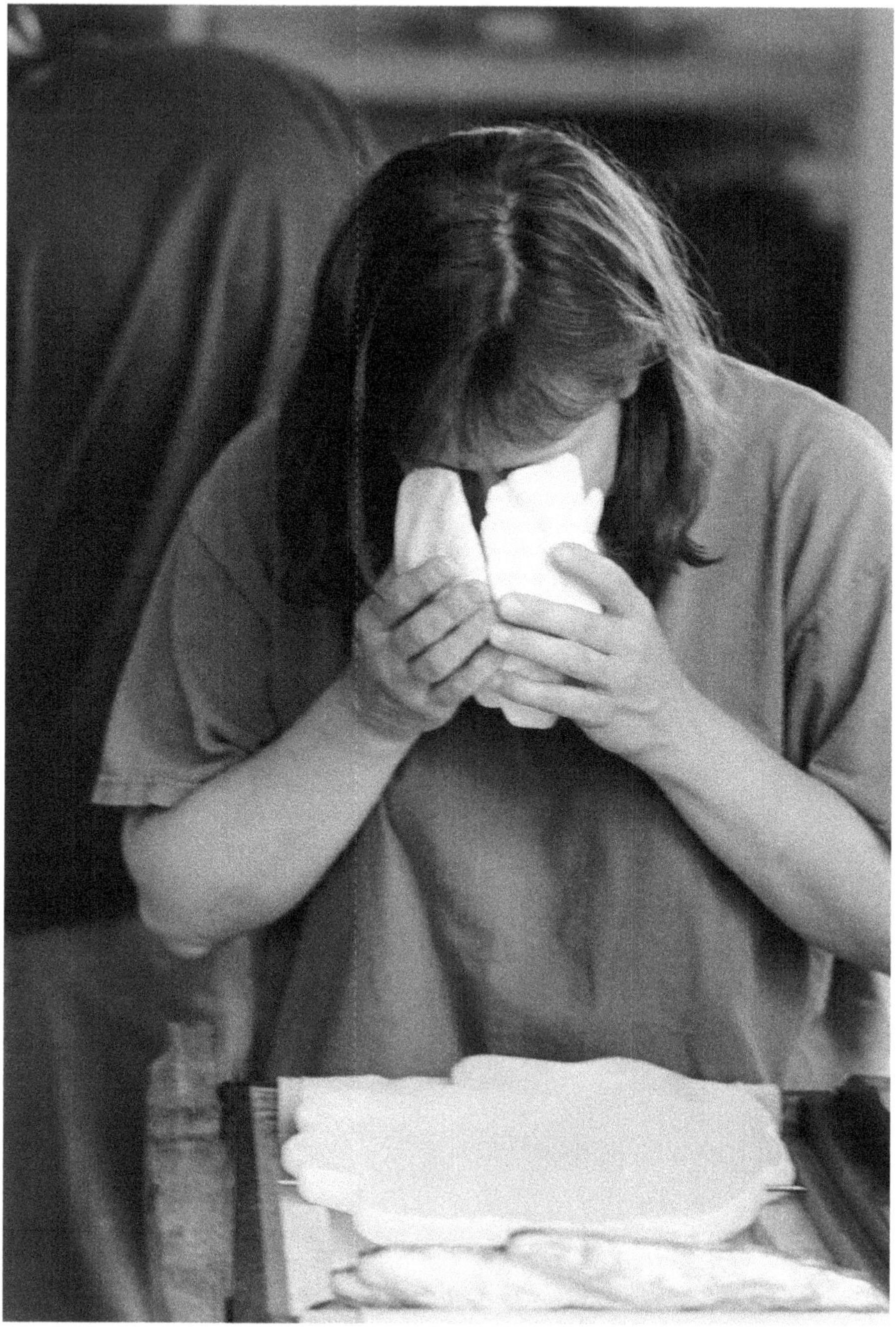

B.5 Rosalyn Driscoll, *What's not meant to be opened (may be opened)*, 25 × 48 × 35 cm / 10 × 19 × 14 in., stone, wood, resin, alabaster, iron, leather, gauze, plaster, copper, 2001 [© Rosalyn Driscoll]

Part III
Identities

8

Beyond the touch tour

Julia Cassim

Background

For a period of 11 years from 1987 I was arts columnist of *The Japan Times* reporting on the museum sector in Japan and elsewhere. Japan was undergoing what was commonly termed the 'third museum boom' with 5,495 museums of every conceivable type constructed between 1960 and 1992.[1] They ranged from small privately-run ones, such as the 'Museum of Scents' in Shizuoka, vanity ones dedicated to a single local artist, or large-scale public and private ones in the major cities. The sheer volume of construction activity and the wholesale acquisition of artworks, artefacts or readymade collections were fuelled by the economic climate of the time where the horizon for growth seemed limitless. Legislation resulting from the 1981 International Year of Disabled People (IYDP) ensured that the 2,793 museums constructed after this date boasted superb physical access while those constructed before were retrofitted to comply with access regulations.

However, the rapidity of activity in the sector and the fact that many museums were created from scratch and had not evolved from any pre-existing private or public collections or history of activity meant that their role and potential as community-based or educational institutions was poorly understood. Art museums were heavily dependent on blockbuster exhibitions originating abroad to continue to bring in visitors after the initial novelty had worn off and, like the burgeoning economy, had the budgets to allow them the pick of the world's collections. Symposia, curatorial or artist lectures and occasional concerts were organised to coincide with temporary exhibitions and academic catalogues were routinely produced, but educational activities were aimed primarily at children and confined to the school holidays.[2] Rare was the museum with a specialist educator or conservator on its staff or one that provided regular programming built around its permanent collection.

Not only was the general public poorly served in educational terms but so too were visitors with disabilities. With no precedents to draw on save the example of the older Japanese museums, and no disability rights organisations hammering on the door, these 'cultural coffins'[3] were under little pressure to change.

The UK context

It presented a stark contrast to the situation in the UK where the introduction of the National Curriculum in 1988 saw a four hundred-fold increase in school visits at the British Museum alone.[4] Museums were actively diversifying their programming and outreach activities in light of their expanded role as providers of educational services to a diversity of audiences. The major conflict lay in how to reconcile the need to preserve the integrity of historic buildings and their collections with the access needs of disabled visitors. Even where longstanding programmes existed at the British Museum, the Victoria & Albert Museum and the Tate, issues of physical access hampered initiatives. It was no coincidence that the second major report on the subject following the 1985 *Arts for Everyone* was entitled *In through the Front Door*, the service entrance having come to symbolise the second-class status of disabled visitors.[5]

Issues of cognitive access

Resident in Japan, curators routinely asked me for comparisons between museum practice in Japan and the UK. Superficial similarities and differences aside, I felt an increasing need to demonstrate that access to the cultural heritage in museums went beyond physical access. Getting people in through the front door was vital but it was only the start of the visitor journey. The issue of cognitive access was central to whether they developed as vibrant community organisations and were able to transcend their static identity of 'temples of art' or 'collections of curiosities' that existed for the benefit of the curators.

The question was how to illustrate this in an unequivocal and practical way that would have more impact than any number of press articles on the subject. What was needed was a demonstration project based on the principle that if museums found ways to make their collections cognitively accessible to their most excluded public (that is, visually and learning disabled visitors), it was likely that such measures would be welcomed by the general public. While the latter may have no problems with their vision, they could not be called visually literate where non-figurative or contemporary artworks were concerned, and shared similar conceptual difficulties of interpretation.[6]

The opportunity came when the Nagoya City Art Museum invited me to co-curate an exhibition with Minako Tsunoda in October 1994 as part of their biannual series aimed at visitors with visual impairments. This is described in detail in a later section of this chapter.

Initiatives at the Nagoya City Art Museum

Art & The Inner Eye # 1 was the third in a series organised since 1989, the year the museum opened. It consisted of small figurative sculptures in bronze and stone that could be handled and had been curated by Harue Murayama of the Gallery TOM, a private gallery in Tokyo and the only permanent touch venue in Japan at the time.[7]

The second in the series in 1992 curated by Tsunoda was an extension of an exhibition of seven contemporary Japanese sculptors who were commissioned to produce or lend existing works for tactile exploration. The majority proved unsuitable in terms of size, material, concept or safety and the exhibition was heavily criticised on these grounds both in the press and by visually impaired visitors for the curatorial lack of consultation with them or any provision of information in alternative formats.

Thus, the third show in the series was an opportunity to trial a new conceptual approach for touch shows in general and expand the boundaries of what was in danger of becoming a standardised format in art museums in Japan and indeed elsewhere – namely that small, mainly figurative three-dimensional works of art in hard stone or bronze, that had been carefully vetted in conservational terms, were made available for tactile exploration by visually impaired visitors.

Early touch shows and ghetto services

Touch shows of this type, irrespective of what they displayed, differed little conceptually from the earliest iterations of the genre. They were to all intents and purposes glorified handling sessions, an outgrowth of the long-standing tradition of loan services that began in the UK in 1864 at the Victoria and Albert Museum.[8] By 1913, we see the first documented initiative for visually impaired audiences by J.A.C. Deas at the Sunderland Museum. A chance remark to him by a teacher at a school for the blind about how difficult it was for his blind students to understand the concept of proportion led him to invite them to explore stuffed animals in the museum collection through touch and to sit on a lion. Five weeks later they made 'outstanding' models of the animals.[9] At the Metropolitan Museum of Art in New York in the same year,

Robert W. de Forest, the museum's secretary ordered two lectures on American sculpture and musical instruments with objects to touch and a Braille text provided.[10]

Eaton's collection of objects

The next conceptual and documented leap for the genre came in 1955 when Allen Eaton assembled a private handling collection for public use in the United States. He detailed his experiences with the 40 objects 'of beauty and wonder' selected from many cultures and their use as a means of communication between visually impaired and sighted people in *Beauty for the Sighted and the Blind*.[11] It provides the first analytical study of the subject of tactile access for visually impaired and sighted museum visitors. Eaton saw the activity not as being aimed purely at a visually impaired audience but as an opportunity for the sharing of experience between people with different sensory vocabularies. This is where the difference lay. He wanted to provide his audience with the widest possible variety of tactile experience and his collection centred on ethnographic or craft items from prehistoric to contemporary times. It included prehistoric hand tools, Sumerian clay tablets, a Navajo silver necklace, a carved wooden drinking cup from the Congo and a set of 12 nested Russian dolls. Much of their fascination, as he noted, lay not only in the tactile beauty of the object but in the cultural or historical story embedded in each, thus touch was seen as a multi-layered experience encompassing the physical, the emotional and the conceptual.

The static touch genre

Since that time, the major emphasis of the standard museum touch experience remains on being able to touch previously forbidden artworks or artefacts that are neither replicas nor duplicates, nor reserve pieces of lower quality, but signature works from the permanent collection. There is rarely any overarching thematic or curatorial narrative beyond tactile exploration or chronology. They centre on 'special' service provision, are aimed primarily at visually impaired visitors not the mainstream audience and are not viewed as a valid exhibition genre in their own right.

This 'ghetto' aspect had been a major criticism of the touch show *Sculpture for the Blind* held at the Tate Gallery in 1981 following its first one organised there in 1976 in collaboration with the Royal National Institute for the Blind (RNIB). It included sculptures by Henry Moore, Jacob Epstein, Barbara Hepworth and Degas arranged in sequence from the naturalistic and progressing to the more abstract.[12]

The 1981 show had been a segregated one for visually impaired people for conservational reasons since the chemical patina of some bronze sculptures in the 1976 show had been damaged by handling. It had caused bitter resentment in sighted visitors who could view the exhibition from outside but had not been able to enter it or handle the works. At a time when the importance of access for disadvantaged audiences was still poorly understood, it was a timely object lesson to sighted visitors of the discrimination disabled people routinely experienced. However, it was clear that the aim should be of universal rather than restricted access in line with recommendations laid down in 1980 by a working party at the Royal Ontario Museum in Canada, declaring itself firmly opposed to the idea of segregated museum experiences: 'We ... reject the concept of special facilities such as "fragrance gardens" or rooms set aside as "tactile galleries" especially for the visually impaired. Every effort should be made to integrate services for the blind with experiences planned for people with normal vision.'[13]

Frozen initiatives

It could be argued that in the intervening 30 years since those recommendations and despite the driver of DDA (Disability Discrimination Act) and Equality Act 2010 legislation, little has changed. Services to disabled people are now routinely offered by museums in the UK. However, for visually impaired visitors, they tend to take the form of touch tours, special handling sessions or audio description and still fall under the category of special services – an add-on devised by the education department for a group of visitors who are seen as equal but in need of separate measures.

It is thus hardly surprising that 'touch' shows within museums have not evolved conceptually as an exhibition form or mainstream interpretative approach despite the promise of the 1990s when the twin forces of the National Curriculum and the growth and interest in multi-sensory shows seemed to offer great scope for this to happen. Then, traditional display techniques were being jettisoned in favour of a more hands-on approach and relevant exhibits designed to withstand the wear and tear of many small hands, the rigorous criticism of young minds and the educational needs of the National Curriculum itself, which stressed resource-based, multi-disciplinary learning and the inclusion of children with disabilities.

The Start project and *Breaking the Mould*

Two pioneering shows that took cognitive accessibility as their starting point and then developed a display that incorporated physical access demonstrated how the needs and aspirations of visually-impaired visitors could be integrated into a mainstream exhibition format, even where this was not explicitly the point of the show. The 1995 Start project at the Walsall Museum and Art Gallery, home to the Garman Ryan collection, placed the interactive exhibit firmly within the context of an art museum with a display based on the collection and geared to three to five year olds. It marked the beginnings of a holistic approach to the permanent collection. Creative artists and designers were commissioned to produce interpretative works, which could be manipulated by the young audience.[14] The same hands-on/minds-on approach for all audiences was adopted at the National Portrait Gallery (NPG) in 1995 for such groundbreaking exhibitions as *Breaking the Mould – Materials and Methods of Portrait Sculpture*.[15]

Since that time, museum shows that have responded to the creative opportunities opened up by these multisensory or interactive shows have been few and far between. *Touch Me: Design and Sensation*' at the Victoria and Albert Museum in 2005 is a rare recent example as are the activities of Blind Art.[16] The emergence of professionally-trained visually impaired artists such as Sally Booth, Jonathan Huxley, Padraig Naughton, Joanna Brendon, Lynn Cox and Maria Oshodi and others working in the area of installation or site specific work has had little influence on the existing status quo. Their work is too often shunted off into the disability arts category and their expertise and insights remain untapped by curators or exhibition designers even where they are in demand for residencies or workshops.

This is even the case for large-scale shows that have centred on issues of visual perception, and cognitive understanding where the linkage between sight, the perceptual impact of its lack and the existence of other sensory vocabularies would seem an obvious curatorial opportunity not to be missed.[17] But missed they most certainly were in *Mirror Image – On Reflection*, Jonathan Miller's show at the National Gallery (Miller, 1998). This dealt with the relationship between painting and perception while *Encounters – New Art from Old*, also at the National Gallery, centred on works by leading contemporary artists including the sculptors Anthony Caro, Louise Bourgeois and Claes Oldenburg, which had been created in response to the permanent collection.[18]

It has been left to initiatives like the globe-trotting *Dialogue in the Dark* installation, and the linkage of research in cognitive psychology and emerging haptic technologies to the subject of touch in museums, for an interest in the broader multi-sensory agenda to be reignited.[19] Whether this will be translated into new exhibition genres or museum initiatives in the UK that transcend the standardised touch tour format remains to be seen. An exhibition at the Sackler Centre at the Victoria and Albert Museum in 2010 would seem to offer a new conceptual direction. Royal College of Art (RCA) sculpture students were given access to the permanent collection, and selected 'uncertain objects' that were then digitally captured, reformed and re-imagined. Each was scanned in x, y and z axes and then worked 'virtually' before being 'printed'

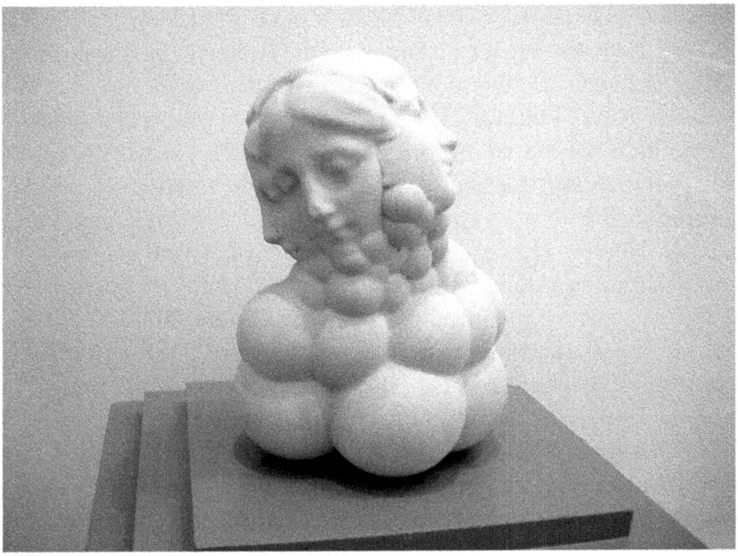

8.1 Dexter Dymoke, *Head of the Virgin*, digitally reformed and re-imagined version of a seventeenth-century statuette after Duquesnoy from the Victoria and Albert Museum's collection of 'uncertain objects'. Dymoke, an RCA sculpture student, digitally captured the work using 3-D scanning technology before producing his version using the rapid prototyping process [© Julia Cassim]

three-dimensionally using rapid prototyping techniques. As an interpretative method, it would seem ripe for an interactive dialogue between visually impaired and sighted artists and visitors (Fig. 8.1).

The impact of art education for blind children on the touch agenda in Japanese museums

In Japan, the roots of interest on the part of the art museum sector in the area of tactile exploration and the broader multi-sensory agenda lie elsewhere. While museum provision for visually impaired visitors is still patchy, the high quality of Japan's art education for blind children has driven interest in the subject. In 1947, Japan's post-war constitution imposed by the occupying American forces guaranteed equality of educational opportunity which included students at Japan's schools for the blind. It ensured that blind children would receive the same educational opportunities as sighted children. Thus the curriculum was identical and specialist art teachers hired, although no teaching materials had been devised to help them. Among them was Shiro Fukurai, an unemployed graphic designer in Kobe who was persuaded, albeit reluctantly, into accepting a position at the Kobe School for the Blind in 1950.

With no tradition of art education for the blind to guide him, Fukurai created a methodology from scratch. He documented the strategies he developed to teach his charges and convince them of the beauty of their work in *How Can I Make What I Cannot See?*.[20] Fukurai's example has deeply influenced his successors in this area, many of whom are practising artists. This in turn has influenced museum professionals, particularly those with an interest in contemporary art as exemplified by the sculptor Yohei Nishimura and the ceramic work he inspired over 23 years as a teacher at the Chiba School for the Blind.

Art education, as defined by Fukurai and Nishimura, is not about the acquisition of specific technical skills, which exemplifies mainstream art education in Japan at school level. They based their teaching on the holistic development of the creative personality of the child and encouraged a whole body approach to the work, with the children standing and using the largest amount of clay possible. Their role is as an enabler who steps back, watches, listens and learns from his students about their world and, based on these observations, prompts them in ways that will help them develop their creative talents through the provision of stimuli such as music, rhythm, movement and so on. There is no question of imposing the aesthetic values of the sighted or urging them to mimic them.[21] This approach, developed as a result of working with children with sensory disabilities, is at the leading edge of art education theory in Japan and has deeply influenced other artists and a new generation of museum educators and curators who are interested in exploring possibilities for new exhibition formats and interpretative methodologies.

Design and curation of *Art & the Inner Eye #1*

It was against this context in Japan of a museum culture that was, on the one hand, new and open to experimental approaches, while on the other reluctant to change the comfortable well-funded status quo in terms of visitor outreach, that *Art & the Inner Eye #1* took place.[22] In curating and designing the show, I wanted it to work on different levels and placed as much emphasis on cognitive and tactile access.

Selection criteria for the artworks

The exhibition consisted of works by 11 contemporary artists from Japan, the UK and the USA. The three two-dimensional works (Jonathan Huxley, Susan Fenton, Yae Asano) were chosen for their strong associative imagery while the painting by Asano could be touched. Asano's technique was coincidentally a reverse of the conventional microcapsule tactile image. He would incise lines into thick white impasto, wait for it to dry and then overlay a thin layer of black paint, which would then be wiped away so that the incised lines were highlighted.

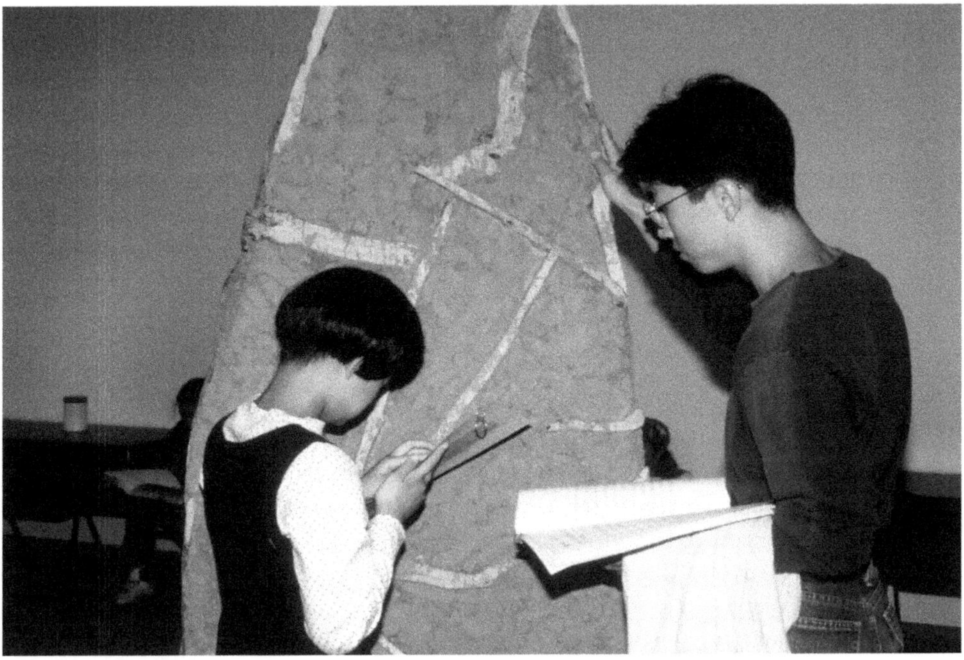

8.2 Blind child reading tactile image of sculpture by Yoshiro Takada at the *Art & the Inner Eye #1* exhibition at the Nagoya City Art Museum, Japan, 1994 [© Julia Cassim]

The eight three-dimensional works were selected to give an idea of the variety and range of materials and techniques used by contemporary artists, to display different surface qualities and be made in strongly contrasting media: rough-smooth, cold-warm, traditional and non-traditional, that is, mud, wood and straw (Yoshiro Takada) (Fig. 8.2), clay (Ayumi Shigematsu), fired paper (Yohei Nishimura), fibreglass (Michio Fukuoka), stainless steel (Shin Kuno), different kinds of fibre and textiles (Masafumi Maeta), industrial or mechanical components (Yukio Fujimoto) and so on. One was deliberately intended for destruction through tactile exploration to challenge the overly respectful Japanese audience. *Art Annual 1992*, by Yohei Nishimura, was a copy of this much-despised Japanese publication that ranks artists according to their market value. Yoshimura had fired it at a temperature of 1000 degrees causing it to burst open into a fat fan shape that was fossilised but fragile and bleached of any text. By the end of the three-week exhibition period this had crumbled to a pile of white ash, which had been Nishimura's conceptual intention.

The three-dimensional works needed a coherence of form and scale, which would allow visually-impaired visitors reliant on touch to understand their overall shape and dimensions without difficulty and permit the general visitor to 'enter' the work directly and not have to approach it via a previous knowledge of art history. No consideration was given to the age, pedigree, relative fame or national origin of the artist and the works were chosen purely on their tactile, conceptual and aesthetic merits. One professional artist with a visual disability (Jonathan Huxley) was included to dispel the notion that such a disability disqualifies anyone from practising a visually-based profession or that the work of people with disabilities is *ipso facto* amateur and not worthy of display alongside examples of 'high art' which were strongly held misconceptions in Japan at the time. We subsequently discovered that Yae Asano was colour blind but had kept this secret for fear that his work would be viewed in a negative light. His painting technique directly reflected this.

Cognitive access measures

The information content of the show was various and in a range of media. The catalogue was designed in large print and had Braille, and raised images with an accompanying colour photograph of each work. The text avoided academic or specialist language and was written for an audience with no previous knowledge of contemporary art in a way that would stimulate them to approach it imaginatively. The audio guide included this and the artists talking about the work. Despite its poor sound quality and length, it proved popular with the result that many visitors spent long periods in the exhibition area.

Two hundred and twenty visually impaired people and a sighted public of 4,082 visited the exhibition during its three-week showing, many travelling from across Japan. Of the total of 4,302 visitors, 1,454 entered the exhibition free-of-charge, indicating that one third was either elderly or disabled. Over 800 people took the time to fill out the detailed questionnaires we prepared in print, large print, Braille and English.

Being able to touch the works was of overwhelming popularity for visually impaired visitors while sighted visitors cited the information content as being key to their enjoyment of each work. By including three works which could not be touched – a painting by Jonathan Huxley and two painted photographs by Susan Fenton – I wanted to test the hypothesis that it is not necessary to physically touch a work to appreciate it. If a tactile image and stimulating description of the work were provided would it be sufficient? The answer was both 'yes' and 'no'. Since the idea of works being touched was quite new in Japan, there was little expectation among the sighted public that they could do this and they were not overly disappointed that three out of the 11 could not be touched. In fact, so ingrained was the idea that artworks should never be touched that some of the sighted audience had to be positively encouraged to touch them by the attendants, which they did with apprehensive and tentative gestures unlike many visually impaired visitors whose handling technique was systematic and professional. Appreciation was expressed in the questionnaires that the artworks were made accessible in this way and many of the general public requested that this should be standard practice for all exhibitions at the museum.

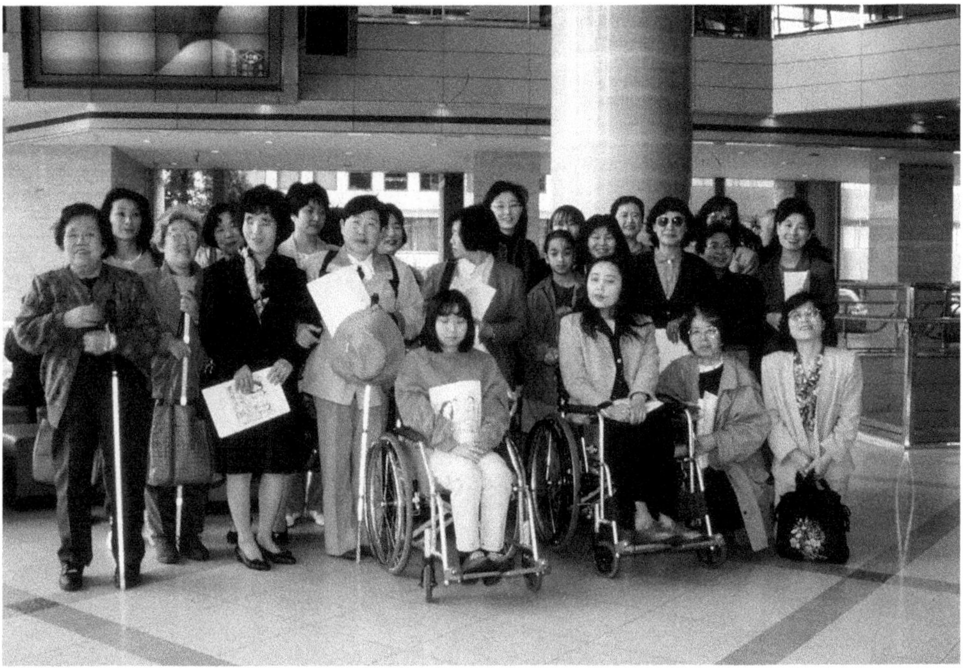

8.3 Access Vision members at the Aichi Prefectural Museum of Art, Japan, 1995 [© Julia Cassim]

The exhibition won the *20th Anniversary Volunteers for Blind Students Award* in the form of a bursary from the College Women's Association. This allowed me to start Access Vision with Yoshimi Harada, head of the Visual Impairment Section of the Nagoya Sports and Rehabilitation Centre who had worked with me on the show. Until my return to the UK in 1998, we organised monthly visits to museums and collections of objects for the group of 26 visually impaired people of different ages (Fig. 8.3). The aim was to develop effective interpretative materials for them, and exert pressure on museums to open up services. Creative workshops were also run where they could expand their understanding their tactile and conceptual understanding of artworks.[23]

Evolved concepts at the Hyogo Prefectural Art Museum

Since that time, there has been a slow expansion of initiatives for visually-impaired museum visitors in Japan with the Kawagoe City Museum, the Sendai Mediatheque, the Gifu Prefectural Museum of Art and the National Museum of Ethnology in Osaka embedding them in their regular programming – driven by a mixture of legislation and individual curatorial interest.

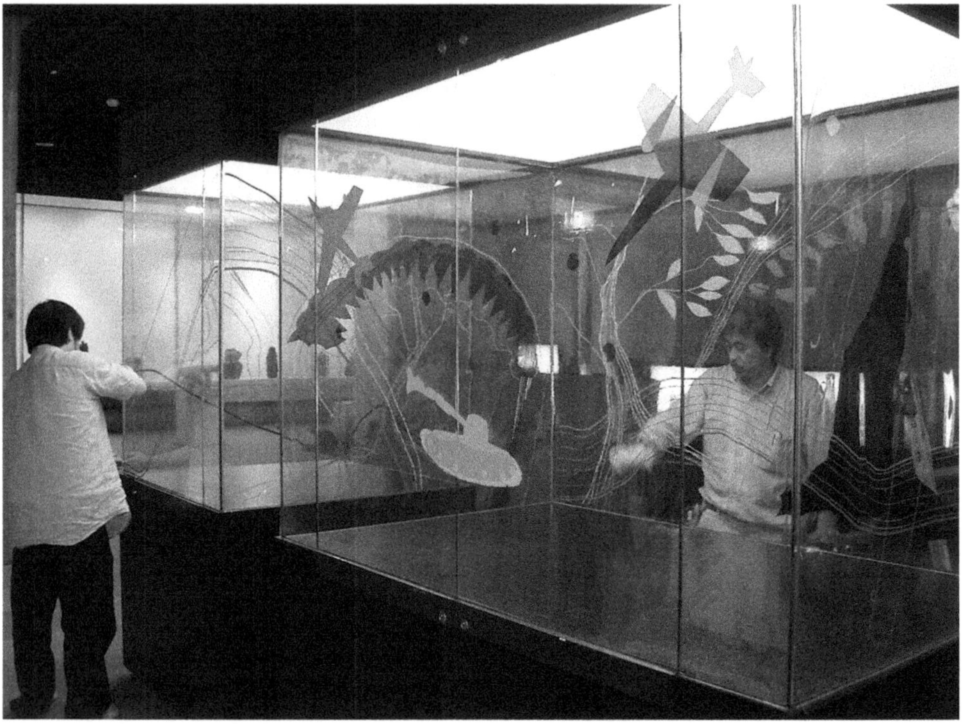

8.4 Blind artist Takayuki Mitsushima (left) prepares vinyl relief drawings on glass cases at the Hayashibara Museum of Art, Okayama, Japan as part of the *Gokan de Miru Kokusai ten* exhibition in October 2004 [© Julia Cassim]

The shining example, however, is the Hyogo Prefectural Art Museum in Kobe, which has organised an annual touch show called *Form in Art* since 1987 aimed at the wider general public. Tadashi Hattori, the curator responsible for many of these shows told me: 'This exhibit is held annually to suggest a new way to appreciate art and to overcome conventional sight-oriented appreciation. We would like all the visitors to think about the visible and invisible, the touchable and untouchable, visually impaired people and so on through this series of exhibitions.'

This consistency and the need to expand exhibition formats for a museum whose focus is modern and contemporary art has allowed for conceptual development of the touch show genre.

Three recent shows demonstrate Hyogo's diversity of approach. Takayuki Mitsushima is a blind artist and graduate of the Access Vision workshops. He creates low-relief drawings using Letraline for linear depictions and thin, coloured, vinyl sheets to express volume. In 2004, he created a large-scale work in this manner for an exhibition of works by visually impaired artists from Japan, Nepal and the UK that I co-curated with Yohei Nishimura at the Hayashibara Museum of Art in Okayama. The museum has a fine collection of traditional art and craftworks encased behind glass and Mitsushima used one of the glass cases as the surface, creating a four-sided 'drawing' (Fig. 8.4) that was illuminated from behind.

In 2002, Mitsushima was invited by Hyogo to select modern works from the permanent collection and interpret them on paper in this way after tactile exploration of them. The show was a means by which the sighted public could have insight into a tactile aesthetic interpreted by someone with high tactile literacy (Mitsushima works as an acupuncturist and masseur) but with an awareness of the visual conventions of two-dimensional depiction since he lost his sight at the age of 10.

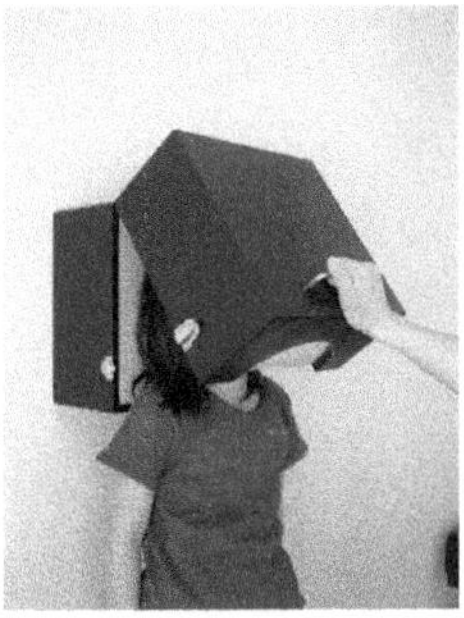

8.5 Takao Sugiura, *Sandwich the Face* (*Ganmen Basamiki*), mixed materials, in the *Form in Art – Everybody Fumbles* exhibition, Hyogo Prefectural Museum of Art, Japan, 2005 [© Takao Sugiura]

In 2005 and 2007, two conceptual artists were invited to create complete installations. The first, called *Everybody Fumbles* by Takao Sugiura, presented the museum with a health and safety nightmare but was one to which the public responded with enthusiasm. One of the galleries was filled to chest height with tiny expanded polystyrene beads in which bronze works from the permanent collection were buried. Children and those under 120 cm in height had to be accompanied and visitors were asked to wade out to the works whose tops could be glimpsed and explore them tactilely wearing eye masks. A dressing room was provided for possessions and visitors given the chilling reminder: 'Please be careful not to fall down ... for we cannot find out or rescue the person under the beads [*sic*].' The second work in the show *Ganmen Basamiki* (*Sandwich the Face*) was a hinged wooden trap-like device hung on the wall in which visitors could literally sandwich their faces for a claustrophobic experience of darkness (Fig. 8.5).

The 2007 installation by project-based artist Noriyuki Yamamura drew on the experience of the 1995 Great Hanshin earthquake in Kobe where the museum is located. The downtown area of the city that had been most devastated by the resulting fires was home to many small shoe manufacturing workshops employing Japanese residents of Korean or *Burakumin* origin – the latter descendants of outcast communities of the feudal era, whose occupations were considered 'tainted' with death or ritual impurity, such as leatherwork. Both groups have suffered significant social discrimination in Japan. Thus Yamamura's work linked three marginalised groups through the medium of a work with historical and social resonance that was also a stand-alone tactile and sensory experience of a high order. Yamamura asked a group of retired female leatherworkers to create a large stuffed outspread hand based on his own in strips of synthetic leather, which replicated its lines. Three bronze sculptures from the permanent collection were placed on different fingers and sighted visitors were asked to explore the installation wearing eye masks (Fig. 8.6).

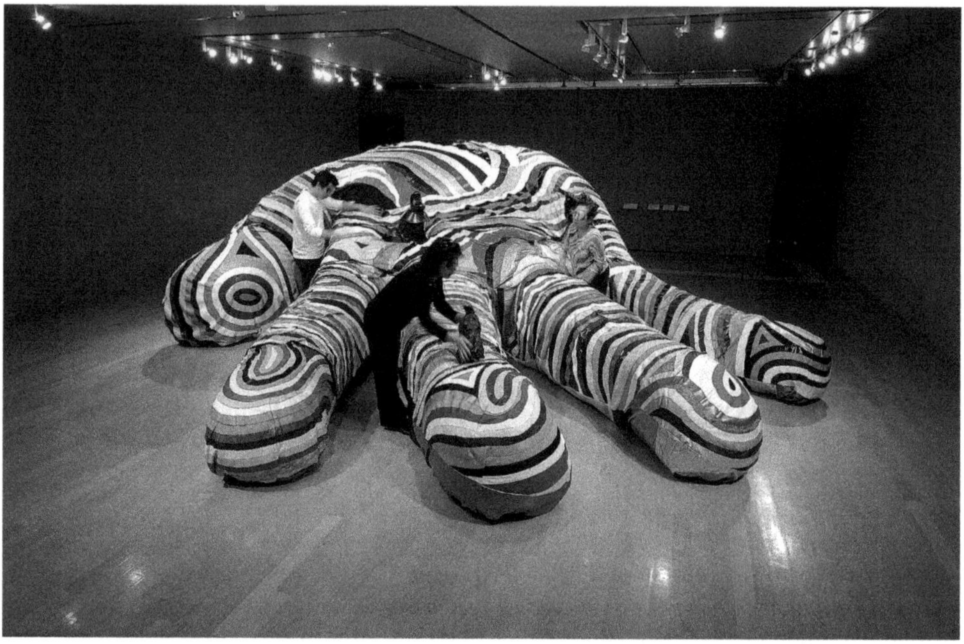

8.6 Noriyuki Yamamura, *Hand*, in the *Form in Art* exhibition, Hyogo Prefectural Museum of Art, Japan, 2007 [© Noriyuki Yamamura]

All three examples and the RCA show demonstrate that touch tours need not be the finite expression of a museum's commitment to an audience that holds the key to new and radical approaches to the interpretation of its collections. If one looks at the history of innovation particularly in the area of communications, many product concepts have their roots in sensory impairments – from the invention of the typewriter in 1808 by Pellegrino Turri for his blind friend the Countess Carolina Fantoni da Fivizzono to enable her to write legibly, to the first applications found for the transistor by Bardeen, Brattain and Shockley as a more reliable, powerful, flexible, smaller, cheaper and cooler power source for hearing aids. It seems logical that the same could happen if the lateral vision and different sensory vocabulary and understanding of visually impaired museum visitors and artists were unleashed to transform the 'special service' of the touch tour into an integrated experience that could be enjoyed by all.

Notes

1. Tansei Sogo Kenkyujo, statistics quoted in 'Cultural Coffins', *AERA*, 2 February 1993 (in Japanese).
2. J. Cassim, 'Letting Kids Get a Feel for Art', *The Japan Times*, Tokyo, 21 July 1991; J. Cassim, 'Toyama Museum Constructed with Care', *The Japan Times*, Tokyo, 21 February 1993; J. Cassim, 'Summer

Programs Keep Kids Busy', *The Japan Times*, Tokyo, 1 August 1993; J. Cassim, 'Keep the Kids off the Streets with Summer Art Workshops', *The Japan Times*, Tokyo, 14 July 1996.

3. Kenkyujo, 'Cultural Coffins'.

4. E. Hooper-Greenhill, *The Educational Role of the Museum*, London and New York: Routledge, 1994, p.324.

5. Museums and Galleries Commission, *Arts for Everyone: Guidance on Provision for Disabled People*, London: Centre for Accessible Environments and Carnegie UK Trust, 1985; and J. Earnscliffe, *In through the Front Door: Disabled People and the Visual Arts: Examples of Good Practice*, London: Arts Council of Great Britain, 1992.

6. See J. Cassim, *Into the Light: Museums and Their Visually-Impaired Visitors*, Tokyo: Shogakkan, 1998 (in Japanese); J. Cassim, 'The Touch Experience in Museums in the UK and Japan', in *The Power of Touch: Handling Objects in Museum and Heritage Contexts*, E. Pye, ed., Walnut Creek, CA: Left Coast Press, 2007, pp.163–83; A. Housen, 'Validating a Measure of Aesthetic Development for Museums and Schools', *ILVS Review: A Journal of Visitor Behavior*, 2 (2), 1992, pp.1–19; A Housen and N.L. Miller, *MOMA School Program Evaluation Study: Report II*, New York: MOMA, 1992; P. Yenawine, *Writing for Adult Museum Visitors*, New York: Visual Understanding in Education, 1997.

7. Cassim, *Into the Light* and Cassim, 'Touch Experience'.

8. A. Whincop, 'Loan Services in Great Britain: Historical and Philosophical Account', unpublished paper, 1983, available from Department of Museum Studies, University of Leicester, Leicester.

9. J.A.C. Deas, 'The Showing of Museums and Art Galleries to the Blind', *Museums Journal*, 13 (3), 1913–14, pp.85–109.

10. American Association of Museums, *The Accessible Museum: Model Programs of Accessibility for Disabled and Older People*, Washington, DC: AAM, 1992, p.13.

11. A. Eaton, *Beauty for the Sighted and the Blind*, New York: St Martin's Press, 1959.

12. Museums and Galleries Commission, *Art for Everyone*.

13. Royal Ontario Museum, *The Museum and the Visually Impaired*, Report, Toronto, Canada: Royal Ontario Museum, 1980.

14. Walsall Museum and Art Gallery, *Children Should Be Seen and Not Heard: Is There a Place for Young Children in the Art Gallery?*, Conference papers, Walsall, 1995.

15. Cassim, 'Keep the Kids off'.

16. S. Khayami, 'Touching Art, Touching You: Blindart, Sense and Sensuality', in *The Power of Touch: Handling Objects in Museum and Heritage Contexts*, E. Pye, ed., Walnut Creek, CA: Left Coast Press, 2007, pp.183–90.

17. O. Sacks, *An Anthropologist on Mars*, London: Picador, 1995; O. Sacks, 'A New Vision of the Mind from Nature's Imagination: The Frontiers of Scientific Vision', in *Nature's Imagination: The Frontiers of Scientific Vision*, John Cornwell, ed., Oxford: Oxford University Press, 1995, pp.101–21; Cassim, *Into the Light*; and Cassim, 'Touch Experience'.

18. R. Morphet, ed., *Encounters: New Art from Old*, London: National Gallery, 2000.

19. South Bank Centre, *Darklight: BT Dialogue in the Dark*, London: BT and Royal Festival Hall, 1995; A. Geary, 'Exploring Virtual Touch in the Creative Arts and Conservation', in *The Power of Touch: Handling Objects in Museum and Heritage Contexts*, E. Pye, ed., Walnut Creek, CA: Left Coast Press, 2007, pp.241–52; C. Spence, 'Making Sense of Touch: A Multisensory Approach to the Perception of Objects', in *The Power of Touch: Handling Objects in Museum and Heritage Contexts*, E. Pye, ed., Walnut Creek, CA: Left Coast Press, 2007, pp.45–61; D. Prytherch and M. Jefsioutine, 'Touching Ghosts: Haptic Technologies in Museums', in *The Power of Touch: Handling Objects in Museum and Heritage Contexts*, E. Pye, ed., Walnut Creek, CA: Left Coast Press, 2007, pp.223–40.

20. S. Fukurai, *How Can I Make What I Cannot See?*, New York: Van Nostrand Reinhold, 1974.

21. Y. Nishimura, *Mita koto nai mono*, Tokyo: Kaiseisha, 1984; Y. Nishimura, *Te no naka no uchu*, Tokyo: Kaiseisha, 1991; Y. Nishimura, *Te de miru katachi*, Tokyo: Hakusuisha, 1995.

22. Nagoya City Art Museum, *Art and the Inner Eye #1*, Nagoya, 1994 (in Japanese – English text available from author).

23. Cassim, *Into the Light* and Cassim, 'Touch Experience'.

Bibliography

American Association of Museums, *The Accessible Museum: Model Programs of Accessibility for Disabled and Older People*, Washington, DC: AAM, 1992.

Cassim, Julia, 'Letting Kids Get a Feel for Art', *The Japan Times*, Tokyo, 21 July 1991.

——, 'Toyama Museum Constructed with Care', *The Japan Times*, Tokyo, 21 February 1993.

——, 'Summer Programs Keep Kids Busy', *The Japan Times*, Tokyo, 1 August 1993.

——, 'Keep the Kids off the Streets with Summer Art Workshops', *The Japan Times*, Tokyo, 14 July 1996.

——, *Into the Light: Museums and Their Visually-Impaired Visitors*, Tokyo: Shogakkan, 1998 (in Japanese).

——, 'The Touch Experience in Museums in the UK and Japan', in *The Power of Touch: Handling Objects in Museum and Heritage Contexts*, E. Pye, ed., Walnut Creek, CA: Left Coast Press, 2007, pp.163–83.

Deas, J.A.C., 'The Showing of Museums and Art Galleries to the Blind', *Museums Journal*, 13 (3), 1913–14, pp.85–109.

Earnscliffe, J., *In through the Front Door: Disabled People and the Visual Arts: Examples of Good Practice*, London: Arts Council of Great Britain, 1992.

Eaton, A., *Beauty for the Sighted and the Blind*, New York: St Martin's Press, 1959.

Fukurai, S., *How Can I Make What I Cannot See?*, New York: Van Nostrand Reinhold, 1974.

Geary, A., 'Exploring Virtual Touch in the Creative Arts and Conservation', in *The Power of Touch: Handling Objects in Museum and Heritage Contexts*, E. Pye, ed., Walnut Creek, CA: Left Coast Press, 2007, pp.241–52.

Hooper-Greenhill, E., *The Educational Role of the Museum*, London and New York: Routledge, 1994.

Housen, A., 'Validating a Measure of Aesthetic Development for Museums and Schools', *ILVS Review: A Journal of Visitor Behavior*, 2 (2), 1992, pp.1–19.

Housen, A. and N.L. Miller, *MOMA School Program Evaluation Study: Report II*, New York: MOMA, 1992.

Kenkyujo, Tansei Sogo, 'Cultural Coffins', *AERA*, 2 February 1993 (in Japanese).

Khayami, S., 'Touching Art, Touching You: Blindart, Sense and Sensuality', in *The Power of Touch: Handling Objects in Museum and Heritage Contexts*, E. Pye, ed., Walnut Creek, CA: Left Coast Press, 2007, pp.183–90.

Morphet, R., ed., *Encounters: New Art from Old*, London: National Gallery, 2000.

Museums and Galleries Commission, *Arts for Everyone: Guidance on Provision for Disabled People*, London: Centre for Accessible Environments and Carnegie UK Trust, 1985.

Nagoya City Art Museum, *Art and the Inner Eye #1*, Nagoya, 1994 (in Japanese – English text available from Julia Cassim).

Nishimura, Y., *Mita koto nai mono*, Tokyo: Kaiseisha, 1984.

——, *Te no naka no uchu*, Tokyo: Kaiseisha, 1991.

——, *Te de miru katachi*, Tokyo: Hakusuisha, 1995.

Prytherch, D. and M. Jefsioutine, 'Touching Ghosts: Haptic Technologies in Museums', in *The Power of Touch: Handling Objects in Museum and Heritage Contexts*, E. Pye, ed., Walnut Creek, CA: Left Coast Press, 2007, pp.223–40.

Pye, E., ed., *The Power of Touch: Handling Objects in Museum and Heritage Contexts*, Walnut Creek, CA: Left Coast Press, 2007.

Royal Ontario Museum, *The Museum and the Visually Impaired*, Report, Toronto: Royal Ontario Museum, 1980.

Sacks, O., 'A New Vision of the Mind from Nature's Imagination: The Frontiers of Scientific Vision', in *Nature's Imagination: The Frontiers of Scientific Vision*, John Cornwell, ed., Oxford: Oxford University Press, 1995, pp.101–21.
——, *An Anthropologist on Mars*, London: Picador, 1995.
South Bank Centre, *Darklight: BT Dialogue in the Dark*, London: BT and Royal Festival Hall, 1995.
Spence, Charles, 'Making Sense of Touch: A Multisensory Approach to the Perception of Objects', in *The Power of Touch: Handling Objects in Museum and Heritage Contexts*, E. Pye, ed., Walnut Creek, CA: Left Coast Press, 2007, pp.45–61.
Walsall Museum and Art Gallery, *Children Should Be Seen and Not Heard: Is There a Place for Young Children in the Art Gallery?*, Conference papers, Walsall, 1995.
Whincop, A., 'Loan Services in Great Britain: Historical and Philosophical Account', unpublished paper, 1983, available from Department of Museum Studies, University of Leicester, Leicester.
Yenawine, P., *Writing for Adult Museum Visitors*, New York: Visual Understanding in Education, 1997.

9

The sculptor is a blind man: Constantin Brancusi's *Sculpture for the Blind*

Sebastiano Barassi

A considerable portion of early twentieth-century art was deeply influenced by contemporaneous, seismic shifts in philosophical and scientific thought. From Friedrich Nietzsche to Henri Bergson, from Albert Einstein to Ernest Rutherford, many of the most innovative thinkers of the period (and thus most fashionable among artists) fundamentally challenged the possibility of absolute, objective knowledge. Under scrutiny in particular was the inadequacy of sensorial experience for the understanding of natural phenomena, with numerous philosophers and scientists also questioning the predominance of sight over the other senses. Along with technological advances in sound recording, photography and film, which offered fresh perspectives for the exploration of the world, these ideas led to the unprecedented widening of the gap between the new, highly abstracted representations of reality put forward by theoreticians and the more established ones based on everyday sensory experience.

In response, a number of forward-looking artists began to develop highly elaborate new vocabularies to address the changing images of the world, most notably leading to the birth of abstract, or non-figurative, art. In most cases these responses were not a mere translation of ideas and theories into a visual language, but very complex creative elaborations and interpretations. Tellingly, the label 'abstract' was rejected by many of those engaged in these enquiries. Constantin Brancusi, for example, famously declared that 'they are imbeciles who call my work abstract; that which they call abstract is the most realistic, because what is real is not the exterior form but the idea, the essence of things'.[1]

At very few other times in history had artists devised such sophisticated means to learn about and analyse reality (whether internal or external). In this sense it is perhaps useful to consider these developments in relationship to contemporary pedagogical thought. From the second half of the nineteenth century alongside conventional educational approaches a number of more progressive methodologies became increasingly fashionable, at least among the intellectual elites. Of particular interest here are those based on the theories of the Swiss educator Johann Heinrich Pestalozzi. Inspired by Jean-Jacques Rousseau's treatise on education, *Émile* (1762), Pestalozzi elaborated a pedagogical system that encouraged perceptual learning and practical activity instead of linguistic repetition, a system in which tactile experience played an especially important role. Throughout the nineteenth century these ideas were developed and popularised across Europe by a number of pedagogues including, in Germany, Friedrich Fröbel. Like Pestalozzi, Fröbel believed that tactile and visual experiences had greater educational value than forms of instruction based exclusively on language. His theories also played an important role in shaping the more forward-looking systems of child education that followed. Maria Montessori's Method, for example, was founded on the centrality of sensory learning and attributed great value to the 'education of the hand'.

Some of the key figures of early twentieth-century art and architecture were schooled following these principles, most notably Vassily Kandinsky, Piet Mondrian, Paul Klee, Le Corbusier and Frank Lloyd Wright. Thus the development of strands of modernist art such as geometric abstraction can be interpreted as resulting from:

> the spread of the Rousseauian model of education as a broad cultural phenomenon [which] was complemented by a growing faith in the power of geometric form ... These beliefs in harmony and the elemental nature of the geometric solids would often be not merely philosophical, but as in the case of theosophy, spiritual in dimension. Indeed, the first historical avant-garde movement to sublate art into life for revolutionary purposes came, not with the ideological sponsorship of socialism or communism, but with that of spiritualism and theosophy. Kandinsky, Paul Klee, Johannes Itten, Wright, Piet Mondrian, and of course Le Corbusier all maintained that turning art toward abstract geometric form would lead to a complete spiritual transformation of society.[2]

With so many and so influential artists educated to observe reality through a widening range of perceptual modes, it was perhaps inevitable that a tendency towards what Martin Jay has described as 'anti-ocularcentrism' should develop.[3] In particular it was within this cultural climate that the role of touch in aesthetic experience acquired new relevance, initially as an alternative to pure visuality. The early 1920s saw several examples of this. In Germany László Moholy-Nagy structured his Preliminary Course at the Bauhaus around the notion of providing a full sensorial education, encouraging students to use touch, hearing and smell to experiment with forms and materials. As he later remarked,

> each of the senses with which we record the position of bodies helps us to grasp space. Space is known first of all by the sense of vision. This experience of the visible relations of bodies may be checked by movement – by the alteration of one's position – and by means of touch.[4]

In Italy Filippo Tommaso Marinetti's *Manifesto of Tactilism* of 1921 exalted the role of touch for its intuitive and psychological value, declaring it a central theme of post-war Futurism. For Marinetti 'the ends of Tactilism must be tactile harmonies, simply; and it must collaborate indirectly towards the perfecting of spiritual communication between human beings, through the epidermis'.[5] Dada and Surrealism also championed the inclusion of tactile elements in art, attracted in equal measure by the 'anti-retinal' value of touch and by its erotic possibilities. In fact Francis Picabia challenged Marinetti's claim to have invented Tactilism, crediting instead the sculptor Edith Clifford Williams, whose *Plaster to Touch* (c. 1915) had been illustrated in 1917 in the only issue of the Dada journal *Rongwrong*.[6]

Rongwrong was one of two short-lived magazines published in 1917 in New York by Marcel Duchamp and his friends Walter Arensberg, Henri-Pierre Roché and Beatrice Wood (the other was *The Blind Man* – on which more later). They were the heart and soul of New York Dada, and the subjects of blindness and touch in art were of great interest to them. The questions surrounding the 'retinicity' of painting was, of course, especially important to Duchamp. From the ready-mades onwards, his work revolved around the tension between presence and representation, challenging fundamentally the centrality of vision in the aesthetic experience. Indeed the radical gesture involved in the ready-mades relied on a conceptualisation of the artistic act that pushed the artwork outside a purely visual contextual framework. Duchamp famously declared he was interested in ideas, not visual products, and that his intention was to put 'painting at the service of the mind'.[7] His rejection of the 'retinal' was so absolute that for a period in the 1920s he abandoned painting in favour of chess, a game he played with considerable success.

One of Duchamp's closest associates was the Romanian sculptor Constantin Brancusi. They first met in Paris around 1912 and remained good friends until the latter's death in 1957. Their friendship was founded on artistic as well as more practical shared interests (for example, Duchamp repeatedly helped Brancusi with the sale of his work), and both greatly enjoyed and roused each other's sense of humour. In the 1910s and '20s, despite having some reservations, Brancusi made explicit declarations of sympathy towards Dadaism, and in the 1920s Duchamp became part-owner of some 30 sculptures by the Romanian, also overseeing the installation of a number of his exhibitions in the United States.

Brancusi was famously reluctant to get directly involved in movements and to contribute grand statements to contemporary debates, generally refusing to write or speak at length about his work. However, thanks to his close

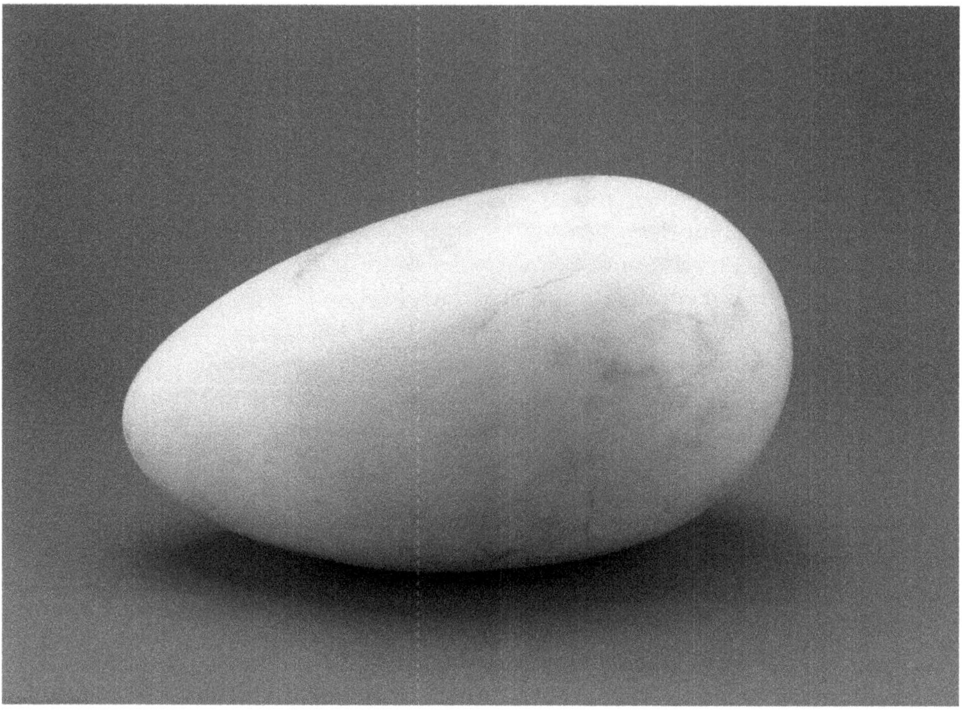

9.1 Constantin Brancusi, *Sculpture for the Blind*, veined marble, c. 1920, Philadelphia Museum of Art, The Louise and Walter Arensberg Collection, 1950 [© 2013. Photo: The Philadelphia Museum of Art / Art Resource / Scala, Florence] [© ADAGP, Paris and DACS, London 2013]

friendship with Duchamp and his circle, he was fully aware of the theoretical discussions around Dada. In fact, at least one work by Brancusi, *Sculpture for the Blind* (Fig. 9.1), can convincingly be interpreted as his contribution, or at least as an outsider's response, to those debates. Remarkably, it remains one of Brancusi's lesser known and studied pieces. This is due in part to the uncertainty that surrounds many aspects of its history, but also to the fact that, if the title and some of the stories around it are to be taken literally, it raises the question of the relationship of blindness with the visual arts, which, for some, remains an uncomfortable subject.

There are only a few established facts about *Sculpture for the Blind*. Firstly, three different versions exist. This is not infrequent with Brancusi, as he liked to re-elaborate a subject in different materials and with more or less substantial formal variations. The earliest version (veined marble, 17.5 × 29.5 × 18 cm) was until recently dated 1916, whereas more recent scholarship suggests pushing it later, towards c. 1920.[8] It was sold by Brancusi to the New York collector and art patron John Quinn in 1922, and then purchased in 1935 by Louise and

Walter Arensberg, with Marcel Duchamp's mediation. In 1950 the Arensbergs donated it, with most of their collection, to the Philadelphia Museum of Art, where it is today. This version is thought to be contemporary with the one in plaster dated 1920–1921 (17.5 × 32 × 24 cm), now in the Atelier Brancusi in Paris. The third version (alabaster, 17.5 × 32.3 × 24 cm) dates from 1925 and is also in the Atelier Brancusi. It was shown at the Salon des Indépendents in Paris in 1926, and at the Brummer Gallery in New York in 1933. As the measurements suggest, the second and third versions are slightly more elongated than the rounder first one.

Although in the past it was suggested that *Sculpture for the Blind* was merely an alternative version of *Beginning of the World* (1920),[9] today the facts that it was Brancusi himself who titled it and that he considered it an individual work are widely accepted. This is an important point, because it is thanks to the title that we can determine Brancusi's intent to associate the smooth and simple forms of the sculpture with blindness, and subsequently with tactile perception. It is also worth pointing out that, in spite of its similarity with the almost perfectly ovoid *Beginning of the World, Sculpture for the Blind* is a less regular piece, as it features shallow planes that are almost invisible to the eye but quite noticeable to the touch.

With this much uncertainty surrounding the most basic historical facts, other information about *Sculpture for the Blind* is even more ambiguous, occasionally amounting to speculation or possibly even myth.[10] A case in point is Henri-Pierre Roché's account of the sculpture's inclusion in the 1917 First Exhibition of the Society of Independent Artists at the Grand Central Palace in New York.[11] No other record of the presence of *Sculpture for the Blind* in the show has been identified to date, and Roché's story (which was published only posthumously) is at odds with the now widely accepted dating of the piece. Yet his recollections are very specific, telling of how the work was shown 'in a closed sack, with two sleeve-holes for the hands … and it was a "revelation for the hands", independent from the eye, although most people thought it was a joke'.[12] As Elio Grazioli points out, most Brancusian scholars tend to treat this claim as Roché's myth-making,[13] or it could simply be a case of misremembering. Alternatively Grazioli, who accepts 1916 as the date of the first version, suggests that the idea of displaying the work in a sack might have been Marcel Duchamp's, possibly as an attempt to place Brancusi more firmly within the Dada camp.[14] What is certain is that no other record has emerged of Brancusi's or Duchamp's plan to exhibit the work this way, in New York or anywhere else, so it seems safe to assume that, if it happened, this remained a one-off gesture.

It is worth noting that the dates of the Independents' exhibition (10 April–6 May 1917) coincide almost exactly with those of the publication in New York of the two issues of the Dada journal *The Blind Man* (no. 1 in April – as *The Blindman* – and no. 2 in May). Both concentrated on the display of contemporary art in America, focusing in particular on the heated discussions that followed the exclusion of Duchamp's *Fountain* from the Independents' exhibition. Thus the journal's title may be taken as both a reference to Duchamp's growing interest in the non-retinal aspects of art and a shot at the inability of public and critics to 'see' the true meaning of his work. It seems plausible that Roché, writing almost 40 years later, might have associated Brancusi's *Sculpture for the Blind* with the Independents' exhibition because of this chronological coincidence, perhaps turning into fact what was only a later thought or a passing humorous comment on the work and its display. The further coincidence of these events with the exhibition in New York and publication in *Rongwrong* of Edith Clifford Williams' *Plaster to Touch* might also have generated some confusion.

Irrespective of the historical accuracy of this anecdote, Roché's essay provides a revealing account of Brancusi's views by one of his closest associates. As the title suggests, the text focuses on *Beginning of the World*, the closest work, stylistically and chronologically, to *Sculpture for the Blind* – a point which Roché himself makes, locating both works within the series of ovoid, recumbent heads. Using the story of the Independents' exhibition as the starting point for an exploration of this strand of Brancusi's work, Roché remarks upon the sculptor's habit of touching and caressing at length his sculptures in the studio, 'placed on his knees, *touched by his hands*, his eyes closed'.[15] This was not only his way of enjoying the finished sculpture, but an integral part of its making; Brancusi was famously very fastidious about the finishing of his works, personally smoothing and polishing them with great care until he obtained the perfect surface qualities he longed for. Thus, Roché writes, Brancusi was twice a blind man, as touch was central to him in both the making and the experience of sculpture.

Roché also cites Brancusi's own words to him about *Beginning of the World* and the other 'egg-skull' pieces: 'I put in it my curiosity for the unknown, an egg in which little cubes ferment, a human brain ... it is a research of depth, of the inside, as the name suggests.'[16] He then describes his own experience of touching *Sculpture for the Blind*, writing of 'veiled forms, contradictory, "the egg", elongated skull, full of angular structures, virtual, underlying'.[17] These are somewhat puzzling statements, which are at odds with the actual forms of the sculpture. Even bearing in mind the gentle modulation of the surface, both Brancusi and Roché rather than describing the work seem to be expressing their feelings and impressions, which originate in the combination of vision (suggesting a human head) and touch (which allows them to perceive deeper than the skull, as far as the 'brain'). The references to the 'inside' and the 'underlying' seem especially meaningful, as they draw attention to the type of non-visual, under-the-surface observation the sculpture is supposed to elicit. So is this what Brancusi thinks is the kind of perception to which the suspension of vision can lead? Are these purely mental images that emerge from an immersion in the darkness of blindness? Are they the result of the different types of memory stimulated by different senses? The suggestion seems to be that through touch we can 'see' more than if we rely on sight alone. Can touch, then, become a sort of 'mother vision'?

Roché discussed again the significance of touch, of the hand and of experiencing with the eyes shut, in two essays he wrote shortly after Brancusi's death in 1957. *L'Enterrement de Brancusi* includes several mentions of hands giving objects, flowers and food (as is common in Romanian funeral customs), and tells of how Brancusi, 'welcoming beautiful women in his atelier, would put a handkerchief over their eyes and little onions and cheese in their mouths saying: "Bite and guess what it is"'.[18] In the second text (titled simply *Constantin Brancusi*), Roché more succinctly refers to the sculptor as a 'wizard with the hands' and a 'sorcerer',[19] introducing a reference to magic that fits in well with the Romanian's inclination towards mysticism and the spiritual sphere.

Roché's insistence on the role of touch and the hand in Brancusi's practice is well justified. Its genesis can be traced back to the beginning of the sculptor's career. In 1907 Brancusi worked for a few months as a technician in Auguste Rodin's workshop, and a Rodinian influence is evident in many of his sculptures from that period. One of Rodin's most celebrated works, *The Gates of Hell*, includes a striking group inspired by Dante's account in the *Inferno* of the ordeal endured by Count Ugolino. Following the poet quite literally, Rodin portrayed Ugolino on his knees, blinded by starvation and groping for his dying children, capturing one of the last moments before 'hunger did what sorrow could not do'.[20] Although Brancusi was never really inclined towards this kind of dramatic story-telling, some of his works from 1906–1907 (in particular the lost *Repose, The Redskins, Sleeping Child* and the three versions of the very Rodinesque *Torment*) were by far the most expressively charged he ever made, and like *Ugolino*, they can be seen to include references – albeit tangential – to blindness.

Crucially, these works introduced forms and themes which were to remain in Brancusi's repertoire for the rest of his career. In formal terms, they are the earliest examples of the sculptor's engagement with the recumbent isolated head, a theme from which originated a sequence of works in which *Sculpture for the Blind* also belongs. In pieces like *Sleeping Child* (1908), *Sleeping Muse* (first version from 1910), *Prometheus* (1911) and *The Newborn* (1915) Brancusi used the unifying formal solution of the recumbent head to explore and bring together themes as diverse as sleep, childhood and torment. *Prometheus* (of which eight versions exist, made between 1911 and probably 1917) is a telling example. The work is titled after the Titan condemned by Zeus to the eternal torment of having his liver eaten daily by an eagle, as a punishment for stealing fire from the Gods. Sydney Geist, pointing out the childishness of the features, wrote that

> the head is inclined to one side in a gesture of pain that Brancusi used in *Torment* and *The Redskins* ... In effect, then we have here a head of a child burdened with the Promethean fate. The head was a portrait of an actual child, now a man whom it still resembles; the title may reveal Brancusi's feelings about the real difficulties surrounding the birth of the child.[21]

This sense of distress which Brancusi associated with birth – he is quoted as saying 'newborns come into the world angry because they are brought into it against their will'[22] – is evident in the open-mouthed scream of *The Newborn*, which formally is quite close to *Sleeping Muse*. And with it we come full circle, as the 1925 version of *Sculpture for the Blind* was exhibited at the Salon des Indépendents in Paris in 1926 with the title *Sleeping Muse (Sculpture for the Blind)*.

Such a complex network of references is frequent in Brancusi's work. *Sculpture for the Blind*, for example, can be interpreted both as part of the recumbent head series, combining the themes of blindness and sleep, and as a much more abstract statement, opening the way for works like *Beginning of the World*. The association of sleep with blindness is particularly meaningful. Sleep can be seen to be a form of temporary blindness, occurring as it does with the eyes shut, in darkness and looking inwards. In sleep, through dreams, we often see things that the eye cannot see; like blindness it involves a suspension of visual perception, and a reliance on different modes of consciousness. The abandonment of vision invites, as we have seen, a stronger reliance on other senses. For Brancusi blindness invites touch, which in turn elicits simple, easily readable forms. This serves perfectly the search for formal purity expressing the 'essence of things' which was one of the central aspects of his art, animated as it was by a modernist version of Neo-Platonism. The essence of things, incidentally, is arguably best captured in the *Beginning of the World*, the egg/seed from which everything is generated, and the most absolute and simplified of Brancusi's forms – and, as we have seen, the closest work to *Sculpture for the Blind*.

Grazioli notes that when John Quinn purchased *Sculpture for the Blind* Brancusi gave him two other sculptures as presents, the marble *Hand of Mademoiselle Pogany* (1920) and the wood *Cup I* (1917), as well as a drawing of *Mademoiselle Pogany* (1912?).[23] This is especially significant in consideration of the great importance attributed by Brancusi to the grouping of his work, as his Parisian studio famously illustrates. Thus thinking about the role of touch in relationship to *Sculpture for the Blind*, its juxtaposition with *Hand of Mademoiselle Pogany* (Fig. 9.2) is loaded with meaning. The latter has been described as embodying 'not so much the anatomical member as the sense of a caress'.[24] Both pieces are smooth, with no suggestion of naturalistic detail such as fingers or facial features. Uncharacteristically Brancusi did not return to the hand as a stand-alone subject, but only as part of more elaborate compositions, most notably in pieces in which it supports a head such as the various versions of *Mademoiselle Pogany* (the earliest of which dates from 1912).

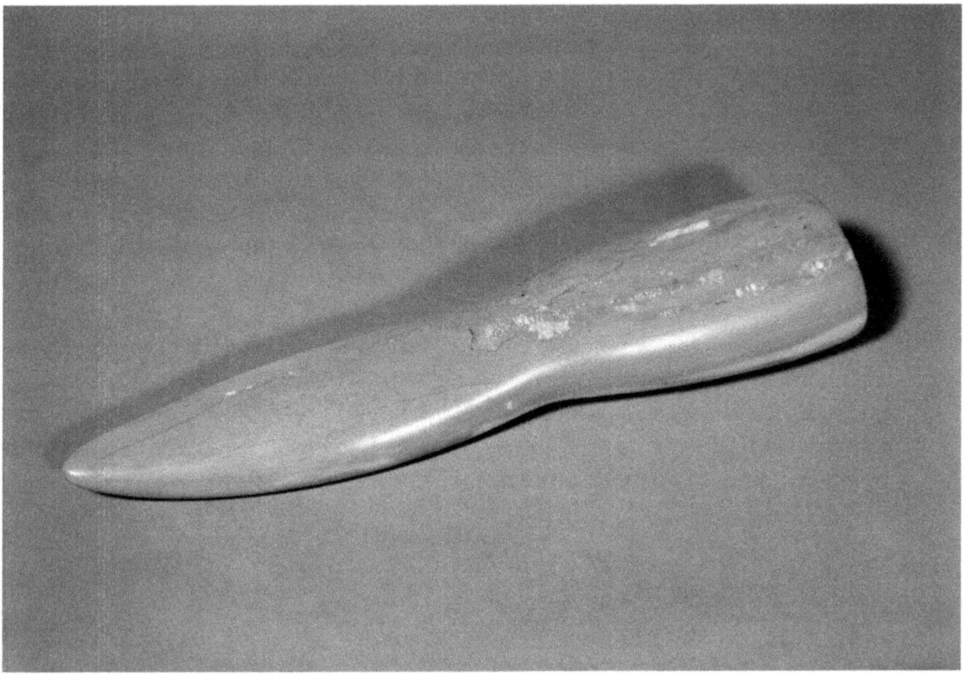

9.2 Constantin Brancusi, *Hand of Mademoiselle Pogany*, 1920, Harvard Art Museums / Fogg Museum, purchase through the generosity of Mr and Mrs Max Wasserman, 1964.110 [Photo: Imaging Department © President and Fellows of Harvard College] [© ADAGP, Paris and DACS, London 2013]

Thus the gift of the drawing seems designed to bring all the elements of the group together, giving it coherence and meaning, and, in light of Brancusi's friendship with Quinn, also suggesting the idea of offering, which is perhaps reinforced by *Cup I*, a piece with a deeply spiritual and ritual feel.

Serge Fauchereau also noted the tactile qualities of *Sculpture for the Blind* and its association with the head sculptures. He observed that the work was 'conceived to be felt with the hands, its roundness is evocative. It is the head and face that a blind person first feels to give shape to someone. A good sculpture makes even those who can see it want to touch it, caress it.'[25] Fauchereau then reads *Sculpture for the Blind* not so much as the primal egg, the beginning of creation, nor as a purely mental picture, but rather as a human head seen and felt as it emerges out of the darkness of blindness.

With its elaborate set of references *Sculpture for the Blind* defines perhaps better than any other work by Brancusi his desire to combine formal simplicity with conceptual articulation and depth. In particular the piece epitomises the tension between figuration and abstraction which many consider one of the most enticing qualities of the Romanian's art. *Sculpture for the Blind* represents, with *Beginning of the World,* one of the starkest statements of Brancusi's quest towards the extreme reduction and simplification of forms. As Sidney Geist put it, it is 'a shape *of* the future'.[26] With it Brancusi completely abandons mimesis, and the sculpture coincides with itself, its title significantly referring to the 'function' of the work, not its subject. So could *Sculpture for the Blind* be Brancusi's answer to the question of abstraction? Does he see abstract art as art for the blind, in that it goes far deeper than the retina? Is he inviting us to look through our inner eye instead? Is he saying we need to be blind to see beyond external appearances and get closer to the 'essence of things'? What is truly remarkable about Brancusi is the fact that his art frequently asks questions with many possible answers, but none ever trivial. Undoubtedly not all his sculptures were made to be touched – certainly not the highly polished metal pieces, whose surfaces are to be enjoyed immaculate. Yet the very fact that with *Sculpture for the Blind* he invites us to close our eyes to really see is without a doubt an extraordinary artistic achievement.

Notes

1. Constantin Brancusi, 'Propos no. 22', in *Theories of Modern Art,* Herschel B. Chipp, ed., Berkeley, CA: California Studies in History of Art, 1968, p.365.
2. Kazys Varnelis, 'The Education of the Innocent Eye', *Journal of Architectural Education,* 51 (4), May 1998, p.214.
3. Martin Jay, *Downcast Eyes: The Denigration of Vision in 20th Century French Thought,* Berkeley, CA: University of California Press, 1993.
4. László Moholy-Nagy, *The New Vision and Abstract of an Artist,* New York: Wittenborn, 1947, p.57.
5. Filippo Tommaso Marinetti, *'Manifesto del tattilismo',* in *Archivi del futurismo,* Maria Drudi Gambillo and Teresa Fiori, eds, Milan: Mondadori, 1958, pp.56–61, my translation. In support of his claim that Tactilism was a Futurist invention Marinetti mentions Umberto Boccioni's pre-War exploration of the tactile qualities of sculpture, in particular the juxtaposition of materials with different properties (iron, porcelain and human hair) in *Fusione di una testa e di una finestra* of 1911.
6. *Rongwrong,* 1, July 1917, p.3. After being shown by Picabia a photograph of *Plaster to Touch,* Guillaume Apollinaire included the work in an article and a lecture on touch in art (Guillaume Apollinaire, 'L'art tactile', *Mercure de France,* 16 February 1918).
7. Marcel Duchamp, 'Painting at the Service of the Mind' (1946), in Chipp, *Theories,* p.395.
8. For the 1916 dating see Pontus Hulten, Natalia Dumitrescu and Alexandre Istrati, *Brancusi,* London: Faber & Faber, 1988, cat. 90, p.290; and Sidney Geist, *Brancusi,* New York: Grossman, 1968, p.56. On grounds of its affinity with *Beginning of the World* and with the plaster version in the Atelier Brancusi, scholars at the Philadelphia Museum of Art and the Musée national d'art moderne in Paris now suggest 1920–21 as the more likely date.
9. See, for example, Athena C. Tacha, 'Legend, Reality and Impact', *Art Journal,* 22 (4), summer 1963, pp.240–41.
10. See Elio Grazioli, 'La *Scultura per Ciechi* di Brancusi', *Riga* (Constantin Brancusi), 19, 2001, pp.325–33. I am indebted to Grazioli for his generosity in sharing the research which provided the starting point for this essay.
11. Henri-Pierre Roché, 'Notice sur le "Commencement du Monde" de Brancusi' (1955), in *Écrits sur l'art,* Paris: André Dimanche, 1998, pp.129–31; all translations from this book are mine.
12. Roché, 'Notice', p.129.

13. Grazioli, 'La *Scultura*', p.326.
14. Grazioli, 'La *Scultura*', p.326.
15. Roché, 'Notice', p.129.
16. Roché, 'Notice', p.129.
17. Roché, 'Notice', p.129.
18. Henri-Pierre Roché, 'L'enterrement de Brancusi' (1957), in *Écrits sur l'art*, p.138.
19. Henri-Pierre Roché, 'Constantin Brancusi' (1957), in *Écrits sur l'art*, p.141.
20. Dante Alighieri, *Divine Comedy*, 'Inferno', canto XXXIII.
21. Sidney Geist, *Constantin Brancusi, 1876–1957: A Retrospective Exhibition*, New York: Solomon R. Guggenheim Museum, 1969, p.47.
22. Hulten, Dumitrescu and Istrati, *Brancusi*, p.100.
23. Grazioli, 'La *Scultura*', p.329. It is perhaps worth noting that Hulten, Dumitrescu and Istrati (*Brancusi*, p.291, cat. 95; and p.296, cat. 117) date the gift of the two sculptures to 1920. If this is correct, the purchase of *Sculpture for the Blind* completed Quinn's small group rather than initiate it. However, the chronological discrepancy does not detract from Grazioli's point.
24. Geist, *Brancusi*, p.76.
25. Serge Fauchereau, *Sur le pas de Brancusi*, Paris: Cercle d'art, 1995, p.76, my translation.
26. Geist, *Brancusi*, p.79.

Bibliography

Apollinaire, Guillaume, 'L'art tactile', *Mercure de France*, 16 February 1918.

Chipp, Herschel B., *Theories of Modern Art*, Berkeley, CA: California Studies in History of Art, 1968.

Fauchereau, Serge, *Sur le pas de Brancusi*, Paris: Cercle d'art, 1995.

Geist, Sidney, *Brancusi*, New York: Grossman, 1968.

——, *Constantin Brancusi, 1876–1957: A Retrospective Exhibition*, New York: Solomon R. Guggenheim Museum, 1969.

Grazioli, Elio, 'La *Scultura per Ciechi* di Brancusi', *Riga* (Constantin Brancusi), 19, 2001, pp.325–33.

Hulten, Pontus, Natalia Dumitrescu and Alexandre Istrati, *Brancusi*, London: Faber & Faber, 1988.

Jay, Martin, *Downcast Eyes: The Denigration of Vision in 20th Century French Thought*, Berkeley, CA: University of California Press, 1993.

Marinetti, Filippo Tommaso, 'Manifesto del tattilismo', in *Archivi del futurismo*, Maria Drudi Gambillo and Teresa Fiori, eds, Milan: Mondadori, 1958, pp.56–61.

Moholy-Nagy, László, *The New Vision and Abstract of an Artist*, New York: Wittenborn, 1947.

Roché, Henri-Pierre, *Écrits sur l'art*, Paris: André Dimanche, 1998.

Tacha, Athena C., 'Legend, Reality and Impact', *Art Journal*, 22 (4), summer 1963, pp.240–41.

Varnelis, Kazys, 'The Education of the Innocent Eye', *Journal of Architectural Education*, 51 (4), May 1998, pp.212–23.

Embracing stone, holding brushes: differentiating touch in the *Unit One* photographs

Fiona Candlin

Within twentieth- and twenty-first-century art writing, touch is often discussed in homogenising terms. Rather than being concerned with the differences between patting and grasping, stroking and holding, or between the varying effects of touch depending on what is touched and who touches, commentators often attribute particular qualities or characteristics to the act of touching. A significant example of this tendency is Nicholas Bourriaud's characterisation of touch within *Relational Aesthetics* where he argues that relational or participatory arts offer 'so many hands-on utopias', are a 'hands-on civilisation', provide 'a tangible symbol' of the state of social encounters today, have a 'tangible dimension as tools serving to link individuals and human groups', and as such provide an alternative to the alienated conditions of contemporary society.[1] At no point does Bourriaud discuss the detail of these tactile encounters or countenance the possibility that tactual encounters may be inequitable, oppressive or alienating.

Similarly homogenising examples of touch can often be found in the association between touch and women's art and experience. During the 1960s and 1970s touch and texture formed part of woman-centred imagery and although these art practices were firmly refuted by feminists who argued against 'the notion of an unchanging female "essence"', a certain equation between touch and women's art and experience has remained current.[2] In these instances contemporary feminists generally use 'touch' as a means of strategically refuting patriarchal conceptions of disembodied vision but, while this approach can be powerful, it can also assume that touch necessarily counters vision, that it is always conceived or experienced as 'embodied', and that it is primarily connected to female experience and notions of femininity.[3]

In this chapter, I examine a short series of photographs to demonstrate how complex, nuanced and historically specific representations and discourses of touch can be. The images in question are from the exhibition catalogue *Unit One: The Modern Movement in English Architecture, Painting and Sculpture* which included photographs of the participating artists' hands. Published in 1934, the images show the artists holding their brushes, pencils or materials, their hands delicately poised, engaging in work or even embracing their sculptures. A close analysis of these images suggests that these variations were significant to the distinction between painters' practices and those of sculptors, to the construction of the artists' gendered personas and to the attribution of authority within their given fields.

The artist's hand

The group Unit One was founded by the painter Paul Nash in 1933 and comprised the architects Welles Coates and Colin Lucas, the sculptors Barbara Hepworth and Henry Moore, and the painters Edward Wadsworth, Ben Nicholson, Frances Hodgkins (later replaced by Tristram Hillier), Edward Burra, John Bigge and John Armstrong; a diverse group whom Paul Nash corralled together under the label 'non-figuratif' and within a general commitment to the modern.[4] Announcing the formation of the group in a letter to the *Times*, he wrote that the 11 participants eschewed repetitions of Pre-Raphaelite or Impressionist styles, and turned away from Nature, in favour of experimenting with design as a structural process and the 'imagination explored apart from literature or metaphysics'.[5] For Nash the group stood 'for the expression of a truly contemporary spirit, for that thing which is recognised as peculiarly of *today* in painting, sculpture and architecture'.[6]

In his introduction to the group's exhibition catalogue, Herbert Read reiterated their shared commitment to 'the forward thrust of modernism' and the contemporary spirit.[7] Their collective agenda was further constructed and reinforced through the design of the catalogue which, despite the diverse contributors and contributions, was highly standardised. Each member of the group was allocated their own section which featured photographs of the artist, their hands, and their work alongside a written statement. The corresponding photographs are all the same size and most of them were shot from the same angle and taken or cropped to maintain a similar distance from the artwork or artist.[8] The differences between the photographs are minimal but they are nevertheless intriguing, particularly as they pertain to the images of the artists' hands, what they hold and how they hold it.

A key distinction is that all the painters are all shown working with paintbrushes, palette knives, set-squares, mixing bowls, pens and pencils, but the sculptors are photographed touching their materials. Rather than holding her tools as the painters do, Hepworth grasps a large globular pebble or possibly a sculpture in process (Fig. 10.1) between her hands while Moore has his arms tightly wrapped around an unfinished (and unidentified) sculpture (Fig. 10.2).[9]

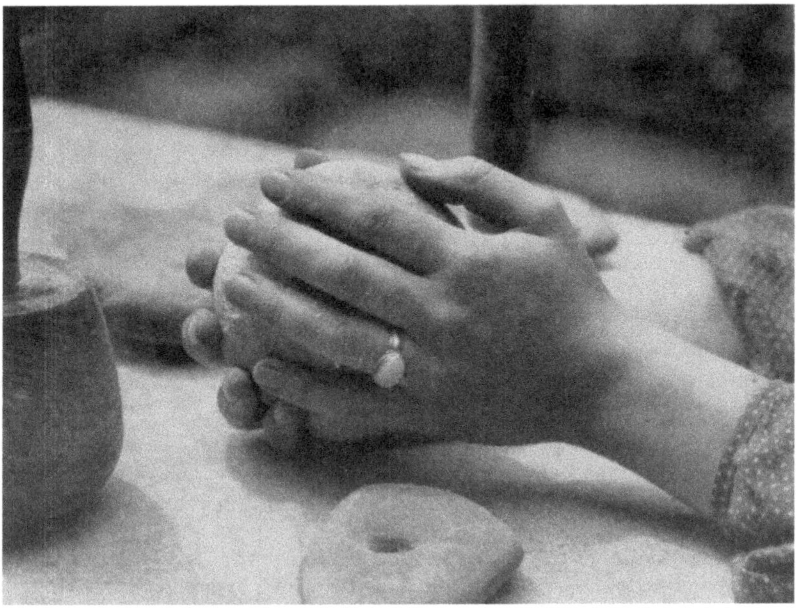

10.1 Barbara Hepworth's hands as published in *Unit One*, photograph by Paul Laib [© Bowness, Hepworth Estate]

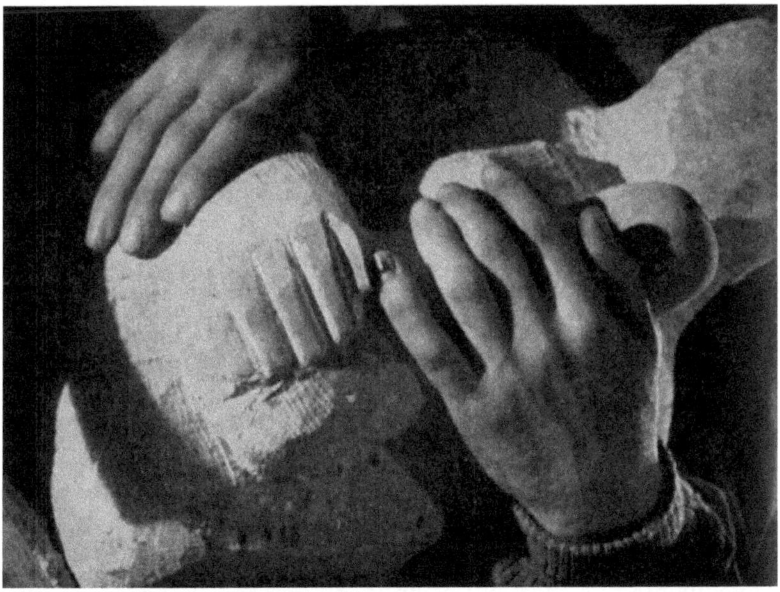

10.2 Henry Moore's hands as published in *Unit One*, photograph by Thea Struve [Reproduced by permission of The Henry Moore Foundation]

It is unlikely that the differences between the images of the painters' and sculptors' hands are accidental since Read commented, that the 'ideals and intentions of the modern movement in art' were articulated within the catalogue, its layout indicates a strong editorial stance and, perhaps more importantly, these poses recur elsewhere.[10] Moore was frequently shown with his arms around his sculptures while Hepworth includes another photograph of herself almost identically positioned in her *Pictorial Autobiography*.[11] What then was at stake here? What did it mean to hold tools rather than to grasp stone?

In 1933, the same year as Unit One was founded, Herbert Read published *Art Now*. The book was clearly read and responded to by his colleagues since John Bigge alluded to it in his *Unit One* artist's statement as did Paul Nash who quoted directly from Read's conclusions. The passage Nash mentioned deals with the notion of the artist's handwriting:

> The ability to express ... which art may have: that is unique in the artist. And by the ability to express I mean literally the technical skill to transpose mental images into linear signs. I mean what has often been called in a very apt metaphor – the artist's handwriting. It is only a metaphor: we must use the word in a large sense, implying that not merely idiosyncrasies, but the whole being of a man is expressed in this act.[12]

Ostensibly straightforward, Read's text makes a series of elisions between artworks, artists and creative production and, in consequence, requires some unpicking. Read refers to artist's handwriting as an act which encompasses the activity of making art and more specifically the transposition of mental images into linear signs (expression). At the same time, the phrase 'not merely idiosyncrasies' implies that handwriting can be read as a noun, referring to the linear signs (form, brushstrokes or image) of the artwork. Read therefore collapses the activity of making art (handwriting) with the style of the artwork (its handwriting), and so the artist's actions and the artwork are rendered synonymous.

In turn, Read closes the distance between the artist's ideas and the artwork. Mental images are conceived of as being transposed into linear signs suggesting that fully formed ideas pass from the mind of the artist, through the hands and brush onto the canvas. The artist's skill lies in his or her unique ability to perform this act of expression and supposedly to convert thought to material object. The artist's idea and the artwork are therefore presented as being straightforwardly conjoined. Finally, Read also advises that handwriting is 'only a metaphor' and that the word must be used 'in a large sense implying that not merely idiosyncrasies', but that 'the *whole being* of a man is expressed in this act'; in other words the handwriting (as material thing) stands for the artist in their entirety.

Thus, within this short but complicated passage, 'handwriting' comes to stand for the artist, the process through which thought becomes image, the unique style of the artist's oeuvre and of individual works, and the act of

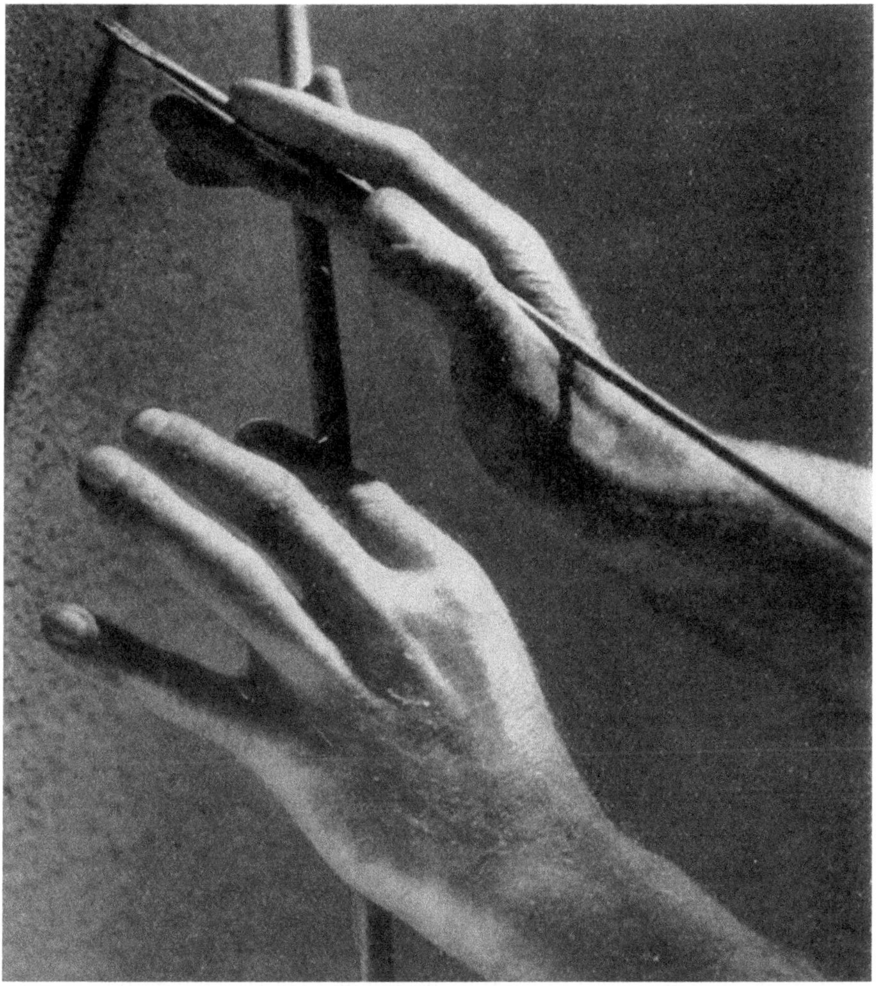

10.3 John Bigge's hands as published in *Unit One*, photograph by Paul Laib [The de Laszlo Collection of Paul Laib Negatives, Witt Library, The Courtauld Institute of Art, London. © The de Laszlo Foundation]

making art. The hand is a synecdoche for the artist, a conduit for thought, the locus of technical skill and the means by which these factors are all transferred onto the canvas (or stone). It is a bravura display of over-determination, but within that context it was neither idiosyncratic nor erroneous. Rather it belonged to a much longer tradition of connoisseurship and art criticism wherein 'the artist's hand' referred to both the style of an artwork (usually a painting) and to the physical hand of the painter, and similarly condensed the applied paint with the activity of painting.[13]

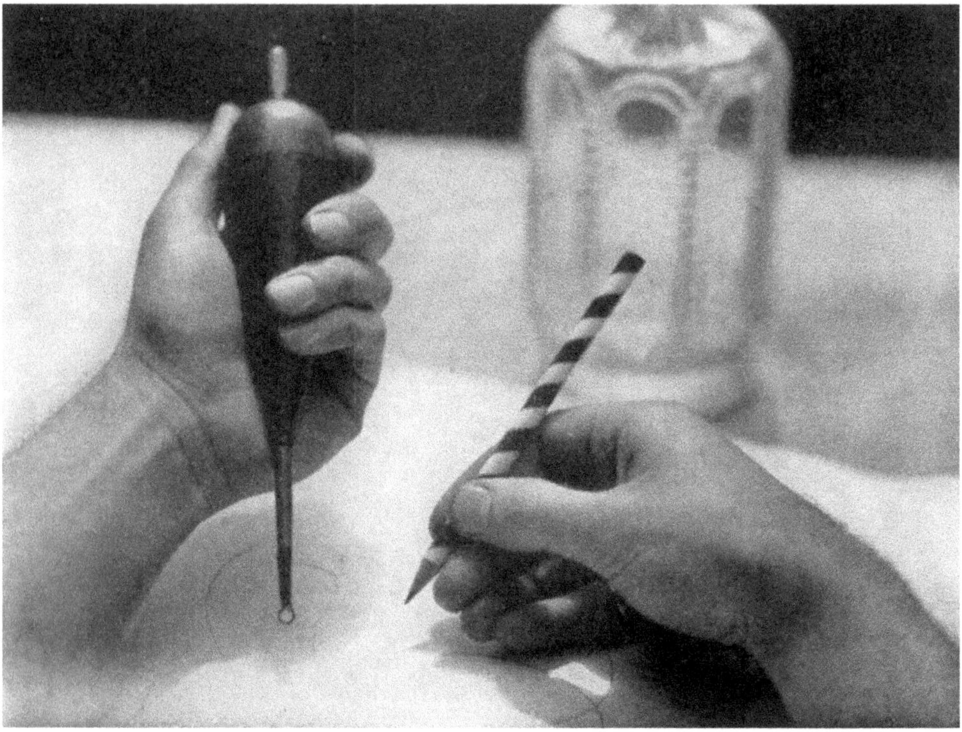

10.4 Ben Nicholson's hands, photograph by Paul Laib [The de Laszlo Collection of Paul Laib Negatives, Witt Library, The Courtauld Institute of Art, London. © The de Laszlo Foundation]

Photographing the artists' hands for the *Unit One* catalogue was therefore a means of signalling the artists' claims to expression, style and personhood, but exactly how these attributes were articulated varied. Depending on what exactly the painters hold and how it is held, the *Unit One* photographs nuance authorship and artistic activity in slightly different ways. The photograph of John Bigge shows him painting using a long slim brush and a mahl stick to keep his hand from touching the canvas, a conventional, even (for then) old fashioned method of painting (Fig. 10.3). At the same time his impossibly poised hands and fingers do not denote actual labour but a moment of pause. This photograph is an image of mastery – perhaps ironically so for Charles Harrison later wrote that 'Bigge's work looked like a ham-fisted version of Wadsworth's'.[14] Ben Nicholson's hands are photographed over his shoulder and appear similarly deft. In his left hand he holds a fishing float, and in his right a striped pencil while in the background, as if it is to be included in an incipient still life, is a glass vase (Fig. 10.4). Nash is shown holding a set-square on an angled architect's desk with one hand and a pencil in the other. In using graphic equipment he is clearly distancing himself from free-hand drawing, but nevertheless his lightly balanced hands serve as an image of control, expertise and skill (Fig. 10.5). Despite their Surrealist and abstract subject matter, the choice and manual articulation of tools within these photographs denotes a traditional 'artistic' persona.

To some degree Read's notion of handwriting and all its correlative assumptions applied to the photographs of the painters and to those of the sculptors, but there was another discourse which related explicitly to carving.

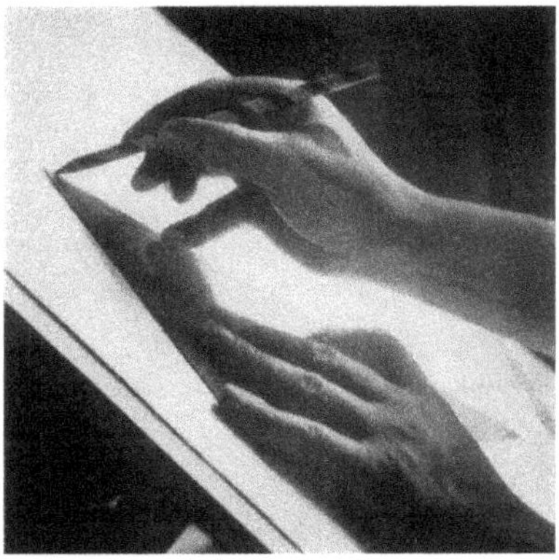

10.5 Paul Nash's hands as published in *Unit One*, photograph by Francis Bruguière

The sculptor's caress

By the time Unit One held their exhibition in 1934, direct carving was widely accepted as *the* mode of practice for advanced sculptors.[15] Although they also used other methods, Hepworth and Moore both carved by hand and in *The Meaning of Modern Sculpture* (1932) R.H. Wilenski defended their work and that of other sculptors on that basis. In a section entitled 'The Modern Sculptor's Creed' Wilenski reprised Jacob Epstein's conception of modellers, that they build 'something out of nothing'.[16] The modeller, he explained, has an idea, makes an armature with 'pliant metal, and on to that he sticks a series of lumps and worms and pellets of clay until the idea has been given form'.[17] The materials provide no inspiration for the artist and are in some manner 'converted to another substance' since the clay is baked or the model is used as a template for a final sculpture. It is this aspect of modelling that particularly offends Wilenski and his contemporaries since it enabled 'marble workers' who are 'merely assistants, operatives or stone masons' to produce scaled up sculptures in quantity: sculpture becomes a mode of manufacture rather than of individual creation.[18]

In contrast, Wilenski claimed that the direct carver 'starts with a block of stone or marble or wood beneath his hand'.[19] Following Michelangelo, he suggested that the final carving is already embedded in the block and that instead of creating it from scratch, as the modeller does, the sculptor is engaged in 'revealing a formal meaning inherent in that substance and no other'.[20] Wilenski conceives of this process as 'collaboration' between the sculptor and the stone. However, the stone also offers the sculptor a 'definite resistance' and 'opposition', and because the work is made 'entirely with his own hand', it is of necessity slow.[21] In consequence, direct carving involves 'greater judgement and difficulty, obstacles and toil' than modelling or

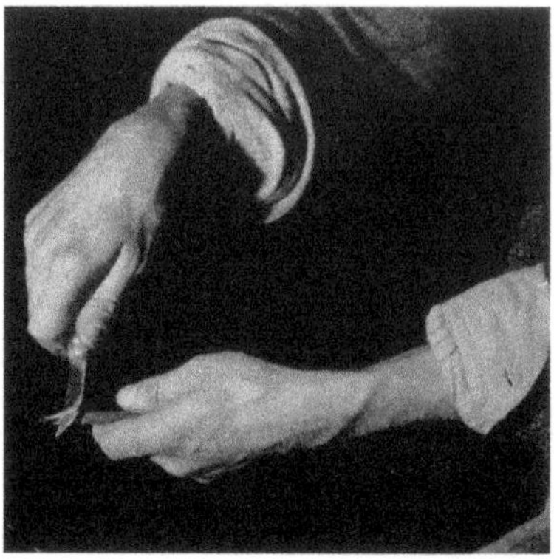

10.6 Tristram Hillier's hands as published in *Unit One*, photograph by Thea Struve

painting, for the sculptor cannot replace what has been removed, alter his decisions, improvise or 'hope that inspiration will turn up'.[22] For Wilenski all these factors cumulatively result in 'the expression of deliberate and considered concepts of permanent and universal significance'.[23] The only way to make modern, serious sculpture of import was to carve it directly.

Throughout *The Meaning of Modern Sculpture* Wilenski emphasises the stone beneath the sculptor's hand and carving by their hand alone. Kineton Parkes also stresses the physical contact between sculptor and stone in his two-volume book of 1931 *The Art of Sculpture*, but rather than construing it as a relation of collaboration and resistance he characterises it as one of love, tenderness and jealousy. He argued that whereas modelling 'implies some severance from personal contact', direct carving establishes an intense emotional bond between the sculptor and his or her stone or wood.

> There is no doubt that the handling of the material of a work of art from start to finish by its creator must result in a more intimate expression ... There is an affection for his product possessed by the sculptor ... which makes him jealous of its handling by any other person, and so are direct carvers made.[24]

In actuality clay models can be made using the hands alone, while direct carving would be impossible without chisels, mallets and drills, but because modelling had become so closely associated with the 'gentleman sculptor of manifold commissions' whose models were scaled up and produced in marble or bronze by a team of skilled assistants, it was characterised as being machine-like and as distanced from the artist's body. Direct carving, since it was conceived as a one-person operation (although Moore acquired his first assistants soon after the publication of *Unit One*), was associated with immediate manual and emotional contact.

By holding their carvings rather than working upon them, Moore and Hepworth are unequivocally represented as direct carvers and therefore as advanced sculptors and not as artists or sculptors in general. This discourse was so potent and the status of direct carvers so exalted, that even the painters tried to ally themselves with it. In his *Unit One* statement Nicholson drew an analogy between his incised paintings and direct carving and Tristram Hillier's catalogue photograph makes a similar connection. He is depicted wearing a flannel shirt with the un-linked cuffs rolled back over a tweed-jacket, his fore-arms bare and flexed and protruding veins highlighted, creating an image that erroneously signifies strenuous manual labour

(Fig. 10.6). In his hands Hillier holds a pencil, sharpening it with a knife by cutting away from himself. Far from adopting a painter's demeanour his pose, grasp and tools connect Hillier with carving.[25]

Gendered contact

Hepworth and Moore both hold stones, in Hepworth's case a pebble, in Moore's an unfinished carving, but there is a crucial distinction in *how* they hold their objects. Both Moore's portrait (Fig. 10.7) and the photograph of his hands (Fig. 10.2) depict him embracing his sculptures. In his close-cropped portrait he looks out, to the right of shot, and leaning against his shoulder is the carving that appears in the photograph of his hands beneath. In this second image he cradles his 'Mother and Child' sculpture against his body, his pose exactly replicating that of the stone 'Mother'. Like Moore, Hepworth also made 'Mother and Child' carvings and three of the four carvings depicted in the *Unit One* catalogue take this theme, but unlike Moore, Hepworth is not depicted in the pose of a mother to her child the sculpture. Rather, Hepworth sits with her arms resting on a table slightly removed from the stone she grasps lightly between her hands (Fig. 10.1). Arguably, the difference between Moore's embrace and Hepworth's loose grasp concerned the attribution of gender roles within discourses of direct carving.

In his reviews of Barbara Hepworth's 1933 exhibition at Lefèvre galleries, Adrian Stokes wrote that the true carver 'attacks his material' and 'he woos the block', smoothing and caressing the stone with love and reverence.[26] '"Advanced" carvers', he continued have 'felt not only the block but also its potential fruit, to always be feminine', a formulation that was clearly problematic in relation to Barbara Hepworth.[27] Stokes sees Hepworth as one of the 'advanced' carvers so in line with his argument she should have assumed a masculine relation to her feminine object. It is therefore somewhat surprising that Stokes asserts that her success is directly connected to being female: 'A man would have made the group more pointed; no man could have treated this composition with such a pure complacence. The idea itself is a spectacular one, but it gains from Miss Hepworth's hands a surer poignancy.'[28]

Perhaps realising that he had, even in this very short review undercut his own argument, Stokes retreats, concluding that 'her carving is astonishingly mature: whereas the appreciation and critique of sculpture is fatuous'.[29]

The following year Stokes' published *The Stones of Rimini* (a response in part to Ruskin's *The Stones of Venice* which also characterises carving as a distinctly masculine pursuit). Removed from the necessity to negotiate an actual female carver, the account of gender that he adduces is clearer if no less bizarre. Like his contemporaries Stokes made a firm distinction between modelling which took its material to be 'no more than so much suitable stuff' and carving as

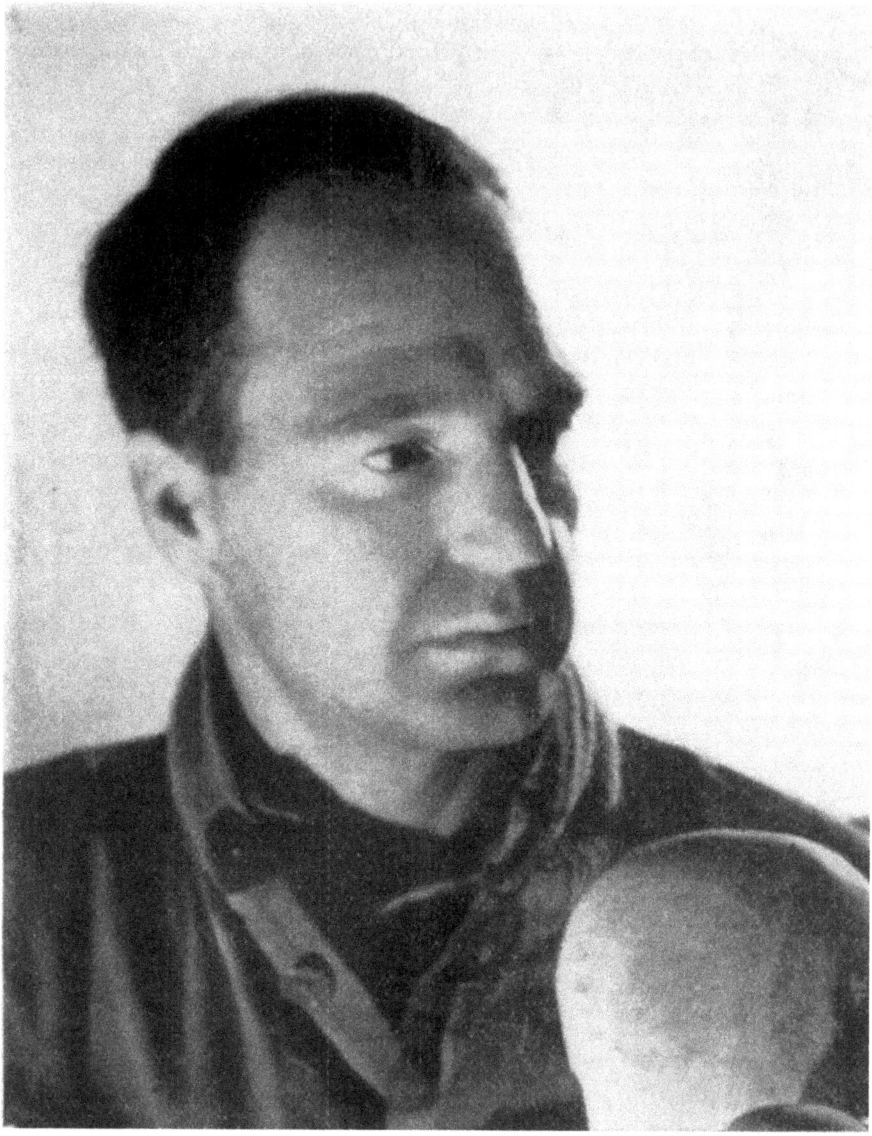

10.7 Henry Moore's portrait as published in *Unit One*, photograph by Thea Struve [Reproduced by permission of The Henry Moore Foundation]

'an articulation of something that already exists in the block'.[30] Stokes developed this point further, claiming that in successful carving 'not the figure, but the stone through the medium of the figure, has come to life'. This animation of the stone takes place under the *hand* of the sculptor: 'Polishing, when it is hand-polish and not a chemical polish ... gives life and light to

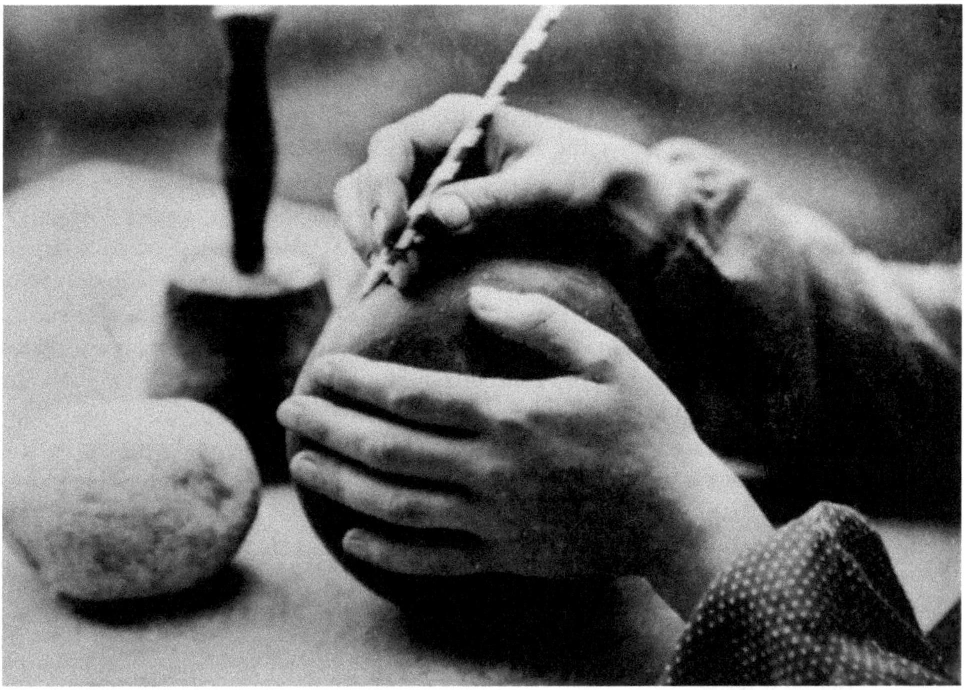

10.8 Barbara Hepworth's hands as published in *Pictorial Autobiography*, photograph by Paul Laib [© Bowness, Hepworth Estate]

the stone', the 'hand-polished marble's glow ... can only be compared to the light on flesh-and-blood'.[31] Even more extremely, polishing stone was 'like slapping the new born infant to make it breathe'.[32]

Crucially, only carvers can animate the stone and carving is the prerogative of 'man, in his male aspect'. The male sculptor woos the female marble whose 'hard luminous surface ... suffers all the stroking and polishing, all the definition that our hands and mouths bestow on those we love' and feels life 'beneath his tool', which Stokes notes is 'masculine' in shape.[33] The sculptures that emerge from the female block of stone, Stokes continues, 'are her children, the proof of the carver's love for the stone'.[34] Having been in analysis with Melanie Klein, Stokes was presumably aware that he was constructing a fantasy of creativity, but his writing nonetheless attributes men with the power to animate raw materials and, in the shape of sculptures, to create offspring. By comparison, women are either linked to the raw material of stone, from which life can be made to emerge by the (male) carver's touch or to the inferior art of modelling. 'Woman', writes Stokes, 'moulds her products', and as moulding cannot endow life, only replicate its forms and figures, modellers are rendered curiously sterile.[35]

Published in the same year as *The Stones of Rimini*, the photographs of Moore and Hepworth in *Unit One* show Moore in two poses traditionally associated with a mother: he cradles his stone carved child in his arms, and held against his chest. Hepworth could almost be modelling, since her thumbs are raised above the stone as if about to start pressing down to mould and shape the material. Here, two more details are pertinent. In the *Unit One* photograph she holds a pale grey pebble whereas the alternative photograph which she included in her *Pictorial Autobiography* shows her holding a larger, darker sphere which resembles clay (Fig. 10.8).[36] This explicit allusion may have been rejected in the selection of the final image but her pose still subtly references modelling. In addition, the rejected photograph shows her without a ring, whereas in the *Unit One* image she has a large (opal?) ring on her wedding finger, the disparity between the images suggesting that it was worn deliberately. The decision may have been made on aesthetic grounds for, located almost exactly in the centre of the shot, its gleaming whiteness focuses the viewer's gaze onto her hands. Nevertheless this punctum also provides a clear reminder of marriage, her femininity, and that Hepworth is (in this context) an anomaly, a woman carver.[37]

Nuanced touch

The overlapping discourses of the artist's hand and the direct carver's touch account for the differences in the *Unit One* photographs. For the painter the hand was the focus and conduit of ability, the thing that connected the artists to the artwork. In 1934, holding a pencil or a brush against the paper or canvas was enough to indicate mastery. Holding stone or a sculpture indicated that the subject of the photograph was a direct carver; embracing it allied Moore to a discourse that privileged masculinity as a creative and procreative force, 'moulding' it feminised Hepworth and placed her lower down the hierarchy of sculpture. Thus, what the artists held and how they held it mattered, since these images of a paintbrush lightly balanced, a knife grasped, or a sculpture embraced all situated the artists in slightly different ways, crediting some with more skill, a greater engagement with modern art, or with the advanced practice of carving than others.

These photographs draw from and articulate a complex and nuanced discourse of touch. Analysing them in detail shows how their signification is highly differentiated – these are not just images of artists' touch – but of sculptors as distinct from painters, direct carvers from modellers, of male and female touch, and of men as mothers. In these photographs touch functions as the conduit of expression, as evidence of expertise and as the guarantee of integrity, authenticity and originality. If the eight small black and white photographs I have discussed in this chapter offer such permutations, then how many more could be found within the conceptualisation, representation and articulation of touch within sculpture or art practice more generally?

Pointing to the nuances of touch and of the discourses that constitute our conceptions of touch does not invalidate the association between touch, participatory art and inclusive social interaction. Nor does it suggest that touch cannot be allied to women's experience or used strategically within a critical feminist art practice. What it does imply is that touch should not be characterised as one thing or another, rather that the nuances of touch should be fully acknowledged and examined. This sited approach to sensory interaction is nothing new for art history or visual culture studies since there have been many fine analyses of vision and visuality over recent decades, but the specificities of gender, history, culture and so forth are regularly evacuated from the study of touch. Perhaps ironically then theorists of touch may need to emulate their colleagues in visual studies to a far greater degree and to write about touch more strategically and with more specificity.

Notes

1. Nicolas Bourriaud, *Relational Aesthetics*, Dijon: les presses du reel, 2002, pp.9, 15, 43.
2. Whitney Chadwick, *Women, Art, and Society*, World of Art, London: Thames & Hudson, 1996, p.323.
3. For example see: Jennifer Fisher, 'Tactile Affects', *Tessera*, 32, 2002, pp.17–28; Constance Classen, 'Feminine Tactics: Crafting an Alternative Aesthetic in the Eighteenth and Nineteenth Centuries', in *The Book of Touch*, Constance Classen, ed., Oxford and New York: Berg, 2005, pp.228–39; and essays in Rosemary Betterton, *Unframed: Practices and Politics of Women's Contemporary Painting*, London: I.B. Tauris, 2004. Contemporary links between women's experience and touch often derive from Luce Irigaray, *This Sex Which Is Not One*, trans. Catherine Porter, Ithaca, NY: Cornell University Press, 1985. For an excellent discussion of the nuances of touch within feminist performance art see: Peggy Phelan, 'The Returns of Touch: Feminist Performances 1960–80', in *Wack! Art and the Feminist Revolution*, Lisa Gabrielle Mark, ed., Los Angeles, CA: Museum of Contemporary Art, 2007, pp.346–61.
4. On the diversity of the artists see Mark Glazebrook, 'Unit One: Spirit of the "Thirties"', in *Unit One: Spirit of the 30's*, London: The Mayor Gallery, 1984.
5. Paul Nash, 'Unit One', *The Times*, Monday 12 June 1933, p.10.
6. Nash, 'Unit One', p.10.
7. Herbert Read, ed., *Unit 1: The Modern Movement in English Architecture, Painting and Sculpture*, London: Cassell and Company, 1934, p.12.
8. According to Harrison, Read modelled Unit One on the Paris group Abstraction Création publications of artworks with accompanying artist's statements. Harrison, *English Art and Modernism 1900–1939*, London: Allen Lane, 1981, p.249.
9. It is likely that Hepworth was holding a pebble since Nash had already likened her work to such. See Paul Nash, 'A Painter and a Sculptor', *The Week-end Review*, 19 November 1932, p.613. Michael Phipps of the Henry Moore Trust, Perry Green has confirmed that Moore's sculpture remains unidentified.
10. Read, *Unit 1*, p.15.
11. Herbert Read's 1934 volume on Moore opens with the sculptor standing beside a finished 'Mother and Child' carving, his left arm draped around its shoulders.

12. Herbert Read, *Art Now: An Introduction to the Theory of Modern Painting and Sculpture*, London: Faber & Faber Limited, 1933, p.144.

13. While Read was no conventional connoisseur, his work as a keeper at the Victoria and Albert Museum between 1922 and 1931 (a home for some of the most eminent English connoisseurs of the early-mid twentieth century) and as editor of the *Burlington Magazine for Connoisseurs* from 1933 meant that he was steeped in that terminology and practice. For biographical details see James King, *The Last Modern: A Life of Herbert Read*, London: Weidenfeld and Nicholson, 1990. For a good overview of European connoisseurship see Mansfield Kirby Talley, 'Connoisseurship and the Methodology of the Rembrandt Research Project', *The International Journal of Museum Management and Curatorship*, 8 (2), 1989, pp.175–214.

14. Harrison, *English Art*, p.248.

15. The stress on direct carving had long antecedents within English art criticism; John Ruskin had written extensively on the ethical and aesthetic superiority of hand-work, ideas that had been expounded by William Morris, both of whom Read and his circle were familiar with. Eric Gill, Gaudier-Breszka and Jacob Epstein had pioneered direct carving techniques in England before the war. For a detailed discussion of direct carving in its European context see Penelope Curtis, *Modern British Sculpture: From the Collection*, Liverpool: Tate Gallery Publications, 1988, p.29.

16. R.H. Wilenski, *The Meaning of Modern Sculpture*, London: Faber & Faber, 1932, p.99.

17. Wilenski, *Meaning*, p.99.

18. Wilenski, *Meaning*, p.96.

19. Wilenski, *Meaning*, p.100.

20. Wilenski, *Meaning*, p.100.

21. Wilenski, *Meaning*, p.96.

22. Wilenski, *Meaning*, p.102.

23. Wilenski, *Meaning*, p.102.

24. Kineton Parkes, *The Art of Carved Sculpture*, 2 vols, vol. 1, London: Chapman and Hall, 1931, p.22.

25. Anne Wagner interprets this image as Hillier whittling a piece of wood (which would further emphasise its allegiance to carving). Anne Middleton Wagner, *Mother Stone: The Vitality of Modern British Sculpture*, New Haven, CT and London: Yale University Press, 2005, p.144.

26. Adrian Stokes, 'Miss Hepworth's Carving', in *The Critical Writing of Adrian Stokes*, ed. Lawrence Gowing, London: Thames and Hudson, 1978, p.309.

27. Stokes, 'Hepworth', p.310.

28. Stokes, 'Hepworth', p.310.

29. Stokes, 'Hepworth', p.310.

30. Adrian Stokes, 'The Stones of Rimini', in *The Critical Writings*, p.232.

31. Stokes, 'Stones', p.231.

32. Stokes, 'Stones', p.232.

33. Stokes, 'Stones', p.235.

34. Stokes, 'Stones', p.231.

35. Stokes, 'Stones', p.230.

36. Barbara Hepworth, *Pictorial Autobiography*, London: Tate Gallery, 1986, p.25.

37. Hepworth was not married at the time. She and her first husband John Skeaping divorced in 1933. The Unit One exhibition was held in April 1934. She married Ben Nicholson in 1938.

Bibliography

Betterton, Rosemary, *Unframed: Practices and Politics of Women's Contemporary Painting*, London: I.B. Tauris, 2004.

Bourriaud, Nicolas, *Relational Aesthetics*, Dijon: les presses du reel, 2002.

Chadwick, Whitney, *Women, Art, and Society*, World of Art, London: Thames & Hudson, 1996.

Classen, Constance, 'Feminine Tactics: Crafting an Alternative Aesthetic in the Eighteenth and Nineteenth Centuries', in *The Book of Touch*, Constance Classen, ed., Oxford and New York: Berg, 2005, pp.228–39.

Curtis, Penelope, *Modern British Sculpture: From the Collection*, Liverpool: Tate Gallery Publications, 1988.

Fisher, Jennifer, 'Tactile Affects', *Tessera*, 32, 2002, pp.17–28.

Glazebrook, Mark, 'Unit One: Spirit of the "Thirties"', in *Unit One: Spirit of the 30's*, London: The Mayor Gallery, 1984.

Harrison, Charles, *English Art and Modernism 1900–1939*, London: Allen Lane, 1981.

Hepworth, Barbara, *Pictorial Autobiography*, London: Tate Gallery, 1986.

Irigaray, Luce, *This Sex Which Is Not One*, trans. Catherine Porter, Ithaca, NY: Cornell University Press, 1985.

King, James, *The Last Modern: A Life of Herbert Read*, London: Weidenfeld and Nicholson, 1990.

Nash, Paul, 'A Painter and a Sculptor', *The Week-end Review*, 19 November 1932, p.613.

——, 'Unit One', *The Times*, Monday 12 June 1933, p.10.

Parkes, Kineton, *The Art of Carved Sculpture*, 2 vols, London: Chapman and Hall, 1931.

Phelan, Peggy, 'The Returns of Touch: Feminist Performances 1960–80', in *Wack! Art and the Feminist Revolution*, Lisa Gabrielle Mark, ed., Los Angeles, CA: Museum of Contemporary Art, 2007, pp.346–61.

Read, Herbert, *Art Now: An Introduction to the Theory of Modern Painting and Sculpture*, London: Faber & Faber, 1933.

——, ed., *Unit 1: The Modern Movement in English Architecture, Painting and Sculpture*, London: Cassell and Company, 1934.

Talley, Mansfield Kirby, 'Connoisseurship and the Methodology of the Rembrandt Research Project', *The International Journal of Museum Management and Curatorship*, 8 (2), 1989, pp.175–214.

Stokes, Adrian, *The Critical Writing of Adrian Stokes*, ed. Lawrence Gowing, London: Thames and Hudson, 1978.

Wagner, Anne Middleton, *Mother Stone: The Vitality of Modern British Sculpture*, New Haven, CT and London: Yale University Press, 2005.

Wilenski, R.H., *The Meaning of Modern Sculpture*, London: Faber & Faber, 1932.

11

Lorenzo Ghiberti and Michelangelo in search of the feeling hand*

James Hall

Whenever the issue of sculpture and touch has been discussed, not enough attention has been paid to what we might term the culture of touch. In fifteenth-century Florence, for example, subtle and novel distinctions were made between touch that is soft and hard, chaste and sexual, and between the touch of the left and right hands. The identity of the toucher – their class, role and gender – was also important. In this chapter, I would like to show how this Florentine culture of touch came to influence the theory and practice of sculpture, especially that of Lorenzo Ghiberti and Michelangelo.

* * *

One of the most important aspects of the Florentine culture of touch is the cult of the left hand, promoted above all by Lorenzo de' Medici, who developed elaborate and innovative theories in relation to it.

The superior beauty and sensitivity of the left hand was already an important component of the courtly love tradition. The Countess of Champagne offers an explanation for the left hand's allure in Andreas Capellanus' classic conduct book, the *Art of Courtly Love* (late twelfth century):

> I should like individual knights of love to be informed that if a lover has accepted a ring from his partner as love-symbol, he should place it on the little finger of his left hand, and always keep the stone of the ring hidden on the inside of the hand. The reason for this is that the left hand normally refrains from all dishonourable and base acts of touch.[1]

The Countess' contention is that since right-handers use the left hand less intensively (and not, it would seem, for acts of hygiene), it is unlikely to be worn, cut or dirty (especially, perhaps, the finger nails). By remaining in a pristine state, the left hand maintains a sort of pre-lapsarian purity and sensuality. The same distinction applies to the hands of women, and Venus frequently wears a ring on the little finger of her left hand in Renaissance depictions.

Lorenzo de' Medici (1449–1492) is the high priest of the Renaissance cult of the left hand, and it is he who sets it on the grandest of moral and cultural pedestals. For Lorenzo, an accomplished poet as well as de facto ruler of Florence, the left hand reigns supreme, and puts the right hand firmly in the shade. His preference for the left hand also has a political dimension, for whereas the right hand picks fights and is bellicose, the left hand is a lover, a pacifist and a healer (the Medici were only too aware of the 'medical' associations of their name). He wants everyone, male as well as female, to cultivate the left hand.

The ultimate privilege is to be offered the left hand of his lady, as happens in this sonnet:

La mi porgea la sua sinistra mano,
Dicendo: – Or non conosci el loco? Questo
È il loco ove Amor pria dar mi ti volle! –[2]

[She offered me her left hand, saying: – Do you still not know this place? This is the place where Amor begs me to do your will!].

By offering her left hand, the lady signals both that she is favouring Lorenzo, and that she trusts he will not take advantage of her. It is a gesture familiar from couple dances, for in these the woman stood with the man on her left, a position of subservience. This was a reversal of traditional hierarchies (brides still stand to the left of the groom in marriage ceremonies) and showed that in the dance the man would 'serve' his lady.

The beauty of the lady's left hand was enhanced by an embroidered sleeve. Throughout the Middle Ages, sleeves were usually detachable, and the most elaborate and costly embroidered motifs were usually confined to one arm – invariably the left. This is why we find so many entries for single sleeves in contemporary wardrobe accounts.[3] Shoulder brooches were also placed on the left side,[4] and most protective charms and amulets.[5] No wonder one's eye was drawn to the left side.

Lorenzo (who composed several dances, and was himself a keen dancer) explains in detail what the left hand means to him in an extended commentary on three consecutive sonnets in which the hand of his beloved is praised. In the first of these sonnets he extols the 'candida, bella e dilicata mano' [white, beautiful and delicate hand] which she uses to draw his heart out of his chest, tying it with a thousand knots and refashioning it anew so that it is disposed to love her. He explains in the commentary that he is referring to her left hand. The left hand is that which:

originates in the heart, and so appears as a more reliable messenger and witness of the intentions of my lady's heart: this is because it is said that in the ring finger, which is next to the finger commonly called the little finger, is a vein that comes directly from the heart, as if a messenger of the heart's intention.[6]

The idea that a nerve or vein passed from the heart directly to the ring finger on the left hand was common currency, and derived from antiquity. In Roman times, a wedding ring was placed on the left hand, but the Christian church seems to have preferred the right hand, and this convention is generally followed when marriage ceremonies are depicted in art. However, the Roman rite seems to have been revived in early fifteenth-century Florence, and several Florentine paintings of *The Marriage of the Virgin* and *The Mystic Marriage of St Catherine* by artists associated with the Medici took the unprecedented step of showing the ring being placed on the bride's left hand. Here, archaeological exactitude (the Virgin and Catherine were all subjects of the Roman Empire) went hand in hand with an intensification of 'heartfelt' feeling.[7]

These ideas represent a crucial fine-tuning of Lucretius' blanket contention in *de Rerum Natura* (Bk. 2, lines 434–7) that touch 'is the sense of the whole body', and the one which performs 'the generative deeds of Venus'.[8] Lorenzo would have us believe that the touch of the left hand is penetrative – but in a psychological and spiritual sense rather than simply sexual. He says that although his lady's eyes made the first wound in his heart, 'then, as often happens, either while dancing or in another equally honest way I was again made worthy to touch her left hand'. He wants us to believe that this is chaste, non-sexual touching, and he adds that he touched her left hand 'because one climbs the ladder of love step by step'.[9] He means climbing upwards – towards spiritual delights – rather than descending to her nether regions. The chastity of this gesture is further guaranteed (he would have us believe) by being performed in the public gaze, at a dance.

Lorenzo de' Medici was not the only fifteenth-century Florentine to be fascinated by the lightest of touches. Idealisation of the most delicate and refined forms of touch is also found in the third book of Lorenzo Ghiberti's treatise *I Commentarii*, which was begun in around 1447 and remained incomplete at his death. For Ghiberti (1378–1455), *refined* touch is a crucial part of his strategy to raise the social and intellectual status of sculpture. He wanted to remind his readers that sculpture is not simply made – as Leonardo would later claim – with sweaty brute force and the 'crashing of hammers'. It can be made, and appreciated, with the lightest – and therefore courtliest – of touches.

In the third commentary, devoted to the scientific study of optics, Ghiberti refers to some antique sculptures which he has seen in diffused light (*una temperate luce*). The first, a statue of a hermaphrodite 'the size of a thirteen year old girl', had been found in a drain in Rome. It was shown reclining on a linen cloth laid on the ground, cleverly posed so that the male and female sexual characteristics were visible, and with the big toe of its extended leg shown caught in the cloth 'with wonderful skill'. Ghiberti concludes his lovingly detailed account: 'In this statue were the greatest refinements. The eye perceived nothing if the hand had not found it by touch.'[10] He makes a similar point about a fragmentary statue found in Florence: 'It has very many refinements the eye cannot see in either a strong or a moderate light; only the hand touching it finds them.'[11] Ghiberti's novel conception of the 'all-seeing-hand' arose in part from his reading of optical treatises, with their discussions of optical illusions that underscored the truancy of sight.[12] Thus although he recommends showing sculptures in a strong light (*luce forte*), strong light only makes '*many* things visible' [my italics] – not all things.[13] For Ghiberti, unreliable eyesight had to be supplemented and corrected by infallible touch.

Although Ghiberti compares the hermaphrodite to a girl at puberty, he would have us believe that the sculptor has carved this risqué statue in such a way that it can only be touched in a supremely refined and non-invasive way. He is, as it were, creating an anti-Pygmalion myth for sculpture – a loving engagement with sculpture that does not revolve around sex or lust. The irony here is that if the carving becomes too subtle and refined, the 'sculptural' qualities – specifically its three-dimensionality – may diminish.

Ghiberti's remarks would seem to apply more to sculpture in low relief rather than in the round, and his insistence on the sensitivity of human fingers does indeed coincide with his own preference for low relief and exquisite gilded finish in the second set of Baptistery doors. Gilding creates a surface dazzle that does indeed trick the eye. Alberti had rejected the excessive use of gold leaf in painting because it 'almost always blinds the eyes of spectators from all angles'.[14] But Ghiberti seems to think he can turn surface dazzle to the sculptor's advantage, or at least use it to furnish an alibi for his theory.

He also seems to be providing an apologia for Florentine *relievo schiacciato* (squashed relief), pioneered by his former apprentice Donatello: *The Ascension with Christ Giving the Keys to St Peter* (Victoria & Albert Museum) is so finely incised that entire sections can disappear, depending on the angle and strength of the external lighting.[15] These reliefs, Ghiberti's theory implies, cry out to be explored by the 'seeing hand'. By the same token, there may be a veiled criticism of the rough vigour of the modelling, and the strong cast shadows, in Donatello's more recent reliefs, like the bronze doors of the Old Sacristy.

Ghiberti's implied preference for low relief sculpture shows interesting similarities with the views of the Eastern Church. The Greek Church had strict views about the form of religious sculpture. A sacred figure was thought to be inappropriate if you could grab hold of it by its nose.[16] For Ghiberti, stroking rather than grabbing seems acceptable. However, in relation to the antique hermaphrodite, Ghiberti seems to want to have it both ways: on the one hand, he praises surface subtleties 'invisible' to the naked eye and accessible only by the softest of touches; on the other hand he praises the sculptor's very visible and no doubt grabable depiction of the male genitals and female breasts.

One of the perennial criticisms of the visual arts, from antiquity onwards, is that unlike, say, poetry, they only reveal the surface appearance of things – the body rather than the soul. Ghiberti implies that great sculpture, because it needs to be touched with great care to be fully apprehended, and is not available to eyesight alone, is an art form that goes beyond 'mere' surface appearances. As such, it is an ingenious modification of a very opaque remark made by Cennino Cennini in his treatise on painting. For Cennini, writing in around 1400, painting not only combines theory (*scienzia*) and manual dexterity, it requires imagination (*fantasia*) 'in order to discover things not seen, hiding themselves under the shadow of natural objects, and to shape them with the hand, presenting to plain sight what does not actually exist'.[17] Ghiberti's own theory claims that great sculpture offers us *real* things that cannot be seen, offering them, as it were, to plain touch.

Ghiberti does not specifically suggest that one hand is more sensitive or decorous than the other, though as a (presumably) right-handed sculptor the skin on his left hand is likely to have been marginally less rough, and so more sensitive. Nonetheless, he did depict a scene on the second set of Baptistery doors in which touch replaces sight as the prime sense, and the 'seeing hand' is a left hand. Ironically, however, this scene – in which the partially blind Isaac mistakenly blesses Jacob – actually demonstrates the fallibility of the sense of touch.

Jacob was the twin brother of Esau, but Esau was born first, with Jacob in his slipstream, clutching his 'elder' brother's heel. In the relief, Esau is seen from the back with his hunting dogs, and his elegantly back-lifted left foot, with the heel projecting out 'in the round', must surely be a witty reference to this story. When their mother Rebecca hears that Isaac will shortly give Esau his blessing, she dresses Jacob (her favourite son, and prophesied to be the chosen one) in Esau's clothes. Because Esau is hairy, she covers Jacob's hands and neck with goatskins. Ghiberti shows Isaac 'feeling' Jacob's goatskin covered neck with the whole of his left hand, while he holds up his right hand in blessing. As Ghiberti himself explained in the autobiographical section of the second commentary: 'Isaac searched for his neck, found it hairy, and gave him his benediction.'

It is no coincidence that Ghiberti's theory of what we might call 'tactful touch' resurfaces in the late eighteenth century, when touching sculpture (especially at night by torch-light) became all the rage. For Herder, in his 1778 treatise on sculpture, *Plastik*, touch was both the most truthful of the senses and, potentially, the most shocking: seeing a gruesome picture, he believed, is far less disturbing than touching a gruesome sculpture. This explained why the Greeks (in contrast to Baroque sculptors) had avoided overly expressive and grotesque subjects, and why modern sculptors should avoid complex surface effects and dramatic convexities and concavities: 'A mouth which shouts is a cave for the hand which touches, and during a smile, the cheeks are a crease.'[18] Hence the smooth and relatively bland surfaces of so many neo-classical sculptures – and the revival of interest in early Italian low relief sculpture, including Ghiberti's, by sculptors such as Flaxman.[19]

Modern art historians have misunderstood the significance of the 'seeing hand' both for Ghiberti and for the age of Neo-Classicism.[20] The Krautheimers, in their great book on Ghiberti, claim that his comments on the 'seeing hand' coincide with the sculptor's reawakened interest in tactile modelling of the human body – an interest that had not been seen in Ghiberti's work since 1401, when he vigorously modelled the naked, twisting body of the sacrificial victim Isaac in the competition relief for the Baptistery doors:

> During the next twenty years he never again focused so directly on the tactile qualities of the human body. Only in the nudes of the Gates of Paradise did he return to modelling similar to that of the Isaac. Indeed, it is only in the late years of his life that he stresses the touch of fingers, the 'seeing hand', when discussing works of ancient art.[21]

They assume that sculpture that caters for the 'seeing hand' will be emphatically 'tactile' – that is, with plenty of surface incident and variation to detain the eye and hand. They must have been influenced at some level by the wide-ranging sensory education promoted by educational reformers such as the Kindergarten Movement and Maria Montessori. Montessori got blindfolded children to feel objects and materials with different textures, shapes and forms: they included steel, glass, silk and sandpaper.[22]

Yet precisely the opposite is the case: pre-modern sculpture that caters for the 'seeing hand' tends to *eliminate* 'tactile' modelling. This may seem counter-intuitive, but the assumption seems to have been that vigorously modelled sculpture can be better comprehended by sight alone, not least because its 'caves' and 'creases' (many with sharp edges) will actually repel the hand. Where Ghiberti is concerned, the nudes on the second set of Baptistery doors are modelled both more schematically and in lower relief than the nude Isaac of the competition relief. Indeed, the second relief sculpture of the nude Isaac is far flatter, smaller in scale in relation to Abraham, and more-self-effacing.

In relation to touch, Ghiberti's ideal was probably something like the body of a beautiful 13-year-old girl: the best sculptural equivalent has to be the marvellous image of the newly-created Eve on the most copied panel of the Baptistery doors. Her small-breasted nude body, streamlined and softly undulating, is shown from the left – the 'heart' side – rising up towards God, borne aloft by the tiny hands of child angels. Altogether, she is touched by six visible hands, including God's left hand (his right blesses her). We can imagine Ghiberti saying of this figure, emerging out of Adam's side like a perfectly preserved antique statue lifted from the ground: 'In Eve were the greatest refinements. The eye perceived nothing if the hand had not found it by touch.'

* * *

Michelangelo is likely to have been exposed to Lorenzo's cult of the left hand in his early years when he was a member of Lorenzo's household between 1489 and 1492 (Lorenzo died in 1492). These were the very years in which Lorenzo's poetic manuscripts were put in order and transcribed, probably for publication. Michelangelo was reputedly a natural left-hander who had learned to draw and paint with his right hand, so he may have had a personal investment in issues relating to handedness.[23]

Michelangelo wrote several poems in which left-right symbolism looms large, and these include two remarkable poetic epitaphs written in the early 1540s which revolve around the supreme beauty of the lady's left hand. He sent the epitaphs to the poet Gandolfo Porrino in 1543 after the death of Porrino's lover Fausta Mancini Attavanti, who was nick-named Mancina – the Italian for left-handed. The poems were a partial compensation for Michelangelo having declined Porrino's request that he do her portrait.

Here Michelangelo suggests that the woman's supreme physical and moral beauty is embodied in her name Mancina:

In noi vive e qui giace la divina
beltà da morte anz'il suo tempo offesa.
Se con la dritta man fece' difesa,
Campava. Onde nol fe'? Ch'era mancina.

[In us there lives and here there lies the divine beauty struck down by death before her time. If she had defended herself with her right hand, she would have escaped. Why did she not do this? Because she was left-handed].[24]

Some critics have assumed Michelangelo is criticising her morals here, using '*mancina*' in its literal sense of 'crooked' or 'lacking'. It has also been called a 'graceless pun'.[25] However, as Porrino was a friend (one who had written praising the *Last Judgment*), and as Michelangelo wrote two epitaphs exploring the same conceit, it is clear he is saying that Mancina's beauty was unrivalled precisely because it was 'left-handed'; and that this meek kind of beauty rendered her as open to death as she had previously been to Porrino's love. There is something here of Isidore of Seville's definition of the 'left hand' in his standard reference work, the *Etymologies*: Isidore believes the Latin word for left '*sinextra*' is derived from '*sinere*', to permit: 'the left hand is so called "as if it 'permitted' something to happen"', he writes.[26] Here, the left hand is the hand that always gives permission, and is hospitable – even unto death.

In Michelangelo's only surviving exercise in 'squashed relief', the *Madonna of the Stairs* (c. 1492), the extended ring finger of the Virgin's left hand is inordinately long and distended, and seems even longer because the other fingers are hidden or clenched. This is, I believe, an expressive and symbolic distortion rather than an accidental disproportion due to Michelangelo's youth and inexperience (anyway, its size could have easily been reduced). The relief exudes sophistication rather than naivety, for it wears its archaeological exactitude on its sleeve. Not only does Michelangelo revive a type of relief that was fashionable half a century earlier, he poses the Madonna seated in profile like a woman in a classical funerary relief.

The naked Christ Child has fallen asleep while feeding at his mother's left breast (a premonition of the *pietà*), so he can probably hear the beating of her heart. Michelangelo's Virgin has always been regarded as rather remote and even unmaternal, because of the lack of eye contact with her son, and the rather limp way in which her left arm and hand rest on her lap.[27] But rather than using conventional body language to demonstrate the maternal bond, Michelangelo uses the outsized ring finger. It not only indicates that we are witnessing a 'heartfelt' scene, but also shows that the Virgin is effectively married to Christ. A 'squashed' relief survives by the Florence-born Agostino di Duccio, the *Virgin and Child with Five Angels* (c. 1450–1460; Victoria and Albert Museum), in which the Christ Child clutches the ring finger on his mother's left hand, making a clear allusion to their mystical marriage.[28]

This quasi-autonomous, airborne finger may also – *pace* Ghiberti – be the 'key' to the spirit in which the marble relief has been carved, and in which it should be experienced. It suggests we are here in a Ghibertian realm of light touches and feeling hands. In Francesco Colonna's prose romance *Hypnerotomachia Poliphili* (1499), the priestess of Venus gets the heroine Polia to 'extend' the ring finger of her left hand, while clenching the others, in order to write love spells, so this gesture seems to have had a special meaning in folklore of the period: 'Then the [High Priestess of the Temple of Venus] had [Polia] curl the fingers of her left hand and extend the ring-finger, then draw in the sacred ashes certain characters, with care and precision just as they were painted in the volume of pontifical ritual.'[29] The finger of Michelangelo's Madonna 'writes', as it were, in the air about her love for her son. In the relief, this maternal realm with its precise and calm hand gestures is contrasted with the world of the boisterous, rough-handed putti standing on the steps in the background.

We can regard the Virgin in Michelangelo's St Peter's *Pietà* (1498–1499) as another sort of honorary '*mancina*' who gives metaphorical permission to us to touch and be touched by the beautiful body of Christ. Whereas her right hand supports Christ's body, its fingers purposefully splayed to the point of dislocation beneath his armpit, the left hand floats free, with fragile fingers parted, as if testing the air (the fingers were broken in the past and restored). The Virgin gestures almost unconsciously towards the viewer who would have first seen the sculpture from that side as he entered the chapel. The gesture is a double invitation – to come closer, and to gaze on her son's body. We are being asked to *imagine* ourselves touching and stroking the body of

Christ, and the Virgin's left hand, with a light, 'left-handed' touch (I doubt Michelangelo wanted people to actually touch his sculptures, with their complex facture, and with so much the potential for damage).[30]

In the 1530s Michelangelo made three works in which we find left-handed archers, and it is here that we have his most explicit exploration of the Laurentian cult of the left hand. Of these, the unfinished statue of *Apollo* (c. 1530) is perhaps his most beguiling and weightless sculpture.[31] The youthful sun-God reaches over his right shoulder with his left hand to take an arrow from his quiver. This means that he is technically a left-hander. It must surely be a depiction of the Delian Apollo (so-called because his principle shrine was on Delos), though Michelangelo characteristically dispenses with iconographic props. This was a benign, loving image of a god famed for his ruthlessness. The Delian Apollo, whose image featured on Greek coins, holds a bow and arrows in his left hand, and the three Graces in his right. According to Macrobius, writing in the *Saturnalia* (c. 400 AD), by holding his weapon in his 'weaker' left hand, Apollo demonstrated that he was 'slower to do harm'; and by holding the Graces in his 'stronger' right hand, he showed he was more ready to do good. Once again, Agostino di Duccio is an iconographic pioneer, for he made a relief of the Delian Apollo (c. 1450) for the Tempio Malatestiano in Rimini.[32]

This interpretation of Michelangelo's statue makes perfect sense when we realise that Michelangelo carved it for Baccio Valori, the victorious commander of the Medici-supporting army that had besieged Florence and overthrown the Republic. Valori was immediately appointed Regent of Florence, and according to Vasari, Michelangelo carved the statue to curry favour as he had been a key figure in the defence of republican Florence. After taking control of the city, Valori issued an order for Michelangelo's assassination, but the artist went into hiding, and was eventually saved by a pardon from the Medici Pope Clement VII.

The fact that Michelangelo made such an entrancing sculpture for Valori has perplexed and disappointed some scholars, and has contributed to its critical neglect. But as soon as we realise its true subject, it becomes one of the most courageous works of political art ever made. It suggests in no uncertain terms that Valori and the Medici should temper their cruelty – and be more like Michelangelo's first Medici patron, Lorenzo the Magnificent.

Although Lorenzo never specifically mentions the Delian Apollo, he believed that Love always shoots his bow with his left hand – a point that is illustrated in Michelangelo's *Design for a Salt-Cellar* (1538; British Museum).[33] The salt-cellar was commissioned by his soldier patron Francesco della Rovere, who was famously 'quick to do harm'. Here a left-handed Cupid, pirouetting on the top of the lid, shoots his bow.[34] Lorenzo further believed that the tips of Love's arrows cause only temporary pain, like the javelin of Peleus and Achilles which was able to heal the wounds it had inflicted. Lorenzo went on to make a pacifist political point that would have especially appealed to Michelangelo in 1530: 'if the right hand has more worth or power, it is owing rather to custom than to nature'.[35]

In Michelangelo's statue, Apollo looks to his left and exposes his left side as if he were offering it up to be touched. Many of Michelangelo's late depictions of the dead Christ – including the crucifixion drawing for Vittoria Colonna and the Rondanini *Pietà* – have a comparable left-leaning orientation. This was unusual as the body of the crucified Christ was traditionally oriented to his right, where the redemptive wound in his side, the good thief and the Virgin are located. The right side was associated with concepts such as light, spirituality and eternal life, while the left side was associated with darkness, temporal things and human love. Thus in crucifixion images the sun was often placed on Christ's right, and the moon to his left.

The most high-profile example of a left-leaning Christ is the *Pietà* (c. 1547–1555) which Michelangelo carved for his own tomb. Christ's head leans over sharply to the left, and the Virgin Mary also takes up a position behind and to his left, with her left hand placed under Christ's left armpit, with the fingers spread over his heart. This scene is presided over by Nicodemus, a towering figure who stands behind Christ and supports his body. Vasari claimed, in a letter of 1565, that Nicodemus' face was a self-portrait of the artist. However, Michelangelo seems to have encountered problems, and he smashed up both of Christ's arms and his left leg. The arms were then restored by an assistant, but the broken leg was dispensed with.

The sculpture's mise-en-scène recalls a vision of Christ described by the medieval German mystic St Gertrude of Elfta. Her writings had been 'rediscovered' after a Latin edition of her revelations had been published in Cologne in 1536. Michelangelo may have learned about Gertrude from Vittoria Colonna. Christ appears before Gertrude and tells her that if she wants to relieve his burden, she should stand on his left and let him lean over and lie on her breast: 'when I lean over to my left', Christ continues, 'I lie on my heart, which is a great solace for my tiredness, and from there I can also look directly into your heart and enjoy the melodious call of your desires'. Few of these sensory intimacies would be possible if Gertrude positioned herself on Christ's right for this is the side of eternity where hearing is the dominant sense. Christ believes that if Gertrude were positioned to his right: 'I would then be deprived of all these sweet things: in the domain where the ear holds sway, the eyes could not easily be delighted, the nostrils could not breathe in, nor the hands grasp'.[36]

In Michelangelo's *Pietà,* Christ does not lie on his mother's breast, but he does 'look' down towards her heart with a faint smile on his face. Christ's head, with its long lock of thick hair, rests directly on her face, and so she really does seem to be breathing him in through her nostrils. She places her left hand firmly over his heart, but with her thumb lodged in his armpit.

Insofar as she cannot see the front of Christ's body, it is a groping 'seeing hand', and her eyes may anyway be closed or clouded by tears. Conversely, the kneeling female figure on Christ's right is very detached – and right-leaning – even as she attempts to support his body. She must be Mary Magdalene, but she is restrained to the point of unrecognisability. She pulls her head away from Christ's body and does not look: it's almost as if she just wants to *listen*. There is very little sensuality about her expression and her pose.

When Michelangelo broke off Christ's left arm, he also broke off the left arm of the Virgin which is attached to it, and we can still see a crack right across her fingers. As we contemplate this key area, we simultaneously experience two very different kinds of touch: a desperate, last-ditch maternal touch, and an iconoclastic and, as it were, self-destructive touch from the distraught artist. If Michelangelo was a natural left-hander, the hammer would have been in his left hand. We are a world away from the idealised Laurentian '*mancina*'.

Notes

* Some of this material is adapted from previous publications, which provide further bibliography: *The World as Sculpture: The Changing Status of Sculpture from the Renaissance to the Present Day*, London: Chatto and Windus, 1999, especially chapter 4, 'Sight versus Touch', pp.80–103; 'Desire and Disgust: Touching Artworks from 1500 to 1800', in *Presence: The Inherence of the Prototype within Images and Other Objects*, Robert Maniura and Rupert Shepherd, eds, Aldershot: Ashgate, 2006, pp.145–60; *The Sinister Side: How Left-Right Symbolism Shaped Western Art*, Oxford: Oxford University Press, 2008.

1. *Andreas Capellanus on Love*, ed. and trans. P.G. Walsh, London: Duckworth, 1982, Bk 2, xxi, #50, p.269.
2. Lorenzo de' Medici, *Comento de' Miei Sonetti*, ed. Tiziano Zanato, Florence: Leo S. Olschi, 1991, vol. 2, no. CXXXVII, ll. 9–11.
3. Jacqueline Herald, *Renaissance Dress in Italy 1400–1500*, London: Bell & Hyman, 1981, p.185.
4. Joanna Woods-Marsden, 'Portrait of the Lady', in *Virtue and Beauty*, exh. cat. National Gallery of Art, Washington, DC, 2001, p.69.
5. Ronald W. Lightbown, *Mediaeval European Jewellery*, London: Victoria and Albert Museum, 1992, pp.96–100.
6. *The Autobiography of Lorenzo de' Medici the Magnificent: A Commentary on my Sonnets*, trans. James Wyatt Cook, Binghamton, NY: Medieval and Renaissance Texts and Studies, 1995, p.123. I have slightly adapted some of these translations.
7. The paintings include Fra Angelico, *Marriage of the Virgin* (1425–26), Prado, Madrid; Rosso Fiorentino, *Marriage of the Virgin* (1523), Florence, San Lorenzo.
8. 'tactus enim, tactus, pro divum numina sancta, corporis est sensus … aut iuvat egrediens genitalis per Veneris res'.
9. Lorenzo de' Medici, *Comento*, p.212.
10. 'In questa era moltissime dolceze; nessuna cosa il viso scorgeva, se non col tatto la mano la trovava'. Lorenzo Ghiberti, *I Commentarii*, ed. Lorenzo Bartolini, Florence: Giunti, 1998, p.108, #III.2. Translation by Elizabeth Gilmour Holt, *A Documentary History of Art, Volume I: The Middle Ages and Renaissance*, Princeton, NJ: Princeton University Press, 1981, p.164. Just before, Ghiberti marvels at the stretched out leg with the big toe caught in the cloth: the same motif occurs in relation to Mars' left leg in Botticelli's *Venus and Mars*, National Gallery, London.
11. Ghiberti, *I Commentarii*, p.108; Holt, *A Documentary History of Art*, p.165.

12. See Martin Kemp, *Behind the Picture: Art and Evidence in the Italian Renaissance*, New Haven, CT: Yale University Press, 1997, pp.104–5.

13. Ghiberti, *I Commentarii*, p.110, #IV.1.

14. Leon Battista Alberti, *On Painting*, trans. Cecil Grayson, ed. Martin Kemp, London: Penguin, 1991, p.85, # 49.

15. There are several images photographed in different light on the V&A collections website.

16. Edwyn Bevan, *Holy Images*, London: G. Allen & Unwin, 1940, p.148.

17. Cennino Cennini, *Il Libro dell'Arte*, ed. Franco Brunello, Vicenza: N. Pozza, 1971; *The Craftsman's Handbook*, trans. Daniel V. Thompson, New York: Dover, 1954, p.3.

18. Johann Gottfried Herder, *Werke*, ed. Wolfgang Ross, vol. 2, Munich: Hanser, 1987, p.523. Hall, *World as Sculpture*, pp.92–9.

19. Engravings of Ghiberti's second set of Baptistery doors were published in the 1770s. Hall, *World as Sculpture*, pp.75–6.

20. See, for example, Jason Gaiger, 'Introduction', in Johann Gottfried Herder, *Sculpture: Some Observations on Shape and Form from Pygmalion's Creative Dream*, trans and ed., Jason Gaiger, Chicago, IL: University of Chicago, 2002.

21. Richard Krautheimer and Trude Krautheimer, *Lorenzo Ghiberti*, Princeton, NJ: Princeton University Press, 1982, pp.282–3.

22. Hall, *World as Sculpture*, pp.253–78.

23. *Vita di Raffaello da Montelupo*, ed. Riccardo Gatteschi, Florence: Polistampa, 1998, pp.120–21.

24. Michelangelo, *The Poems*, trans. and ed. Christopher Ryan, London: Dent, 1996, no. 177.

25. Michelangelo, *Poems*, p.306, n. 177.

26. *The Etymologies of Isidore of Seville*, trans. Stephen A. Barney et al., Cambridge: Cambridge University Press, 2006, xl: I: 68, p.235.

27. James Hall, *Michelangelo and the Reinvention of the Human Body*, London: Chatto and Windus, 2005, chapter 1, 'Mothers'.

28. In another relief by Agostino in the Louvre, the Christ child holds the ring finger of her right hand, a gesture that alludes to the traditional Christian iconography of marriage. In a relief in the Bargello, his fingers lightly touch the thumb of her left hand, but this seems to have no symbolic significance.

29. Francesco Colonna, *Hypnerotomachia Poliphili*, trans. Jocelyn Godwin, London: Thames and Hudson, 1999, pp.227–8.

30. There is a similar dichotomy in the depiction of hands in Michelangelo's *Creation of Adam* on the Sistine Ceiling (1508–12). Despite being closest to God's animating finger, Adam's raised left hand remains a miracle of languid grace, whereas his own right arm, on which he leans, is more energised and tense. Similarly, God's right hand, with its extended index finger, is sublimely purposeful and instrumental, whereas the impossibly long index finger of his left hand is double-jointed and unfurls itself luxuriantly over the shoulder and neck of an attendant boy. To us it looks rather grotesque and tentacular; but it is clearly meant to be the epitome of craggy elegance.

31. I discuss the disagreements over the identification of the subject – Apollo or David? – in *The Sinister Side*, p.290.

32. Macrobius, *Saturnalia*, I: 17; Rudolf Pfeiffer, 'The Image of Delian Apollo and Apolline Ethics', *Journal of the Warburg and Courtauld Institutes*, 15, 1952, p.21.

33. Hall, *Sinister Side*, pp.300–302.

34. The third example of left-handed archers occurs in the presentation drawing *The Archers*, for which see *The Sinister Side*, pp.303–4.

35. *The Autobiography of Lorenzo de' Medici*, p.131.

36. Gertrude d'Helfta, *Oeuvres Spirituelles*, trans. and ed. J-M. Clément, Paris: Editions du Cerf, 1978, vol. 4, pp.164–6. Cited by Nigel F. Palmer, '*Herzeliebe*, weltlich und geistlich: Zur Metaphorik vom "Einwohnen im Herzen" bei Wolfram von Eschenbach, Juliana von Cornillon, Hugo von

Langenstein und Gertrud von Helfta', in *Innenräume in der Literatur des deutschen Mittelalters*, B. Hasebrink, H.-J. Schiewer, A. Suerbaum and A. Volfing, eds, Tübingen: De Gruyter, 2007, pp.220–21.

Bibliography

Alberti, Leon Battista, *On Painting*, trans. Cecil Grayson, ed. Martin Kemp, London: Penguin, 1991.

Andreas Capellanus on Love, ed. and trans. P.G. Walsh, London: Duckworth, 1982.

Bevan, Edwyn, *Holy Images*, London: G. Allen & Unwin, 1940.

Cennini, Cennino, *The Craftsman's Handbook*, trans. Daniel V. Thompson, New York: Dover, 1954.

——, *Il Libro dell'Arte*, ed. Franco Brunello, Vicenza: N. Pozza, 1971.

Colonna, Francesco, *Hypnerotomachia Poliphili*, trans. Jocelyn Godwin, London: Thames and Hudson, 1999.

Ghiberti, Lorenzo, *I Commentarii*, ed. Lorenzo Bartolini, Florence: Giunti, 1998.

Hall, James, *The World as Sculpture: The Changing Status of Sculpture from the Renaissance to the Present Day*, London: Chatto and Windus, 1999.

——, 'Herbert Read's "The Art of Sculpture"', in *The A.W. Mellon Lectures in the Fine Arts: Fifty Years*, , Washington, DC: National Gallery of Art, 2002, pp.35–8.

——, *Michelangelo and the Reinvention of the Human Body*, London: Chatto and Windus, 2005.

——, 'Desire and Disgust: Touching Artworks from 1500 to 1800', in *Presence: The Inherence of the Prototype within Images and Other Objects*, Robert Maniura and Rupert Shepherd, eds, Aldershot: Ashgate, 2006, pp.145–60.

——, *The Sinister Side: How Left-Right Symbolism Shaped Western Art*, Oxford: Oxford University Press, 2008.

Herald, Jacqueline, *Renaissance Dress in Italy 1400–1500*, London: Bell & Hyman, 1981.

Herder, Johann Gottfried, *Werke*, ed. Wolfgang Ross, Munich: Hanser, 1987.

——, *Sculpture: Some Observations on Shape and Form from Pygmalion's Creative Dream*, ed. and trans. Jason Gaiger, Chicago, IL: University of Chicago Press, 2002.

Holt, Elizabeth Gilmour, *A Documentary History of Art, Volume I: The Middle Ages and Renaissance*, Princeton, NJ: Princeton University Press, 1981.

Kemp, Martin, *Behind the Picture: Art and Evidence in the Italian Renaissance*, New Haven, CT: Yale University Press, 1997.

Krautheimer, Richard and Trude Krautheimer, *Lorenzo Ghiberti*, Princeton, NJ: Princeton University Press, 1982.

Lightbown, Ronald W., *Mediaeval European Jewellery*, London: Victoria and Albert Museum, 1992.

Medici, Lorenzo de', *Comento de' Miei Sonetti*, ed. Tiziano Zanato, Florence: Leo S. Olschi, 1991.

Michelangelo, *The Poems*, trans. and ed. Christopher Ryan, London: Dent, 1996.

Palmer, Nigel F., '*Herzeliebe*, weltlich und geistlich: Zur Metaphorik vom "Einwohnen im Herzen" bei Wolfram von Eschenbach, Juliana von Cornillon, Hugo von Langenstein und Gertrud von Helfta', in *Innenräume in der Literatur des deutschen Mittelalters*, B. Hasebrink, H.-J. Schiewer, A. Suerbaum and A. Volfing, eds, Tübingen: De Gruyter, 2007, pp.197–224.

Pfeiffer, Rudolf, 'The Image of Delian Apollo and Apolline Ethics', *Journal of the Warburg and Courtauld Institutes*, 15, 1952, pp.20–32.

The Autobiography of Lorenzo de' Medici the Magnificent: A Commentary on my Sonnets, trans. James Wyatt Cook, Binghamton, NY: Medieval and Renaissance Texts and Studies, 1995.
The Etymologies of Isidore of Seville, trans. Stephen A. Barney et al., Cambridge: Cambridge University Press, 2006.
Virtue and Beauty, exh. cat. National Gallery of Art, Washington, DC, 2001.
Vita di Raffaello da Montelupo, ed. Riccardo Gatteschi, Florence: Polistampa, 1998.

Pictorial essay C: The touch of the oracle

Michael Petry

In the past hands ventured in, often without asking, with only minimal permission, a look in the eyes, a slight smile or upturned lip, a glance, or the lightest, feathery touch as two passed, a spark of static electricity that foretold a flood of touch and touching of tongues and toes interlocked. In the past I slid into the sylvan glade and stroked the wood that was a nymph, the limb that was the hunter's, the pond that reflected the echo of my love. I was the grass beneath my lover's foot, the sand that flowed through their fingers that stuck to their leather clothing. In the past I was the wind that whistled through the aperture to tickle my lover's navel, to kiss them coolly and I was the rain that fell across their face, fresh, not the salty water of our parting. In the past, I was the sun that warmed my lover's skin like passion and lit their way into me, I was the wine that flowed between our lips and down our throats, a gift to the gods, a libation to those that are us.

In the past, men toiled in forests to raise the wood that I would work, that I would hold and mould into the skin of the gods, our skin, yours and mine and those we would touch, seemingly hard yet soft, almost yielding, inviting to the hand while rebuffing the eye. In the past women would finger the wool that was spooled into yarn that I would work, that I would twist and knot and cord and form into a secret voice of time, knots like ruffled hair after pleasure, tangles formed into a maze of desire, a history of touch. In the past children would roam the fields minding animals, while our animal desires, our animal nature allowed me to record that pleasure on the skins of animals, skinned for our desire, hung, up, and blood flowing through our veins, racing even, and down drains where animals gave up their life force for us, the gods.

In the past, you would come to me, and on me desire would show like the rays of the sun, and with me, to a place foretold called so many things so many times and under such guises and disguises that all hope of recognition should be lost, and yet when our forces collide who can change the thread of time, the shirt woven for us by fate. In the past I slipped you on, a second skin, bejewelled with the pearls of our love, the white treasure of happiness the sand in the flesh turned to a kind of gold, a white that is like the lotus blossom, the bringer of sleep and forgetfulness, the bringer of death, of desire, of touch, of the gods.

In the past, you would touch the wooden hole that yearned for you to stroke it, to oil it with your fingers that allowed the sun and light through its orifice, that foretold a coming storm, that retold a story of alignment and placement of standing stones and falling down, of swaying gently in the breeze of hovering over another, of the waiting, the intense longing moment of flesh suspended by the knowledge that in one more fraction of time desire would merge into action and forever be lost to knowledge and only a rebirth of desire, an unending treadmill of expectation would suffice. In that never-ending moment time slows, as if the gods themselves took a break to see if in the libation a new world would emerge from the bed of lovers, for only lovers make time, not even the gods can do so, not even in their own lust, for time is ours, of our human making and spending. In that moment of suspense when eyes say yes and lips part and breath quickens and blood flows throughout and skin feels the most alive, the art of living is all we know.

In the past, the oracle would touch us deeply in an unconscious vibration of the air, a sound would come, into our ears, and in the translation of it our actions would be vouchsafed and made wholly our own. I would spring, you would fall, and together we would go forth to spread the news of our wholeness, our oneness with the time of time, our completion of the cycles that tick, in our ears, just out of hearing, that unending clatter of the birth of the now, and the oracle would curse time itself, would shout down the ages an anger at the impotence of flesh and bone to withstand the forces that even the gods fear. In the past the oracle warned of the blackness, the bleakness of an never-ending time and the quickness of time's flow, today the bud, tomorrow the flower and no stilled lives ever brought to bear, only the decay of molecules and the stilled tongues, the frozen fingers and skin like parchment, written on mine, the times of our lives, those we have loved, those who have left their mark upon us and we them, skinned. In the past the oracle would silently shout and grab our chests and hold us close and tear our hair and drink of our joy.

In the past we found ourselves in a garden, we found ourselves in an oasis of calming heat, waves visible to the eye as hands shaded eyes to seek out the path to the oracle, a path marked on no map but instilled in each living thing, loaded into their very being like an arrow in a bow, waiting to meet its mark, to pierce its rightful owner, to bring about the change, the moment of light filling the space of us. In the past the light was brighter, stronger and able to bend round holes in time, and space itself out across us, and bring us safely home, to the home inside, the oracle's promised land of longing fulfilled, home to us, the home of us, the home of your hand on mine, the home of my lips to your ear whispering, *the path to me, was always through you*.

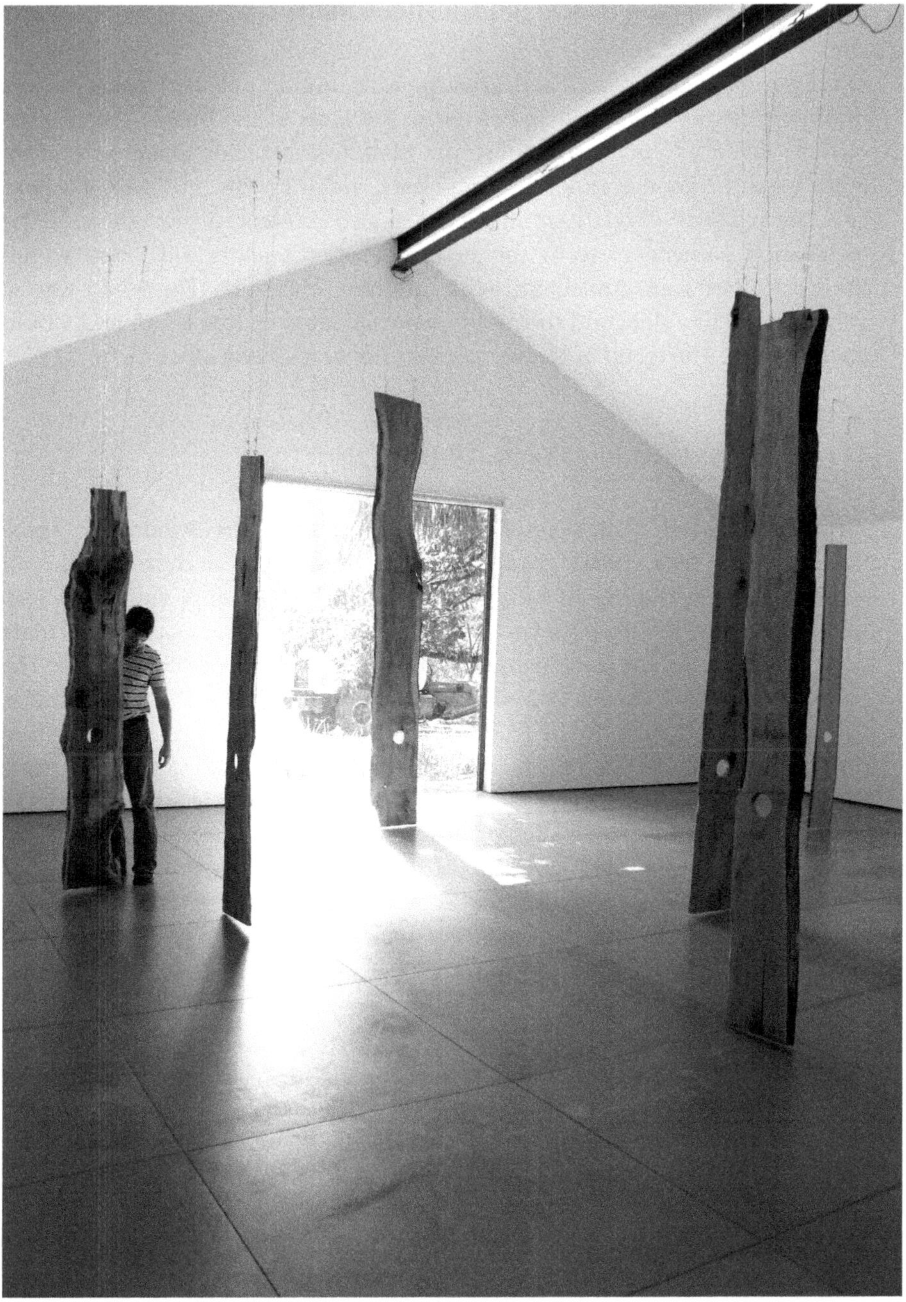

C.1 Michael Petry, *In the Garden of Eden* (Devin Borden Hiram Butler Gallery, Houston, 2007) [© Michael Petry]

In the Garden of Eden (Devin Borden Hiram Butler Gallery, Houston, 2007)

In the Garden of Eden comprised 12 suspended, highly polished vertical slices of timber, with a circular hole cut out at the level of the pelvis. The incised oculus references Duchamp, Moore, pre-historic star-gazing machinery, glory holes used for anonymous sex in gay bars, video booths and public toilets, and Jasper Johns' *Target* paintings (which also referenced glory holes). The installation was meant to be touched, and when visitors did interact with the pieces they were confronted with different sensations. The wood was so velvety it felt like skin, and the pieces were activated by that touch and would start to sway. The smell of the wood was intense and evocative.

The Lovers (*WAS: White as Snow*, DBHBG, 2004)

The Lovers is a direct link to previous works the *Fairy Tales* (Sundaram Tagore Gallery, New York, 2004), made of leather and pearls, and stretched over wooden frames. The size of each stretcher was exactly that of one of a pair of real male lovers. To create the pearl templates each lover was asked to ejaculate onto their partner, the documentation of these shapes forms the portrait. The pattern was traced from a Polaroid in an attempt to de-sex the image and to fictionalise the process. In the *Fairy Tales*, the ejaculates were produced within the fictional construct of a pornographic movie (I used a video still to capture the patterns), for *The Lovers*, the ejaculates were from people who were really lovers and who often make such patterns on each other, but not for exhibition. In agreeing to make the piece, the couple fictionalised their relationship, as they do not document their ejaculates as a matter of course, and in so doing created a fiction. The resultant painting depicts ejaculates from real lovers but in a fictional setting (as all portraits are).

Spent (Westbrook Gallery, London, 2006)

The Spills series looks at formal aspects of ejaculates, made from sterling silver bought for that purpose (*Spill Bottom, Spill Top*). However, in *Spent,* I melted my childhood silver coin collection. It now resembles a large ejaculate, having had many coins, which are now truly spent. *Spent* speaks of childhood and the passage into adulthood, the physical changes allowing boys to become men, and the work is loaded with autobiographical information. Yet the melting of the collection into a mass, reduces the whole to a mass of memories. The melted silver was spilt onto a jeweller's stone into its present form, creating sexual fictions. *Spills* reference Richard Serra's hot lead *Castings* (1969)

C.2 Michael Petry, *The Lovers* (*WAS: White as Snow*, DBHBG, 2004) [© Michael Petry]

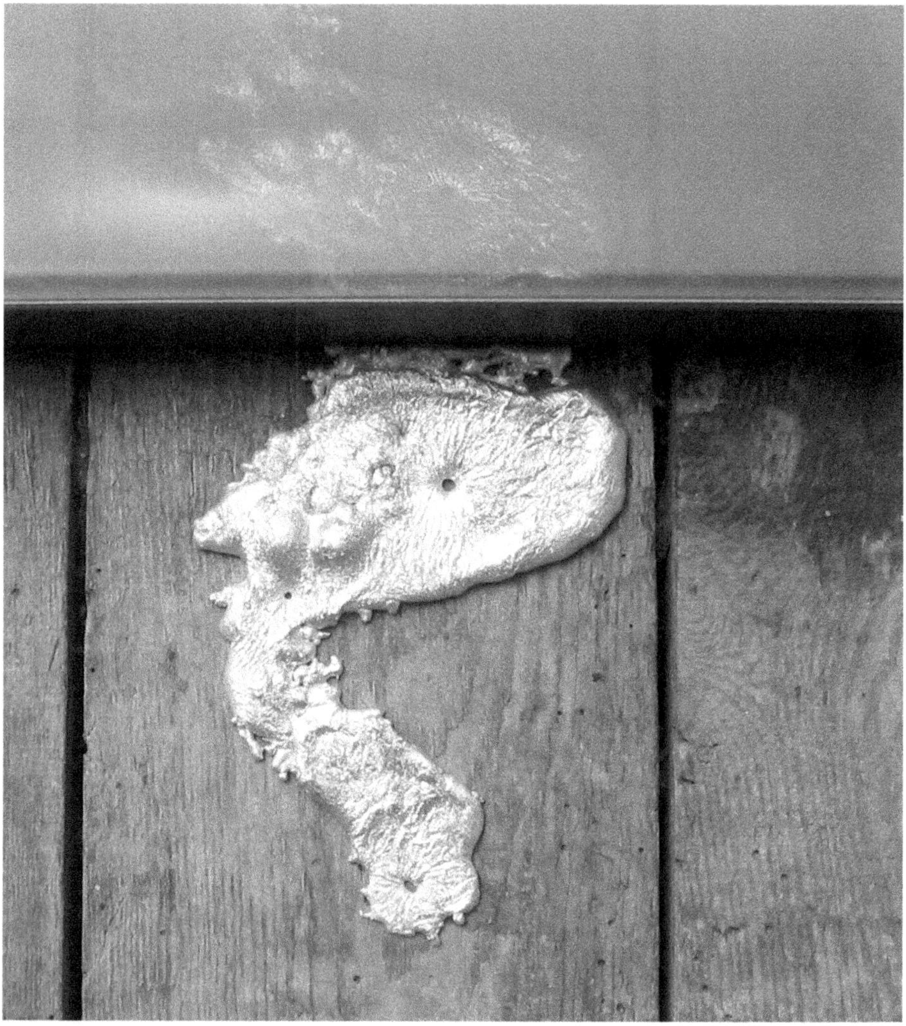

C.3 Michael Petry, *Spent* (Westbrook Gallery, London, 2006) [© Michael Petry]

where he made sculptures in situ by flinging molten lead. His seminal work is referenced by Mathew Barney in his *Cremaster 3*, having Serra fling what appear to be ladles of semen. The filmic bonding sees the two men as links in a hetero-dominant art history. Serra the grand old flinger passes on the artistic torch to the up and coming man. My *Spills* link me to Robert Gober and Warhol. Dave Hickey in *In the Dancehall of the Dead: Robert Gober* describes his work as 'interior decorating with a vengence (sic)' and Warhol the echt florist, camouflaged his work behind his personality, and also made works with semen on canvas. It is ejaculate that links all said players to Duchamp's *Paysage fautif* (1946) one of the first known uses of semen in modern art.

Tie A Knot In It (detail, Zane Bennett Contemporary Art, Santa Fe, 2012)

The *Tie A Knot In It* (*TAKII*) series is based in the action of masturbation, where each knot represents an orgasm (male or female). Each sees different lengths or types of rope, string or wire used to make a series of knots. The distance between each knot may give the work its title (*Nipple Pinch, Rough Neck* – both are over 10 metres long and can be played with in the gallery) or it might come from the material (*Sewing Seed* works use garden cord) but all reference the sexual notion inherent in the series' title. The phrase is used as a brush off for unwanted sexual advances, or as a term of stoppage when the desire to urinate is not met with an available facility. A forget-me-not shows the desire for one of a pair to be remembered in their absence. Indigenous peoples used belts of knots to pass messages from one end of South America to the other in a matter of days. Knots have a history; the Gordian gave Alexander the key to ruling the world. The first *TAKII* was made from white yarn and is exactly my height in length. Every few centimetres a large clot of knots resembles dripping semen, or just knots. Each of these clots is made from tens of individual knots. The process took over three months to complete, and the work was installed in a way as to be almost invisible, like the time it took to make it.

La petite mort III (*True Love*, Muzeum Mierdzi, Legnica, Poland, 2007)

The French for orgasm, *la petite mort* (the little death), posits the small passage of time from one state of being to another. These works are spent; time well spent, and also worthless pieces of string. The series addresses the craft/art divide; made from craft materials, each is similar to macramé, but is not. They speak of traditional women's handicraft, lace-making, sewing and gender issues in fine art production, they document a man making knots,

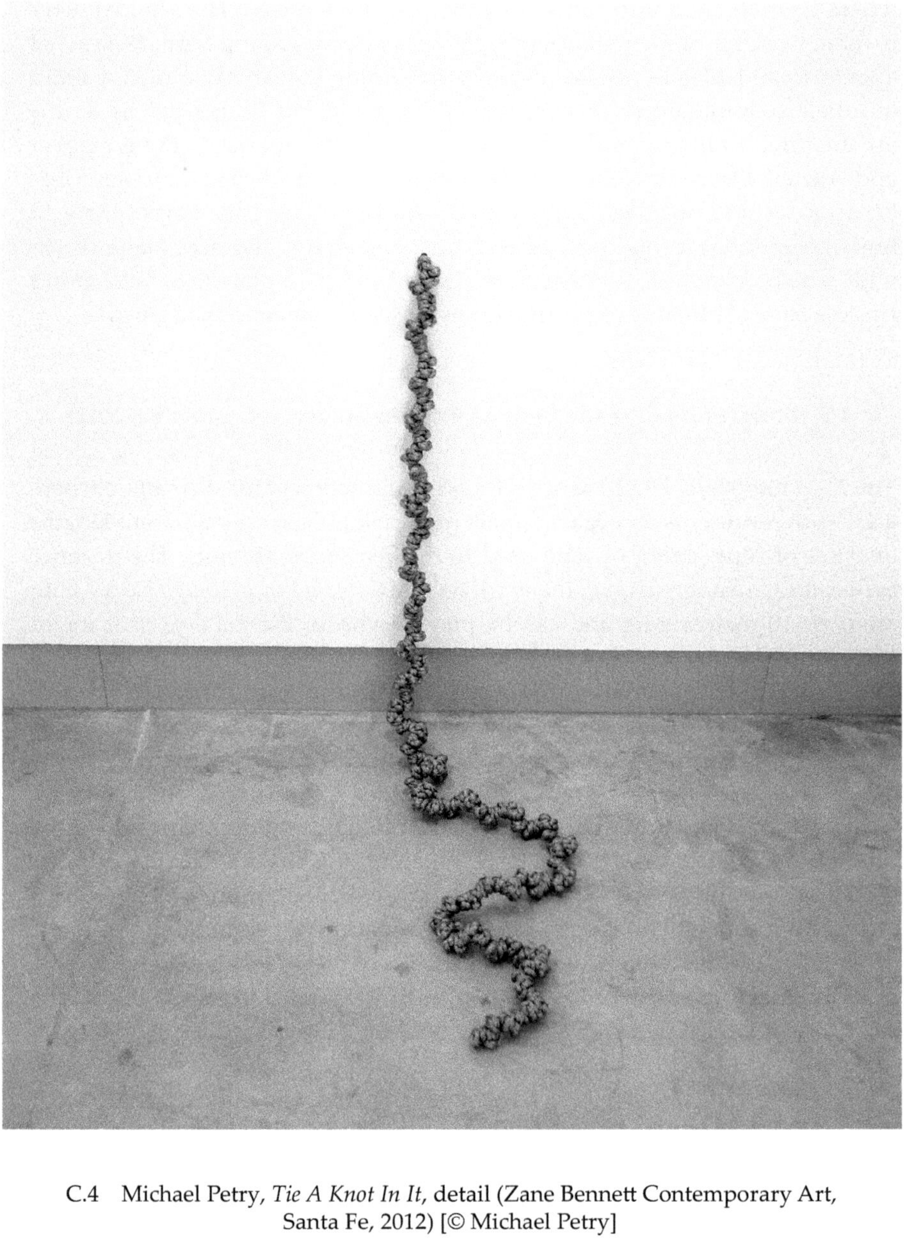

C.4 Michael Petry, *Tie A Knot In It*, detail (Zane Bennett Contemporary Art, Santa Fe, 2012) [© Michael Petry]

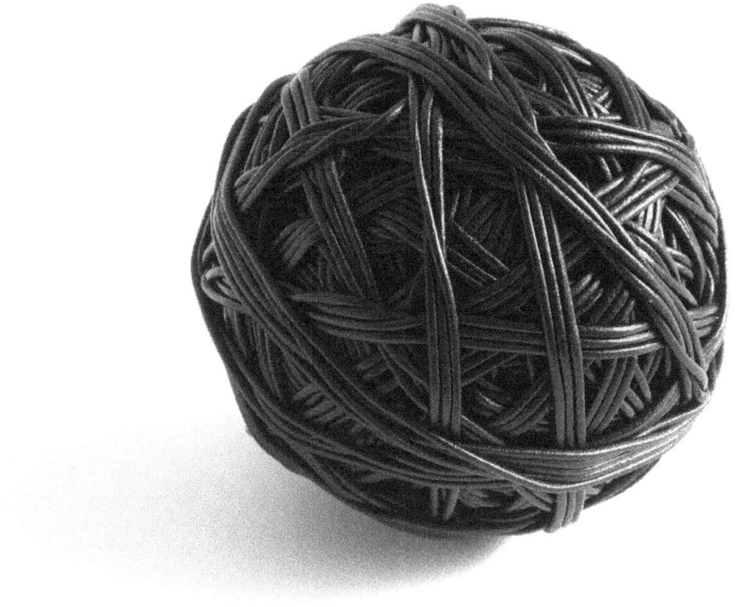

C.5 Michael Petry, *La petite mort III* (*True Love*, Muzeum Mierdzi, Legnica, Poland, 2007) [© Michael Petry]

tying string, making/wasting time. If I were a sixteenth-century woman tying knots, making lace, the resultant artefact would have little value compared to a work in silver or a work made on canvas made by a man. How such objects were and generally still are seen as craft or as fine art alters not only their artistic reception but also the price people are willing to pay for them. In effect I am a man who performs a *womanly* act, yet my knots are not craft, they are minimal sculptures, but sculptures all the same, and men's work in the visual arts generally (sadly) has a higher value than the work of women. These mean objects still perform as art, doing so in a gallery setting that gives them gravitas by inhabiting those environs.

In the illustrated works and in much of my production, regardless of material (blown glass, polished wood, knotted cord), the haptic is at play, and *play* is offered for consideration. I allow touch but sadly most institutions do not. Yet visitors almost always find a way to transgress as their marks attest on my once shiny surfaces ...

Select bibliography

This bibliography is not comprehensive but intended only as a general guide to the literature on this topic. Further bibliographical references will be found after the individual chapters in this volume and in the bibliographies to the works contained below.

Bacci, Francesca, 'Sculpture and Touch', in *Art and the Senses*, Francesca Bacci and David Melcher, eds, Oxford: Oxford University Press, 2011, pp.133–48.

Baker, Malcolm. 'Some Object Histories and the Materiality of the Sculptural Object.' In *The Lure of the Object*, edited by Stephen Melville, 119–34. New Haven and London: Yale University Press, 2005.

Bauer, Douglas F., 'The Function of Pygmalion in the Metamorphoses of Ovid', *Transactions and Proceedings of the American Philological Association*, 93, 1962, pp.1–21.

Bilstein, Johannes and Guido Reuter, eds, *Auge und Hand*, Oberhausen: Athena, 2011.

Boetzkes, Amanda, 'Phenomenology and Interpretation Beyond the Flesh', *Art History*, 32 (4), 2009, pp.690–711.

Bolland, Andrea L., 'Desiderio and Diletto: Vision, Touch, and the Poetics of Bernini's Apollo and Daphne', *The Art Bulletin*, 82, 2000, pp.309–30.

Braungart, Georg, *Leibhafter Sinn: Der andere Diskurs der Moderne*, Tübingen: Niemeyer, 1995

——, 'Die tastende Hand, die formende Hand: Physiologie und Ästhetik bei Johann Gottfried Herder', in *Hand, Schrift, Bild*, Toni Bernhart and Gert Gröning, eds, Berlin: Akademie Verlag, 2005, pp.29–39

Brook, Donald, 'Perception and Appraisal of Sculpture', *The Journal of Aesthetics and Art Criticism*, 27 (3), 1969, pp.323–30.

Candlin, Fiona, 'Blindness, Art and Exclusion in Museums and Galleries', *Journal of Art & Design Education*, 22, 2003, pp.100–110.

——, 'Don't Touch! Hands Off! Art, Blindness and the Conservation of Expertise', *Body and Society*, 10, 2004, pp.71–90.

——, 'The Dubious Inheritance of Touch: Art History and Museum Access', *Journal of Visual Culture*, 5 (2), 2006, pp.137–54.

——, 'Museums, Modernity and the Class Politics of Touching Objects', in *Touch in Museums: Policy and Practice in Object Handling*, Helen Chatterjee, ed., London: Berg, 2008, pp.9–20.

——, 'Touch and the Limits of the Rational Museum', *Senses and Society*, 3 (3), 2008, pp.277–92.
——, 'The Touch Experience in Museums in the UK and Japan', in *The Power of Touch: Handling Objects in Museum and Heritage Contexts*, E. Pye, ed., Walnut Creek, CA: Left Coast Press, 2007, pp.163–83.
——, *Art, Museums and Touch*, Manchester: Manchester University Press, 2010.
Chatterjee, H., *Touch in Museums: Policy and Practice in Object Handling*, Oxford: Berg, 2008.
Classen, Constance, ed., *The Book of Touch*, Oxford and New York: Berg, 2005.
——, and David Howes. 'The Museum as Sensescape: Western Sensibilities and Indigenous Artefacts.' In *Sensible Objects: Colonialism, Museums and Material Culture*, edited by Elizabeth Edwards, Chris Gosden and Ruth Phillips, 119–222. Oxford: Berg, 2006.
——, 'Museum Manners: The Sensory Life of the Early Museum', *Journal of Social History*, 40 (4), 2007, pp.895–914.
——, *The Deepest Sense: A Cultural History of Touch*, Urbana, Chicago and Springfield: University of Illinois Press, 2012
Claude Heath: Drawing from Sculpture, Leeds: Henry Moore Institute, 1999.
Cranny-Francis, A., 'Touching Skin: Embodiment and the Senses in the Work of Ron Mueck', in *Cultural Theory in Everyday Practice*, Nicole Anderson and Katrina Schlunke, eds, South Melbourne, Victoria: Oxford University Press, 2009, pp.36–46.
——, 'Semefulness: A Social Semiotics of Touch', *Social Semiotics*, 21 (4), 2011, pp.463–81.
——, 'The Art of Touch: A Photo-Essay', *Social Semiotics*, 21 (4), 2011, pp.591–608.
——, 'Sculpture as Deconstruction: The Aesthetic Practice of Ron Mueck', *Visual Communication*, 12 (1), 2013, pp.3–25.
Crowther, Paul, *Phenomenology of the Visual Arts: (Even the Frame)*, Stanford, CA: Stanford University Press, 2009.
Derrida, Jacques, *Memoirs of the Blind: The Self-Portrait and other Ruins*, Chicago: University of Chicago Press, 1993.
Deschênes, Michèle, 'De quelques definitions de la sculpture au XXe siècle', *Espace Sculpture*, 31, 1995, pp.32–5.
Diaconu, M., 'The Rebellion of the "Lower" Senses: A Phenomenological Aesthetics of Touch, Smell, and Taste', in *Essays in Celebration of the Founding of the Organization of Phenomenological Organizations*, H. Chan-Fai, I. Chvatik, I. Copoeru, L. Embree, J. Iribarne and H.R. Sepp, eds, 2003 [online] available at www.o-p-o.net (accessed: 3 March 2014).
——, 'Reflections on an Aesthetics of Touch, Smell and Taste', *Contemporary Aesthetics*, 4, 2006 [online] available at www.contempaesthetics.org (accessed: 3 March 2014).
Di Bello, Patrizia, 'Photography and Sculpture: A Light Touch', in *Art, History and the Senses: 1830 to the Present*, Patrizia Di Bello and Gabriel Koureas, eds, Farnham: Ashgate, 2010, pp.19–34.
——, '"Multiplying Statues by Machinery": Stereoscopic Photographs of Sculptures at the 1862 International Exhibition', *History of Photography*, 37 (4), 2013, pp.412–20.
Didi-Huberman, Georges, *La resemblance par contact: archéologie, anchronisme et mode nité de l'empreinte*, Paris: Ed. de Minuit, 2008.
Driscoll, Rosalyn, *Aesthetic Touch/Haptic Art: Proceedings of the Eurohaptics 2006 Conference*, Paris, 2006.
——, 'Aesthetic Touch', in *Art and the Senses*, Francesca Bacci and David Melcher, eds, Oxford: Oxford University Press, 2011, pp.107–14.
Fisher, Jennifer, 'Relational Sense: Towards a Haptic Aesthetics', *Parachute*, 87, 1997, pp.4–11.

Fisher, Jennifer, 'Tactile Affects', *Tessera*, 32 (Summer), 2002, pp.17–28.
Franzini, Elio, 'Art and the Body: A Philosophical Perspective', *Leitmotiv*, 0/2010, pp.27–49 [online] available at http://ledonline.it/leitmotiv (accessed: 6 March 2014).
——, 'Rendering the Sensory World Somatic', in *Art and the Senses*, Francesca Bacci and David Melcher, eds, Oxford: Oxford University Press, 2011, pp.115–31.
Freedberg, David, *The Power of Images: Studies in the History and Theory of Response*, Chicago, IL: University of Chicago Press, 1989.
Gallace, Alberto and Charles Spence, 'Tactile Aesthetics: Towards a Definition of Its Characteristics and Neural Correlates', *Social Semiotics*, 21 (4), 2011, pp.569–89.
Geary, A., 'Exploring Virtual Touch in the Creative Arts and Conservation', in *The Power of Touch: Handling Objects in Museum and Heritage Contexts*, E. Pye, ed., Walnut Creek, CA: Left Coast Press, 2007, pp.241–52.
Getsy, David J., *Body Doubles: Sculpture in Britian, 1877–1905*, New Haven, CT and London: Yale University Press, 2004.
——, 'Tactility or Opticality, Henry Moore or David Smith: Herbert Read and Clement Greenberg on "The Art of Sculpture", 1956', *The Sculpture Journal*, 17 (2), 2008, pp.75–88.
——, *Rodin: Sex and the Making of Modern Sculpture*, New Haven, CT and London: Yale University Press, 2010.
Goslee, Nancy M., 'From Marble to Living Form: Sculpture as Art and Analogue from the Renaissance to Blake', *The Journal of English and Germanic Philology*, 77 (2), 1978, pp.188–211.
Grazioli, Elio, 'La Scultura per Ciechi di Brancusi', *Riga* (Constantin Brancusi), 19, 2001, pp.325–33.
Greenberg, Clement, 'Roundness Isn't All: Review of the Art of Sculpture by Herbert Read', in *Clement Greenberg: The Collected Essays and Criticism*, John O'Brian, ed., Chicago and London: University of Chicago Press, 1993, pp.270–72.
Gross, Kenneth, *The Dream of the Moving Statue*, Ithaca, NY: Cornell University Press, 1992.
Hall, James, *The World as Sculpture: The Changing Status of Sculpture from the Renaissance to the Present Day*, London: Chatto and Windus, 1999.
——, 'Herbert Read's "The Art of Sculpture"', in *The A.W. Mellon Lectures in the Fine Arts: Fifty Years*, Washington, DC: National Gallery of Art, 2002, pp.35–8.
——, 'Desire and Disgust: Touching Artworks from 1500 to 1800', in *Presence: The Inherence of the Prototype within Images and Other Objects*, Robert Maniura and Rupert Sheperd, eds, Aldershot: Ashgate, 2006, pp.145–60.
Harvey, Elizabeth D., ed., *Sensible Flesh: On Touch in Early Modern Culture*, Philadelphia, PA: University of Pennsylvania Press, 2002.
Hetherington, Kevin, 'The Unsightly: Touching the Parthenon Frieze', *Theory, Culture, Society*, 19 (5/6), 2002, pp.187–205.
Hecht, Peter, 'The Paragone Debate: Ten Illustrations and a Comment', *Simiolus*, 14 (2), 1984, pp.125–36.
Hecker, Sharon, '"Sealed Between Us": Wax and the Role of the Viewer in Luciano Fabro's *Tu*', *Oxford Art Journal*, 36 (1), 2013, pp.13–38.
Hemsterhuis, Frans, *Lettre sur la sculpture*, Paris: École nationale supérieure des Beaux-Arts, 1992.
Herder, Johann Gottfried, *Sculpture: Some Observations on Shape and Form from Pygmalion's Creative Dream*, ed. and trans. Jason Gaiger, Chicago, IL and London: University of Chicago Press, 2002.
Hersey, George L., *Falling in Love with Statues: Artificial Humans from Pygmalion to the Present*, Chicago, IL and London: University of Chicago Press, 2009.

Hildebrand, Adolf von, *Das Problem der Form in der bildenden Kunst*, Strasbourg: J.H.E. Heitz, 1893.
Hinz, Berthold, 'Statuenliebe: Antiker Skandal und mittelalterlich Trauma', *Marburger Jahrbuch für Kunstwissenschaft*, 22, 1989, pp.135–42.
Hohenemser, Richard, 'Wendet sich die Plastik an den Tastsinn?', *Zeitschrift für Ästhetik und allgemeine Kunstwissenschaft*, 6, 1911, pp.405–19.
Hopkins, Robert, 'Touching Pictures', *British Journal of Aesthetics*, 40 (1), 2000, pp.149–67.
——, 'Sculpture', in *Oxford Companion to Aesthetics*, J. Levinson, ed., Oxford: Oxford University Press, 2003, pp.572–82.
——, 'Sculpture and Space', in *Imagination, Philosophy, and the Arts*, M. Kieran and D. Lopes, eds, Abingdon and New York: Routledge, 2003, pp.272–90.
——, 'Painting, Sculpture, Sight and Touch', *British Journal of Aesthetics*, 44 (2), 2004, pp.149–66.
——, 'Molyneux's Question', *Canadian Journal of Philosophy*, 35 (3), 2005, pp.441–64.
——, 'Sculpture and Perspective', *British Journal of Aesthetics*, 50 (3), 2010, pp.1–17.
——, '*Re*-imagining, *Re*-Viewing and *Re*-Touching', in *The Senses: Classic and Contemporary Philosophical Perspectives*, Fiona Macpherson, ed., Oxford: Oxford University Press, 2011, pp.261–83.
Huber, Jörg, ed., *Taktilität: Sinneserfahrung als Grenzerfahrung*, Zürich: Institut für Theorie (ith), 2008.
Jansson-Boyd, C. and N. Marlow, 'Not Only in the Eye of the Beholder: Tactile Information Can Affect Aesthetic Evaluation', *Psychology of Aesthetics, Creativity, and the Arts*, 1, 2007, pp.170–73.
Johnson, Geraldine, 'Touch, Tactility, and the Reception of Sculpture in Early Modern Italy', in *The Blackwell Companion to Art Theory*, P. Smith and C. Wilde, eds, Oxford: Blackwell Publishing, 2002, pp.61–74.
——, 'The Art of Touch in Early Modern Italy', in *Art and the Senses*, Francesca Bacci and David Melcher, eds, Oxford: Oxford University Press, 2011, pp.59–84.
——, 'In the Hand of the Beholder: Isabella d'Este and the Sensory Allure of Sculpture', in *Sense and the Senses in Early Modern Art and Culture Practice*, A. Sanger and S.T. Kulbrandstad Walker, eds, Farnham: Ashgate, 2012, pp.183–97.
Jolles, Adam, 'The Tactile Turn: Envisioning a Postcolonial Aesthetic in France', *Yale French Studies*, 109, 2006, pp.17–38.
Jung, Jacqueline E., 'The Tactile and the Visionary: Notes on the Place of Sculpture in the Medieval Religious Imagination', in *Looking Beyond: Visions, Dreams, and Insights in Medieval Art and History*, Colum Hourihane, ed., University Park, PA: Penn State University Press, 2010, pp.203–40.
Kemske, Bonnie, 'Embracing Sculptural Ceramics: A Lived Experience of Touch in Art', *The Senses and Society*, 4 (3), 2009, pp.323–44.
Kessler, Hans-Ulrich, 'Pietro Bernini's Statues for the Cappella Ruffo in the Church of the Gerolamini in Naples', *The Sculpture Journal*, 6, 2001, pp.21–9.
Khayami, S., 'Touching Art, Touching You: Blindart, Sense and Sensuality', in *The Power of Touch: Handling Objects in Museum and Heritage Contexts*, E. Pye, ed., Walnut Creek, CA: Left Coast Press, 2007, pp.183–90.
Kluxen, Andrea, 'Plastisches Sehen: von Johann Gottfried Herder bis Adolf von Hildebrand', in *Ästhetische Probleme der Plastik im 19. und 20. Jahrhundert*, Andrea M. Kluxen, ed., Nürnberg: Aleph-Verlag, 2001, pp.23–45.
Koed, Erik, 'Sculpture and the Sculptural', *The Journal of Aesthetics and Art Criticism*, 63 (2) 2005, pp.147–54.
Kopania, Kamil, *Animated Sculptures of the Crucified Christ in the Religious Culture of the Latin Middle Ages*, Warsaw: Wydawnictwo Neriton, 2010.

Körner, Hans, 'Der fünfte Bruder: Zur Tastwahrnehmung plastischer Bildwerke von der Renaissance bis zum frühen 19. Jahrhundert', *Artibus et Historiae*, 21 (42), 2000, pp.165–96.

——, 'Die entäuschte und die getäuschte Hand: der Tastsinn im Paragone der Künste', in *Der stumme Diskurs der Bilder: Reflexionsformen des Ästhetischen in der Kunst der Frühen Neuzeit*, Valeska von Rosen, Klaus Krüger and Rudolf Preimesberger, eds, Munich: Deutscher Kunstverlag, 2003, pp.221–41.

——, 'Die Erziehung der Sinne: Wahrnehmungstheorie und Gattungsgrenzen in der Kunstliteratur des 18. und frühen 19. Jahrhunderts', in *Perception and the Senses: Sinneswahrnehmungen*, Therese Fischer-Seidel, Susanne Peters and Alex Potts, eds, Tübingen: Francke, 2004, pp.125–42.

——, 'The Invisible Hand: Distant Touch and Aesthetic Feelings in the Late 18th Century', *Predella*, 29, 2011 [online] available at http://www.predella.it/archivio/index0558.html?option=com_content&view=article&id=177&catid=65&Itemid=94 (accessed: 6 March 2014).

La Barbera Bellia, Simonetta, *Il paragone delle arti nella teoria artistica del Cinquecento*, Bagheria: Cafaro, 1997.

Lamia, Stephen, 'Souvenir, Synaesthesia, and the "Sepulcrum Domini": Sensory Stimuli as Memory Stratagems', in *Memory and the Medieval Tomb*, Elizabeth Valdez del Alamo with Carol Stamatis Pendergast, eds, Aldershot: Ashgate, 2000, pp.19–41.

Lichtenstein, Jacqueline, *The Blind Spot: An Essay on the Relations between Painting and Sculpture in the Modern Age*, trans. Chris Miller, Los Angeles, CA: Getty Research Institute, 2008.

Lopes, Dominic M.M., 'Art Media and the Sense Modalities: Tactile Pictures', *The Philosophical Quarterly*, 47 (189), 1997, pp.425–40.

——, 'Vision, Touch, and the Value of Pictures', *British Journal of Aesthetics*, 42, 2002, pp.187–97.

MacGregor, G., 'Making Sense of the Past in the Present: A Sensory Analysis of Carved Stone Balls', *World Archaeology*, 31, 1999, pp.258–71.

Malsch, Wilfried, 'Herders Schrift über die Skulpturkunst in der Geschichte der Unterschiedung des Plastischen and Malerischen oder Musikalischen in Kunst und Literatur', in *Johann Gottfried Herder: Language, History and the Enlightenment*, Wulf Koepke, ed., Columbia, SC: Camden House, 1990, pp.224–35.

Maragliano, Giorgio, 'La visione che tocca: una metafora assoluta da Herder a Wölfflin', in *La polifonia estetica: specificità e raccordi*, Massimo Venturi Ferriolo, ed., Milan: Guerini, 1996, pp.129–38.

Marinetti, F.T., *Il tattilismo: manifesto futurista*, Milan: Direzione del Movimento Futurista, 1921.

Martin, F. David, 'The Autonomy of Sculpture', *The Journal of Aesthetics and Art Criticism*, 34 (3) 1976, pp.273–86.

——, 'On Perceiving Paintings and Sculpture', *Leonardo*, 11 (4), 1978, pp.287–92.

——, 'Sculpture, Painting, and Damage', *The Journal of Aesthetics and Art Criticism*, 37 (1), 1978, pp.47–52.

——, 'Sculpture and "Truth to Things"', *Journal of Aesthetic Education*, 13 (2), 1979, pp.11–32.

Mazzocut-Mis, Maddalena, *Voyeurismo tattili: Un'estetica dei valori tattily e visivi*, Genoa: il melangolo, 2002.

Mendelsohn, Leatrice, *Paragoni: Benedetto Varchi's Due lezzioni and cinquecento art theory*, Ann Arbor, MI: UMI Research Press, 1982.

Molesworth, Helen, 'Duchamp: By Hand, Even', in *Part Object Part Sculpture*, Helen Molesworth, ed., University Park PA: Pennsylvania University Press, 2005, pp. 179–201.

Mülder-Bach, Inka, 'Eine "neue Logik für den Liebhaber": Herders Theorie der Plastik', in *Der ganze Mensch: Anthropologie und Literatur im 18. Jahrhundert*, Hans-Jürgen Schings, ed., Stuttgart: J.B. Metzler, 1994, pp.341–70.

——, 'Ferngefühle: Poesie und Plastik in Herders Ästhetik', in *Im Agon der Künste: paragonales Denken, ästhetische Praxis und die Diversität der Sinne*, Hannah Baader, Ulrike Müller Hofstede, Kristine Patz and Nicola Suthor, eds, Munich: Fink, 2007, pp.451–65.

Museo Tattile Statale Omero, ed., *L'arte a portata di mano: Verso una pedagogia di accesso ai Beni Culturali senza barrier (Atti del convegno Portonovo di Ancona 21–23 ottobre 2004)*, Rome: Armando, 2006.

O'Rourke Bolye, Marjorie, *Senses of Touch: Human Dignity and Deformity from Michelangelo to Calvin*, Leiden: Brill, 1998.

Peña, Carolyn de la, 'Saccharine Sparrow (Circa 1955)', in *The Object Reader*, Fiona Candlin and Raiford Guins, eds, Milton Park, Abingdon, Oxon; New York: Routledge, 2009, pp.506–9.

Perricone, Christopher, 'The Place of Touch in the Arts', *Journal of Aesthetic Education*, 41 (1), 2007, pp.90–104.

Petrelli, Micla, *Valori tattili e arte del sensibile*, Florence: Alinea Editrice, 1994.

Pfotenhauer, Helmut, 'Gemeißelte Sinnlichkeit: Herders Anthropologie des Plastischen und die Spannungen darin', in Helmut Pfotenhauer, *Um 1800: Konfigurationen der Literatur, Kunstliteratur und Ästhetik*, Tübingen: Niemeyer, 1991, pp.79–102.

Pierre, Caterina Y., 'The Pleasure and Piety of Touch in Aimé-Jules Dalou's "Tomb of Victor Noir"', *The Sculpture Journal*, 19 (2), 2010, pp.173–85.

Pinotti, Andrea, 'Un'immagine alla mano: note per una genealogia dello spettatore tattile', in *Il luogo dello spettatore: forme dello sguardo nella cultura delle immagini*, Antonio Somaini, ed., Milan: Vita e Pensiero, 2005, pp.119–40.

——, 'Guardare o toccare? Un'incertezza herderiana', *aisthesis*, 2 (1), 2009, pp.177–91.

Plunkett, John, '"Feeling Seeing": Touch, Vision and the Stereoscope', *History of Photography*, 37 (4), 2013, pp.389–96.

Podro, Michael, 'Herder's "Plastik"', in *Sight and Insight: Essays on Art and Culture in Honour of E.H. Gombrich at 85*, John Onians, ed., London: Phaidon Press, 1994, pp.341–53.

——, 'Un traité de Herder: Plastik', in *Histoire de l'histoire de l'art*, Édouard Pommier, ed., Paris: Klincksieck, 1995, pp.327–43.

Potts, Alex, 'Male Phantasy and Modern Sculpture', *Oxford Art Journal*, 15 (2), 1992, pp.38–47.

——, *The Sculptural Imagination*, New Haven, CT and London: Yale University Press, 2000.

——, 'Tactility: The Interrogation of Medium in Art of the 1960s, *Art History*, 27 (2), 2004, pp.282–304.

Powell, K.H., 'Hands-on Surrealism', *Art History*, 20, 1997, pp.516–33.

Protzmann, Heiner, 'Die visuelle Ästhetik der Skulptur und das Problem der Wechselvertretung von Auge und Tastsinn', *Jahrbuch der Staatlichen Kunstsammlungen Dresden*, 13, 1981, pp.17–28.

Prytherch, D. and M. Jefsioutine, 'Touching Ghosts: Haptic Technologies in Museums', in *The Power of Touch: Handling Objects in Museum and Heritage Contexts*, E. Pye, ed., Walnut Creek, CA: Left Coast Press, 2007, pp.223–40.

Read, Herbert, *The Art of Sculpture*, London: Faber & Faber, 1956.

Russo, Luigi, ed., *Estetica della Scultura*, Palermo: Aesthetica, 2003.

San Juan, Rose Marie, 'The Horror of Touch: Anna Morandi's Wax Models of Hands', *Oxford Art Journal*, 34 (3), 2011, pp.433–47.

Schneider, Helmut J., 'The Cold Eye: Herder's Critique of Enlightenment Visualism', in *Johann Gottfried Herder: Language, History and the Enlightenment*, Wulf Koepke, ed., Columbia, SC: Camden House, 1990, pp.53–60.

Schwarte, Ludger, 'Taktisches Sehen: Auge und Hand in der Bildtheorie', in *Auge und Hand*, Johannes Bilstein and Guido Reuter, eds, Oberhausen: Athena, 2011, pp.211–28.

Segal, Naomi, 'Words, Bodies and Stone', *Journal of Romance Studies*, 6 (3), 2006, pp.1–18.

Smith, T'Ai, 'Limits of the Tactile and the Optical: Bauhaus Fabric in the Frame of Photography', *Grey Room*, 25, 2006, pp.6–31.

Sonderen, P.C., *Het sculpturale denken: De esthetica van Frans Hemsterhuis*, Leende: DAMON, 2000 [online] available at http://dare.uva.nl/document/82526 (accessed: 6 March 2014).

Spence, Charles, 'Making Sense of Touch: A Multisensory Approach to the Perception of Objects', in *The Power of Touch: Handling Objects in Museum and Heritage Contexts*, E. Pye, ed., Walnut Creek, CA: Left Coast Press, 2007, pp.45–61.

——, 'The Multisensory Perception of Touch', in *Art and the Senses*, Francesca Bacci and David Melcher, eds, Oxford: Oxford University Press, 2011, pp.85–106.

Spence, Charles and Alberto Gallace, 'Making Sense of Touch', in *Touch in Museums: Policy and Practice in Object Handling*, H. Chatterjee, ed., Oxford: Berg, 2008, pp.21–40.

Stewart, Peter, *Statues in Roman Society: Representation and Response*, Oxford: Oxford University Press, 2003.

Stoichita, Victor I., *The Pygmalion Effect: From Ovid to Hitchcock*, trans. Alison Anderson, Chicago, IL and London: University of Chicago Press, 2008.

Thomas, Ben, 'The Paragone Debate and Sixteenth-century Italian Art', D.Phil., University of Oxford, 1996, 2 vols.

Van Vliet, Muriel, 'Phénoménologie de la perception et théorie de l'art chez Ernst Cassirer: l'ouverture d'un dialogue avec Maurice Merleau-Ponty', in *Ernst Cassirer et l'art comme forme symbolique*, Muriel Van Vliet, ed., Rennes: Presses Universitaires de Rennes, 2010, pp.117–44.

Verbeek, Caro, 'Prière de toucher!: Tactilism in Early Modern and Contemporary Art', *The Senses and Society*, 7 (2), 2012, pp.225–35.

Walsh, Linda, 'The "Hard Form" of Sculpture: Marble, Matter and Spirit in European Sculpture from the Enlightenment through Romanticism', *Modern Intellectual History*, 5 (3), 2008, pp.455–86.

Wenderholm, Iris, *Bild und Berührung: Skulptur und Malerei auf dem Altar der italienischen Frührenaissance*, Munich and Berlin: Deutscher Kunstverlag, 2006.

Winter, Gundolf, 'Skulptur und Virtualität oder der Vollzug des dreidimensionalen Bildes', *Skulptur – zwischen Realität und Virtualität*, Gundolf Winter, Jens Schröter and Christian Spies, eds, Munich: Fink, 2006, pp.47–74.

——, 'Bild – Raum – Raumbild: zum Phänomen dreidimensionaler Bildlichkeit', in *Das Raumbild: Bilder jenseits ihrer Flächen*, Gundolf Winter, Jens Schröter and Joanna Barck, eds, Munich: Fink, 2009, pp.47–63.

Winter, Gundolf, Jens Schröter and Christian Spies, eds, *Skulptur – zwischen Realität und Virtualität*, Munich: Fink, 2006.

Wood, Jon, David Hulks and Alex Potts, eds, *Modern Sculpture Reader*, Leeds: Henry Moore Institute, 2007.

Zeuch, Ulrike, *Umkehr der Sinneshierarchie: Herder und die Aufwertung des Tastsinns seit der frühen Neuzeit*, Tübingen: Niemeyer, 2000.

Zuckert, Rachel, 'Sculpture and Touch: Herder's Aesthetics of Sculpture', *The Journal of Aesthetics and Art Criticism*, 67 (3), 2009, pp.285–99.

Index

Illustrations are indicated by page numbers in **bold**.

For Product Safety Concerns and Information please contact our EU
representative GPSR@taylorandfrancis.com
Taylor & Francis Verlag GmbH, Kaufingerstraße 24, 80331 München, Germany

www.ingramcontent.com/pod-product-compliance
Ingram Content Group UK Ltd.
Pitfield, Milton Keynes, MK11 3LW, UK
UKHW022022201125
465320UK00008B/67
9780367669379